GAJAPATI

GAJAPATI

A KING WITHOUT A KINGDOM

ASHOK KUMAR BAL

Foreword by Dr Karan Singh

Konark Publishers Pvt Ltd
New Delhi · Seattle

Konark Publishers Pvt. Ltd
206, First Floor,
Peacock Lane, Shahpur Jat,
New Delhi 110 049
Phone: +91-11-41055065
e-mail: india@konarkpublishers.com
website: www.konarkpublishers.com

Konark Publishers International
8615, 13th Ave SW,
Seattle WA 98106
Phone: (415) 409-9988
e-mail: us@konarkpublishers.com

Copyright © Ashok Kumar Bal, 2022

All rights reserved. No part of this book may be reproduced or utilized in any form or by any means, electronic or mechanical, including photocopying, recording, or by any information storage and retrieval system, without prior permission in writing from the publisher. The views and opinions expressed in this book are the author's own and the facts are as reported by him, based on his extensive research of the subject, which have been verified to the extent possible, and the publisher is not in any way liable for the same.

Most of the photographs used in this book are from the collection of Shri Debi Prasanna Ganguly, belonging to an old family of photographers of Puri, and used with permission except where stated otherwise.

ISBN: 978-81-949286-2-1

Edited by Ranjana Narayan
Cover Credit: Chuguli Sahu & Sudarshan Shaw
Typeset by Saanvi Graphics, Noida
Printed and bound at Thomson Press (India) Ltd

Bapa & Bou,
who would have been happiest to see this
and
Maya, beloved granddaughter,
for being the source of pure joy during this journey, and
hoping she reads the book one day when she grows up!

ଭୁଜତଳେ ମୋତେ ରଖ ମହାବାହୁ !
ବାହୁତଳେ ମୋତେ ରଖ
ବିପୁଳ ଭୁଜ ବିସ୍ତାରି ଦେଲେ ଛାର
କି କରି ପାରିବ ଦୁଃଖ ॥

Bhujatale mote rakha mahabahu!
Bahutale mote rakha
Bipula bhuja bistari dele chhaara
Ki kari pariba dukhah II

Oh Almighty, give me shelter
Keep me under your shoulder,
If you lay your infinite arms round me
What misery can touch me!

[*A stanza of Gajapati Birakeshari Deb's (AD 1736–1793)*
prayer to Lord Jagannath]

CONTENTS

Foreword by Dr Karan Singh   xi

Review by Dr Sitakant Mahapatra   xiii

Review by Princess Aswathi Thirunal Gouri Lakshmi Bayi   xiv

Acknowledgements   xv

Introduction   xix

1. Gajapati   1
2. Gajapati King: The Foremost Servitor   20
3. Suryavanshi Gajapatis: Grandeur and Glory   47
4. Mukunda Deb: The Last Independent Hindu King   77
5. Ramachandra Deb I: Abhinava Indradyumna   89
6. Purushottama Deb: The Most Attacked King   101
7. Gajapatis on the Run: Turbulent Times for Both the Lords   107
8. Ramachandra Deb II: Fallen King, Unfailing Devotion   123

9. Birakeshari Deb I: Gajapati Goes Mad	140
10. Mukunda Deb II: The Fall of the Last Pillar	153
11. The Fort of Barabati: The Pride and the Prison	182
12. Dibyasingha Deb III: Crown to Conviction	199
13. Rani Suryamani Patamahadei: Woman Extraordinaire	226
14. Plight of Pattaranis: The Sordid Story of Pension	260
15. Mukunda Deb III: A Confirmed Oddity	285
16. Ramachandra Deb IV: Tryst with Gurudev, Fight with Priests	305
17. Gajapati *versus* Gajapati: Beginning and End of Hostility	315
18. Dibyasingha Deb IV: The Golden Jubilee King	334
19. And It Never Ends…	352
Appendices	379
Notes	401
Bibliography	419
Index	429

Dr. KARAN SINGH

3, NYAYA MARG,
CHANAKYAPURI
NEW DELHI - 110 021

FOREWORD

In the broad strokes of Indian history that we find in our educational system we learn mainly about national issues, the freedom movement, partition, and so on. In this process the rich and varied history of our former regional kingdoms tends to get neglected. The present book is a case in point which gives us the fascinating story of how the Gajapati Maharaja of Puri holds a unique position of Adyasevak (the first and foremost servitor) of Lord Jagannath. It takes the history back to the Ganga dynasty of the 11th century which established the strong foundations for a Hindu-Odishan empire, and mentions the Ganga and Suryavanshi rulers who built a strong and prosperous kingdom stretching from the Ganges to the Cauvery along the coast of India. It was King Gajapati Prataprudra Deb's tenure that saw the emergence of the great Chaitanya Mahaprabhu who is revered as a Amshavatara of Lord Vishnu himself. This resulted in a remarkable resurgence of the Bhakti cult when the King himself became his devoted follower.

The Hindu kingdom of Odisha was the last to fall prey to the ruthless Islamic invasions during which the great Jagannath Temple itself was subjected to a barbarous attack and the kingdom reduced to a semi-autonomous status with much smaller territory. After 200 years of Muslim Rule came the arrival of the Marathas in 1750 and the Gajapati was reduced to the status of an 'insignificant local zamindar'. After the British conquest of Odisha in 1803 Raja of Khurda became the Raja of Puri with no territory but with an assigned role of Temple Superintendent. Several proposals made by the British Government were strongly opposed by the eminent lawyer Madhusudan Das.

With Independence in 1947 the administration of the Temple was taken away from the Raja of Puri by an Act of Parliament and entrusted to a Management Committee with the Gajapati as its Chairman. Thus we have a situation where the Gajapati now, although having no territory, is deeply revered by all devotees of Lord Jagannath around whom a great deal of Odishan culture : dance, sculpture, music & painting revolves. The present Gajapati Dibyasingha Deb has completed fifty years as a fully dedicated servant of Lord Jagannath. I may add that the present Maharani is from Jammu and is distantly related to me. This provides a significant link between North and East India.

It is my pleasure to write a Foreword to this well researched book written by Shri Ashok Kumar Bal. This will fill a gap in the history of Odisha, and will be of interest not only to historians but to the general public. I dedicate this book to Lord Jagannath Himself.

Sri Jagannath Swami Nayanapathgami Bhavatu me

Karan Singh
19 July 2021

TEL. : (011) 2611-5291 2611-1744, FAX : (91-11) 2687-3171
Email : karansingh@karansingh.com

REVIEWS

I was so happy to find a book written in English on the Gajapati of Puri, the King so intertwined with the all-pervasive Jagannath Cult. In one of Anangabhima's last inscription of 1238 (*anka*) is given as the regnal year of Lord Purushottam. The identification between the King and the State deity reached in fullest form under Anangabhima's son Narasimha I (AD 1238–64). Narasimha I was the first Orissan king to take the title of the 'Lord of the Elephants' (Gajapati), a title which is still used by the present King of Puri and by which he is referred by the mass of pilgrims during the yearly Car Festival.

The author has put commendable effort in traversing the history of Gajapatis, their changing fortunes and telling many fascinating stories. The uniqueness of this royal institution has few parallels. Epigraphical and iconographical evidences suggest that the King is considered as a personification of Deity. The author, by his narration and explication, has nicely brought out the distinctive aspects of the association between the kingly nature of the State deity, Jagannath, meaning the Lord of the World, and the godly persona of His earthly representative, the King or the Gajapati.

I am sure the readers will find the book informative, enlightening and enthralling.

—**Dr Sitakant Mahapatra**
Padma Vibhushan and Jnanpith Award winner

Kaudiar Palace Thiruvananthapuram - 695 003, Kerala, India
Tel: (O) 0471- 2431393

I am delighted to have come across this beautiful book on the Gajapatis of Puri. The age-old ritual association between the Gajapati Maharaja and the revered temple of Lord Jagannath is unique in conception and in practice. In the annual Rath Yatra festival of Jagannath, Balabhadra and Subhadra, the Gajapati Maharaja as *Adyasebak* performs the *Cherrapanhara* service—or sweeping of the street before the chariot of the Lord—symbolizing the king as the servant and subordinate of the supreme and sovereign Lord. However, it is interesting to learn that the Gajapati Maharaja of Puri is venerated as Chalanti Vishnu, i.e., a living reflection of Lord Vishnu.

There is a great similarity between the Gajapati of Puri and the Travancore Royal Family. The Maharaja of Travancore and the Travancore Royal Family are known down the ages as *Sree Padmanabha Dasas*, a title they hold to their hearts as most supreme.

The author has come out with a book of great historical and religious significance which, I am sure, the readers will welcome. This is a praiseworthy venture which explores and presents our rich history and great heritage to the people.

Thiruvananthapuram,
12 August 2021

Princess Aswathi Thirunal
Gouri Lakshmi Bayi

ACKNOWLEDGEMENTS

This book is an endeavour which could not have been possible without the support and contribution from such people to whom I owe a debt of gratitude.

My soulful gratitude to Jagadguru Shankaracharya Nischalananda Saraswati-ji Maharaj of Govardhan Peeth, Puri, for granting me an opportunity of his divine audience, taking time to discuss the topic and blessing my mission.

I express my sincere gratitude to Shri Jyoti Prakash Panigrahi, Minister of Tourism and Culture, Government of Odisha, and his predecessor Shri Ashok Chandra Panda for being very kind in facilitating my research work by granting access to various sources in different libraries, archives and institutions in Odisha. My special thanks to Shri Manoranjan Panigrahi, former Secretary, Culture, Government of Odisha, who extended a helping hand in exploring and obtaining information from various rare resources.

Mr Mahimohan Tripathy, former Administrator of Jagannath Temple, Ex-Member of the Shree Jagannatha Temple Managing Committee and a great scholar on Jagannath culture, has offered valuable advice and insights into numerous aspects of the Temple and its tradition. I owe my deep gratitude to him. My sincere thanks to Prof. Kailash Chandra Dash, an erudite scholar on the history of Odisha, for the several discussions with him that helped in getting clarity on various academic aspects. Consultations with Prof. Subash Dash of Sanskrit Department, Utkal University, were helpful in understanding many texts and documents in Sanskrit, for which I am thankful to him. Prof. D.S. Patnaik of Geology Department, Utkal University, was instrumental in helping me connect with various resource persons in the University who provided valuable support and guidance. My sincere thanks to him and his colleagues. I greatly benefitted from the discussions with Prof. Sidheswar Mahapatra, Head Priest of the Shri Jagannath Temple. I owe my sincere thanks to him for such enriching discourse.

I am thankful to Dr Soleman Ali, Superintendent, and Mr Prasanta Mahakud, Reprographer of Odisha State Archives, for their unfailing support in providing access to old literary sources; archival, historical and many unpublished documents. The Kedarnath Gavesana Pratisthan in Bhubaneswar is a great repository of valuable documents and books. I would like to thank the Librarian, Mrs Binodini, for her support and cooperation. No research on Odisha's past can be complete without a visit to the Odisha State Museum, a treasured place for materials of cultural and historical value. I would like to record my deep gratitude to Mrs Jayanti Rath, former Superintendent of the State Museum, Mrs Bhagyalipi Malla, present Superintendent, Mrs Bharati Pal, Curator, and Mr N.K. Samal, Librarian, for their invaluable help, guidance and providing unfettered access to rare journals, books, documents, epigraphic inscriptions and unpublished manuscripts. I am thankful to Mrs Suchismita Mantry of Odisha Sahitya Akademi for her help in providing various literary records and information. The Harekrushna Mahtab State Library of Government of Odisha has been a great resource centre for my study. Mr Santosh Chatterjee, Dy. Director, and Mr Kartik Sahoo, Attender, were extremely helpful in making available a large number of books and study materials for my work. My sincere thanks to them.

ACKNOWLEDGEMENTS

I am indebted to Mr Subhranshu Panda of Penin Books for showing interest in my work and voluntarily providing interesting materials and valuable books which enriched my knowledge. Discussions with Mr Hara Prasad Das, a great writer, critique and thinker, provided deep insights and different perspectives of looking at history. My grateful thanks to him.

Ms Supriya Prasant, a translator and writer of repute, was very forthcoming in rendering support to my work and study. I am grateful to her. Special thanks to Prasanta Biswal, my friend, for going through some of the chapters and offering valuable suggestions.

I cannot thank Bhagyalaxmi Nayak enough, for her ever willing and painstaking efforts in getting the manuscript neatly typed, corrected, rearranged several times. Her contribution in such a critical area of work deserves my grateful acknowledgement and gratitude. I would also like to record my sincere thanks to Sudhansu Bhuyan, Manoj Mishra, Sarat Tripathy, Satyanarayan Mahapatra, T.K. Jayakrishnan, Sourav Choudhury, Manu Dash, Dharanidhar Behera, Pradeep Rout and Seshadev Sahu for their unflinching help at all times. My special thanks to Mitali Madhusmita for her invaluable support. My thanks are due to Dr Basant Kumar Panda, former Professor, Viswa Bharati, for his inputs. I am grateful to Shri Lalit Mohan Deb, a family member of the erstwhile Athagarh King, who was quite helpful in providing some rare and useful documents. I owe a lot to Debi Prasanna Ganguly of Puri for providing rare and relevant photographs.

Acceptance by Mr K.P.R. Nair, Founder and Managing Director of Konark Publishers, New Delhi, to publish my maiden book is a matter of great excitement for me. I owe my deep gratitude to him. I am extremely thankful to Ranjana Narayan, Commissioning Editor, for undertaking the editing work and her valuable contributions. Big thanks to Jiza Joy, Coordinating Editor, for her excellent efforts. Special thanks to Binita Roy, who has been a valued help in going through the manuscript and doing the preliminary editing job of the book. Chuguli Sahu, Priyadarsini

Mohanty and Sudershan Shaw have done a wonderful design of the cover. My heartfelt thanks to them.

I am fortunate to have got enormous support and encouragement from my family and I take this opportunity to acknowledge their contribution. Abhilasha, Sohum and Chiranjiv deserve special mention and thanks for their continuous encouragement all through the journey. Above all and as always, my greatest thanks to my biggest critique and cautious admirer Chhanda, my soulmate. Her constructive criticism and measured appreciation provided the much-desired balance to stay on course in an endeavour of this kind. I owe a special debt to her for her endurance and support.

Always, many unnamed contributors and collaborators play a silent but significant role in the outcome of a project. I am indebted to them for their invaluable support.

A reader is the ultimate judge and jury of a book. It's the reader who alone and always matters. I owe my gratitude to all my readers for their indulgence in the book.

INTRODUCTION

This book is a humble attempt on my part to tell the story of the Gajapati tradition of Odisha where the Gajapati of Puri, the unique king without a kingdom, who is more revered than any other royal due to his ritualistic association with Lord Jagannath. The book presents fascinating narratives, anecdotes and perspectives on the Gajapatis of Odisha.

As a child, I always felt intrigued by the personality of the Gajapati and his influence on the psyche of the people of Odisha. I would like to share some captivating aspects of my reminiscences about the Gajapati, which may find resonance with many of my generation from Odisha.

During my school days, I would memorize the long title of great Gajapati King Kapilendra Deb (AD 1435–1467) while learning the glorious past of Odisha's history. The title was no ordinary one. The title runs as under:

Shree Shree Shree Virashree Gajapati Gaudeswara Nabakoti Karnatotkala Kalabargeswar Viradhivirabara Bhuta Vhairaba Sadhu Sasanotirna Rautaraja Atula Bala Parakram Sahasra Bahu Kshetriyakula Dhumaketu Maharajaadhiraja...

Our teachers used to explain to us each term of the title, which was full of meaning reflecting the glory and grandeur of the King. One would cram and memorize the entire title to be able to say it in one go. This title, needless to say, was a source of delight for us; as school students, we took enormous pride in the heroic achievement of one of the great Odishan kings.

Another childhood memory, which is a source of motivation for writing the book, is my palm leaf horoscope (*jataka*) made after my birth by the village astrologer. The horoscope not only recorded the details of the date and time of birth as per the lunar calendar like any other horoscope but it also mentioned the name of the reigning Gajapati and his regnal year (*anka*). It is a tradition, which is even followed today in Odisha where the horoscope of a person bears the name of the Gajapati and his regnal year. It reflects a deep personal bond between the people and the Gajapati which starts with the birth of a child. This intrigued me. I used to wonder why the name of the Gajapati was mentioned in my horoscope! This curiosity propelled me to know more about the Gajapati kings and the institution they have symbolized over the years.

The lingering memory that most people have of the Gajapati is the narrative repeated every year through the radio commentary (before television came into our life) of the Rath Yatra in which the king performs the *chherapanhara* ritual. We would listen in rapt attention about the king's arrival at the venue and sweeping the floors of the three chariots with a broom. This story left an indelible imprint of the Gajapati in our mind since childhood.

Another fond childhood memory is a play called *Kanchi Abhijana* that used to be performed during the annual function of the school. This musical play was about the legend of the great association between the Gajapati Purushottama Deb (AD 1467–1497) with Lord Shri Jagannath, where Shri Jagannath played the role of the Commander of the Odishan king, led the king's army and defeated Kanchi King Saluva Narasimha Deva. The victorious Purushottama Deb brought with him Roopambika (later known as Padmavati), the daughter of the defeated Kanchi king. This popular play is a very important part of the folklore in Odisha and has remained a favourite since my childhood.

These stories led me to delve deep into the subject and find out more about the Gajapatis, Jagannath culture and the history of Odisha that are so intensely and intricately interwoven. Some of the narratives revolving around the Gajapati though based on facts are as absorbing as fiction.

During my studies and later career outside Odisha, I used to visit Jagannath Temple on every trip back home. I used to be fascinated by one aspect of the Temple—the solo deity of Lord Jagannath, known as Patitapabana, placed near the *Singha Dwara* (Lion's Gate, the main door at the entrance) of the Temple. In every temple, the main deity is placed inside the *Garbha Griha* (sanctum sanctorum), and this is true also for the deities of Lord Jagannath, Balabhadra and Subhadra, which is the familiar sight at any Jagannath temple in India. I realized that all people (including non-Hindus) could have a *darshan* of Patitapabana (Lord Jagannath as the Lord of the fallen) from outside without entering the Temple.

A personal experience that reignited the curiosity may be apt to describe. My father left for his heavenly abode on 30 May 2017 and like most Odias, he had his last wish to be cremated at the *Swarga Dwara* in Puri. When we reached Puri for the cremation, it was very late in the night, but we decided to take a route going past the Temple. To our surprise, the gate at *Singha Dwara* was open even at such a late hour postmidnight which was unusual and we could see Patitapabana from outside. It was as if Lord Jagannath was waiting to witness the last passage of one of his devotees. We stopped outside the Temple and offered our prayers. For us it was some sort of divine coincidence. This made me more curious as to why the deity was placed just inside the Lion's Gate at the main entrance of the Temple. And as luck would have it, I dived deep into my research on the Gajapati tradition and learnt that the lone image of Lord Jagannath was installed near the main entrance to ensure that a Gajapati, a great devotee of the Lord who had converted to Islam, would be able to offer his prayers without entering the temple as non-Hindus were not allowed inside.

Apart from this, there are many such fascinating stories. There was a Gajapati who adopted a son as his heir, then disowned him in favour of another adopted son leading to a prolonged court case. There was also a king accused of murder and sent away to the Andamans. There are also incredible stories of how kings and priests on numerous occasions protected the Jagannath Temple from invaders and shifted the deities to secret locations. The story of Pattarani (Queen) Suryamani Patamahadei is an exceptional narrative of an extraordinary woman. These stories and events take us through a scenario where the Gajapati of Odisha, once a king of a vast empire, got reduced to the status of the Gajapati Maharaja of Puri, a king without a kingdom. The continued ritual association of the Gajapati with the Jagannath Temple has, however, placed him in a unique position of honour and reverence among people. Although a king without the usual trappings of royalty, he is revered as *Chalanti Vishnu*, that is a living embodiment of Lord Vishnu.

This book is not a chronological historical narrative. Through various chapters of stories, events and perspectives, it seeks to present the important facts and facets of history. The chapters are so arranged that each chapter can be read independently. A reader has a choice of randomly starting the book from any of the chapters.

As students, we have studied, rather have been indoctrinated into a curriculum of Indian history which was a manifestation of the colonial rule in India. This has been adopted and continued even after the end of colonial rule. Indian history, as taught in schools and colleges, is not the real history of India. The history of India is the history of people and royalties, its villages and towns, of its temples and monuments, and its culture and tradition. The history of India lies in its vast diversity: diverse cultures, disparate people, different languages and dispersed localities. Indian history that we study deprives us of the knowledge about our rich, varied and divergent cultural heritage, particularly the important facets of history of different localities, regions, states, provinces or even villages. This book is a modest attempt to bring out some aspects of a regional history, the story of the Gajapatis of Odisha.

Everyone has a history and a story to tell. Everyone is a bit of a historian in himself, though with all humility I must confess that 'I am not a historian'. A historian's history has its limitations in terms of its domain and detail. In some books on the history of India, the Gajapati of Odisha finds reference in a paragraph or two. The reference is either casual or occasional. This is quite understandable as the focus of that Indian history is different. The history of India in prescribed texts has followed a doctrinaire approach of a discipline and curriculum. In the process, its coverage and context has suffered. Any regional or local history suffers from the twin limitations of perspective and proportion. The history of India from the perspective of an author is exclusionary in nature as it tends to exclude regional, sub-regional and local histories of different parts of India. An attempt to make an inclusive character of Indian history also suffers for it often lacks the propensity to accommodate the diverse character and content of our varied history.

I claim no originality as the book is based on compilation of materials from varied sources. Some prominent aspects have been highlighted broadly conforming to chronological sequences though not necessarily implying a complete chronological narrative. Though the narrative is based on historical facts, this is not a book of history. The factual perspectives of various intriguing and lesser known incidents have been highlighted. History has its limitations in matters of an institution of such antiquity and importance. Not everything can be captured by history. Legends, folklores, and stories handed down over generations do constitute an invaluable part of our heritage. These constitute the faith and belief of the people, thus assuming the character of inviolable truth.

Readers may find the book useful and some may express a sense of indifference or even dislike it. Good, bad or indifferent may be the usual and expected reception to the book. I owe my deep gratitude to each and every one—those who found it informative, those who offered criticism or suggestions, and those who were indifferent and kept me on the tenterhooks of speculation and apprehension.

1
GAJAPATI

Gajapati is a title used by the kings in Odisha as a royal honour and status, and as a dynastic privilege and practice. During the rule of the Gangas and then under the Suryavanshi Gajapatis, Odisha was a strong and vast Hindu kingdom stretching from river Ganga in the north to river Cauvery in the south along the east coast of India.

With the Afghan conquest of Odisha in 1568, the region lost its independence and the king of Odisha became a semi-independent ruler known as the Raja of Khurda with a reduced territorial domain. The British conquest of Odisha in 1803 saw the complete territorial dispossession of the Raja of Khurda. The King of Khurda relocated to Puri in 1807, and came to be known as the Raja of Puri; his formal role restricted to the traditional ritual domain of temple affairs as the superintendent of the Jagannath Temple.

The title of Gajapati has been the privilege of all those kings who had ritual association with the Jagannath Temple in Puri. Therefore, whether as the king of Odisha or the Raja of Khurda or the Raja of Puri, all from the line have been using the title of Gajapati as a dynastic hereditary practice. Their exclusive association with the ancient Jagannath Temple provided a distinct identity to the Gajapati kings of Odisha since the Ganga period. The title has been inherited as a legacy and honour since the time of Kapilendra Deb (AD 1435-1467), and his successors enjoy it till date.

The Four Princely Races

Gajapati is one of the four principal titles conferred on Hindu kings who ruled over India. The other three are—Narapati, Aswapati and Chhatrapati. Since Kali Yuga (in Hinduism, Kali Yuga is the fourth and present age of the world cycle of four *yugas*, or 'ages'), Hastina (Hastinapur) had been the capital and seat of power of the united empire in the Indian subcontinent. The fou princely races ruled the country in acknowledgement and obedience of the sovereignty of Hastina. They were in charge of four different dominions under the aegis of the greater sovereignty. In their respective dominions they functioned as independent royalties. The Narapatis ruled over what is in current times the Deccan, Telangana and Karnataka. The Aswapatis ruled the Maratha regions, i.e., ancient Maharashtra; the Chhatrapatis, a celebrated line of Rajput princes, ruled over Rajasthan; and the Gajapatis were the monarchs ruling over Odisha or Utkalkhand.

The literature describing these princely races is not confined to Odisha alone.[1] The *Raj Padhati* of Karnata (a treatise on royal practice referred to by historian Sterling) also refers to the three races of Narapati, Aswapati and Gajapati. According to this, the princes of the Narapati line ruled over the south, the Aswapatis ruled over the west, and the Gajapatis were lords of the east.[2] Thus, we see that the classification of royal kings was very ancient, starting from the Kali Yuga; and the Gajapatis of Odisha have occupied a place in that classification of royalty since ancient times.

According to eminent historian and epigraphist D.C. Sircar, Aswapati, Gajapati and Narapati are foremost in terms of royal titles in the inscriptions of the Kalachuri kings of northern India. The most famous of these kings, Karna (r. 1041–1071) adopted the epithet 'Asvapati-Gajapati-Narapati-Raja-Traya-Adhipati'. The same epithet was later adopted (in its Kannada translation,

Asvapati-Gajapati-Narapati-Muvara-Rayara-Ganda) by the Vijayanagar kings. Sircar believes that the expressions refer to the king as adopting it as 'lord of the threefold sovereignty', i.e., of the three wings of sovereignty—the cavalry, elephant force and infantry.

Sircar further explains that 'some of the medieval Indian kings considered themselves sufficiently strong in all the three wings of sovereignty and claimed the comprehensive title referred to above, while their neighbours were inclined to apply to them any one of the three epithets with reference to the wing in which they were regarded as especially strong. This is how the latest rulers of the Imperial Ganga dynasty of Orissa and their Suryavanshi successors gradually became famous as Gajapati'.[3]

There is an interesting passage in the *Ain-i-Akbari* (a 16th-century document detailing the administration of the Mughal Empire under Akbar), written by his court historian Abu'l Fazl, which refers to the 'Game of Cards'. In this instance, the author mentions four types of royal kings used in classifying the cards. The first is the *Aswaput*, the king of horses. He is depicted on horseback like the king of Delhi, with the *chhatr* (umbrella), *alum* (standard), and other insignia of royalty. The second is the *Gujput*, the king of elephants. He is mounted on the elephant like the king of Odisha. The third is the *Nurput*, the king of men. Like the king of Vijayapur (Bijapur in Karnataka), he is seated on a throne and has different kinds of soldiers attending him on foot. The fourth is *Chhatrapati*, the king or bearer of the imperial umbrella.[4]

The Elephant in Indian Culture

Etymologically, the word 'Gajapati' is a combination of 'Gaja' which means an elephant and 'pati', meaning lord or owner. The word 'Gajapati' owes its origin and significance to the term 'Gaja', i.e., the elephant. The Gaja or the elephant occupies a prominent place in Hindu religion and royalty, also being a part of Indian culture and custom. The elephant denotes majesty, strength, authority, dignity, wisdom, wealth, patience, valour and royalty. These are essential attributes of kingship. The creature's grand size conveys a sense of authority, strength and power. Since time immemorial, elephant has been associated with royal tradition and majesty, and was an indispensable part of royal procession and congregation.

In Indian tradition, lotus and elephant have a mythical association. Lakshmi—the principal goddess of fertility, abundance, prosperity and wealth—is depicted as a lotus goddess. She is lotus-born (*Padmaja*), lotus-eyed (*Padmakshi*) and she carries a lotus in her hand (*Padmahasta*). It is significant that the lotus goddess is also called Gajalakshmi—Lakshmi who is accompanied by elephants. In many Hindu houses, one can see images of Lakshmi emerging from a lotus, and two elephants pouring gold coins standing at her right and left sides. The elephant, thus, symbolizes wealth, abundance and prosperity. These are essential and aspirational attributes of a king.

Apart from that, elephants are also known for their memory and wisdom. Kings used to have learned men and erudite scholars in their courts who were repositories of knowledge in *sashtras, vidhis, nyaya, vyakarana, sanskar*, etc. (texts, practice or rituals, law, grammar, culture, etc.). These learned men acted as conscience keepers and advisors to the king who relied on them for their wise and informed counsel. *Rajadharma* (duties of a king towards the State) and governance depended on the wise counsel of learned scholars. Elephants, thus, had a connection with wisdom, which was very important for a king.

India has been described as the land of elephants by historians and poets. In the *Indica* of Megasthenes, written in 302 BC, many passages are devoted to elephants. Greeks and Romans were particularly impressed by the supposed invincibility of elephants as a weapon of war. Elephants also acquired significance as an instrument of improving diplomatic relations. In this context, there are two instances of gifting of elephants. One is an ancient custom where the elephant was gifted as a tribute to a teacher, and the other a recent one where the elephant was held as an emissary of peace. In both the cases, the values that the elephants stand for have been highlighted.

The first instance of an elephant as a gift refers to a tribute to a great teacher. Many years ago, Alexander's defeat of Porus in 326 BC was a major achievement and triumph for the great conqueror. He was, however, humbled by the great fight that Porus put up in the battle. The war elephants in Porus' army drew the particular attention of Alexander. He was amazed by the mighty animals. As a mark of his victory, Alexander paid tribute to his teacher Aristotle by gifting him an elephant. He sent an elephant captured from the banks of the Indus to the Acropolis in Athens, 2,000 miles away, in the 4th century BC. The elephant was accompanied by Leon of Atrax, a cavalry commander. This is described in a book titled *An Elephant for Aristotle* (1958) by American writer L. Sprague de Camp. Though the novel is predominantly a travelogue about a soldier accompanying the elephant in a long arduous journey, the significance of the elephant as a sign of victory and a token of tribute needs special emphasis.[5]

The second instance was comparatively a recent occurrence. In October 1949, Jawaharlal Nehru, the then Prime Minister of India, received letters written by hundreds of students from Japan requesting him for a gift of an elephant. He felt intrigued by the strange request. Incidentally, Japan had lost two of their last elephants in World War II. The elephants in Tokyo's Ueno Zoo were a great attraction for children. Opened in 1882, Ueno Zoo was Japan's oldest and most loved zoo.

In 1943 zookeepers were ordered to kill all wild and dangerous animals fearing their escape from Ueno Zoo during bomb raids by the Allied forces. The request for relocation of the animals was rejected. Two of the zoo's longest used elephants survived but starved to death subsequently. After the wartime killings, the zoo held a memorial service for the martyred animals in 1943. The Japanese children missed the creatures and thus had written to the Indian Prime Minister to gift them an elephant.

Responding to their request, Nehru sent an elephant, Indira, named after his daughter. He wrote to the children of Japan that they should 'treat Indira as a gift not from me, but from the children of India to the children of Japan. The elephant is a noble animal, much loved in India and typical of India. It is wise, patient, strong and gentle. I hope all of you will develop these qualities.' Indira was thus sent as an emissary of peace and a symbol of friendship between Japan and India.

After dispatching the gift, Nehru wrote a letter to the children in India:

> Grown-ups have a strange way of putting themselves in compartments and groups. They build barriers of religion, caste, colour, party, nation, province, language, custom and of rich and poor. Fortunately, children do not know much about these barriers, which separate. They play and work with each other and it is only when they grow up that they begin to learn about these barriers from their elders. I hope you will take a long time in growing up....
>
> Some months ago, the children of Japan wrote to me and asked me to send them an elephant. I sent them a beautiful elephant on behalf of the children of India. This noble animal became a symbol of India to them and a link between them and the children of India.
>
> I was very happy that this gift of ours gave so much joy to so many children of Japan, and made them think of our country... remember that everywhere there are children like you going to school and work and play, and sometimes quarrelling but always making friends again. You can read about these countries in your books, and when you grow up many of you will visit them. Go there as friends and you will find friends to greet you.[6]

In both the cases mentioned here, the noble elephant represents wisdom, patience, strength and gentleness. These attributes find expression in the virtuous animal as an emissary of peace, mark of victory and symbol of friendship.

Elephants in the History of Odisha

Odisha was known for her war elephants. One of the earliest references of it is found in the celebrated work of the greatest-ever literary genius Kalidasa in *Raghuvansam* (5th century CE). Canto 6 of *Raghuvansam* describes the *swayamvara* of princess Indumati of Vidharbha. Hemangada, a prince from Kalinga, was present at the *swayamvara* of Indumati as a participant.

Sunanda, the counsel of the princess, described his glorious achievements, strength and kingdom to her. Hemangada was the lord of Mahendra, a prominent hilly region in ancient Kalinga (Odisha), and the Mahodadhi, as the Bay of Bengal was known in that area. When the king marches at the forefront of his army with a fierce appearance and with his energetic bloodthirsty war elephants behind him, he himself appears like the mount of Mahendra (stanza 54). In the 58th stanza, Kalidasa writes that Indumati, who was usually drawn to physical appearance and strength, turns away from Hemangada as the goddess of fortune turns away from an unfortunate person. The elaborate description of Hemangada in *Raghuvansam* indicates that he was a powerful warrior king who had control over islands of the sea and was known as Lord of the Ocean; he also had a powerful army on the land with a large number of elephants at his command which had fought many battles. Kalidasa addressed him as Kalinganatha or Lord of Kalinga and Mahodadhipati or Lord of the Ocean in his work.[7]

In the *Arthashastra* of Kautilya (300 BC) the elephants of Kalinga are admired as the best of the type in India. Yuan Chwang (Hsuan Tsang), the Chinese pilgrim-scholar, visited Odisha and the neighbouring provinces in 639 AD. From his chronicles, it appears that Kalinga was home to large, dark elephants, which were prized in the neighbouring kingdoms.[8]

The Muslim geographers of the 9th and 10th centuries have also written that large elephants were one of the chief commodities of trade for Odisha in the Bhauma-Kara period (AD 736–940).

Ibn Rustah, an Arab geographer, in AD 920, speaks of Odishan elephants as the tallest of the region. The anonymous writer of *Hudud-al-Alam*, who began his work in AD 982–983 for Abul Harith Muhamad Iban Ahmad, the prince of the province Guzgan or Guzganan located in the North West of modern Afghanistan, mentions about Odisha that 'extremely large elephants are found there, such as in no other place of India.'[9]

Kautilya elaborated the significance of the use of elephants in war. According to him, the duties of elephantry were:

i. To lead the army,
ii. To help in making roads, houses, etc.,
iii. To destroy enemy troops,
iv. To measure the depth of streams, rivulets and rivers,
v. To climb up and down the slopes of hills,
vi. To make headway into uneven lands and places covered with shrubs,
vii. To consolidate the scattered troops of one's army,
viii. To defend own troops,
ix. To exhibit the prowess of own army,
x. To release own troops from the clutches of enemy,
xi. To frighten the enemy troops by its menacing attitude,
xii. To destroy the carriages of the enemy,
xiii. To break the walls, forts and camps of enemy,
xiv. To disrupt the well-organized enemy formation,
xv. To trample the enemy,
xvi. To capture enemy soldiers and finally to establish victory.[10]

Various scholars of ancient India laid stress on the elephant corps in an army. Sage Palakapya, the author of *Hastyayurveda* (an ancient treatise on elephants and treatment of their disease) writes, 'The sunrise is the ornament of the world, the moon of the night, learning is the ornament of men and the elephant of the army. ... Where there is truth, there is religion, where there is religion, there is prosperity, where there is beauty, there is nobility and where there are elephants, there is victory.'[11] Ancient political treatises like the *Nitisara* by Kamandaka, *Nitivakyamrita* by Somadevasuri, the *Agni Purana* and other texts speak in glowing terms of the importance of elephants in war. One source indicates that a well-trained and well-equipped elephant is capable of destroying 6,000 well-caparisoned horses in a war.[12]

The elephants of Odisha were so prized that in AD 1353 Shamsuddin Ilyas Shah (founder of the Bengal Sultanate) invaded the region and retreated only after obtaining a few elephants. In AD 1361 Sultan Firoz Shah Tughlaq (ruler of the Tughlaq dynasty) invaded the Ganga Kingdom during the reign of Bhanudeva III. The Sultan concluded his victorious campaign with an elephant hunt at Padmatola in the old Baramba state (present-day Cuttack district). Bhanudeva III entered into a treaty with the Sultan by offering him 20 big elephants and agreeing to supply him a number of elephants as an annual tribute.[13]

During the reign of Bhanudeva IV (AD 1414–1434), son of Bhanudeva III, Odisha was raided many times by outsiders to obtain elephants. A Muslim chronicle states that Hushang Shah, the Sultan of Malwa, was in need of elephants for his war with Gujarat, and since Odisha was the fabled country of the best elephants, he led an expedition to it in the guise of a dealer in horses. The Sultan brought with him horses of different colours that the king of Odisha prized the most. When Bhanudeva IV with a small band of followers wanted to examine the horses brought by Hushang Shah, he was treacherously seized and made captive and was not released till he promised to give the Sultan some of his best elephants.[14]

The sultans of Delhi, Bengal, Jaunpur (in present-day Uttar Pradesh) and Malwa are stated in the Muslim chronicles to have invaded Jajnagar or Odisha for elephants. It is mentioned in the *Sirat-i-Firuz Shahi* that Sultan Firoz Shah Tughlaq, while returning to Delhi from Odisha, set out along the banks of the Mahanadi, 'where elephants like stars prowl about'. The author of the *Sirat-*

i-Firuz Shahi gives another interesting piece of information. 'Rai Bhandeo' or Bhanudeva III made a present of his famous elephants to Firoz Shah, keeping only one for himself 'so that the name of Gajapati handed down by his forefathers might not be obliterated'.[15]

Elephants have always been the proud possessions of the kings of Odisha. Besides being a status symbol, as mentioned, elephants were extensively used in warfare. The number of elephants owned by a king determined his relative strength and status. Anantavarman Chodagangadeva (AD 1078–1150), the famous king of the Ganga dynasty, had a large army of elephants. Famous epigrapher and historian Dr S.N. Rajguru in his seminal work *Orissa's Cultural History*, relying on epigraphic evidence, has written that Chodagangadeva had a troupe of 99,000 elephants. He was crowned with the title *Nabanabati Sahasra Gunjaradhisvara* (Lord of 99,000 Elephants).[16] This is referenced in the Ronanki stone inscription.[17] No other kingdom in India had that large an army of elephants.

Muslim sources give varying estimates of elephants owned by different kings of Odisha. In *Burhan-i-Ma'asir* it is stated that Kapilendra Deb (AD 1435–1467) possessed 2,00,000 elephants.[18]

Elephants were abundantly available in Odisha, playing a significant role in warfare, and this has been highlighted by various authors. Noted Indologist A.L. Basham writes:

> They [elephants] were trained with great care and attention, and, marching in the van of the army, acted rather like tanks in modern warfare, breaking up enemy's ranks, smashing palisades, gates, and other defences; a line of elephants might also act as a living bridge for crossing shallow rivers and streams. Elephants were often protected by leather armour, and their tusks tipped with metal spikes. The Chinese traveler Sung Yun, who visited the kingdom of the Hunas in the 6th century, speaks of fighting elephants with swords fastened to their trunks, with which they wrought great carnage, but there is no confirmation of this practice in other sources. As well as the mahout, the elephant

usually carried two or three soldiers, armed with bows, javelin and long spears, and advanced with a small detachment of infantry to defend it from attack.[19]

The legendary war elephant that Robert Clive rode to fight and eventually led to the victory of the East India Company was from Odisha. The elephant was Clive's favourite.[20]

The elephants from the jungles of Odisha were engaged extensively in war by various rulers. The Odisha elephants were sought after everywhere across India. In a war or a truce, the winning side always demanded and was compensated by elephants. Elephants from Odisha had a pan-India demand and presence among royalties.

During Akbar's reign (AD 1556–1605), Odisha was under the control of Afghans. Akbar sent his trusted general Man Singh to take control of Odisha. Man Singh reached an understanding with the Afghans and entered into a treaty with them. As per the treaty, Odisha came under the sovereignty of Mughal King Akbar. The Afghans were appointed as loyal subordinates of the Mughal emperor. The Jagannath Temple and nearby districts were to be transferred to Emperor Akbar. Nasir Khan, the young Afghan king, presented 150 elephants to Man Singh as a token of gift. The treaty with the Afghans was signed on 15 August 1590. As a sign of victory, Man Singh sent 1,004 elephants to the Mughal durbar.[21]

Shah Jahan was the Mughal emperor from 1628 to 1658. He had a large band of elephants in his army, headed by a *musaraf* (a high-ranking military official in charge of the elephantry division). During Shah Jahan's time, this post was occupied by Rai Brundaban Das, a native from Odisha. As a matter of fact, none other than an Odia was qualified to head the elephant corps of the Mughal army during Shah Jahan's reign. This was because of the dexterity and competence of Odias in training, taming and managing elephants used in war to trample and terrorize the enemy and their riders.[22]

Information highlighting elephants and their role in war can be found in various literary works in Odia. Godavara Mishra was a minister of peace and war or *Sandhivigrahika* and a *Rajguru* (king's advisor) under Gajapati Prataparudra Deb (AD 1497–1540). In his work *Harihara Chaturanga,* a treatise on the art of warfare, he has discussed the importance of elephants in a battle. The eight chapters of the work are devoted to the science of war. In the first chapter, the author highlights the importance of elephants. It is significant that the title of Gajapati used by kings since the late Ganga rulers is due to the possession of invincible and enormous elephant corps which played decisive roles in all the battles. Godavara Mishra writes:

Sahi raja yasya chambah sa tamuryatra hastinah
Tasmattam vibhriyadraja sa yuddhayogya gunanvatah

(He is verily the king who has an army and that indeed is the army which comprises elephants. Hence the king with qualitative disposition should possess an army capable of encounter.)

Ratriyatha sasankena youvanena yatha striyah
Tatah sena gajendrena taya raja cha sobhate.

(A king shines forth with the army comprising elephants as the night is pleasant with the moon and as women in their youth.)

The writer has gone further in describing the methods of capturing, taming and maintaining elephants for the purpose of war. The entire chapter containing 813 hymns is devoted to discussing elephants and their use in wars.[23]

Brundabana Nathasharma, a renowned writer from Deogarh in western Odisha, wrote a series of essays on elephants and elephantology in the weekly *Sambalpur Hitaisini* published from 1889 to 1923. Nathasharma's article on *Hastitatwa* (elephantology) was published in different issues of the above weekly in 1908. He has cited lucidly in Odia the names given to the elephant in Indian literature, the categories of war elephants, elephant riding techniques, white elephants, foreign names of elephants, the size of elephants, *musth* in elephants, etc. He also calculated that twice the circumference of the front foot gives the height of an elephant.[24]

The Gajapatis of Odisha

As we have seen, 'Gajapati' is a title used by the kings of Odisha. The title was unknown in the region before the 10th century AD.[25] Since then, various kings of Odisha have used the title of Gajapati in some manner or the other. The title of kings associated with the elephant or Gaja is interesting and important in the history of Odisha. Anantavarman Chodagangadeva (AD 1078–1150), the greatest ruler of the Ganga dynasty, is the earliest king to have been associated with a title involving elephants. As we have seen, some inscriptions ascribe to him the title *Nabanabati Sahasra Gunjaradhisvara*, meaning Lord of 99,000 elephants.

As per the Simhachalam Temple inscriptions, Narasimhadeva I (AD 1238–1264) seems to have used the title of 'Gajadisha' for the first time. The Kapilash Temple (Dhenkanal, Odisha) inscriptions of Narasimhadeva are very instructive and revealing. The inscriptions contain a passage which calls the ruler both *Anantavarman* and victorious, '*Birashri* Narasimha Deb', and seems also to endow him with the title Gajapati. 'We know that the successor of Anantavarman Chodaganga enjoyed the secondary name Anantavarman. Our inscription seems to show that the title Gajapati, which is known to have become a distinguishing epithet of the later rulers of the Ganga family, was enjoyed by Narasimha I about the middle of the 13th century.'[26]

It is significant to note that Narasimha I was the Ganga ruler who used the title of Gajapati for the first time. In the Draksharama temple (in Andhra Pradesh) inscriptions, Bhanudeva I, son of Narasimha I, has been described as *Gaja Ghatapati* and *Gajapati*. Narasimhadeva III also used the title of Gajapati. Narasimhadeva IV has been described as *Gaja Nibahapati*. Bhanudeva IV (AD 1414–34) is titled *Gajadhish*. There is a reference of Bhanudeva IV, the last Ganga king, bearing the title of Gajapati, which is evident from three inscriptions in his name at Simhachalam.[27] As per Simhachalam inscriptions, the king is styled as *Gajapati Pratapa Vira Nissanka Bhanudeva*. The title of Gajapati is a legacy of the Gangas, and the title of many Ganga kings had an association with the word Gaja or the elephant. Some of the Ganga kings used the title of Gajapati, but they, however, did not use it as a matter of dynastic practice or tradition on a continuous basis.

Kings of the solar dynasty (Suryavamsi) succeeded the Ganga dynasty. Kapilendra Deb (AD 1435–1467) was the founder of the great solar dynasty. He was the first king to have used the title of 'Gajapati' with grandeur. He and his descendants styled themselves as Gajapati or Lord of Elephants. Although the solar dynasty is said to have heralded the Gajapati era, the title of Gajapati was used by successive kings even after the solar dynasty. The title became their dynastic and regal title, a royal entitlement. Only those kings who had control over the territory of Puri, the abode of Lord Jagannath, were entitled to the Gajapati title. It gave them the honour of status or equivalence as ruler of Odisha. Just as Lord Jagannath was revered as *Rastradevata*, God of the kingdom, the Gajapati got the honour of the king of the province. The complimentary linkage between Shri Jagannath and Gajapati played a very important role in social and political identity and the character of Odisha.

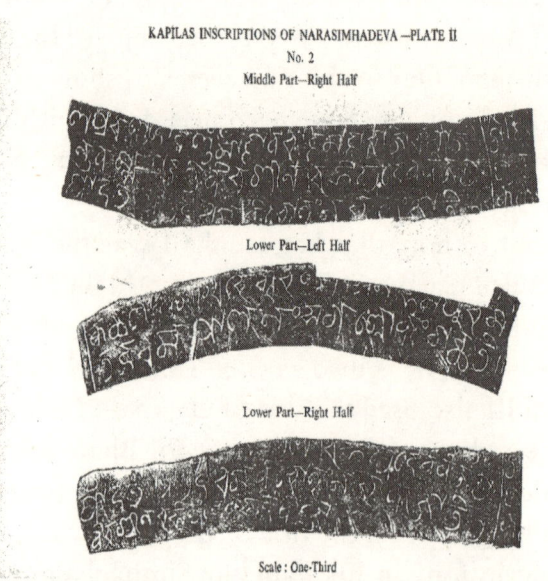

Fig. 1: Kapilas Inscriptions of Narasimhadeva

Source: D.C. Sircar, Epigraphia India, vol. XXXIII.

In Plate II, line 4 (see Fig.1), the word 'Gajapati' appears for the first time. The line reads as under:

4 para[m]ēśvara[ḥ*]   Gaṁ(Ga)ṅg-ānvay-āvalama(mba)na-stambha[ḥ*]⁰   śrīmad-A[na*]
  ntavarma-[Gaja]tti²-vira-śī-Narasiṁhadēva⁸ vijay[ī] [|*]

Kapilendra Deb ascended the throne in AD 1435 and is regarded as the greatest among Gajapati kings. He laid the foundation of a great empire and his reign has been the most glorious chapter in the history of Odisha. When he became the king, the territory extended up to the river Godavari in the south. Kapilendra Deb further extended the border of his kingdom up to the river Cauveri in the south. In the north it spread up to the river Ganga. He conquered Gauda kingdom (present-day Bengal), and Karnata (Vijayanagar country), Kalabarga (Bahmani) in the south.

Kapilendra Deb defeated Sultan Nasiruddin Mahmud Shah of Gaud and assumed the title of 'Gaudeswar' to commemorate his victory after offering a *saree* (headdress) called *Pundarikagopa* to Lord Jagannath.[28] The titles of Gaudeswar and Gajapati were used for the first time in a Jagannath Temple inscription dated AD 1450.[29] Golbarga or Kalabarga was the old capital of the Bahmani kingdom, and later Bidar became its capital. Kapilendra Deb defeated Bahmani Sultan Humayun Shah and assumed the title of 'Kalabargeswar'. With the help of his son Hamavir he conquered Vijayanagar in the south. Thus, by defeating the kings of Bengal, Bidar and Karnata, he claimed sovereignty over them and was crowned with the title of 'Gajapati Goudeswara Nabakoti Karnata Kalabargeswar Trikalingaadhipati'. Dr S.N. Rajguru writes that by conquering Gauda in eastern India, Golbarga or Kalabarga in the west and Karnata in the south and capturing nine forts, Kapilendra Deb acquired control over Trikalinga.[30]

The term *Nabakoti* in the above title has been interpreted variously by historians. Some historians think this is a conventional expression that denotes his sovereignty over nine crore people.[31]

Some others, however, are of the view that the term *Nabakoti* refers to nine forts.[32] Telugu poet K. Lakshman Rao, in his book *Hindu Desa Katha Sangraha,* identified these nine forts as Udaygiri, Konda, Vidu, Kondapalli, Bellamkonda, Nagarjunakonda, Abdanka, Ammanabroku and Tangedu. These were important forts in the Vijayanagar kingdom and were in the possession of Prataprudra Deb (AD 1497–1538, the grandson of Kapilendra Deb) when Krishnadevaraya, ruler of the Vijayanagar Empire, set out to conquer the Odisha kingdom.[33]

An inscription found from South Arcot district of Tamil Nadu reveals that by the end of AD 1464, Kapilendra Deb had spread his empire up to the lower Cauveri. Hamavir's son Kapilendra K. Mahapatra was put in charge of nine forts which were Kondapalli, Thiruvarur, Addanki, Binukonda, Dandapada, Padaividu, Baludulumpattusabadi, Trichurapally and Chandragiri.[34]

The title 'Nabakoti Karnata Kalabargeswar' appears for the first time in the Veligalani plates (in present-day Andhra Pradesh) of Kapilendra in AD 1458. According to well-known historian R. Subrahmanyam, the real significance of the word *Nabakoti* has not been properly understood so far. According to him, 'Nabakoti Karnata Kalabargeswar' is found in every colophon given at the end of every *ucchvasa* (a division or chapter of a book) of *Saraswativilasam*. He has tried to correlate the Nabakoti of the title with the *Srikhandadri* of the Gopinathpur (near Cuttack) inscription. According to him, *Srikhandadri* for *Nabakoti* and *Kanchipura* for *Karnata* are synonyms used for metrical purposes. The nine forts indicated by the epithet are Bellamkonda, Vinukonda, Nagarjunakonda, Rajamundry, Peddapuram, Kaluvalapalli, Oddadi and Potnuru. Therefore, *Nabakoti* or *Srikhandadri* are expressions to indicate the whole region from Simhachalam in the north to Nellore in the south.[35]

The title of Gajapati was expanded at different times. The extended titles denoted conquest of new kingdoms and exhibition of greater might and power. Some examples of different titles used by the Gajapatis in different times as available from records are mentioned below:[36]

a) *Gajapati, Goudeswara, Nabakoti Karnata, Kalabargeswar Trikalingaadhipati*

b) *Virashree Gajapati Gaudeswar Nabakoti Karnat Kalabargeswar Avirai Bhuta Bhairaba Dusaha Dusasana Anikarane Rautarai Atula Bala Parakrama Sangram Sahasrabahu khetriyakula Dhumaketu Shree Shree Gajapati Shree Shree Khetrapati Biradhibirabra Shree Shree....*

c) *Shree Shree Shree Virashree Gajapati Gaudeswara Nabakoti Karnatotkala Kalabargeswar Viradhivirabara Bhuta Vhairaba Sadhu Sasanotirna Rautaraja Atula Bala Parakram Sahasra Bahu Kshetriyakula Dhumaketu Maharajaadhiraja....*

Andrew Sterling, in his celebrated work *Orissa: Its Geography, Statistics, History, Religion and Antiquities* (1822), has referred to the title as 'Vira Sri Gajapati, Gaureswar Navakotikernatotkalavaregeswaradhirai, Bhuta bhairava deva, Sadhusaanotkarna, Rawat Rai, Atula balaparakramsangrama Sahasra Bahu, Kshetriya Kuladhumraketu, & c'. Translating it in English, he writes:

'The illustrious Hero, the Gajapati (Lord of Elephants,) Sovereign of Bengal, Supreme Monarch over the rulers of tribes of Utkala; Kernata, and the nine forts, a divinity terrible as Bhairava to the wicked, the protector of the grants enjoyed by the pious; king of kings; like the lord of a thousand arms in the field of battle by his unequalled might, and a comet to the martial race.'[37]

Nevertheless, the core title is 'Gajapati Goudeswara, Nabakoti Karnata, Kalabargeswar'. This title was earned and assumed by Kapilendra Deb. As a dynastic rule, the same title has been used by all successive Gajapatis till date.

The title 'Gajapati' has been used by some chiefs in south India too, but the title has been predominantly and uninterruptedly used by the kings of Odisha since the days of Kapilendra Deb. A list of Gajapatis of Odisha is given below:

- Gajapati Kapilendra Deb (1435–1467)
- Gajapati Purushottama Deb (1467–1497)
- Gajapati Prataprudra Deb (1497–1538)
- Gajapati Mukunda Deb (1560–1568)
- Gajapati Ramachandra Deb I (1568–1600)
- Gajapati Purushottama Deb (1600–1621)
- Gajapati Narasimha Deb (1621–1647)
- Gajapati Balabhadra Deb (1647–1657)
- Gajapati Mukunda Deb I (1657–1689)
- Gajapati Dibyasingha Deb I (1689–1716)
- Gajapati Harekrushna Deb (1716–1720)
- Gajapati Gopinath Deb (1720–1727)
- Gajapati Ramachandra Deb II (1727–1736)
- Gajapati Birakeshari Deb I (1736–1793)
- Gajapati Dibyasingha Deb II (1793-1798)
- Gajapati Mukunda Deb II (1798–1817)
- Gajapati Ramachandra Deb III (1817–1854)
- Gajapati Birakeshari Deb II (1854–1859)
- Gajapati Dibyasingha Deb III (1859–1887)
- Gajapati Mukunda Deb III [recorded as Makunda Deb III] (1888–1926)
- Gajapati Ramachandra Deb IV (1926– 1956)
- Gajapati Birakeshari Deb III [recorded as Birakishore Deb III] (1956–1970)
- Gajapati Dibyasingha Deb IV (1970–till present)

Although the regnal name of Mukunda Deb started in 1560, it discontinued for some time and recommenced from 1657. In all practical purposes, the practice of using regnal name started in 1657 with Mukunda Deb I. Even after 1657, there are certain periods which saw some Gajapatis not using the conventional regnal names. A pattern of four regnal names is followed in the order of Dibyasingha Deb, Mukunda Deb, Ramachandra Deb and Birakeshari Deb. Similarly, the regnal names of queens or ranis also follow a corresponding pattern: Leelavati Patamahadei, Padmavati Patamahadei, Chandramani Patamahadei and Suryamani Patamahadei. The practice of using regnal names was optional and some Gajapatis retained their original names. However, for more than 300 years this practice has been followed. To distinguish between similar names, the regnal names are suffixed by a numeral such I, II, III, IV or their period of rule is mentioned against their names to differentiate one from another having the same regnal name. The reason behind following such a tradition of specific regnal names of royalty is not known. However, such a practice is seen to be followed in English monarchy, where a king or queen is known by a regnal name with suffix of a numeral.

Interestingly, there are two minor aberrations in the regnal list. Mukunda Deb III is recorded as Makunda Deb III and Birakeshari Deb III is recorded as Birakishore Deb III.

2

GAJAPATI KING

The Foremost Servitor

The Jagannath culture has evolved over centuries of social, religious and cultural tradition, with its roots in the worship of Lord Jagannath as the God of the masses and the Lord of the Universe. It is a manifestation of the faith, beliefs, history, tradition, rituals, legends and myths, accumulated and assimilated in the evolving culture with Lord Jagannath as the epicentre. An important aspect of this culture is the traditional association between the Gajapati and Lord Jagannath. Lord Jagannath is held as the paramount monarch of the kingdom of Odisha, and the Gajapati is considered as His deputy to govern the kingdom. This tradition owes its origin to the ancient past. The linkage between the Gajapati and Lord Jagannath is unique in concept as well as in practice.

The surrender and subordination to God is a part of Hindu philosophy. It is believed that wealth, fame, fortune, position and status of a person are God's gifts—a person owes all these to the Almighty. This philosophy finds vibrant demonstration in the relationship between the Gajapati kings in Odisha and Lord

Jagannath, where the Gajapati acknowledges that both the Seat and the State belong to Jagannath—He being the presiding monarch of the country and the Gajapati as His loyal servant. This association is manifested in religious as well as political dimensions. The centrality of Lord Jagannath in forming and framing this tradition is significant. The Lord and the royalty and their association form an indispensable and inseparable part of this evolved living tradition.

It is learnt from the *Madala Panji,* the chronicles of Jagannath Temple, that much before the arrival of the greatest Ganga King Chodagangadeva (AD 1078–1150), Shri Jagannath (Lord Purushottama) was accepted as 'Lord of the King of Odisha' (*Odisa Rajara Prabhu Shri Jagannath*). Once, King Yayati Keshari (of Soma or lunar dynasty of Kosala AD 922–955), finding that Lord Jagannath was missing from His temple for years, asked a gathering of learned sages, Brahmins and mendicants: 'Where is Shri Jagannath, considered to be the Lord of the King of Odisha?' He learnt from them that the Lord had been taken to a secret place near Sonepur (Subarnapur, Odisha) and buried there following an invasion of the *Yavana* (Muslim) king Raktabahu.[1] King Yayati then started an expedition to locate and recover the idol. He found the idol hidden beneath the ground. Since the idol was damaged and decayed, King Yayati got a new wooden idol made and installed it in a new temple erected for the purpose at Puri.

There is a difference of opinion regarding King Yayati—on whether it was Yayati I or Yayati II. However, the point here is not the relevant regime but to highlight the fact that Jagannath has been referred to as 'Lord of the King of Odisha'. This demonstrates for the first time from scriptural writings that Lord Jagannath was held over and above the king of the day and the king of the state. It also shows that Lord Jagannath was accepted as the ultimate Lord of the Kings of Odisha. This has been followed by all successive kings or Gajapatis of Odisha.

All the kings of the Ganga dynasty beginning with Chodagangadeva worshipped Purushottama-Jagannatha as the state deity of Odisha. There are epigraphical sources based on which historians confirm that Anangabhimadeva III (AD 1211-1238, Chodagangadeva's great-grandson) was the propounder of the tradition or ideology that Jagannath was the supreme Lord and the king was His deputy or *rauta*. There is, however, a view that Chodagangadeva had accepted himself as the *rauta* (deputy) of Purushottama-Jagannatha.[2]

The debate centres round the reference to Chodagangadeva as *rāutarajula* in the inscriptions of the the Vijayanagar Empire, Saka year 1061 (AD 1137). This is the only inscription of Chodaganga that refers to him as *rautaraja*, which does not appear to be a ritual title. Therefore, without getting into the debate on the issue, we can say that Anangabhimadeva III is regarded as the propounder of this philosophy, which is supported by corroborating evidences. He is the earliest imperial Ganga monarch who is known to have assumed the subordinate title *rāutta* and claimed theoretically at least to have been a feudatory of the God Purushottama-Jagannatha.[3]

Anangabhima III

According to the *Madala Panji*, King Anangabhima abdicated his throne and declared Jagannath to be the sovereign Lord of Odisha and himself merely as His vassal. The *Panji* states:

> His son Anangabhima* of his free will declared that his name shall be Purusottama (Jagannath). Though stationed at Cuttack city, he remained a vassal chief by dedicating everything to Lord Jagannath. He ruled for twenty-one years five months and six days. Anangabhima as also Purusottama did not celebrate his coronation. 'Jagannath is the Sovereign of the kingdom of Odisha', so saying he did not perform his coronation rites.[4]

---

* Here Anangabhima refers to Anangabhimadeva III and he was the son of Rajaraja III, son of Anangabhimadeva II. Anangabhimadeva III was the great-grandson of Chodagangadeva (in 'Odisha Itihas', *Ama Odisha*, edited by Pritish Acharya, Bhubaneswar, 2012, p. 69).

This king, according to a tradition recorded in the *Madala Panji*, became a ruler of the *rauta* (feudatory, from Sanskrit Rajaputra) class after dedicating all his possessions (including the kingdom) in the Lord's favour (*e nagara- Katake thai Sri-Purusottama-Sri-Jagannatha-devanku samasta samarpi Rauta-pane thaanti*). The same work also says how from that time the Ganga kings did not enjoy formal coronation at the time of accession, as God was considered to be the ruler of the country (*raja 2 anka abhisheka na hele; Odisha-rajya-raja Sri-Jagannatha-Mahaprabhu emanta kahi abhisheka nohile*). The Bhubaneswar inscription of Anangabhima III refers to Anangabhima's kingdom as *Purusottam Samrajya* (i.e., the empire belonging to Purusottama-Jaganantha); and in some records of Bhanu II (c. 1305–27 A.C.), the great-great-grandson of Anangabhima III, the God Purushottama-Jagannatha is mentioned as his overlord.[5]

The Bhubaneswar inscription of Bhimadeva, an alternate name of Ganga monarch Anangabhima III, is quite significant. In that inscription there are many epithets describing the king, of which the first one is of considerable interest. It says that the Ganga monarch, described as a subordinate ruler, was the son of Purushottama (i.e., the God Purushottama-Jagannatha of Puri). This inscription is different from the rest, as in other inscriptions, Anangabhima III is described as dedicating his kingdom in favour of the Deity and considering himself a *rauta or rautta* (feudatory) of the latter. The claim to be God's son was undoubtedly meant to be the same as that preferring to be God's feudatory. The second epithet in the inscription represents him as the lord of the whole earth as far as the four oceans. This appears to be a conventional claim preferred by the imperial rulers of ancient and medieval India. The third epithet seems to say that the king was surrounded by a large number of learned men.[6]

There are four interesting epigraphs of Anangabhima III found on the walls of the Patalesvara shrine within the inner compound of the Jagannath Temple in Puri. Inscription II records the grant of two *vatis* and five *manas* (both refer to measurements) of land in a village (of Kshatayi-Utapalli) 'by the footman (*Padataka*, modern

Odia *paika*) Khanda, who was the son of Chandana, on Monday, Makara-badi 7, in Saka 1158 and in the *anka* year 29 of *Rautta* Anankabhimadeva (Anangabhima III) falling in the victorious reign of God Purushottama'. It is clear from this inscription that Anangabhimadeva considered himself as viceroy (*rauta*) of the God whom he regarded as the real lord of his kingdom.[7]

The philosophy of the king being subordinate to Lord Jagannath also led to a transformative change in religious allegiance from *Saivaism* to *Vaishnavism* by the Ganga kings. The early Gangas were worshippers of Shiva and devoted to *Saivaism*. The early rulers of the imperial Ganga dynasty including Chodagangadeva assumed the title of *Parammaheswara* since 1112 AD, though he as well as his forefathers were *Parammaheswara* for about 600 years. In some earlier inscriptions like the Korni copper plate, Chodagangadeva styled himself both as *Parammaheswara* and *Paramvaishnava* (ultimate follower of Vishnu). Later, in the Vizagapatam (in Andhra Pradesh) inscription, Chodagangadeva is referred to in many names including *Paramavaishnava*,[8] but significantly the title of *Parammaheswara* was missing. However, it is important to observe that even though the Ganga kings followed a gradual transformation from Saivaism to Vaishnavism, they continued to patronize and support Saivite tradition and culture. Without getting into much detail, it would suffice here to conclude that religious catholicity of the imperial Gangas was of a very high order.[9] However, it is beyond doubt that the successive Ganga and Suryavanshi kings became ardent promoters of the Vaishnava cult.

Anangabhimadeva's ideology of subordination to Lord Jagannath had two aspects. *First* was popularizing of the notion that the kingdom of Odisha was the territory of Jagannath and the Ganga king governed on His behalf as a deputy. *Second* was based on a premise that the king derived his authority from Jagannath and, therefore, he styled himself as the son of Jagannath/Purushottama. These two aspects are akin to the concept of the divine right of a king, where the king acts as an agent or appointee of God or as God's representative. These two aspects may be independent, but derived strength from each other.

The Ganga kings used this ideology for political and religious purposes. It was a very powerful tool for acquiring royal legitimacy, consolidation and expansion of the empire by Anangabhimadeva. This ideology was followed by his successors. This principle aimed at unifying the local forces, particularly local chiefs, against potential Islamic invaders as well as neighbours like the Kakatiyas (a powerful dynasty that ruled most of eastern Deccan between the 12th and 14th centuries). Anangabhimadeva realized the importance of a unified kingdom with support from all quarters to ward off external aggression. Therefore, the strategy was to engender a feeling that any attack from outsiders was viewed as an act of aggression not against the king but against the Lord of the Kingdom. By donning the title of *rauta*, Anangabhimadeva secured the unfailing trust of his people. People accepted this deputy ideology because for them religion was more important than political power; it made them repose full faith in the king's actions. This was coupled with the second aspect of the ideology that all the king's actions were sanctioned by the Lord. These two aspects also helped in securing sustained support from other Hindu chiefs who held the Ganga kings as agents of the presiding deity of the state, the *rastradebata*, i.e., Lord Jagannath.

Explaining the uniqueness of Jagannath as the emperor of the state, R. Balakrishnan, an avid writer on the subject, makes a comparative analysis. He takes the examples of Tamil society where Lord Murugan (Karthikeya) is called the God of Tamil; in Andhra Pradesh Lord Balaji of Tirumala is considered the most important deity, or in the case of Kasi Viswanath of Benares that is dedicated to Lord Shiva, and so on. According to Balakrishnan, the story of Jagannath is significantly different from these examples as Lord Jagannath is literally and figuratively venerated as the State God. In the case of other examples, 'the sovereign aspect of identity is missing'.[10]

This philosophy was not a theoretical exercise. A declaration of suzerainty or overlordship of Lord Jagannath was not enough or complete in itself but had to be demonstrated in practice. In the social, religious and political life of the kingdom, Lord Jagannath as the overlord or supreme monarch was required to be given the full honour and reverence as was due to a monarch or king in regular course.[11]

The declaration of Jagannath as the sovereign of Odisha by Anangabhimadeva III started *svaratvidhi* or the practice of theocracy. This was accompanied by elaborate *Rajabhogas* (kingly services).[12]

Lord Jagannath Treated as a Royal

Lord Jagannath was a humanised deity, personified and treated like a royal. As per the tradition in royal households, the menu of offerings to Lord Jagannath consisted of rich food, pleasant drinks, flavoured *pithas* (cakes) and sweet delicacies. The menu was a lavish spread consisting of dishes of 56 varieties (popularly known as *Chhappan Bhog*), which increased over time. Attire, ornaments, cosmetics, articles of use, furniture and the bed of the deity were designed to suit a king. Jagannath's daily routine from waking up early in the morning till going to bed late at night is associated with detailed paraphernalia involving rituals befitting a king. The midday nap and courtesan's singing and dancing before going to bed at night were part of royal tradition. Quite a few specific annual functions of Lord Jagannath were observed by the kings. On certain occasions, the rituals such as *ekadasi* (11th lunar day), *rajaniti* (a ritual performed by the Gajapati), etc. were observed. On specific occasions, Lord Jagannath was dressed in special garments called *besa*. Jagannath puts on *rajabesa* or royal dress on five occasions: on full moon days of *Kartika, Pousa, Phalguna* (months of the Hindu calendar) and on *Vijayadasami* (10th day of the Navaratri festival) and on the 11th day of the bright fortnight of *Asadh*. These *besas* are called *Suna besas* (attires of gold).

Some words and expressions that are exclusively used in relation to kings have been adopted for Lord Jagannath. Some notable examples in the native dialects are *abakasa, anabasara, beharana, chamu, cula, ekanta, mailama, mukhapakhala, pahuda, singara, ulagi, srianga,* etc. These words are used in relation to kings and royal personages, but are always used in relation to Jagannath too.[13]

These rituals and practices followed are specific to Lord Jagannath. The tradition and practice of *Rajbhoga* identifies the deity with the king, but the ideology of subordination reinforces it by promoting and propagating the deity as very special and unique, being the supreme monarch of the state. This is a unique phenomenon where an idol is assigned the status of the sovereign of a state.

Far-Reaching Consequences of Anangabhimadeva III's Ideology

Anangabhima's professed ideology of surrender and subordination to Lord Jagannath had far-reaching consequences. It helped Anangabhimadeva III in achieving the task of complete formation of the Ganga Empire. He faced three powerful political forces, namely the Kalachuris of Ratnapur (ruled parts of present-day Chhattisgarh), the Muslims of Bengal, and the Kakatiyas of Andhra. He defeated the Kalachuri king and occupied the Sonepur tract (western Odisha). He took effective steps to check the two important forces in the northern and southern frontiers—the Muslims in Bengal and the Kakatiyas in Andhra. Although he defeated the Muslims, Anangabhima became conscious of the political implications of the rise of Muslim power in the border of his kingdom. So, he unified the local Hindu chiefs under his imperial control and strengthened the integrity of the gigantic kingdom to safeguard it from foreign invasion. He used his professed ideology of being the *rauta* of Lord Jagannath, which helped him in this endeavour. The political situation prevailing in India on the eve of his coming to power impelled him to bring about a coordination between polity and religion, a novel experiment in statecraft. Muhammad Ghori conquered the powerful kingdom of Delhi and Ajmer of Prithviraj Chauhan in AD 1192. Within a couple of years the Muslims conquered Kanauj (in Uttar Pradesh) and continued their triumphant march eastward, and by AD 1197 the whole of Bihar was under their control. Then they moved southwards. In the beginning of the 13th century, Hindu India received great blows from Muslim invaders: they destroyed temples, stupas, monasteries and pillars, and on those sites mosques were erected. The lack of unity among the Hindu kingdoms facilitated the ingress of Islamic invaders. The result was that one by one all succumbed to the onslaught, though Odisha could raise her head against it for four centuries more.

There was disarray and disunity among the Hindu kingdoms, namely the Chedis of the west, the Chalukyas of the south and the Senas of Bengal. Such discord resulted in fighting among the Hindu kingdoms and posed a possible threat to the neighbouring coastal tract of Odisha. The dedication of the throne to Lord Jagannath by Anangabhimadeva was a great political experiment and it helped in curbing the ambition of other Hindu kings of the bordering states to acquire the property of a renowned deity, which was *devasva* (belonging to God), at the risk of popular disapproval as also for fear of inviting divine displeasure. On the other hand, Anangabhima's ideology was based on the belief that any move to acquire the territory which belonged to Lord would lead to religious inspiration among the people of Odisha to protect the integrity of the kingdom. *Devasva* property is considered to be immune to outside interference. In that sense Anangabhima's tactical strategy of dedicating the kingdom to Jagannath and declaring the entire territory as Lord's territory or *devasva* was a novel experiment. Declaring Jagannath as the supreme monarch provided protection and shelter to the king.

The idea of monarchy of Jagannath achieved its purpose. Odisha was the only region that was able to withstand repeated Islamic onslaughts for several centuries. During the 13th century, when the whole of north India was under Muslim rule, Odisha under an illustrious ruler like Anangabhima III was able to ward off the Muslims. The Khiljis reached as far south as Rameswaram by AD 1310; soon the Tughluqs succeeded the Khiljis and their ambition to effectively subjugate the Deccan became clear from the transfer of the capital from Delhi to Daulatabad in south India. It is significant to note that of all the Hindu kingdoms of India, Odisha could retain its independence against frequent Muslim attacks from all quarters till AD 1568 while the entire north India and practically the whole of Deccan was under the sway of Muslims.

Sovereign Supremacy of Lord Jagannath

In conformity with the doctrine of considering the supremacy of Lord Jagannath, Anangabhimadeva appointed *Chhatisniyogas*, i.e., 36 types of servitors or temple servants for the service of the Lord. The tradition was retained by his successors, although under the banner of *Chhatisniyogas*, the category of temple servants increased subsequently. This tradition was akin to a tradition of kingship where a retinue of servants were engaged for various services. The royal officers included the *rajguru* (royal servitor), *mahapatra* (minister), *mudiratha* (the king's representative in absence), *chamukhutia* (who declares the king's presence wherever the king moves), *tadhau* (the recorder), *purohit* (the king's priest), *pratihari* (the royal attendant), *mahajana* (the king's nobles), *vaidya* (the physician), and so on. The retinue of servants included both Brahmins and non-Brahmins. The inclusive character of the servants is significant and distinct from many other temples. This diverse and secular character of services and servants upholds Lord Jagannath as a monarch and not a purely religious head.

The practice of investing with *saree* (headdress) is a very unique tradition and akin to a royal practice. Many of the servitors of Lord Jagannath are invested with *saree*, which formally confers permission to serve. Without this investiture, a servant or a *sebak* is not eligible to serve Lord Jagannath. This essential prerequisite shows a kind of royal association of the servants with the Lord. It confers entitlement to serve the Lord and permits access to the ritual domain of services. It is pertinent to mention here that some of the temple services such as of *daitapatis* and *swar*s (performed by a category of temple servitors) do not require such investiture of sarees as their association with Lord Jagannath is very ancient and existed prior to the advent of the Ganga kings.

The *Nabanka* (new year) festival of Lord Jagannath on the eve of *Makara Sankranti* (winter solstice) is reflective of another royal tradition. *Nabanka* means the day on which the regnal year (*anka*)* of the monarch begins. The counting of regnal year is a royal prerogative. It is known from the inscription of Ganga kings that Jagannath's regnal years were officially used. Even now, the same is being followed.

The composition of the *Madala Panji* is another example of royal service. A part of the *Panji* is also called *Rajabhoga itihas*. Kings of the late medieval period used to employ court-writers called *karanas* to write the important events of their kingdom. As Jagannath was the king of Odisha, his writers recorded the history of Odisha. The word *Madala* is derived from *mudula* or *muddala* (found in old Telugu and Odia inscriptions and in the *Madala Panji*), which means an official record. It is pertinent to mention

---

*The regnal years of the rulers of Orissa were being calculated in the *Ankasrahi* method in which the numbers 1 & 6 and the numbers ending with 6 and 0 except 10 were omitted at the time of calculation. A notable feature of this is the counting of the *Anka* year which always starts from *Bhadra Sukla* 'Dvadasi' of the lunar year which is called *Sunia*. But in the case of coronation of a king on some day before the *Sunia* day, his second *Anka* will be reckoned from the *Sunia* day of the year. Consequently it may so happen that in a lunar year three *Anka* years—the last *Anka* of deceased ruler and the 2nd and 3rd *Ankas* of the successors—were taken to be current (K.N. Mohapatra, *A Descriptive Catalogue of Sanskrit Manuscripts of Orissa*, vol. 4-12, Government of Orissa, Dept. of Cultural Affairs, 1963).

here that apart from the Jagannath Temple there is no instance of any other temple maintaining such a chronicle of recorded history of a region.

A remarkable feature and demonstration of the sovereign supremacy of Lord Jagannath is the festival of Rath Yatra (Car Festival) that was prominently highlighted during the Ganga period. The celebrated Car Festival, representing the annual visit of the deities to Gundicha Temple (three km from the Jagannath Temple), begins from the *Asadha sukla dwitiya* (the second day of the bright fortnight of *Asadha* which coincides with June–July). The duration of this festival is 12 days till *Asadha sukla trayodasi* (the 13th day of the bright fortnight of *Asadha*). The festival starts with *Pahandi Bije* (ritual) on the first day and concludes with *Niladri Bije* on the 13th day. This is also known as *Gundicha Yatra* when the deities with elaborate adornments set out for the Shri Gundicha Temple for a sojourn after which they return to their abode. The deities are taken in an elaborate ritualistic procession to their well-decorated chariots.

Before the chariots are moved, the Gajapati performs a very important ritual called *chherapanhara* (ceremonial sweeping ritual). The Gajapati Maharaja, the first servitor (*Adyasebak*) of Lord Jagannath, comes out of his palace in a ceremonial attire in a traditional palanquin (*Tamjhan*), led in a procession with the accompaniment of musical instruments. He walks up the three chariots Taladhwaja, Devadalana and Nandighosha for Balabhadra, Subhadra and Jagannath respectively to perform various rituals, with *chherapanhara* as the most symbolic of his duties as a servant of the Lord. The *Rajguru* sanctifies a broom with golden handle and offers it to the king who performs *chherapanhara*, or sweeping of the floor of the chariots with the broom. After completing the ritual, the Gajapati Maharaja returns to his palace and the chariots get ready to move. The *chherapanhara* tradition is the most visible public demonstration of the supremacy of Lord Jagannath. It is performed before the vast multitude of people who assemble to witness this sacred and significant annual event.

Since non-Hindus are not allowed inside the Temple, it is the only occasion in a year when the deities come out of their abode and move and mingle with the masses irrespective of their religion, caste, creed, status and sect. This occasion conveys the ultimate supremacy of the Lord to whom people come in large numbers to pay their respects. The *chherapanhara* service performed before the public also conveys that even the king, the Gajapati Maharaja, performs the service as an ordinary human being before the Lord. The service of sweeping the floor of the chariots in full public view reinforces and reiterates both the high esteem of the Gajapati Maharaja and his status as a *sebak* and subordinate to the deity. The *chherapanhara* service is the most vibrant demonstration of the doctrine of surrender and subordination in public view.

The establishment of Jagannath as the presiding deity of the Odishan Empire, the declaration that the Ganga kings were His *rauta*, and an elaborate arrangement for regular worship akin to royal service led to the widespread popularity of Lord Jagannath and the Temple of Puri across India. This also contributed to the rising power of the priestly class in Puri. The philosophy of the Gangas came in handy for the priestly class as they also held the Lord as Supreme and considered the Gajapati as a mere deputy. This philosophy provided a space for the priestly class to occupy and assert their position in the elaborate framework of rituals and services in the temple. In this scenario, some later kings of the Ganga dynasty attempted to dilute the ideology by repositioning themselves vis-à-vis Lord Jagannath.

The last two Ganga kings—Narasimha IV (ruled till AD 1425) and Bhanudeva IV (his son)—in their inscriptions clearly referred to their own sovereignty without mentioning Jagannath as their overlord or king of Odisha.[14] Such attitude of disregard and discourtesy evoked severe opposition from the priests of Puri. The people of Odisha could not accept this as they had always endorsed the Ganga king's doctrine of the overlordship of Jagannath. The aberration was short-lived.

Kapilendra Deb – An Elect of Lord Jagannath

Gajapati Kapilendra Deb (AD 1435–1467) succeeded the last Ganga dynasty ruler Bhanudeva IV and established the powerful Suryavanshi dynasty. There are many stories related to Kapilendra's accession to the throne. It is outside the scope of this work to discuss all those stories. However, what is pertinent to our discussion is that Kapilendra did not belong to the previous lineage and was an outsider who occupied the throne. According to legend, Kapilendra Deb had been chosen as the successor of Bhanudeva by Lord Jagannath Himself. As per the *Madala Panji*, Bhanudeva IV was childless and prayed to Jagannath to be blessed with a successor. The Lord appeared in his dream and indicated that he would find his successor near the Bimala Temple (located within the Jagannath Temple complex). Next morning Bhanudeva went to the temple of Bimala and found a boy whom he later adopted, and the boy succeeded the king. This story is corroborated by the Gopinathapura Stone Inscription engraved under the orders of his minister Gopinath Mahapatra. The relevant verse has been translated as follows:[15] 'By the order of the Lord of Nilagiri (blue hill) (who is) the lord of the three worlds (Jagannatha), there was born in the Odradesa a king named Kapilendra, the ornament of the Solar Line.'

A new doctrine was established by Kapilendra Deb, wherein, he propounded himself as 'an elect of Lord Jagannath'. As this required acceptance and affirmation, he sought the support of the priestly class to legitimise this doctrine. This was necessary for his survival as he was not a direct lineal descendant of the previous king. The priestly class accepted him as the founder of a new dynasty called *Suryavansha* (Sun dynasty). After his accession to the throne, he faced stiff opposition from several feudatory kings. In order to establish himself and suppress the rebellion, he made a declaration addressed to the feudatory kings (in his 4th *anka*), which is available in one of the inscriptions of the Jagamohana (assembly hall) of the Lingaraj Temple of Bhubaneswar. It states:

'All the kings in my Orissa kingdom should work for the good of the (paramount) sovereign, should keep up virtuous ways, should not remain in bad ways. If they act badly towards the sovereign, they will be expelled from the kingdom and all their property confiscated.'[16]

To further consolidate his position and to secure the support of people, he resorted to remittance of taxes. He followed a carrot and stick policy by conveying a stern message to rebellious feudatories and displaying a benevolent approach towards people by lessening their tax burden. There is an interesting and important inscription to this effect engraved on the Jaya-Bijaya door of the Jagannath Temple during his 4th *anka*. This is the door through which devotees and pilgrims pass to have darshan of the deities. In this inscription, Kapilendra Deb warns the kings, 'The tax payable on salt and cowries (money) which is due to us of our kingdom of Orissa I have remitted, I have…remitted! (He) who being a king, violates this, rebels against the deity Sri Jagannatha.'[17]

Through this order, Kapilendra Deb also sent a message to the feudatory kings that anyone who dared to revoke the remittance of these taxes would incur the wrath of Jagannath, the Lord of the Universe. He tried to earn legitimacy by projecting that he had secured the sanction of Lord Jagannath and conveyed that any opposition or attack on the Gajapati (Kapilendra Deb) would be an offence against Jagannath Himself. Kapilendra Deb thus introduced an interesting facet into the doctrine, wherein he conveyed that all his actions had the sanction of Lord Jagannath, and while establishing the legitimacy of his actions, he warned others to refrain from doing anything against Lord Jagannath.

The Gopinathapura inscription mentions that Kapilendra became the king of Odisha by the decree of Jagannath. Thus, his acceptance became smooth and Kapilendra Deb could create an impression that he was the chosen one by Jagannath, the overlord of Odisha. To strengthen this notion further, it is learnt from inscriptions on the Jaya-Bijaya door, that he made a significant submission before Lord Jagannath: 'Whom so ever You favour this territory is his, it is verily not mine' (*E bhumikhanda tu yahaku anugraha karu, mohara se kebe nuhe*).[18]

This assertion and submission was an extension of his doctrine of being the elect of the Lord. This was intended to show that the throne belonged to Lord Jagannath and he had no intention of taking it away. He had merely succeeded a servant of the Lord, Bhanudeva. It was to be considered as replacement of one servant by another, or one servant taking over the duties of another servant.

Kapilendra Deb, as a true *sebak*, surrendered all his wealth to Lord Jagannath. As a servant of the Lord, he always considered that all his wealth and possessions belonged to his Master. In an inscription in the Puri Temple, his vow before the deity Jagannath bestowing all his jewellery on Him and as much wealth as possible on Brahmins is recorded.

He issued the following decree for inscription:[19] 'Oh Jagannath, Thou knowest indeed all (things) of mine—(both) within and without. Whatever jewellery I have, that is Thine, whatever treasure (wealth) I possess, other than this, I shall bestow on Brahmins, as much as I can. Favour anyone with this kingdom (lit. patch of land) He (will be) my....'

In a subsequent inscription, Kapilendra Deb is recorded to have bequeathed several ornaments and jewellery of 1,400 varieties for the decoration of the deities with a list of the ornaments mentioned in the inscription. The inscription states: 'King Kapileswara (*sic*) bequeathed these to Jagannatha, the Great Lord. He who entertains in his mind (the idea) 'I shall take these away' rebels against Holy Jagannatha'.[20]

He started the practice of consultation with the Lord before taking any difficult decision. He is probably the first Gajapati who in his inscriptions is said to have asked for Jagannath's advice. In 1464, he undertook an expedition against his opponents. Before starting the expedition, he paid a visit to Jagannath and complained: 'Oh Jagannath! Thus prayeth Thy servant (*sebaka*). Throughout the kingdom, I have maintained from childhood, these feudal lords including the infantry and cavalry, and gave them wealth. All of them have forsaken me. I shall deal with them and punish them as they deserve. Oh Lord Jagannath! Thou judge this fact whether I am right or wrong.'[21]

Kapilendra Deb, by adopting this policy of communication with the presiding deity or *Rastradebata*, made Lord Jagannath both a witness to and an approver of his decisions. This had a dual purpose. First, he showed his abiding loyalty to the Lord as his supreme authority who was required to be informed of his decisions. This approach made the people in general subscribe to the view that his decisions had the approval of the presiding deity of whom he was a mere *sebak*. This also helped him in securing the support and loyalty of several feudatory kings as a measure of unity to safeguard his vast empire. It provided him with the ammunition to silence his opponents who did not accept him and treated him as a usurper to the throne or an illegal claimant by not being a direct descendant of the preceding Ganga king.

Further, by giving magnanimous grants and donations to the Puri Temple, Kapilendra secured the support of the powerful priestly class and other *sebaks* of the temple. This approach gave him strength, power and support from all sections of the society, including the feudatory kings, to expand and consolidate his empire. This immensely contributed to making him a fine administrator and earned the continued goodwill of his subjects. People looked up to him with immense respect and reverence, both from the point of view of the Gajapati being a *sebak* of the Lord and subordinate to the presiding deity. This instilled a widespread feeling among people that whatever the Gajapati was doing, he was doing so as a servant and representative of Lord Jagannath.

Secondly, people looked upon him as a strong king and extolled him for his expansionist drive that made the Odishan Empire one of the largest Hindu kingdoms at that time, starting from the Hooghly River in the north to Cauvery in the south. No other king of Odisha since Kharvela (209–170 BC of the Chedi dynasty) had ruled over such a vast territory as Kapilendra Deb did.

Though of humble origin, Kapilendra Deb proved himself a genius in surpassing all his predecessors in conquest, suppression of rebellions, generosity, efficient administration and all other qualities which went to make him the greatest monarch of Odisha of that period. This was singularly possible because of his articulation and implementation of a well-calibrated Jagannath-centric philosophy. His act of surrender to the presiding deity of Odisha as a *sebak* and continued patronage of the priestly class and the temple tradition helped him in enlisting the desired support for pursuing a focused approach towards achieving his objectives. His long reign of 34 years was one of the most stable and glorious periods in Odisha's history.

It is significant to mention that Kapilendra Deb introduced a new concept of *sebak* of Lord Jagannath. This is how the concept of the king as the *Adyasebak*, first servitor of Jagannath, originated. The title *Adyasebak* denoted a transformative change from the earlier concept of *rauta* to *sebak*, without changing the core philosophy of surrender and subordination to Lord Jagannath. This change had significant implications. The growing emergence of the priestly class provided the context for the change.

By declaring himself a *sebak* of Lord Jagannath, Kapilendra Deb adopted a two-fold approach. First, he needed the support of the priestly class to be accepted as the king. This was an exercise in legitimising his position. Secondly, the legitimisation or acceptance required a functional status; since he was not of royal lineage, Kapilendra Deb chose to be a servant of the Lord. This ensured that the priestly class, particularly the Brahmins, accepted him into the fold of the servitors of Lord Jagannath. This enabled him to enter into the framework of temple services and the network of temple servants.

It is also pertinent to mention that the concept of *rauta* that was diluted by some of the later Ganga kings was corrected and strengthened by Kapilendra Deb through his concept of *sebak*, whereby the king formally positioned himself in the *sebak* fold for attending to temple services. Later, this was formalised and the Gajapati was treated as the *Adyasebak* with prescribed services to offer to the Lord.

Purushottama Deb – The Lord Fought for Him

Purushottama Deb (AD 1467–1497) succeeded his father Kapilendra Deb. He was not the rightful claimant to the throne as he deprived his elder brother, Hamvira. The doctrine of elect was again applied to aid in his acceptance and legitimacy. He pursued a liberal and lavish approach of donating expensive gifts to Lord Jagannath. He also donated villages as offering. By making lavish presents to the Brahmins, he secured their support. He advised the other regional kings of Odisha: 'Never deprive Brahmins of these four matters—wealth, wife, life and land.'[22]

The Puri inscription of Purushottama Deb records his order as follows: 'Feeling, hearing and seeing, I advise the kings of Odisha, as long as this world lasts, all ye kings! ye are to make gifts to the brahmanas with peaceful and attentive mind, never deprive brahmanas of these four items—wealth, life and land…'.[23] The fourth item mentioned in the inscription is not legible. However, Hermann Kulke, German historian and Indologist, relying on M.M. Chakravarti, has deduced that the fourth item is 'women'. Famous writer K.B. Tripathi too lists the four items as wealth, women, life and land.[24]

We have more evidence of Purushottama Deb's vigorous policy of pleasing the priestly class. In one of his Puri inscriptions, he states, 'Oh Jagannatha, Thou knowest everything of mine both external and internal. Whatever precious things I have, I will bestow on the Brahmans as much as I can.'[25]

It is the reign of Purushottama Deb that has given us one of the most popular folklores of Odisha, known as the Legend of *Kanchi Abhijan*. This legend is a narrative of a fascinating story of reinforcing the supremacy of Lord Jagannath and portraying the Gajapati Purushottama Deb as his *sebak* or deputy.

The death of Kapilendra Deb saw his enemies becoming powerful and aggressive. Sultan Mohammad Shah III of the Bahmani Empire immediately called a war council and appointed Malik Hassan Bahari as the commander of the army, and he brought under his occupation Rajahmundry, Kondavidu and some other forts. Saluva Narasimha, the King of Kanchi, capital of the Vijayanagar Empire, taking advantage of the situation tried to extend his kingdom at the expense of Odisha's ruler. When Hassan Bahari occupied Rajahmundry and Kondavidu, Saluva Narasimha recovered his lost territories by occupying the east coast between Udayagiri in the north and Cauvery in the south.

Purushottama Deb faced a crisis; he found parts of his territory, acquired by his father Kapilendra Deb, being usurped. This territorial loss spurred him to fall back on the presiding deity of the state for help. In this context, the popular *Kanchi Abhijan* story depicts the glory of Purushottama Deb through the participation of Lord Jagannath and Lord Balabhadra in the war against Kanchi.

The popular play *Kanchi Abhijan* is very dear to the people of Odisha. The story goes as follows: Saluva Narasimha of Kanchi had a beautiful daughter, Roopambika. Purushottama Deb wanted to marry her. The Kanchi King, however, refused to give his daughter to a king who performed the menial duty of a sweeper on the great occasion of the Car Festival of Lord Jagannath every year. The Kanchi King looked down on the Odishan King whom he equated with a *chandal,* a man of low caste doing the menial job of a sweeper.

Purushottama Deb took this as an insult not only to him but also to Lord Jagannath. He decided to take revenge and vowed to get the Kanchi Princess Roopambika married to a sweeper. Purushottama Deb led an expedition to Kanchi but lost in the war. The failed Purushottama Deb then sought the shelter of Lord Jagannath. He prayed and propitiated Lord Jagannath who promised him in a dream that he would help in the war. As per the legend, in the second expedition, Lord Jagannath and his brother Balabhadra proceeded to Kanchi ahead of the Gajapati in the guise of two horsemen, one sitting on a black horse and the other on a white one.

As per the legend, the brothers bought butter milk to quench their thirst from a milkmaid named Manika on their way to

Kanchi. But instead of paying her in cash, they gave her a ring asking her to present it to the king who was coming behind, to pay her in exchange for the ring. When Purushottama Deb and his army passed the same place, he was stopped by the milkmaid asking to be paid for the milk she had given to his two soldiers some time back. On seeing the ring which was that of Lord Jagannath, the king realised the divine support.

In the war, the king of Kanchi was defeated. Purushottama Deb succeeded in taking the Kanchi princess into custody and brought her to Odisha. To avenge the earlier insult, Purushottama Deb instructed his Minister to solemnise her marriage with a sweeper. But his clever minister saved the situation by presenting the princess to him as his bride when the king was doing the duty of a sweeper (*chherapanhara*) at the time of the Car Festival in Puri, thus doing his duty as per the instruction of the king. Purushottama Deb agreed to marry her and the story ended happily. She was known as Padmavati after marriage.

This war finds pictorial expression on the walls of the Jagamohan hall inside the Jagannath Temple, where the stucco structural representation of Lord Jagannath and his brother Balabhadra in the guise of horsemen proceeding to Kanchi can be seen. These representations have been referred to as *Vedha Parikrima* in the Odia work of Balaram Das, a contemporary of Prataprudra, son and successor of Purushottama Deb. The work was meant to be a pilgrim's guide, and it states, 'After visiting this you will find the representation of two brothers [Lord Jagannath and Balabhadra] galloping valiantly towards Kanchi, on the wall of Jagamohan.'[26]

The legend has such an impact on the culture of Odisha that the images of the two horsemen and the milkmaid are frequently depicted as subjects in the famous *Pattachitra* paintings of Odisha that evoke the imagination of the people of Odisha about the *Kanchi Abhijan* and devotion to Lord Jagannath.

Purushottama Deb's Kanchi expedition shows the height of the enduring dependence and faith of the Gajapati on Lord Jagannath.

In this case, the presiding deity came to the help of his *sebak* to restore his dignity and honour by saving him from the insult of Saluva Narasimha. Though the Kanchi-Kaveri expedition is part of a legend, evidence points to the historicity of the events depicted. This is also supported by the fact that Purushottama Deb after he defeated the Kanchi king, brought with him three things: an image of Lord Ganesha which was a favourite of the Kanchi king and installed the idol in the Jagannath temple premises; an image of *Sakhigopala*—which is now found in the Temple of Sakhigopala in Puri district—and a jewelled throne known as the *Ratna Singhasana* or *Ratna Bedi,* on which the three deities Jagannath, Balabhadra and Subhadra are seated or installed.

The expedition demonstrated that Lord Jagannath was the supreme monarch of the Odisha Empire and Purushottama Deb was His *sebak*. The failure of the first expedition, when the king himself led the war against Saluva Narasimha but lost, led him to turn to the ultimate saviour Lord Jagannath, the supreme commander, to come to his rescue and lead the war against the Kanchi king, which was finally won by Gajapati Purushottama Deb.

Purushottama Deb invaded the Bahmani kingdom in AD 1476. He took advantage of the famine situation in the Bahmani kingdom and internal revolt in the Bahmani army. As a result, the Bahmani Sultan lost both Rajahmundry and Kondavidu to the Gajapati.

Purushottama Deb, in order to exercise his control over various services of Lord Jagannath, prepared a manual titled *Gopalaracanavidhi*, which became a tool to control the priests through 'elaborate prescription and descriptions of daily and other special rituals'.[27]

Prataprudra Deb

Prataprudra Deb, son of Purushottama Deb, succeeded him in AD 1497. The *Gitagovinda* was composed by Jayadeva in the 12th century AD. This lucid composition became very famous because of its introduction in the rituals of Jagannath culture. With the patronage of the Ganga emperors, *Gitagovinda* was sung every day in the temple as a result of which it became popular in every household in Odisha and India as well. Purushottama Deb wrote a variation of *Gitagovinda* known as *Abhinava Gitagovinda*. His son Prataprudra Deb introduced the singing of *Abhinava Gitagovinda*, in place of the *Gitagovinda* of Jayadeva, which was a long-standing tradition. This brought him in conflict with the priests.

Prataprudra Deb had to withdraw his order and restore Jayadeva's *Gitagovinda*. This finds mention in a Puri inscription where there is a clear order of Prataprudra that reads, 'Four Vaishnav singers will only sing Gita Govinda'. The said inscription prohibited any other songs to be sung.[28] The priestly class tried to assert their power over the Gajapati as far as temple services and rituals were concerned. At this time, the arrival of Chaitanya Mahaprabhu (Indian saint) became a golden opportunity for Prataprudra Deb. The increasing popularity of Chaitanya made a big dent in the power and position of the priestly class. The support provided by Chaitanya and the patronage of Prataprudra Deb was able to somewhat check the power and influence of the Puri priests.

The relationship between the king and the deity, however, remained intact with adherence to the ideology introduced by Anangabhimadeva III and followed by his successors in a great measure up to AD 1568, with minor aberrations in between. The tradition of this relationship remained a redeeming and predominant feature of the Jagannath cult and culture. As a matter of fact, the identity, existence and continuity of the Gajapati kings in Odisha revolved around their inevitable dependence on Lord Jagannath, and was a key factor in the survival of kingship in Odisha. This is because of a three-way matrix of close association and correlation of vital elements in the social, religious and political dynamics of the society.

The crucial base is the intimate relationship that the people of Odisha had (and continue to have) with Jagannath. Lord Jagannath is no ordinary symbolic deity for worship. He occupies a deep and permanent place in the hearts and minds of the people of Odisha.

He is held as a popular living God and worshiped in each and every Hindu home, and the connection of the people with the Lord is deeply spiritual and emotional. Jagannath is their ultimate destination, the last refuge, oasis of shelter and undying ray of hope. Jagannath is viewed as their companion and friend. On every occasion of life, be it birth, death, marriage, prosperity, or adversity or any other occasion, people have a bond with Jagannath. There is a vast body of literature that has developed over time depicting this association between the people and Jagannath. This axis of relationship is paramount for the survival of two other aspects: the relationship between the king and the people on one hand, and the king and the Lord on the other.

The Gajapatis were conscious that any act of theirs which incurs the displeasure of the supreme authority Lord Jagannath or is perceived to be offensive to Him or is thought to be an act of insubordination to Him would distance them from the people. Therefore, their existence and continuity depended upon strengthening and sustaining the faith and bond of people with Jagannath. The Gajapatis, therefore, secured the trust of the people by demonstrating their unflinching devotion and loyalty to the Jagannath cult by acting as the Lord's most devoted and humble servant. The principle of divine right and of subordination or surrender thus became the foundational philosophy of the Jagannath cult, which was nurtured over the ages.

AD 1568 and Beyond

This tradition faced challenges after AD 1568. Several factors contributed to its dilution. The Gajapati kings lost their independence to the Afghans in 1568. The king of Odisha became the Raja of Khurda with loss of his territory and independence from 1568 till 1751. Frequent attacks by the Mughals led to a situation where the deities were secreted out frequently from the temple at Puri, and the Gajapatis were often imprisoned; both the Lord and the Gajapatis were on the run. The destabilized regime of the Raja of Khurda became more chaotic due to internal feuds, greed, and conspiracy among the Hindu kings of the region. Barring short intermittent periods of respite, the Khurda Rajas were under great stress to save themselves and protect the honour and sanctity of their revered deity Lord Jagannath. This was a period of great turmoil, uncertainty and instability for the Khurda Rajas.

The takeover of Odisha by the Marathas in 1751 was of no comfort. Gajapati Birakeshari Deb I (AD 1736–1793) lost vast territories with loss of control over four parganas, which included the Jagannath Temple, to the Marathas. Thus, the dissociation of the Khurda Raja from the Puri Temple was almost complete during the rule of the Marathas.

The coming of the British in 1803 brought in an interesting dimension. The British followed a policy of distancing themselves from the rituals and religious affairs of the temple by entrusting the matter in the hands of the Raja of Khurda, who became the Raja of Puri when Gajapati Mukunda Deb II (AD 1798–1817) relocated to Puri after being released from prison. The linkage between the Gajapati and Lord Jagannath was restored in a formal sense but the Raja of Puri was not the same as the powerful Gajapatis of yesteryears.

The Raja of Puri, a king without any kingdom, a titular monarch, a ruler only in name, was no king at all. He was an appointee of the British and totally dependent upon their benediction. After India's Independence, with the enactment of the Shri Jagannath Temple Act 1954 the dissociation became complete except for the formal association of the Gajapati as Chairman of the Shree Jagannatha Managing Committee. However, the ritualistic tradition of the Gajapati being the *Adyasebak* continued.

In the changed scenario, only the traditions in the sphere of religious rituals appear to have survived. The Raja of Puri's customary association with Lord Jagannath in terms of performing rituals acquired an aspect of immortality. He still commands widespread respect and reverence because he is the *Adyasebak* of Lord Jagannath. In the eyes of people, he is the

Gajapati. People look up to him not for his power and position but for his revered and loved role as the first and foremost servitor of Lord Jagannath. People long to have a glimpse of him, and when they see him they feel as if they are seeing their *Chalanti Vishnu* (living God). He is also honoured by being called *Thakura Raja*. The important ritual of *chherapanhara* during the Rath Yatra continues to sustain and uphold the Gajapati's connection with the people. Therefore, the perception and admiration of the Gajapati in the minds of the people have not been affected in spite of the vicissitudes over time.

The Ekadashi Tradition

A visible display of the age-old tradition of the linkages between the deity and the king finds expression in a ritual observed on every *Ekadashi* (11th day of both the *Shukla* or bright phase of the moon and *Krushna* or dark fortnight) when the *mahadeepa alati* (the great lamp offering) is performed at night. After the evening *dhupa* (offering of incense), the *puja pandas* (temple priests) first perform the *mahadeepa alati* near the *Ratna Singhasana*, then go around it and thereafter pass the *Jaya-Bijaya* door to go in front of the Bimala Temple. Then they give three *kalashas* (earthen pots) and some *tulsi* (basil leaves) to the *Chunara sebaks*. The *Chunara sebaks* are hereditary servitors who perform the service of *mahadeepa alati* to the *Neelachakra* (blue wheel) at the top of the temple and also tie the temple flag every day. The *Ghantuas* (a category of *sebaks*) prepare 12 *chandraudiyas* (specially made lamps). The three *Chunara sebaks* climb up the temple with the *mahadeepa* and *chandraudiya*. Standing below the *dadhinauti* (circular base of the topmost portion of the temple below the *Neelachakra*), they offer *tulsi* and sandal paste to the *Neelachakra* and then go around it thrice and light three *chandraudiyas* in each of the four directions. While moving around they recite the *prasasthi* (hymn) in the name of the ruling Gajapati and then pray aloud to Lord Jagannath as under:

'May the Lord save,

Virashree Gajapati Gaudeswar Nabakoti Karnatotkala Kalabargeswara Abhirai Bhuta Bhairabha Duhsaha Duhshasana Anikarane Routrai Atula Bala Parakrama Sangrama Sahasrabahu Khetriyakula Dhumaketu Viradhivirabara Pratapi Sri Sri Sri Dibyasingha Deb Maharaja (here the name of the ruling Gajapati is taken) sheltering him inside the conch shell and shielding him by the disc.'

They chant *Hari Bol* while going around the *Neelachakra* and also pray to Jagannath for the well-being of the people. This ritual on every *Ekadasi* day is a prayer to Jagannath to protect the king and keep him safe. The above *prasasthi* (hymn) is recited on *Ekadasi* days even now. This symbolises Lord Jagannath as the ultimate protector and custodian of the Gajapati. Though in the present times the Gajapati is just a nominal title unlike the powerful kings in the past, the ritual is observed elaborately on every *Ekadasi* night.

3

SURYAVANSHI GAJAPATIS
Grandeur and Glory

The Gajapati kings starting with Kapilendra Deb inherited a strong foundation and legacy from the Ganga dynasty. Chodagangadeva (AD 1078–1150) is regarded as the founder of the Ganga dynasty in Odisha and he ruled for a period of 72 years, establishing a strong, prosperous and vast kingdom. During his long reign—a rare phenomenon in history—he shifted his capital from Kalinganagar (present-day Mukhalingam in Srikakulam district of Andhra Pradesh) to Baranasi Kataka (the present-day Cuttack). By relocating the capital, he shifted the seat of power closer to the centre of his empire and close to the religious nerve centre of Odisha, i.e., Lord Jagannath at Puri, where he began building the now-famous and highly revered Jagannath Temple. The Gangas, who originally came from the Andhra-Telangana region, ruled for 14 generations from Cuttack and were completely assimilated with the local population to become Odias.

By starting to build the Jagannath Temple, Chodagangadeva gained great popular acclaim and respect; he also helped in imparting a pan-India character to the temple that has increased over the centuries. Subsequent Ganga kings, such as Anangabhimadeva III, contributed significantly to the growth of the Ganga kingdom by expanding the territory. At its height of splendour under Anangabhimadeva III, the Odishan kingdom occupied the vast area stretching from the Ganga River in the north to the Cauvery in the south and included the erstwhile Somavanshi kingdom to the west. It is reckoned that this was the largest Hindu kingdom existing at that time. Anangabhimadeva III also earned immortal fame by completing the construction of the Jagannath Temple at Puri, which was begun by Chodagangadeva. As described in the previous chapters, being a great devotee of Lord Jagannath, Anangabhima installed Lord Jagannath as the state deity, the supreme monarch, and he assumed the position of the Lord's deputy (*rauta*), a tradition that was carried on by the subsequent kings.

Narasimhadeva I (AD 1238–1264), also known as Langula Narasimha, was the son and successor of Anangabhimadeva III. A great warrior, he gained fame by defeating Islamic invaders from the north. Narasimhadeva's brilliant military strategy frightened and kept the invaders away during his reign. His strategy of aggression as the best defence proved effective and kept Odisha independent for a long period. Narasimhadeva's contribution in the field of art and architecture was also path-breaking. The great monumental marvel, the Sun Temple at Konark, was built under his patronage. The Konark temple is the most magnificent, delicate, and the finest and grandest celebration of art, architecture and sculpture by any king in Odisha till date. The magnificent monument has no equal and continues to surprise and hold successive generations spellbound through its exquisite craftsmanship and splendid sculptural depictions. Konark presents the pinnacle of the Ganga dynasty's achievements both from the point of view of their military might and patronage of art.

The Ganga rule established a vast empire and a strong administrative structure. It was during this period that the construction of many temples and architectural works of significance were undertaken. The period also witnessed the rise to prominence and pre-eminence of Lord Jagannath. The Ganga kings became ardent followers of Vishnu. The foreign invasions were kept at bay. Their great legacy was passed on to their successors.

Kapilendra Deb

Kapilendra Deb, the founder of the Suryavanshi Gajapatis, ascended the throne in AD 1435 after the last Ganga king, Bhanudeva IV. Kapilendra Deb's ascension provides a turning point in the Gajapati history in Odisha because he was not a lineal descendant of the Gangas but claimed to belong to the Suryavansha dynasty. His legitimacy to the throne was based on a claim that he became the ruler by an *adesa* (order) of Lord Jagannath.

Besides the Gopinathapura Stone Inscription that lends support to the narrative of Kapilendra having been adopted by Bhanudeva following a dream wherein he was directed by Lord Jagannath to do so, other sources, namely *Katakaraja-vamsavali* and *Kaifiyat of Jagannatham*, narrate similar stories with minor differences. The boy whom Bhanudeva found at the temple of Bimala-Parvati was given the name Kapila Samanta Rao. During the last days of Bhanudeva's rule, the Mughals invaded the country and demanded a large ransom. The king paid a portion of it, and for the remainder left his son Kapila Samanta Rao as hostage. The king died soon after. The Mughals then released Kapila Samanta and allowed him to rule this country.[1]

It is learnt from two sources, namely the *Madala Panji* and *Gangavansanucharitam*, that before ascending to the Ganga throne, Kapilendra Deb had assumed three titles at three different periods of time—*Rauta, Mahapatra* and *Brahmarabara*. These three titles represented his different status and position in the military. *Rauta* was a military title which indicates that holder of the title was a horseman. *Mahapatra* was a title conferred on a distinguished officer of the Ganga army. *Brahmarabara* was a very high rank in the army, generally adorned by members of the royal families. These titles reflect his humble beginnings and meteoric rise in the army—from a horseman to *Brahmarabara*.

Though there are different versions from various sources about how he ascended the throne, the undisputed fact remains that Kapilendra Deb was not a lineal descendant of the Gangas. Thus, he was not the rightful claimant to the throne of the Odishan kingdom. Bhanudeva IV was a weak king who engaged in frequent battles with the Reddys of Rajahmundry. When the Ganga king was thus preoccupied fighting with the Reddys, taking advantage of the king's absence and preoccupation in the south, Kapila Samanta usurped the throne with the support of disgruntled officials. Kapilendra Deb immediately took upon himself the task of protecting Odisha from twin dangers: one from impending foreign invasion from the north and the other, retaliation from Bhanudeva IV, who was not able to withstand the earlier invasion from the south.

Kapilendra Deb also faced the challenge of credibility and acceptability. He faced serious tests both internally as well as externally. In the south, the Vijayanagar emperor Devaraya II (AD 1422–1446) had infiltrated into and occupied the territory up to Simhachalam (Vizagapatam, Andhra Pradesh). The Reddy rulers were extending their frontiers further into the north. There was also the danger of Islamic invasion from the Sultan of Bengal. In addition, the Malwa ruler tried to take advantage of the complex situation in Odisha. Even within Odisha, local chiefs refused to acknowledge Kapilendra Deb as their king and began to act as independent sovereigns. Under these trying circumstances, Kapilendra Deb wanted to consolidate his position by proclaiming an order against the rebellious chiefs, and hence he adopted a tough line. The proclamation threatened expulsion from the kingdom and confiscation of property of the feudatory and local kings if they acted against the sovereign.

He followed a two-fold approach. He formulated and executed a policy to keep the masses happy by addressing their welfare.

At the same time, he pursued an aggressive agenda against his detractors and invaders.

As mentioned earlier, the feudatory chiefs became powerful and declared themselves as independent and did not recognize Kapilendra Deb as the king. The powerful chiefs of Silavamshi of Nandapura (present-day Koraput in Odisha), Matsyas of Oddadi (Jeypore, in Koraput) and Vishnuvardhana Chakravartins of Panchadharala (Vizagapatam) did not recognize Kapilendra Deb's accession. In pursuance to his proclamation, these chiefs were suppressed and subjugated by the Gajapati during the early part of his reign. It is also learnt that he suppressed the revolt in Khemidi, which appeared to be one of the chiefdoms of present-day Ganjam district bearing the names of *Sanakhemidi*, *Badakhemidi* and *Parlakhemundi*.[2]

As a part of the legitimization process, Kapilendra Deb donated land and valuable items to the Jagannath Temple and the priestly class; declared Lord Jagannath as the supreme authority or the *Rastradebata* and considered himself as His *sebak*. This doctrine, discussed in detail in the previous chapter, was followed to reinforce his credentials and legitimacy. This also helped him in gaining acceptance by the people and the other feudatory kings of Odisha.

An inscription of Jagannath Temple incised in the 19th *anka* of Kapilendra Deb's reign (AD 1450) refers to his victory over Malik Parisa (Malik Padshah), the Sultan of Gaud. To celebrate the victory, the Gajapati presented Lord Jagannath a precious *saree* named *Pundarikagopa*. In the same inscription, Kapilendra Deb assumes the title of 'Gaudeswara' which clearly indicated that he defeated Sultan Nasiruddin of Bengal (probably another name for Malik Parisa) sometime around AD 1447.[3]

In the south, the King Deva Raya II of the Vijayanagar Empire died in AD 1446 and was succeeded by his weak son Mallikarjuna Raya. The Reddys of Rajahmundry did not get any support from their weak ally. Kapilendra Deb took advantage of this position and sent his son Hamvira to defeat the Reddys. Hamvira succeeded and the kingdom of Rajahmundry was brought under Kapilendra Deb in AD 1448. After the death of Deva Raya II, the whole of Vijayanagar and the king of Kondavidu (present-day Guntur, Andhra Pradesh) became weak. Kapilendra Deb occupied these kingdoms in AD 1454. Thus, he became the master of the Krishna–Godavari delta, and this brought Odisha face-to-face in conflict with the Bahmani kingdom of the Deccan. When Bahmani Sultan Humayun Shah attacked Devarakonda (in Nalgonda, Telangana) Kapilendra Deb, on being approached by the Velema chief of the Deccan (Telangana), attacked the Bahmani army and occupied the region in AD 1458. Following this success, Kapilendra Deb entrusted his son Hamvira the task of conquering the entire Telangana. Hamvira defeated his enemies and occupied their forts.

By AD 1464, Kapilendra Deb had acquired a vast empire stretching from the river Ganga in the north to Tiruchirappalli in the Cauvery valley in the south along the coast. From epigraphic records, it is seen that he had assumed the titles *Gajapati, Gaudeswara, Nabakoti, Karnata,* and *Kalabargeswar*. Each of these titles has significance. The title of Gajapati, as mentioned earlier, was used as a title of status and position by Kapilendra Deb. He conquered a part of Gauda within Bengal and became Gaudeswara. His conquest of the Bahmani kingdom and expedition to Bidar earned him the title of Kalabargeswar. The capital of the Bahmani kingdom was earlier known as Gulburga from which Kalabarga is derived as an Odia aberration. After conquering part of the Vijayanagar Empire, Kapilendra Deb assumed the title of Nabakoti Karnata; Vijayanagar at that time was known as Karnata. As regards the meaning of *Nabakoti*, there are different interpretations (discussed in Chapter 1). *Nabakoti* (nine crores), according to some historians, referred to the total population of Bahmani and Vijayanagar which he conquered. *Nabakoti* has also been interpreted as nine forts which were very important.

Although Kapilendra Deb had a vast empire, he continued to face rebellions by local chiefs which bothered him. One of his inscriptions in the Jagannath Temple dated AD 1454 states: 'Oh! Jagannath, thy servant thus informeth the high officers in the kingdom. From soldiers and servants (illegible, probably up to them) I looked after (all) from boyhood. Now they have forsaken me. I will treat them as they deserve. Lord Jagannatha, judge the correctness or incorrectness of mine (acts).'[4]

Kapilendra Deb initially held a lowly rank in the Ganga army. He rose from humble roots to establish a vast empire. Whereas his predecessors, the Ganga and Somavamsi kings, had all come from outside Odisha, he was an Odia. It was after many centuries that a native Odia was ruling over his own people, which gave them a sense of pride and self-respect. He deepened his connection with his kingdom by associating himself with the Jagannath Temple and calling himself his *sebak*. This provided him a truly unique identity and status that enabled him to galvanize support and ensure his subjects fought in battlefields, since his success in military pursuits depended on the same.

After Kharvela (209–170 BC of the Chedi dynasty), Kapilendra Deb stands the tallest king in building a great Odishan empire. He provided a role model to the people of Odisha to assert their identity and pride and enlisted their support for the protection and expansion of his kingdom. He could instil the idea in the minds of the people that defending and expanding the kingdom was the joint responsibility of the ruler and the ruled. This militarism penetrated deep into the ranks of people, irrespective of their caste or social status.

Kapilendra Deb's regime marked a new beginning for prosperity of Odia literature, and the Gajapati occupies a place of distinction for promoting Odia language. Being a native of Odisha, he declared Odia as the *Rastrabhasa* or the language of the people and promoted and patronized its growth. Under the Ganga dynasty, Sanskrit was the *Rajbhasa* (language of the court) as well as the *Devbhasa* (language of God and Brahmins). There was a divide between the ruler and the ruled in the absence of a popular *Lokbhasa* (language of the people). Kapilendra Deb realized the need to popularize the native local language, i.e., Odia, to bridge the gap and come closer to the people. Before him and particularly during the Ganga period, poets, writers and learned scholars were patronized and encouraged to work in Sanskrit language. The development of Odia language and literature was scanty and limited. Absence of royal patronage was the biggest impediment to the growth of Odia literature. This situation was addressed by Kapilendra Deb, who himself was a great writer and scholar in both Sanskrit and Odia literature. As a celebrated writer in Sanskrit, he wrote the play *Parasuram Vijay* in Sanskrit. This was very popular in those days. He accorded royal recognition to the Odia language. Many of his inscriptions were written in Odia. He believed that popular spread of his works could happen only when they were written or communicated in people's language. In his Sanskrit play, *Parasuram Vijay*, he introduced songs in Odia language. In fact, in this play the character Rani Chandravadana sings songs in Odia instead of Sanskrit. This shows Kapilendra Deb's initiation and patronage of Odia language and literature. The composition of Odia songs was appreciated very much by the people.

Sarala Dasa, the *Adikavi* (first poet), was a contemporary of Kapilendra Deb. He is considered as the Father of Odia literature. His *Mahabharata* was the most significant contribution to Odia language and literature during the time of Kapilendra Deb. He wrote two other books, *Bilanka Ramayan* and *Chandi Purana*. These two works contain about 2,800 and 5,500 verses respectively.

Sarala Dasa, originally known as Siddheswar Parida, was a Sudra by caste. A non-Brahmin composing the magnum opus of *Mahabharata* in Odia was a revolutionary step in those times. According to a rough estimate, the *Sarala Mahabharata* contains 83,000 verses, each of two lines, and covers 2,309 printed pages.[5] In the *Musali Parva* of *Mahabharata,* Sarala Dasa opens with a long invocation addressed to Lord Jagannath, who enjoys unquestioned supremacy among Hindu gods and goddesses of Odisha. Sarala Dasa describes the manifold powers and qualities of Lord Jagannath and tells us that Maharaja Kapileswar (another name of Kapilendra Deb) with innumerable offerings was serving this great deity and thereby destroying the sins of the age. This extraordinary work was not limited to or a literal translation of Ved Vyas's *Mahabharata*. It is a regional variation of the original epic, where the core content remained intact, with wider variations designed and described to contextualize the local situations, places, people, stories, myths, legends and folklore. It was an innovative experiment in literature, introducing a new genre which became popular among the people. The people related to the stories and understood the essence of the *Mahabharata* easily because of the familiar regional contexts and its local adaptations. Sarala Dasa's unique form of narration of this epic continues to be adored, recited and discussed even today by common people.

Dr Mayadhar Mansinha in his *History of Oriya Literature* aptly observed:

> Sarala Dasa, the peasant genius, not only wrote a great book but practically created a whole literature. The whole subsequent development of Odia literature was possible just because this peasant left behind this grand composition in a language that was still contemptible in the eyes of the learned and the rulers. This Sudra's successful adventure supplied inspiration and encouragement to all his immediate successors. And its influence on poets down to modern times is also deep and expansive.[6]

An attempt was made to compare the *Sarala Mahabharata* with the original *Mahabharata*. Sarala Dasa did not limit his work to the original text containing 18 *parvas* (chapters). He added three more *parvas*, namely *Madhya Parva*, *Gada Parva* and *Kansika Parva/Ansika Parva*.

Coming from a peasant family and not educated, Sarala Dasa dedicated his work to the grace of Goddess Sarala (Goddess of knowledge and wisdom).[7] Sarala Dasa highlighted the attributes of a king who ruled his subjects according to the rule of *Dharma* (duty of king towards his subjects). Gajapati Kapileswar, according to the poet, by being a *sebak* of Lord Jagannath had removed the sins of Kali Yuga (dark age), and in his conception, Kapilendra Deb was following *Raj Dharma* or Rule of Dharma. In the *Santi Parva* of Sarala's *Mahabharata*, Bhishma's instruction to Yudhisthira is significant:

> Oh king Yudhisthira! Rule the country according to the principles of Dharma. Happiness of the people is the happiness of the king. Distribute charity to the subjects at proper time and on appropriate occasions. Don't believe things without personal surprise visits. Ascertain truth through spies and cut off the heads of real enemies of the country. It is not a sin to punish evil-doers. Respect gods and Brahmins. Never covet another's wife or wealth. Entrust your administration only to a very trustworthy minister and discharge your royal duties in accordance with his advice. Do not permit foreign spies to live in the capital. Distribute free food and drinks at the places of pilgrimage. Do not harass cultivators. Station your commanders of the army at places where they are needed. Be liberal in the maintenance of horses and elephants and leave plenty of pasture land for cattle, show respect to the talent of learned and honour it; never be miserly towards poets.[8]

Raj Dharma or rule of law as enunciated by Sarala Dasa mirrors the vision and conduct of Gajapati Kapilendra Deb. He was not only the mighty ruler of a vast empire but also a just and judicious one. He followed these principles as a model king setting an example for his successors.

During Kapilendra Deb's reign, a new age of renaissance began in Odisha.

Purushottama Deb

Gajapati Kapilendra Deb was succeeded by his son Purushottama Deb, who acceded to the throne in AD 1467. A *Rajavanshabali* (historical document) provided by the former Bamanda state (present-day Deogarh, Odisha) refers to Purushottama Deb as a *Bhogini Nandana* (son of mistress). Another historian mentions that Purushottama Deb's mother was a *Phula-vivahi*. *Phula-vivahi* represents a class of wives of the rulers of Odisha who occupied an intermediate position between concubines and queens.[9] The Persian work *Tarikh-i-Ferishta*, while writing about events of Odisha, observes that 'Mangal Ray, a Brahmin and adopted son of the "late king" was ruling Odisha in 1470–71 AD.' As per epigraphic inscriptions, Purushottama Deb was the ruler of Odisha during the same period. Hence the name of Mangal Ray by Ferishta is said to be identical to Purushottama Deb.

In *Saraswatvilasam*, composed by Purushottama Deb's son Prataprudra, it is described that his father (Purushottama Deb) was the son of Kapilendra Deb by Parvati. The work is silent about the status of Parvati.

As per some sources, Kapilendra Deb had many wives. He had 18 sons from his wives, and Purushottama Deb was the son of Parvati, who was likely a mistress. On the death of Kapilendra Deb, the succession of Purushottama Deb was marred by a war of succession and dispute. Hamvira, the eldest son of Kapilendra Deb (although this fact is not free from doubt), was a great warrior and general during his father's regime; by the law of primogeniture, he was the rightful successor to his father's throne. Hamvira was instrumental in contributing to the success of his father in achieving a mighty and large empire. There is no historical account of Purushottama Deb's achievement or involvement in empire-building during his father's time. However, he became the Gajapati after Kapilendra Deb. The *Madala Panji* records that Purushottama Deb was anointed on the banks of the Krishna River by Kapilendra Deb around AD 1465–66. According to the *Madala Panji*, Kapilendra Deb could not decide who among his 18 sons should inherit his kingdom. He prayed to Lord Jagannath to help him. Lord Jagannath is said to have appeared in his dream and elected Purushottama Deb as his successor. The king, therefore, retired with his son to the banks of the Krishna where he anointed him as his successor. Kapilendra Deb died subsequently.

There is another version as to why Kapilendra Deb did not choose Hamvira, his most celebrated eldest son, who, by hereditary practice, would have been the natural choice. During the last years of his reign, Kapilendra Deb faced serious rebellions from various kingdoms, particularly from the south. Once, having decided to suppress some rebels, he visited the south. He conveyed his decision to the presiding deity Lord Jagannath and embarked on a southern expedition to rein in the rebels. By this time, due to old age, Kapilendra Deb's health was failing. He learnt that his trusted son Hamvira, who was his general as well as chief architect of the southern expansion, was not able to deal with the rebels. It was around this time that Saluva Narasimha Deva Raya (AD 1431–1491), the king of Vijayanagar, was becoming very powerful. He started grabbing territory from the Odias, taking under his rule the Arcot district (in Tamil Nadu) in AD 1466, which was under the authority of Dakshina Kapileswar Kumar Mahapatra, son of Hamvira.[10] The rising power of Saluva Narasimha Deva Raya also posed a threat to Kapilendra Deb's territory on the east coast. Kapilendra Deb was apparently disappointed in Hamvira for his failure to ensure the loyalty of royal officials under him. This probably made him select his youngest son Purushottama Deb as successor.

After Kapilendra Deb's death, the accession of Purushottama Deb was not easy. However, some factors favoured him to claim legitimacy to the throne. The fact that he was 'nominated' by Lord Jagannath was a great tool used for his justification to ascend the throne. As Lord Jagannath had 'commanded' Kapilendra Deb in a dream to choose Purushottama as his successor, it became a divine directive and people willingly accepted it. The doctrine of divine elect (chosen by God), experimented and exhibited by Kapilendra Deb when he took over as ruler, was used by his son and successor Purushottama Deb. The new Gajapati followed a conscious and active policy of pleasing the most powerful priestly class. Some inscriptions in the Jagannath Temple show that he gained the gratification of the Brahmins by abolishing the *chaukidari* tax on them and by renewing the old grants to them.[11] These moves helped Purushottama Deb in two ways. First, it helped him in the process of legitimizing his accession to the throne. Secondly, the 'divine command' protected him from his rival brother Hamvira, who posed great challenges in the early years of his rule as Gajapati.

Purushottama Deb in the early years of his reign faced great problems from two rivals—his elder brother Hamvira and Saluva Narasimha of Vijayanagar. Hamvira too faced problems from Saluva Narasimha, who constantly threatened the kingdom with his push northwards. Hamvira, in a bid to overthrow Purushottama Deb, sought the assistance of the Bahmani King Muhammad Shah III (AD 1463–1482). Muhammad Shah III agreed to help Hamvira and sent Nizam-ul-Mulk Hassan Bahri to help the Odishan prince. Their combined army captured Kondapalli (in Krishna district) and Rajahmundry and proceeded to Cuttack. Purushottama Deb was defeated and Hamvira became the king of Odisha (1472). However, his tenure was short-lived as Purushottama Deb regained his authority (1476). According to the *Saraswativilasam,* Purushottama Deb successfully brought Hamvira to his knees. The defeated Hamvira was allowed to go to Khemidi (Gajapati district, Odisha), where he ruled as a vassal of Purushottama Deb.[12]

Purushottama Deb now faced two great adversaries. One was Saluva Narasimha and the other was the Bahmani Sultan. During the initial years of his rule, Purushottama Deb saw a shrinking of his territories, which were lost to his southern enemies. He had to wait for some years before he could galvanize a strong enough force to retrieve his lost territory and prestige. It was his good fortune that around this time the Bahmani Empire was plunged into disorder as a result of the murder of the great statesman Mahmud Gawan, who was prime minister in the court of Muhammad Shah III, in 1481.

The following year, Muhammad Shah died, plunging the Bahmani Empire into crisis with all the internal fissures coming into the open. Taking advantage of this, Purushottama Deb mobilized his army, and as per epigraphic records he not only captured the strategic fort of Kondavidu but also the whole of the Godavari–Krishna doab region including Guntur district. After dispersing the Muslim intruders, Purushottama Deb's army proceeded to the south with a determination to reconquer the dominion which belonged to his great father in the past. He defeated the powerful Saluva Narasimha, and brought along the latter's daughter, Roopambika, who was later known as Queen Padmavati after his marriage to her (this story of *Kanchi Abhijan* is described in Chapter 2).

Two notable aspects of Purushottama Deb's regime are worth mentioning. The first is about Hamvira, a great military general and the eldest son of Kapilendra Deb, who was denied the throne after his father's death. Records suggest that he was unable to displace Purushottama Deb permanently as ruler. He appears to have occupied the throne for about four years before Purushottama Deb regained his position. It is an intriguing fact that a great military general like Hamvira could not hold on to the throne after occupying it for four years, that too with the support of the Bahmani rulers. From this, it seems evident that Hamvira did not have the popular support, while Purushottama Deb, being the 'choice' of Lord Jagannath, tilted the balance in his favour. The two brothers appeared to have reached some kind of understanding, which resulted in Hamvira being put in charge of Khemidi and worked as a vassal of the Odishan king.

This probably was one of the historical factors that led to the animosity and conflict between the ruler of Parlakhemundi, who also assumed the title of Gajapati, and the Raja of Puri (for more details, see Chapter 17). Parlakhemundi as a part of the larger Khemidi kingdom was ruled by the Gangavanshi kings. The rulers of Parlakhemundi being lineal descendants of the Ganga kings always claimed to be the real Gajapatis by hereditary practice. The advent of Hamvira in Khemidi probably brought in an element of conflict and antagonism between the Suryavamsi Purushottam Deb with the Raja of Parlakhemundi.

It is very surprising that there is no historical record of Hamvira after he was shifted to Khemidi. What happened to him is not known and is a matter of speculation and conjecture. Hamvira's son Kapileswar Kumar Mahapatra was appointed as the viceroy of the conquered territories of the south by his grandfather Kapilendra Deb. His whereabouts are also not known from history. Hamvira had another son called Narahari Patra, who survived him and was later captured along with Birabhadra, son of Prataprudra Deb, when he was in charge of Kondavidu when Krishnadevaraya conquered it. Had Hamvira inherited his father's empire, history would have been different. Hamvira, one of the foremost generals of his age, would have probably averted the disintegration of the empire soon after Kapilendra Deb's death. Kapilendra Deb's dream, in which Shri Jagannath favoured Purushottama Deb, not only deprived Hamvira of his rightful claim, but also relegated Hamvira and his son, Kumar Mahapatra, to obscurity and oblivion of history.

Prataprudra Deb

Prataprudra Deb succeeded his father to the throne in AD 1497. Although his father Purushottama Deb had lost a substantial part of his kingdom in the early years of his reign, he was fortunate to reconquer the territory as far as Pennar River in the south during his last years. Thus, Prataprudra Deb inherited a vast kingdom extending from the Ganga River in the north to Nellore (on the banks of the Pennar in Andhra Pradesh) in the south.

Prataprudra Deb's accession happened at a time when the prevailing political situation in his kingdom was very fragile. The Deccan as well as Bengal regions were in chaos. In the Deccan, the Bahmani sultanate was divided into five principalities. The immediate result was that Muslim power in the Deccan became sufficiently reduced. In 1491 AD, a dying Saluva Narasimha entrusted the kingdom of Vijayanagar and his minor sons to the care of his general Tuluva Narasa Nayaka. The Tuluva regent tried his best to carry out the orders of his master but met with little success. Narasa Nayaka died in 1503, which plunged Vijayanagar into utter political confusion. From 1505 till the accession of Krishnadevaraya in early 1510, there was political turmoil in Bengal and the hold of Ala-ud-Din Muzaffar Hussain Shah was not very firm. Prataprudra Deb failed to utilize this opportunity to consolidate his own position; as a result, the strength of his enemies grew and the political horizon of the Odisha Empire became overcast with dark clouds.

Krishnadevaraya, the greatest monarch in the history of Vijayanagar, came to the throne in the beginning of 1510. Krishnadevaraya's accession to the throne was a defining moment for Prataprudra Deb as it had a great impact on the future of the Odishan kingdom. Krishnadevaraya had two great ambitions. First, to snatch from Odisha the supremacy of the east coast, and second, to humble the Muslim power in the Deccan.

Krishnadevaraya began a meticulous and well-planned war against Odisha in 1512 that lasted for seven years. He succeeded in breaking up the Gajapati's empire during these years, achieving one brilliant victory after another. The Vijayanagar forces occupied Udayagiri in 1513 and the siege lasted for 18 months. Tirumala Rautraya, an uncle of Prataprudra, was captured and taken captive. Krishnadevaraya then turned his attention to Kondavidu, the strongest fort in the south in possession of the Gajapati that was considered to be the most unassailable fort. Ultimately the starving inmates of the fort were captured at the end of a prolonged siege.

Portuguese traveller Fernao Nuniz writes that immediately after the fall of Udayagiri, Krishnadevaraya called his prime minister Saluva Timma and told him that 'he was not content [with] that trivial victory [presumably Udayagiri] and that he wished to go forward a hundred leagues into the kingdom of Oriya; and he ordered him to make ready provisions and pay fully the salaries of the forces'. According to evidence found from contemporary inscriptions, before laying siege to the fort of Kondavidu, Krishnadevaraya took in a single campaign some of the forts including Addanki, Vinukonda, Bellamkonda, Ngarajunakonda, Tangeda and Ketavaram.

The siege of Kondavidu has been described differently in various works. The *Amuktamalyada*, a great literary work by Krishnadevaraya, states that the Odiyas, assembled in the fort of Kondavidu, 'went to heaven without any wounds on their bodies'. The Mangalagiri temple (Vijayawada) pillar inscription records that Saluva Timma starved the Odiyas to death. It states that the real cause of the Odiyas going 'to heaven without wounds on their bodies' was that they were starved and the water supply in the fort either ran short or was cut off. In the Kondavidu conquest, Birabhadra, son of Prataprudra Deb, was taken captive along with other nobles and feudatory chiefs.

Emboldened by these victories, particularly the conquest of Kondavidu, Krishnadevaraya pushed further into Odisha. His army crossed the Krishna river and invaded the fort of Kondapalli near Vijayawada. Prataprudra Deb made a last attempt to stop the invasion by sending his best troops to Kondapalli. However, the Odishan army was no match to the army of Krishnadevaraya. As per the Kalahasti Temple (Chittoor, Andhra Pradesh) inscription, a large number of people were taken captive in this battle. Nuniz's account shows that the queen of Prataprudra was also taken captive.

Krishnadevaraya reached Simhachalam. He set up a *Jaya Stambha* (a pillar of victory) commemorating his success in his advance towards Odisha. When Krishnadevaraya was preparing to move further from Simhachalam, a sad incident occurred. Birabhadra, the brave son of Prataprudra Deb who had been taken captive at Kondavidu, committed suicide. Regarding the death of Birabhadra, there are different versions, of which one is very popular. Birabhadra, who was very dexterous with both sword and dagger, was entrusted with the administration of Kondavidu by his father. Krishnadevaraya once summoned Birabhadra to a fencing duel. Birabhadra wanted to please Krishnadevaraya by showing off his skill, but when he learnt that his opponent was a man of lower rank, he felt insulted and killed himself. The prince preferred death to dishonour. The death of his beloved son Birabhadra had a huge impact on the mind of the Gajapati, who decided to go for a treaty with Krishnadevaraya in 1519. As a result of the treaty, the river Krishna was regarded as the boundary between the two states.

Also, according to the terms of the treaty, Prataprudra Deb gave his daughter, princess Jaganmohini, in marriage to Krishnadevaraya. In some records Jaganmohini is referred to as Annapurna, Bhadra or Tukka, the latter being a Telugu name that was given to her after marriage.[13]

The marriage of the Gajapati princess with Krishnadevaraya is a less known fact in history, and few records are available on this marriage. The Gajapati, in order to overcome the trauma of his son's death, to rescue his wife who had been taken captive and also to prevent further ingress of Krishnadevaraya into Odisha, decided to give his daughter in marriage to the Vijayanagar King. According to R. Subrahmanyam, the story of Portuguese traveller Fernao Nuniz suggests that Krishnadevaraya made his marriage with the daughter of the Gajapati a necessary condition for signing the permanent treaty, and to achieve this he used the captive queen of Prataprudra as a powerful tool. To secure the release of his wife Prataprudra was compelled to give his daughter in marriage to Krishnadevaraya. For Krishnadevaraya, it was a kind of vindication for the earlier historic defeat of Saluva Narasimha. At the time of that battle, Gajapati Purushottama Deb had taken the daughter of Saluva Narasimha, Roopambika, from Kanchi, Vijayanagar, as a mark of victory. So, for Krishnadevaraya taking the daughter of Prataprudra Deb was like paying back in the same coin.

However, the marriage was a political exigency and it did not succeed. According to one account, the marriage was never conjugated. On the wedding night, the sword belt of the newly-wed princess, worn at the time of the nuptials, loosened and fell to the ground. The fallen gem-studded sword made

Krishnadevaraya suspect his bride. He thought that the princess had hidden the sword with the intention of killing him. He believed it to be a design by the Gajapati princess to avenge the insult meted out to her father. He left the room immediately never to return.[14] Krishnadevaraya had deserted Jaganmohini on a great misunderstanding, thinking that the sword was a weapon to kill him. However, in reality, wearing a sword was a royal practice. The Gajapati princesses used to wear a sword belt as a mark of honour and defence. Deserted and deprived, Jaganmohini, an accomplished princess who was well-versed in Sanskrit, spent her whole life in loneliness in Kambham (also spelt as Cumbum) in Kurnool district. She was a very kind woman and with support from her father and by selling her jewellery she obtained money and excavated a very large water reservoir near Kambham. She also wrote a Sanskrit poem titled *Tukka Panchakam* (The Lament of a Woman). She speaks of neglect by her husband and her separation from him. It is a fine rendition and portrayal of her sadness and the agony of separation. The poem is extracted as under.[15]

तुक्का नाम गजपतिपुत्री कृष्णदेवरायपत्नी।
चरन्वनान्ते नवमञ्जरीषु न षट्पदो गन्धफलीमजिघ्रत्।
सा किं न रम्या स च किं न रन्ता बलीयसी केवलमीश्वराज्ञा ॥ १ ॥
मा किंशुक प्रकटयात्मनिमेषमात्रं मन्मस्तके विहरतीति मधुव्रतोऽयम्।
किं मालतीविरहवेदनया त्वदीयं दृष्ट्वा प्रसूनमचिरादनलभ्रमेण ॥ २ ॥
भ्रमर भ्रमता दिगन्तराले कचिदास्वादितमांक्षितं श्रुतं वा।
वद सत्यमपास्य पक्षपातं यदि जातीकुसुमानुकारि पुष्पम् ॥ ३ ॥
कुसुमानि लिखन्तु नाम चित्रे कतिचित्कारुविशेषरूढशिक्षाः।
सुरभित्वममूनि किं लभन्ते किमु चैतेषु रसं पिबन्ति भृङ्गाः ॥ ४ ॥
किं मालति म्लायसि मां विहाय चुचुम्ब तुम्बीकुसुमं षडङ्घ्रिः।
लोके चतुर्भिश्चरणैः पशुस्स्यात् स षड्भिरत्यर्थपशुर्न किं स्यात् ॥ ५ ॥

The English translation is as follows:

That is to say, the bumblebee, while wandering amidst the fresh flowers, drifts away from the Champak, unable to take in its smell. Does that give the Champak a bad name that it lacks in beauty or fragrance? Only that the laws of the Almighty are binding and unsurpassable. (It is only under the licence of the Almighty that the bumblebee does not dare any proximity to the Champak. Unable to bear its fragrance, it flies way in fear.) |1|

O Kinshuk (Palash flower)! Your momentary happiness at the bumblebee circling over you is as out of place as is the sorrow of the Malati at the bumblebee deserting it. The bumblebee has mistaken the Palash flower for fire because of its redness and in that illusion, it has gone near it. (The bumblebee, being a tiny and silly insect, grows excited at the mere sight of fire.) |2|

While wandering across the horizon, if the bumblebee does not drink honey from a flower brimming with delightful fragrance, like the Jati flower (Malati) and goes somewhere else, does that take away from the glory and essence of that flower? |3|

If a skilled artist, with the finest of craftsmanship, draws flowers on the canvas minutely detailing all the intricacies, will the bumblebee be able to derive any fragrance from it? Will it be able to drink its honey? |4|

O Malati! You are bothered by the bumblebee deserting you and kissing a Bottle Gourd flower. But do remember that a beast has neither conscience nor knowledge. Because, it is four-legged. As the bumblebee has even a greater number of legs (it has six) than that of a beast, is it not supposed to be even more lacking in knowledge than a beast is? |5|

There is a Telugu version of the episode which is also quite interesting and different. The version in *Rayavacakamu* presents the perspective from the point of view of King Krishnadevaraya. In his northward victory he conquered a portion of the territory of the Gajapati and deep inside this territory he erected a pillar of victory near Potlur-Simhadri. After putting up the pillar he called Gajapati's agent Subuddhi and told him, 'I want you to realize that I have come solely for the sake of increasing my glory, not with any desire of annexing your kingdom. The Gajapati kingdom I leave for the Gajapati. I shall return now to my territory.' [16]

On being informed by Subuddhi, the Gajapati had a meeting with Krishnadevaraya. Feeling no distrust for Rayalu (Krishnadevaraya), he began to speak to the king. The Gajapati began by reciting a Sanskrit verse:[17]

Nastam kulam bhinna-tatakakupan
Vibhasta-rajyam saranagatam ca
Go-brahmanan deva-ganalayamsca
Yaduddharet purva-catur-gunam tat.

A broken family, damaged tanks and wells,
A fallen kingdom, one who comes seeking refuge,
Cows and Brahmans, and temples of gods–
Supporting these is four times as meritorious!'

Rayalu then said to the Gajapati, 'After all, is there any real difference between you and me?' Saying nice things in this way, he presented many presents and gifts to the Gajapati and gave him four ornamented garments. For his part, the Gajapati presented his daughter Jaganmohini to the king and poured water to seal their marriage.

To honour his new son-in-law and his daughter he offered them ornaments that were truly worthy of being presented as gifts. 'Instead of the usual silks, scents, and treasures that are given as dowry, I give for my daughter all the kingdoms in the south of the river Krishna that are under my control, with all their forts, fortresses, and bastions. And the elephants, horses, and foot soldiers of those lands I give as her servants and attendants.' He also gave swings, and evening carriages, cattle and livestock, fine furniture, and a goose-down bed with legs of coral. All this and more he gave to his dear daughter. He also gave all the worthy things his new son-in-law deserved.

For one, he gave endless quantities of ornaments made from nine gems, which were of unparalleled quality and were taken from his palace treasury. He gave elephants and horses, swords and shields, and other such gifts as befit a king. Rayalu was pleased beyond measure. He ordered royal drums to be sounded and mounted his elephant. He then began his march back to his capital.[18]

The story of the marriage between Prataprudra Deb's daughter and Krishnadevaraya has different versions as per Odia and Telugu sources. However, there is no mention about the same in the *Madala Panji*. There is neither any reference about the treaty between Krishnadevaraya and Prataprudra Deb nor any mention about the marriage in the temple chronicle. Two Portuguese travellers had visited the Vijayanagar state under Krishnadevaraya. Domingo Paes and Fernao Nuniz visited Vijayanagar and stayed there during 1520–25 and 1535–37, respectively. Their travel accounts have been narrated by various authors in their works. Nuniz mentions that Krishnadevaraya had three wives, although the names of two, Chinna Devi and Tirumala Devi, are found in some inscriptions. In her book *Vijayanagar Empire*, historian Vasundhara Filliozat writes, 'In some literature, the daughter of the King of Orissa whom Krishnadeva Raya married was called Jaganamohini. Nuniz says that King Krishnadeva Raya had three Principal Queens, though only two Queens Chinna Devi and Tirumala Devi figure in the inscriptions. Then who was this queen?'

She was none else but the daughter of Prataprudra Deb. Robert Sewell, in his celebrated work *A Forgotten Empire: Vijayanagar—A Contribution to the History of India* (2002 edition), writes that Krishnadevaraya married a daughter of the Odisha king. According to him, there is a long inscription in the temple of Varadaraja Swami at Conjeevaram (Kanchipuram) confirming this story.

In *Annapurna*, a historical novel in Odia published in 1934, it is mentioned that Krishnadevaraya had two queens before his marriage with the Odishan princess. His first wife was Chinamma, a Kshatriya princess, and his second wife Tirumala was the princess of Srirangapattam (near Mysuru). Historically it may be noted that Krishnadevaraya entered into the treaty with Prataprudra Deb in 1519. Before this, he had defeated Prataprudra Deb by conquering Kondavidu, Udayagiri and Rajahmundry. Soon after conquering these, he went to the Simhachalam temple and offered large donations to Lord Narasimha. His two queens had accompanied him and offered jewelled ornaments to the temple. This finds mention in the Simhachalam Temple Inscription, writes Dr N. Mukunda Rao in his book published in 1986.

After the treaty with the Odisha Gajapati, Krishnadevaraya was said to have gone to Tirupati temple. He made lavish gifts of gold and cash and worshipped the Lord with all sorts of ornaments. He had got made a copper image of himself, with his hands folded in respect and flanked by his queens Tirumala Devi and Chinna Devi so that he could always remain standing there in the eastern doorway to attend on his lord. It is certain that by that time even though the marriage with Jaganmohini was solemnised, the new queen was not staying with the king. This is the most plausible explanation of absence of the queen Jaganmohini in the copper image in the Lord Venkateswara temple at Tirupati.

There is another variation to the story of Jaganmohini's marriage. Jaganmohini, after the marriage, could not adjust to the situation. The death of her brother, defeat of her father and loss of territory, detention of her mother, and the deal involving her marriage haunted her. She held Krishnadevaraya responsible for the humiliation, defeat of her father, and death of her brother. On the first night of their marriage, when Krishnadevaraya wanted to be close to his newly-wed but resisting wife, the jewel-studded belt sword (called *odiani* in Odia) tied to her waist became loose and fell on the ground, thus making Krishnadevaraya suspicious of her motive. This has been discussed earlier. Though Krishnadevaraya left the palace, in deference to her desire to be left alone, later he built a house where she stayed separately. The story of the sword remained wrapped in mystery; Krishnadevaraya had harboured a feeling that it was secretly hidden by her to kill him to avenge the humiliation meted out to her father and family.

Jaganmohini led a lonely, pious life dedicated to the welfare of people and completely detached from her husband. She devoted herself to Sanskrit literature. Years later, she started realizing the futility of leading a lonely life. She developed a yearning for her husband. When the king was on a visit to Kambham earlier in Kurnool district and now in Prakasam district in Andhra Pradesh, she learnt about it and sent a message to the king expressing a desire to meet him. The king was pleasantly surprised, and immediately fetched her. At the meeting after so many years she presented the five verses she had written, or *Tukka Panchami*, to him. The king, himself a learned man of letters and literature, understood the agony and desire of his lonely queen after reading the poem. He became emotional and speechless. Forgetting everything, he went into a deep conversation with his queen. The real story of the waist sword on the first night of marriage was unravelled. The king felt ashamed and a sense of guilt overshadowed him. He felt sorry and begged forgiveness for the misunderstanding. Jaganmohini felt equally remorseful. The king then brought her to the capital with much fanfare, celebration and rejoicing. The two queens welcomed her and received her with much affection and care as the true Chinnamma (youngest one). Their life of togetherness was, however, short-lived. Krishnadevaraya died in 1529 shortly after the reunion.

The treaty with Krishnadevaraya and the attack by Quli Qutb Shah of Golconda (the fifth sultan of the Qutb Shahi dynasty) led to the Odishan Empire losing territory between Kondavidu and Simhachalam, and this substantially reduced the size of the Odishan kingdom during Prataprudra Deb's regime. He, however, after this period of 'infamous defeat and territorial losses' ruled for a long period of 20 years. This period was otherwise a remarkable time in the region's history, as it witnessed the great emergence of spiritualism and the Bhakti cult under Sri Chaitanya. It also saw the resurgence of Odia literature under five learned men, scholars and litterateurs, popularly known as *Panchasakhas* (five associates).

The arrival of Sri Chaitanya Mahaprabhu at Puri in 1509 was a turning point in the religious history of Odisha. He stayed there for 18 years until his death and greatly influenced the minds and thoughts of Vaishnavas in Odisha. He went to Puri to visit the shrine of Lord Jagannath. He felt greatly attracted to Lord Jagannath and spent his remaining days of life in Puri.

The leading principle that underlines Chaitanya's philosophy is Bhakti or devotion, which is illustrated by the mutual love of Radha and Krishna.

Chaitanya's propagation of Bhakti cult through the popular *sankirtans* had a great impact on the people of Odisha. They joined in large numbers in the *kirtan* (devotional chanting and dancing) procession whenever they heard the sound from a distance. The *Panchasakhas* and the common masses joined the *kirtan* procession and danced with Chaitanya. His brand of Vaishnavism got incorporated into the Jagannath culture, which had considerable impact on millions of Vaishnava devotees. It had such a widespread impact that the king, the subject, the high, the low, everyone became ardent supporters and followers of Sri Chaitanya. Panchasakha literature, *Vaishnava Nilambrata* by Madhava Patnaik, *Chaitanya Bhagavata* of Vrindavana Dasa, *Chaitanya Mangala* of Jayananda, *Chaitanya Charitamrita* of Krishnadas Kaviraj Goswami and various other contemporary works contributed to the popularization and large-scale propagation of the Bhakti movement in Odisha.

People started following the new creed. The first follower was Basudev Sarvabhauma, a great *nyaya* (logical realism school of philosophy) scholar. Patronized by Gajapati Prataprudra Deb, Chaitanya travelled to the south in 1509, and met Ramananda Raya, a governor of Prataprudra Deb, a great scholar and a bhakta, on the banks of Godavari. The *Chaitanya Charitamrita* gives a long account of the dialogue between them, wherein at the bidding of the master, Ramananda described the various stages of bhakti. Ramananda, after his interaction with Chaitanya, resigned from his position as governor and went to Puri to live with Chaitanya.

Gajapati Prataprudra Deb himself was greatly influenced by Sri Chaitanya. The *Chaitanya Charitamrita* describes how Prataprudra Deb urged Sarvabhauma to arrange for him a meeting with Chaitanya. But Chaitanya refused to see him. The king wrote a letter to Sarvabhauma to 'entreat the bhaktas or the master to intercede with him for me; through their favour, I may reach his feet; and like not my kingship if I cannot gain his grace. If Chaitanya doesn't take pity on me, I shall give up my throne and turn a religious mendicant.'[19]

Ramananda pleaded the Gajapati's cause before Sri Chaitanya and at last got his permission to allow the son of Prataprudra to see him for the 'son is one's own born again'. Ramananda took pains and accompanied Prataprudra Deb's son who was 'handsome and dark, clad in yellow robe, reminding him of Krishna'. Chaitanya lovingly received him and repeatedly embraced him. Ramananda then took the prince back to the king, who rejoiced at his son's good fortune. An opportunity soon arrived for Prataprudra Deb to see Chaitanya. Krishnadas Kaviraj writes that during the chariot festival, after the enthusiastic singing of *sankirtan*, Chaitanya fell unconscious in the courtyard of Kashi Mishra (the high priest). Prataprudra Deb, instructed by Sarvabhauma, suddenly came out into the assembly and fell at his feet. Chaitanya after regaining consciousness exclaimed, 'Woe to me, I have touched one given the worldly power and wealth.' When the Gajapati heard this, he burst into tears and said, 'Here do I forgo all my power and wealth and surrender them at your feet. Take me master, as the meanest of those that love you.'[20]

Ramananda Raya in his celebrated work *Jagannath Ballabh* refers to this incident. 'This is indeed a marvel. Raja Prataprudra Deb who is a terror to the Pathans and whose physical might surpasses that of most men, whose iron contact is dreaded by the strongest of wrestlers, had melted like a soft thing at the touch of Chaitanya.'[21] Govinda Das in a contemporary biography of Chaitanya records, 'Whenever Chaitanya walked in the streets with a large crowd of men following him with song, music and dance, Raja Prataprudra walked on bare feet behind them all like the humblest of his subjects.'[22]

Nagar Kirtane yebe Mahaprabhu Yaya,
Dina bese maharaja pechhu pechhu dhaya.

The Gajapati was mesmerized by the magnetic influence of Sri Chaitanya. Chaitanya's continuous stay in Puri, his divine personality and his philosophy and preaching entered the palace. The queens were also greatly influenced by Chaitanya's teachings and became great devotees. Prataprudra Deb was initiated formally into Gaudiya Vaishnavism (founded by Sri Chaitanya).

The resurgence of Chaitanya's Bhakti cult and preaching was associated with the political decay of the Odishan kingdom under Prataprudra Deb. The Gajapati's defeat at the hands of Krishnadevaraya and Quli Qutb Shah may have been the beginning of this political decline. Sri Chaitanya's movement during Prataprudra's time has drawn a sharp division among historians. A section of eminent historians feels that Chaitanya's influence on the society and the administration of the king was the main reason for the fall of Prataprudra Deb. Another section of historians offers a contrarian view. In *Chaitanya Bhagavata* written by Vrindavana Dasa in AD 1550, Sri Chaitanya is said to have given the following advice to the king of Odisha: 'Your mind should be attached to Sri Krishna only and nothing else. Always have the name of Sri Krishna on your lips.'

Ramananda Raya and Gopinatha Badajena were governors of Rajahmundry in the south and Midnapur in the north, respectively. Ramananda Raya was an ardent follower of Sri Chaitanya. Krishnadas Kaviraj had written that Ramananda Raya was so absorbed in his devotion towards Sri Krishna that he was unable to maintain the accounts of collection and expenses of the state revenue. He finally gave up the service and dedicated his life in following Chaitanya's preaching. Ramananda Raya's conduct as governor of a province when two powerful enemies, Vijayanagar and Golconda, were knocking at the door, throws ample light on the state of administration. His conduct made foreign invasion easier. At a time when the 'Oriya nation needed the service of every honest and capable man for the defence of political prestige and empire, Ramananda Ray betrayed his trust to his own people by retiring from his position on the weakest frontier of the country.'[23] Gopinatha Badajena's role in the drastic fall in state revenue annoyed Prataprudra Deb, who even ordered his execution. It is mentioned in *Chaitanya Charitamrita* that Sri Chaitanya intervened in the matter and asked the king to forgive Gopinatha Badajena. He was not only pardoned but reinstated.

Famous historian R.D. Banerjee held Sri Chaitanya responsible for the political decline and ultimate fall of Odisha. According to him, the acceptance of Vaishnavism, rather neo-Vaishnavism, was the real cause of the Muslim conquest of Odisha 25 years after the death of Prataprudra Deb.[24]

A similar view is expressed by noted historian Dr Harekrushna Mahtab. According to him:

> A doctrine that preaches inaction and sentimentalism is harmful to the ordinary man in his daily walk of life and it is simply fatal to an administrator who holds the destiny of millions. The attempt to make the Bhakti cult a mass religion and to influence the king and his officers by his sweet pessimistic philosophy had no doubt been fatal to the social and political life of the country.[25]

This view has its share of counter. Prabhat Mukherjee, while contesting R.D. Banerjee, states, 'We have given a description of the Chaitanya Age in Odisha. In the process of time, the history of Chaitanya movement in Odisha has been overlaid by sentiment and prejudice. R.D. Banerjee has done great injustice to the memory of the great saint by holding him responsible for the military decline of Odisha in the reign of Prataprudra, and indirectly for the fall of Odisha.'[26] Another historian, R. Subrahmanyam, also agrees with his views. According to him:

> We cannot agree with Mr Banerjee when he says that Caitanya is mainly responsible for the decline of martial spirit in Orissa. Nor was Caitanya responsible for the fall of Orissan power. The inferior war-machine of Orissa and the treachery of some of the selfish officers like Govinda Vidyadhara, who betrayed Prataprudradeva in his wars against the sultan of Bengal, mainly accounted for the failure of Prataprudradeva in his numerous wars.[27]

The era of Prataprudra Deb witnessed the emergence of five comrades or *Panchasakhas* who played a stellar role in bringing literature and spiritual values closer to people. Balarama Dasa, Jagannath Dasa, Achyutananda Dasa, Yasobanta Dasa and Ananta Dasa collectively are referred to as *Panchasakha*. Their lasting contribution to society and literature is ever remembered. *Panchasakha* or the saint scholars of Odisha belonged to the 16th century. They were all contemporaries of Prataprudra Deb and Sri Chaitanya. They greatly influenced the literary, cultural and social life of Odisha. These five associates came together when Sri Chaitanya and the Bhakti movement with royal patronage from Prataprudra Deb were at high momentum.

Prataprudra Deb's last days saw the emergence of powerful enemies in the south. The already weakened kingdom was further diminished after the death of Prataprudra Deb in 1532. According to the *Madala Panji*, he was succeeded by two minor sons: Kalua Deb, who reigned for one year and five months, and Kakharua Deb, who ruled for three months. They were killed one after another by Prataprudra Deb's minister Govinda Vidyadhara, who usurped the throne. He founded the Bhoi dynasty in Odisha. He ruled for seven years and was followed by Chakrapratap, who reigned for eight years. He was succeeded by Narasimha Deb Ray, who died after one year of rule, leading to Raghudeb Ray ascending the throne. Mukunda Deb usurped the throne by removing Raghudeb Ray. Between the death of Prataprudra Deb and the rise of Mukunda Deb, there were six rulers in 19 years. The Odishan Empire entered a new phase of extreme instability where succession to the throne was achieved through violence, murder, betrayal and conspiracy.

4

MUKUNDA DEB

The Last Independent Hindu King

Mukunda Deb became the Gajapati in 1560 and founded the Chalukya dynasty in Odisha, claiming descent from the Eastern Chalukyas of South India. His accession to the throne was followed by a period of turmoil and bloodshed marked by internecine warfare as well as internal conspiracy and conflicts, which finally led to the downfall of the Hindu rulers of the kingdom.

Path to the Throne

To understand the story of Mukunda Deb's rise, we must first learn the story of Govinda Vidyadhara, a general in the army of Gajapati Prataprudra Deb. Vidyadhara, an ambitious man, plotted to seize power from Prataprudra and he accomplished his goal by finishing off the bloodline of the Gajapati. He is said to have murdered the two minor sons of Prataprudra, thereby usurping the Gajapati's throne.

According to another version, as detailed in the *Madala Panji*, we are informed that Prataprudra Deb had 16 sons who survived him, but they were all murdered by Govinda Vidyadhara. This led to the founding of the Bhoi dynasty by the new ruler. This marked the beginning of the deplorable practice of killing the incumbent Gajapati by pretenders to the throne to fulfil their personal ambitions. For the first time, greed and ambition leading to conspiracy, treachery and murder became the vehicle for establishing a new dynasty.

Mukunda Harichandan, who would later assume the title of Mukunda Deb, hailed from the south of Odisha. He was a brave and skillful soldier of repute in the army of Prataprudra Deb. When Vidyadhara took over the reins, he appointed Mukunda as the general in charge of the Cuttack Fort. Displaying greater trust in Mukunda Harichandan, Vidyadhara entrusted the state to his custody while he continued his southern campaign to extend his kingdom. While Vidyadhara was fighting with the Sultan of Golconda, one Raghubhanja Chhotaraya started a rebellion against him, attacking and seizing Cuttack. It seems Raghubhanja Chhotaraya was the son of the sister of Prataprudra Deb. He wanted to capture the Gajapati throne after the murder of Prataprudra Deb's sons.[1] Left with no other option, Vidyadhara returned from the south to defend his capital, successfully warding off the usurper and pushing him over the Bengal border.

However, Vidyadhara could not enjoy the fruits of his labour. On his way back to Cuttack he was taken ill and died, leaving his son Chakrapratap Deb to take his place. Chakrapratap proved to be an oppressive and cruel king and entrusted the administration of the kingdom to Danai Vidyadhara, who was a lieutenant in his father's army. Soon, Chakrapratap was killed by his son Narasimha Jena, who then occupied the throne. It is at this point that we find Mukunda Harichandan returning to the scene; he and his accomplices are said to have entered the palace of Narasimha Jena in the guise of women and killed the king. With Narasimha's demise, his brother Raghuram Chhotaraya was placed on the throne.

But a struggle was underway for the throne as there were three aspirants: Danai Vidyadhara, Mukunda Harichandan and Raghubhanja Chhotaraya. Danai Vidyadhara was stationed in the south of the kingdom at that time. He returned to stake his claim as ruler but was imprisoned by Mukunda Harichandan; Danai Vidyadhara never made it out as he died in prison. Taking advantage of the chaos, Raghubhanja Chhotaraya tried to seize power by declaring war against Mukunda Harichandan. However, Mukunda prevailed as he was able to defeat, imprison and later execute Raghubhanja.

Thus, we see that after the death of Prataprudra Deb, the throne of the Gajapati became the object of intense strife and competition leading to a lengthy and bloody struggle. Internal feuds, greed and conspiracy became the order of the day for 19 years after Prataprudra Deb died; six Gajapatis came and went, each ruling for a very short duration till Mukunda Deb took over.

The focus of the Gajapatis shifted to defending their seat of power and dealing with internal strife. In this process, the general population suffered. The absence of a strong and stable administration ultimately led to the rapid decline of the rajas.

Mukunda's Mistake

Although Mukunda Deb associated himself with the Chalukya dynasty, there is no independent source to verify that claim. But we do have some other information about him.

In an inscription from the Bhimeswar Temple in Draksharamam in East Godavari district, Mukunda Deb is described as the son of Sarvaraju and grandson of Singharaju. He was also known as 'Telenga Mukunda Deb', an epithet that shows that he did not hail originally from Odisha and was considered an outsider. This proved to be something of a drawback in his claim of becoming the Gajapati. Added to this was the inescapable fact that his path to the coveted title had been splattered with blood as he was responsible for almost decimating the Bhoi dynasty. This posed a challenge to his credibility as the legitimate ruler. Also, at the same time, the frequent internal squabbles and strife surrounding the Gajapatis led to feelings of disgust among the general people, who were losing their faith in their rulers. But Mukunda Deb successfully managed to overcome all these hurdles in his path, and in the short span of eight years that he ruled, was able to restore the status and esteem associated with the Gajapati to a great extent.

Mukunda Deb was a skilled soldier and a good military strategist. He defeated the King of Gauda and expanded the kingdom up to Tribeni (in Hooghly district of West Bengal). This is corroborated by epigraphical evidence available in the Bhimeswar Temple inscriptions. Also, a flight of steps constructed on the banks of the Ganga at Tribeni is known as 'Mukunda Ghat' attesting to the Odia king's conquest of the region. Even today, the Mukunda Ghat is considered a very holy place among Hindus.

But Mukunda Deb's tactical mind did not stand him in good stead for long. He got embroiled in the politics of Bengal and found himself caught in the midst of a fight between the Mughals and the Afghans, which would eventually lead to his downfall.

When Akbar ascended to the throne of Delhi in 1556, Ibrahim Khan Sur, his rival, was badly defeated and had to flee to Bengal to save himself. However, Sulaiman Karrani, the Sultan of Bengal, considered Sur as a potential threat and tried to apprehend him. Left with no other option, Ibrahim Sur fled to Odisha, where Mukunda Deb gave him shelter. This would prove to be a blunder. As was to be expected, Mukunda Deb's actions incurred the wrath of the Afghan Sultan of Bengal. Initially, Mukunda Deb did not see it as a threat because by that time he had developed a very good relationship with Emperor Akbar and thought that would give him adequate insurance against the Afghans, who were adversaries to the Mughals.

In 1566, Akbar sent Hassan Khan Khajanchi to the court of Mukunda Deb as his ambassador along with an Odiya musician of the Mughal court, named Bhatta Mahapatra, who according to the *Akbarnama* had no equal in music and composition of Hindi songs.² Mukunda Deb in exchange had sent a Hindu ambassador named Paramananda Rai to the court of the Mughal emperor. With the establishment of such cordial diplomatic relationship, Mukunda Deb felt confident of repelling the Bengal Sultan as he presumed the assurance of the Mughal Emperor's support and patronage in the event of a conflict with the Afghans.

This presumption proved to be a costly mistake on his part. Akbar's real intention was to extend his rule to Bengal in due course of time. If by that time Odisha was to be annexed by the Bengal sultans, it would, in fact, give the Mughal emperor the upper hand as he would manage to gain Odisha along with Bengal by defeating the Afghans. Till such an event came to pass, however, it was in Akbar's interest to gain the support of the Hindu kingdom of Odisha to gain strategic advantage over Bengal. It was never the intention of Akbar to strengthen the position of Mukunda Deb. A naïve Mukunda Deb could not read the Mughal Emperor's game plan and committed a historic blunder by making an enemy of the Bengal Sultan.

Sulaiman Karrani was waiting for an opportune moment to exact revenge on Mukunda Deb for having granted asylum to Ibrahim Sur. The perfect opportunity presented itself in 1568, when Akbar's military attention was engaged in Chittor. Sulaiman Karrani sent his troops under the command of his son Bayazid and General Kalapahad to attack Mukunda Deb. Karrani had astutely judged that the friendship of Mukunda Deb with Akbar was superficial and there was little chance that the Mughal emperor would come to the aid of the Hindu king. But Akbar was in the midst of a bigger mission in Chittor and would not be able to spare time for the Gajapati. This is exactly what came to pass and Mukunda Deb did not get any support from Akbar in his defence against the Bengal army. None of the other feudatory rulers of Odisha came to Mukunda Deb's aid and the Gajapati found himself all alone in the battle.

While Mukunda Deb's forces were fighting at the border, Bayazid and Kalapahad found an alternate route and tactically proceeded to Cuttack. On the other hand, with Mukunda Deb preoccupied with the Afghan forces, Ramachandra Bhanja, the commandant of the Sarangagada Fort (near Bhubaneswar), declared himself as king of Odisha taking advantage of the Gajapati's absence from Cuttack. Caught in a bind, Mukunda Deb was left with no choice but to enter into a treaty with the Afghans so that he could return to fight with Ramachandra to defend his position. Mukunda Deb after submitting to the Afghan invaders rushed back to Cuttack to suppress the rebellion. He, however, was killed by Ramachandra in Gohiritikiri (near Jajpur, Odisha). Immediately thereafter, Bayazid killed Ramachandra. It is ironical that Mukunda Deb was not killed by Sulaiman Karrani or his forces, but by his own general, who declared himself as the king of Odisha, however short-lived that might have been.

Another version of the conflict speaks of two traitors, Sakhi and Manai, who were generals of the king of Odisha. They guided the Afghan army led by Kalapahad to Mukunda Deb's army and surprised the unprepared Odishan army by their sudden presence, leading to the rout of the Odias. Thus, Mukunda Deb fell victim to the same method of betrayal that he himself had adopted to usurp the throne. He first became a cause and then a consequence of a vicious game of treachery and murder.

Whichever version of events is considered, we find that Mukunda Deb's downfall exposed the fragile and volatile political situation in Odisha, where the internecine feud was the main reason for the fall of the kingdom.

The Achievements

Ruling over a kingdom extending from the Ganga in the north to the Godavari in the south, Mukunda Deb showed remarkable abilities as an administrator. In his short reign of eight years he not only built a great kingdom but also became a favourite of the people. He created many Brahmin villages also known as *sasanas* and commissioned several sculptures to be built within the compound of the Jagannath Temple. Mukunda Deb was also a great patron of art and literature.

He paid special attention to strengthening the defences for his kingdom. For instance, he strengthened and rebuilt the Barabati Fort (in Cuttack). He also built a palace with nine storeys inside the fort. The first storey was taken up for housing the elephants and the stables; the second was occupied by the artillery and the guards and had quarters for attendants; the third was used by the patrol and gatekeepers; the fourth had workshops; the fifth housed the kitchen; the sixth contained the public reception rooms; the seventh had the private apartments; the eighth contained the women's apartments; and the ninth housed the sleeping chamber of the governor.[3] Two English merchants, William Bruton and R. Cartwright, who visited the fort 63 years after the death of Mukunda Deb, were surprised at its splendor and described it as the 'Court of Malcandy'. Bruton's account of the Barabati Fort is as follows:

> To the north of the city, at the bifurcation of the Mahanadi and the Kathjuri, stood the citadel of Cuttack, Fort Barabati, a spacious area, a mile and half in circumference, defended by a broad ditch faced with masonry by double walls of stone and by square sloping bastions, which clearly bespoke its indigenous origin. Fifty years before the coming of the English, Mukunda Deo, the last Hindu ruler of Orissa, had built within it a castle of gray granite, with nine lofty courts, but he had lost his kingdom to the Moslem, and Agha Muhammad Zaman of Taharan, a Mugul Viceroy, now abodes in the stately palace of Malcandy.[4]

Whereas the English merchants described the fort as having nine courts, we have Abu'l Fazl's account of the nine-storeyed structure of the fort. Although this does point to a discrepancy, what is beyond dispute is that Mukunda Deb was able to refortify the fort to make it a strong military base during his rule.

Kalapahad's Sacrilege

The 1568 Afghan conquest of Odisha is incomplete without a reference to the attack by General Kalapahad and the desecration of the Jagannath Temple perpetrated by him. We turn to the *Madala Panji* for a description of the events that transpired.

When the temple priests and *sebaks* heard of the fall of Cuttack, they smuggled the idols of Lord Jagannath, Balabhadra and Subhadra from the temple and fled to an island on Chilika Lake for safe upkeep of the deities. But this information reached Kalapahad. First, he proceeded to the Jagannath Temple at Puri, looted valuables and jewellery from the temple and wreaked massive damage and destruction there. Then, based on the details received from an informer, he went to the place where the idols had been hidden. He seized the idols, placed them on an elephant, and took them to Bengal, where they were burnt on the banks of the Ganga. As per legend, a Vaishnav devotee named Bishar Mahanti followed Kalapahad to the place where the idols were burnt. He managed to recover the *brahmas* (core material) from the thrown burnt images and put them inside a *mridanga* (drum) and brought them back to a place called Kujanga in Odisha.

Kalapahad unleashed a reign of terror and left an indelible print of horror and tragedy in the minds of people. This has been described in various historical documents. The account described in the *Madala Panji* is supported by various other sources too. Abu'l Fazl writes, 'Kalapahar, the general of Sulayman Karani on his conquest of the country, flung the image [of Jagannath] into fire and burnt it and afterwards cast it into the sea.'[5]

Historian Abd al-Qadir Badauni, a contemporary of Akbar, writes, 'In this year also Sulaiman Kirarani (*sic*), ruler of Bengal who gave himself the title of *Hazrati A'la* and had conquered the city of Katak-u-Banaras, that mine of heathenism, and having made the stronghold of Jagannath into home of Islam, held sway from Kamru [Kamrup in Assam] to Orissa, attained mercy of God.'[6]

Neamet Ullah, in his *History of The Afghans* compiled during the reign of Jehangir between AD 1609–1611, writes thus:

> He [Suleiman Kerrani (*sic*)] conceived a scheme to subdue the fort of Orissa, which they call Juggernauth and its troops it being the strongest fortress of infidels into which the Mohammedans had not yet set a foot. The town was surrounded on four sides with temples and a deep water, to cross which, Suleiman mounted the Afghans upon three hundred elephants and by that means demolished the temples. In one of them there stood an idol, weighing thirty *mauns* of gold; its two eyes were rubies; and it was surrounded by seven hundred other idols, all of a different make, and made of gold; they all fell into the hands of the holy warriors. The female inhabitants of the town, ornamenting themselves in a pompous way, concealed themselves behind different temples of Jagannath, without thinking of flight; 'For' said they 'is there anyone so mighty and powerful, to do any harm to the worshippers of God?' When a body of Mohammedans rushed into that temple, and took the women prisoners, they were struck with the greatest surprise: which was excited by this fact also, that religious men who had accompanied Suleiman in that expedition had asserted, that no single soldier would come off without at least securing one idol of gold; the weight of no one of them being under a *maun* of gold. But most surprising of all, is the fact, that all of those who had co-operated in sacking these idols, died within a space of a year, reduced to misery and distress.[7]

Another version of this notable event runs thus:

> The largest temple of the Hindus is situated in the kingdom of Orissa and is known by the name of Jagannatha. He [Kalapahad] turned his attention towards its destruction and marched with the images of god Krishna which was decorated in elegant and beautiful ways and whose limbs were made up

of red gold and pair of eyes formed of Badakshani ruby to be broken into fragments and cast into gutter.[8]

The destruction of religious places was part of a conscious strategy followed by the Afghans to break the spirit of a people. They were aware that the heart and soul of the Odia people were immersed in religiosity and this devotion manifested itself in deities and temples. The Afghans, therefore, resorted to damage and desecration of temples and other religious places, while plundering the riches stored therein, which helped in demoralizing the general population and also weakened the kings of Odisha.

The Afghan attack also coincided with the period when internal feuds had already weakened the institution of the Gajapati, which was beset with factional disputes. It became clear to the invaders that it would be easy to conquer the kingdom at such a vulnerable time by attacking the faith (*astha*) of the people, which resided in temples and deities. This would, in turn, serve to finally destroy the cherished claim of the Hindu rulers because, as mentioned earlier, Lord Jagannath was the presiding deity of the kingdom from whom the Gajapati kings drew their existential authority and inspiration.

In this context, it would be appropriate to explore some legends associated with General Kalapahad, who vandalised the Jagannath Temple. Although the veracity of the legend regarding Kalapahad is not supported by any historical evidence, it is worthwhile to examine it here.

It is believed that Kalapahad was originally a Hindu Brahmin. The daughter of the Sultan of Bengal fell in love with him and ultimately married him. Kalapahad intended to remain Hindu even though he had married a Muslim princess but faced societal backlash.[9] He came to Puri to perform a ceremony of expiation in the Jagannath Temple, but the Brahmins did not permit him to perform the ritual, objecting on the grounds that such reconversion or return to the fold of Hinduism was not permitted in the religion. Kalapahad was obviously angry and annoyed with the Brahmins, and the humiliated general was said to have turned into a great

Muslim fanatic and fundamentalist, taking a vow to seek revenge for the humiliation meted out to him.

This legend has taken firm hold in the imagination of the Odia people. Such stories, a part of folklore and popular belief, are deeply rooted in the minds of the general populace and very widespread, and are passed down over generations. While these may be dismissed on the grounds of historicity or lack of evidence, it is difficult to erase them from people's minds and faith.

The legend of Kalapahad has had such a deep impact on the Odia folklore that even children are familiar with it. A popular children's song has kept alive in the minds of the people the story of Kalapahad and the tragedy of Mukunda Deb's death with the loss of his kingdom to the Afghans.

This Odia song is as follows:

Aila Kala Pahad
Bhangila Luhara Bada
Peila Mahanadi Pani
Subarnathalire heda
Parasile Mukundanka Rani.[10]

The stanza translated in English reads as under:

Kalapahada arrived,
Broke the iron fence, and
Drank water of Mahanadi
Mukunda's queen
Served *heda* in a golden plate.

The song is meant to be an obituary of the last independent Hindu Gajapati of Odisha, with whose death the region lost its independence. The reference to the serving of *heda* (cooked cow meat; forbidden for Hindus) in a golden plate by the rani of Mukunda Deb to Kalapahad speaks of the sad and sordid end of the Odisha Empire and the eventual victory of the Afghans.

The capture of the Barabati Fort, which was the ultimate citadel of power and the seat of authority, was an indication of the deplorable state to which the Gajapati had fallen to. This pitiable state was achieved by violent use of brutal force to damage and defile the deities and the temples that people revered. This created great insecurity and fear in the minds of people. Their indescribable helplessness finds expression in the song where the queen of the deceased Gajapati is shown as surrendering herself to the conquerors by serving beef to them.

It should be mentioned here that some authors refer to a slight variation to the above poem, wherein instead of *heda* the word used is *heera*.[11] '*Heera*' in Odia means diamond and represents all the valuable possessions of the rani. Whether the word *heda* or *heera* was used in the original poem, the essence conveyed through the serving of *heda* or offering of *heera* on a golden platter was to portray the utter despair of the Odias over their defeat at the hands of Kalapahad and the abject surrender by none else than the queen of the deceased king Mukunda Deb. There is hardly any such comparable instance of a society narrating its own deplorable situation in such a pitiable manner.

5

RAMACHANDRA DEB I
Abhinava Indradyumna

Ramachandra Deb I (AD 1568–1600) of the Bhoi dynasty acceded to the throne of Khurda at a defining moment in Odisha's history after Mukunda Deb, the last independent ruler of the kingdom, lost to the Afghans.

With the loss of independence of the kingdom and the ransacking of the Jagannath Temple by General Kalapahad, the populace was plunged into deep despair and anxiety. There was apprehension regarding the new Muslim rulers, aggravated by reports of widespread attacks on Hindu places of worship. It was at this tumultuous time that Ramachandra Deb, a Gopala by caste, acceded to the throne of Khurda. As he did not belong to any royal lineage and was from a lower caste, his being invested with the kingship was an unusual phenomenon.

Ramachandra Deb had his task cut out for him; he had to tackle a twofold challenge—first, proving his credentials and legitimacy as ruler of Khurda, and second, restoring the honour and dignity of the Jagannath Temple. The second task was especially important as the Gajapati derived his authority from Lord Jagannath Himself.

On the other hand, the new king had to ensure that the people from higher castes, led by the Brahmins, would not rise in rebellion against him. Thus, it became imperative for him to secure his acceptance by the higher *varnas*, particularly the Brahmins.

Becoming the Gajapati

From various sources, including the *Madala Panji* and accounts of Muslim historians such as Abu'l Fazl and Ferishta, we learn that Ramachandra Deb I, known as Ramai Routraya alias Ramachandra Routraya Mahapatra before his coronation, was the son of Danai Vidyadhara (also referred to as Janardhan Vidyadhara). Ramachandra was the prime minister and general of Govinda Vidyadhara (AD 1533-1541) and of his successors up to AD 1559 when he was imprisoned by Mukunda Harichandan (Mukunda Deb) in the fort of Barabati.

At the time of Mukunda Deb's death in AD 1568, Ramachandra Deb was being interned in the fort of Rajahmundry, but after the king's death, the chieftains in the south proclaimed Ramachandra Deb as the king of Odisha. He was installed at the fort of Kotam,* as Cuttack, the traditional seat of power, was under the Afghans during that time. Three years after his investiture at Kotam, Ramachandra Deb established a fort in the village of Khurda at the foot of the Barunei hills, which stood midway between Cuttack and Puri. The name of this new capital was Jagannathpur Kataka named after Lord Jagannath, and the idols were brought from Kujanga and reinstalled here after the infamous attack by Kalapahad.[1]

---

* The Kotam Fort, also referred as Gotam where Ramachandra Deb ruled for three years, is located five miles to the east of Srungavarapukota town of the Vizagpatam district of the Andhra State (vide Sewell's List of Antiquarian Remains, vol. I, p. 14). This also finds reference in K.N. Mohapatra's article 'Gajapati Ramachandra Deva I', *OHRJ*, vol. VI, no. 4 (January 1958).

The *Madala Panji* gives a brief account of the accession of Ramachandra Deb I as follows: 'After the death of Mukunda Deb, the king of *Yaduvamsa* began to rule. The son of Danai Vidyadhara was living in the fort of Totama. He became king as Ramachandra Deva and built a fort in Khurda at the foot of Barunei hills which was also called Jagannathpur Kataka.'²

It is significant to note here that with the shifting of the capital from Cuttack (under the domination of the Afghans) to Jagannathpur Kataka, the realm and status of the Gajapati was reduced. His dominion now extended over the newly created state of Khurda, and he was christened as the Raja of Khurda.

This new administrative division was soon cemented by the division of the erstwhile independent Odisha kingdom into three separate states. The region between river Godavari and river Rushikulya (in Odisha) came under the Golconda Sultan. The region from river Kathajodi (an arm of the Mahanadi River in Odisha) till Hooghly, the region that was initially under the Afghans, ultimately went to the Mughals. The balance of the coastal area came under the Raja of Khurda. It may be pertinent to mention that Raja Todar Mal during Akbar's time visited Odisha in 1580 to supervise the introduction of his settlement of crown lands, founded on a measurement and valuation called *Taksim Jamma* and *Tankha Raqmi*.

The settlements were finally completed by Raja Man Singh. During Man Singh's time, the Raja of Khurda was recognized with a rank, as a *Mansabdar* of 3,000 soldiers and 500 cavalry, and his estate composed of the jurisdiction called Killa Khurda with the *mahals* Rahanga, Limbai, Purushottam Chattar, etc. Andrew Sterling writes: 'The jurisdiction thus left to the Raja of Khurda, extended from the Mahanuddy to the borders of Kimedy in Ganjam, comprising 129 killahs, gerhs, or hill estates, exclusive of those situated within his own zemindari.' The above number agrees exactly with that given in the *Ain-i-Akbari*—'in Cuttack are one hundred and twenty-nine brick forts (killahs), subject to the command of Gajapati'.³ Thus, under the Raja of

Khurda's direct rule, there was one zamindari with 71 *killas* or forts. Additionally, under his command there were 30 *zamindaris* containing 129 *killas*.

Ramachandra Deb I's assumption of the title of the Raja of Khurda was not without challenges. Mukunda Deb's descendants also staked their claim to the crown. We find evidence from the 1590 inscription of Athagarh that Mukunda Deb's brother Narasimha Bahubalendra had declared himself the Gajapati and the true successor with the help of the Golconda Sultan. But Bahubalendra's machinations fell through and he was not recognized as the Gajapati by the people. On the other hand, Mukunda Deb's son (also known as Ramachandra Deb, more specifically as Telenga Ramachandra Deb) approached Emperor Akbar claiming the throne of Odisha. However, by that time, Ramachandra Deb I had established himself and was widely accepted by the people as the Raja of Khurda. It was left to the Mughals to resolve the conflict between Mukunda Deb's son and Ramachandra Deb. The dispute on the issue of succession to the Khurda throne was thus between two claimants, namely Ramachandra Deb I, son of Danai Vidyadhara of the Bhoi dynasty who acceded to the throne after the death of Mukunda Deb, and Telenga Ramachandra Deb, son of Mukunda Deb.

Raja Man Singh, the Mughal agent, had to decide whom to accept as the legitimate ruler. He had a soft corner for Telenga Ramachandra Deb for his loyalty to the Mughals. On the other hand, he could not trust Gajapati Ramachandra Deb as he had been an ally of the Afghans who were enemies of the Mughals. The Gajapati was, therefore, very skeptical about Man Singh's action when he invited both claimants to the Khurda throne to the Jagannath Temple at Puri.

However, Ramachandra Deb directly reached out to the Mughal emperor, which changed the equation. Man Singh was in a dilemma. Though he suppressed the Afghan rebellion at Jaleswar (in Balasore district, Odisha), he found the Gajapati as a defiant yet powerful force to reckon with. Man Singh also found that the priests, Brahmins, temple *sebaks* and the general populace were sympathetic to Ramachandra Deb. The Gajapati was very popular among people. The other claimant Telenga Ramachandra Deb did not have popular support. The dilemma of Man Singh got resolved when he got a directive from Mughal Emperor Akbar to withdraw his forces from attacking Ramachandra Deb for which he had made elaborate arrangements. The Gajapati expressed his loyalty to the Mughal emperor and accepted his suzerainty.

The *Madala Panji* describes the resolution of dispute between the two claimants to the throne. During *Chandan Yatra* (a 21-day temple festival in April), Khurda Ramachandra Deb and Telenga Ramachandra Deb accompanied Man Singh to the Jagannath Temple. The servitors asked Man Singh to whom they should give the *khadi prasad* (temple offering). Man Singh offered the *khadi prasad* to the Khurda Raja Ramachandra Deb in front of the Bimala temple and recognized him as the Thakur Raja of Odisha. As Man Singh did not want to displease Telenga Ramachandra Deb, he was made the king of Aul (in Kendrapara). The other son of Gajapati Mukunda Deb, Chhakadi Brahmarabara, was made the raja of Patia (in Bhubaneswar district) by succession. Thus, the dispute was resolved.[4]

The Pious Ruler

As his first act after establishing his capital at Khurda, Ramachandra Deb I appointed Bardhan Mahapatra, son of Kabi Dindima Mahapatra, and the court poet of the late Gajapati Prataprudra Deb, as the *rajguru* (royal preceptor). This move appeased the Brahmin community and they applauded the appointment of the learned Bardhan Mahapatra. The rajguru played an important role in legitimizing Ramachandra Deb as the Gajapati, and the King, in turn, depended on the Brahmin's wise counsel and followed his advice very religiously. On behalf of the Gajapati, the rajguru reached out to the masses through various means, such as introducing many religious festivals in the state.

In order to gain widespread support of the local community as well as the Brahmins, Bardhan Mahapatra started the autumnal celebration of Durga Puja on a massive scale. He compiled the *Durgaustav Chandrika* after consulting Mukti Mandap (about whom we shall read later) and the Gajapati. Durga Puja was celebrated as a *Samarika Utsav* (martial celebration) and was conducted using elaborate rituals. The ceremony of *Durga Madhaba Yatra* in Puri was also started at this time and this established a deep link between Durga Puja and the Puri Jagannath Temple. After the ceremonial procession and worship, the idol of Durga Madhaba used to be brought back to the temple. Then the darbar of Durga Madhaba used to be held there, with Gajapati Ramachandra Deb I attending it, as the representative of Lord Jagannath and Goddess Durga, along with the other royal dignitaries. The Gajapati would sit in front of the idol; the Rajguru would sit to the south of the king and on his north side were seated the various feudatory lords. All the state officials ranging from commanders-in-chief to village heads participated in this celebration.

The worship of Durga was a form of Shakti Puja; it was a celebration of the great power of the Goddess and was symbolized through the worship of arms and ammunition. The royal preceptor, by introducing and then popularizing Durga Puja, succeeded in achieving two purposes. First, the worship of Shakti and its association with the Jagannath Temple helped to establish the legitimacy of Ramachandra Deb's rule among all sections of society. Second, it instilled and inculcated the spirit of courage, sense of triumph and penchant for martial skill in the hearts of the Odia people and their Gajapati. This was very timely to save the society and the community from the growing influence of the Bhakti philosophy and Sri Chaitanya's Vaishnavism in Odisha, which had seriously blunted the military and fighting spirit of the people.

Although the institution of Shakti puja in Odisha was very impressive, the most remarkable achievement of Ramachandra Deb I was the reinstallation of the idols of Jagannath, Balabhadra and Subhadra, which had been destroyed by Kalapahad, in the temple at Puri. According to the *Madala Panji*, the Gajapati brought the *'brahman'* (the core material in the unburnt portion of the original image) from Kujanga in the ninth year of his reign and had the idols of Jagannath, Balabhadra and Subhadra constructed and consecrated in Khurda Jagannathpur Kataka after performing necessary sacrifices. These images were installed on the *Ratna Singhasana* of the Jagannath Temple on the 18th day of Karkataka, which was in Srabana, Sukla Navami in Ramachandra Deb's 11th year as king. According to astronomical calculations, the date corresponds to 17 July 1575 in the Gregorian calendar.[5] This was obviously an occasion of great celebration for all sections of the Hindu society who hailed this historic event and honoured the king with the title *Dwitiya Indradyumna* or 'Second Indradyumna' for this noble work. This event of significance is well recorded in the *Madala Panji*.

King Indradyumna was the legendary original founder of the Jagannath Temple. The King was a great devotee of Lord Vishnu and had a burning desire to build a Vishnu temple. He sent his priest Vidyapati to meet Sabara (tribal) King Viswabasu, who knew the sacred location of the idol of Nila Madhaba. On being informed by Vidyapati, King Indradyumna in the *Satya Yuga* (Age of Truth) proceeded to Utkal to bring back that image to his kingdom. He was disappointed as he could not find the image of Nila Madhaba. After doing the *Ashwamedha Yagna* (ritual performed by ancient kings to prove their imperial sovereignty), he finally found a wooden log floating on the sea bearing the insignia of Lord Vishnu. From this log, the images of Jagannath, Balabhadra, Subhadra and Sudarshan were carved. He built the great temple and installed the images there. Indradyumna prayed to Lord Brahma to consecrate the temple. Brahma told the King that Lord Jagannath would grace the temple and he would hoist the flag in the blue wheel, at the *darshan* of which people would attain salvation. Gajapati Ramachandra Deb I is compared with Indradyumna as after Kalapahad's barbarous attack he was able to restore and re-establish the newly-made deities in the famous temple. Ramachandra Deb's action brought a new lease of life to the temple and the people. For this great act, he was called the Second Indradyumna or *Dwitiya Indradyumna*.

After the installation of the new idols, the Gajapati reintroduced the *Mahaprasad Seva* (offering of 56 food items to Lord Jagannath), which had been discontinued since the fall of Mukunda Deb's kingdom. The *Madala Panji* mentions that prominent Brahmins gathered for the *Mahaprasad Seva* at the temple. Ramchandra Bhatt, Gobardhan Praharaj and Misra Goswain took *Mahaprasad* from the hands of Ramachandra Deb I and touched their foreheads with it in reverence. The congregation of Brahmins, sanyasis, saints, mendicants and *sebaks* chanted *Hari Bol* and the King was honoured and called Thakur Raja and *Chalanti* Vishnu.[6] In the annals of Gajapati history, no other king has been acclaimed, applauded and held in such high esteem as Ramachandra Deb I because of his immense and unequalled contribution towards reinstating the idols of Jagannath, Balabhadra and Subhadra at their rightful place.

This glorious occasion generated a wave of great happiness and relief among the people, who believed that Lord Jagannath had finally returned to His abode after a long spell of absence which would augur well for everyone. With reinstallation of the idols in the Jagannath Temple, the Rath Yatra or the Gundicha Yatra (Car Festival), which was discontinued for eight years, was also restarted with new vigour. Recommencement of this festival brought immeasurable joy and rejoicing to the people. To mark this joyous occasion, Gajapati Ramachandra Deb I wrote a play titled *Sri Krishna Bhakta Vatsalya Charitam*, which was staged at the time of the Car Festival.

Chandakabi, an Odiya poet from Ramachandra Deb's time, eulogized the king in his *Indradyumna Avtar*. The poet writes that by bringing the deities to their abode, Ramachandra Deb had achieved a rare feat that would immortalize the king for ages to come. In his famous work *Basanta Ustav Mahakabyam*, Pandit Haladhar Mishra, a famous Sanskrit poet of Odisha in the first half of the seventeenth century, has described Ramachandra Deb I as *Naba Indradyumna* for reviving the worship of Jagannath in the great temple.

Ramachandra Deb I carried on his work to revive and promote Hinduism by establishing 16 *sasanas* (Brahmin villages or settlements) around Puri. Some of these prominent *sasanas* are Bira Ramachandrapur, Shri Ramchandrapur, Bijaya Ramchandrapur, Pratap Ramchandrapur and Ubhayamukhi Ramachandrapur. It may be useful to mention that when Cuttack was the capital of the Odishan kingdom, Gajapati Purushottama Deb had planned to set up 16 Brahmin *sasanas* near Cuttack. Many *sasanas* were set up, the first being Prasanna Purusottampur, which was inaugurated on 17 February 1469. After the occupation of the state by the Afghans, the importance of these 16 *sasanas* declined. In order to revive and strengthen Hinduism, Ramachandra Deb I again established 16 *sasanas* around Puri.

During his regime, the Mukti Mandap at the Puri Temple also got a facelift and acquired renewed importance. The Mukti Mandap, the holy seat and the congregation of learned Brahmins/scholars was considered as the highest authority for interpreting Hindu religious practice and principles, and its decision was considered as final and binding on all Hindus. Learned men from 16 *sasanas* used to sit in the Mukti Mandap, which had 16 pillars, each representing a *sasana*. Subsequently, this number was increased to 21 by extending its coverage to more *sasanas* and including additional members. Epigraphical evidence shows that by 1511, the Mukti Mandap was very well established and deep rooted. From the *Madala Panji* as well as the *Ain-i-Akbari* we come to know that the present Mukti Mandap was re-constructed to commemorate Man Singh's visit to the Jagannath Temple in AD 1592 by his wife Gaura Rani.*

---

* Balarama Dasa, a great poet of the Panchasakha period during Prataprudra Deb's time, in his work *Vedantasara Gupta Gita* has referred to the Mukti Mandap and certain dates mentioning about a great scholar called Balabhadra Rajguru. The period referred to is in

Almost a century earlier, Gajapati Purushottama Deb (AD 1467–1497) had brought the idols of Sakhigopala and Ganesh to Cuttack as tokens of his victory against Kanchi.[7] In 1568, before Kalapahad could damage or destroy the temple and these idols in Cuttack, they were smuggled out. When he set up his capital at Khurda, Ramachandra Deb I constructed a temple there to house these idols in order to preserve their sanctity.[*]

Conflict with Man Singh

Man Singh, the general of Emperor Akbar, moved to Cuttack in 1592 to wage war against the rebel Afghan sardars, who had been provided shelter by Ramachandra Deb I at the Sarangagada Fort. Purushottam, son of Ramachandra Deb I, joined the Afghans in their opposition to the Mughal attack, which further enraged Man Singh. Man Singh managed to seize the fort but did not succeed in capturing the Afghans as they fled to the jungles. This left Man Singh's mission incomplete. A frustrated Man Singh decided to punish Ramachandra Deb I for the impertinence displayed by his son. He planned to attack Khurda and stationed a large contingent of Mughal soldiers at Pipili.

As per the *Akbarnama*, sensing impending defeat, Ramachandra Deb I asked his son to surrender to the Mughal emperor and sent

---

the 17th regnal year of Prataprudra Deb, which began from 16 August 1510 and continued till 4 September 1511. This would help to erase a misplaced impression that the Mukti Mandap was set up by Man Singh [Kedarnath Mahapatra, *Khuruda Itihasa*, Grantha Mandir (Cuttack, 1999), p. 15, and Kedarnath Mahapatra, *A Descriptive Catalogue of Sanskrit Manuscripts of Orissa*, vol. I (Smriti Manuscripts, 1960), p. 22].

[*] These idols became the object of attack time and again. For instance, when Taqi Khan attacked the temple at Rathipur, the idols were already taken to a place near Chilika Lake for safekeeping. During the time of the Marathas, the present-day temple at Satyabadi was constructed and the idols were finally moved there.

him to Man Singh. However, Man Singh was not appeased and demanded the personal presence of Ramachandra Deb I in order to accept his surrender. The Gajapati refused to bow down and comply with Man Singh's order. Enraged, Man Singh decided to crush the Raja's arrogance and sent an army led by his son Jagat Singh who was accompanied by several other important military men like Mir Sharif Sarmandi, Mir Qasim Badakhashi, Barkhurdar, Adul Baqa, Muhamud Beg Shamlu and Shihabu-d-din Diwana to wage war against Ramachandra Deb.

News reached Emperor Akbar about this massive preparation for the attack on the Raja of Khurda. According to some documents, Ramachandra Deb I expressed his loyalty to Emperor Akbar and complained about Man Singh's move to attack him. Annoyed at this misadventure of Man Singh, Akbar conveyed his displeasure and advised his general to refrain from the planned attack. Man Singh had no option but to put his war plans on hold and sign a treaty with Ramachandra Deb I. We can infer from this episode that Man Singh and Emperor Akbar were aware of the might of Ramachandra Deb I. Ferishta also describes Ramachandra as 'a prince of great power and fame'.[8] General Man Singh had decided to send no less than seven war veterans along with his son to take on Ramachandra Deb I, and in spite of the military superiority of the Mughal army, Akbar had thought it prudent to avoid a clash with the Gajapati.[9] Subsequently, Ramachandra Deb I established a good relationship with Emperor Akbar. As mentioned earlier, he was recognized as the King of Khurda and also the custodian of the Jagannath Temple.

Patron of Literature

Gajapati Ramachandra Deb I was a man of letters and a great patron of literature. As we have seen, the *Durgotsava Chandrika* was composed during his reign, which was very successful in promoting the autumnal worship of Goddess Durga. The Sanskrit drama *Sri Krishna Bhakta Vatsalya Charitam* is also attributable to him, as mentioned earlier. Kabi Chintamani Misra, a contemporary of Ramachandra Deb, was the author of *Sambararicharita*, *Kadambarisara*, and other works. The most notable writer and poet during his period was Biswanath Samantaray, whom Gajapati Ramachandra Deb I had honoured with the title of *Kavichandra* for his poetic achievements and learning. Kavibhusan Govinda Samantaray, an illustrious descendant of Biswanath Samantaray, has also written about him in his book *Suri Sarvasvam*.

When Man Singh came to Puri in 1592, Kavichandra Biswanath got an opportunity to meet him and presented his work *Ratnasara* to him. Man Singh was so overwhelmed with his poetic talent and discourse that when he returned to Delhi in 1594 he took along the poet to present him to Emperor Akbar. Pleased with Biswanath Samantaray's talent, the Mughal emperor introduced him to the learned and erudite scholars in his court. Biswanath also received grants of land and jewels from the emperor. Abu'l Fazl in his *Ain-i-Akbari* mentions about this poet who was honoured so highly in the Mughal court. After returning from Delhi, Samantaray settled in Pratapramchandrapur.[10]

The ascent of Ramachandra Deb I to the throne of Khurda came about in extremely adverse circumstances. The ruler had the formidable and daunting task of re-energizing a demoralized population after the fall of the Jagannath Temple at the hands of Afghan marauders. All the while, he also had to ensure that his legitimacy as the Gajapati was recognized by his subjects. Ramachandra Deb I achieved both his objectives by reinstating the idol of Lord Jagannath in His venerated temple and thus he came to occupy a unique position in the history of the region. During his long reign of almost 30 years, Ramachandra Deb I proved to be an able administrator and benevolent king. For his many achievements, he was honoured with the title of Abhinava Indradyumna and will forever be remembered in the history of Odisha.

6

PURUSHOTTAMA DEB
The Most Attacked King

Purushottama Deb succeeded his father Gajapati Ramachandra Deb I as the Raja of Khurda (AD 1600-1621). Purushottama Deb had been trained from a young age by his father in administrative and military tactics and had been prepared for his future role as the Gajapati. By the time he ascended the throne, he was considered a knowledgeable and experienced leader.

With friendship established between Ramachandra Deb I and Emperor Akbar, Purushottama Deb, a young prince at that time, visited Moghul Durbar and met Akbar. He was accompanied by Man Singh. This was a period when the Gajapati had successfully established friendly and cordial relations with the Mughal administration.

However, with the death of Akbar in 1605, the period of peace and friendship ended. Jahangir was crowned the Mughal emperor, and from the outset he made it clear that he would not follow in his father's footsteps of liberalism and religious tolerance. This proved to be very unfortunate for Purushottama Deb. After all, as the custodian of the Puri Temple, which was one of the most important Hindu religious centres of that time, he became an obvious target of attack by the Mughal forces that wanted to establish their supremacy.

It was also during Purushottama Deb's reign that Odisha was made into an independent administrative region by the Mughals, by carving it out of the Bengal *subah* (province). In 1607, Cuttack was made the capital of this newly-established *subah* by the Mughal *subedar* (the governor/ruler of a *subah*). The Mughal subedars, in order to assert their authority and to demonstrate their loyalty to the Mughal emperor, initiated a policy of frequent attacks on the Hindu kingdoms of the region which till then functioned like near-independent states.

Hasim Khan was appointed as the first subedar of Odisha in AD 1607. He soon started targeting Hindu rulers to please the Mughal emperor. It was under his rule that one of the most daring attacks was made on the Jagannath Temple by one of his *jagirdars* (landlords), Kesho Das Maru. Although a Hindu himself, Kesho Das's allegiance was firmly with his Muslim overlords. To prove his loyalty, he found no better way than to attack the revered shrine of Lord Jagannath at Puri. He went to the shrine pretending to seek *darshan* (blessings) of the Lord, but chose a time when the idols were at the Gundicha Temple during the Car Festival. With everyone busy at the Gundicha Temple 3 km away, Kesho Das and his army of Rajput soldiers faced no hurdle in entering the Jagannath Temple and plundering the temple treasury of its fabulous riches, all the while creating panic and striking fear in the hearts of all those in the temple. As soon as Gajapati Purushottama Deb heard the news of the sudden attack, he set out for Puri from Khurda with his forces consisting of cavalry and chariots to defend the shrine.

A Persian source mentions that the Khurda Raja moved with a force of 10,000 cavalry, 3,000–4,000 infantry and a large number of chariots to besiege Kesho Das who was inside the temple.[1] In a strategic move, he surrounded the temple and chariots were positioned all along the boundary wall. But as Purushottama Deb mounted a fierce attack, Kesho Das adopted a novel form of counterattack. His soldiers collected bamboo sticks and long poles, wrapped them with cloth, and dousing them in ghee and oil from the temple storeroom, set fire to these making them into effective fireballs. They hurled the fireballs at the chariots surrounding the temple, thus causing immense panic and damage. The Gajapati's forces were thrown into disarray as the chariots got burnt down and the men ran away to save their lives.

While this fighting was underway, Hasim Khan was making other plans. He approached the subedar of Bengal, Islam Khan, for seeking additional reinforcements and assistance to Kesho Das. Islam Khan dispatched General Khwaza Tahir Muhammad Bakshi with a strong military contingent to fight alongside Hasim Khan. Thus strengthened, the subedar of Odisha proceeded to Puri to join the attack against the Gajapati. However, before the additional forces reached Puri, Kesho Das decided to take upon himself the task of defeating Purushottama Deb without any support and prove himself before the emperor. He, therefore, launched a fierce attack.

Realizing that he was outmanoeuvred and outnumbered, Purushottama Deb made a quick decision to avert certain defeat at the hands of the Mughals. He negotiated with Kesho Das and entered into a treaty with him. However, having trapped the Gajapati in an impossible situation, Kesho Das took advantage of the circumstances to inflict humiliating conditions on Purushottama Deb as part of the treaty. He raised three demands, all of which the Gajapati had to meet. First, Purushottama Deb had to agree to offer his daughter to Jahangir. Second, he had to pay a *peshkash* (tribute) of Rs 3 lakh to the Mughal emperor. Third, Purushottama Deb had to give his sister in marriage to Kesho Das as well as pay a dowry of Rs 1 lakh. The treaty imposed extremely humiliating conditions on the Raja of Khurda. And the humiliation did not end there. It soon became clear that the treaty was only used as an excuse by Kesho Das, who violated its terms by killing many hundreds of the Gajapati's soldiers known as *Paiks*, to inflict more harm on the Raja.

Having thus achieved his objective, Kesho Das left for Khurda even before Hasim Khan with his forces could reach Puri. At Khurda, Kesho Das was married to the Gajapati's sister. Here too

Kesho Das created a conflict. When he was offered an elephant as part of the dowry, he was enraged to find that the pachyderm was weak and injured. He, therefore, forcibly took away six elephants belonging to the Raja instead.

After Kesho Das returned to Cuttack, he was honoured by Jahangir for his great loyalty. The Mughal emperor conferred upon him a standard, a robe of honour, a bejewelled sword, a belt, a horse, a bejewelled saddle and reins, in order to draw the attention of others to such deeds of valour. He also elevated Kesho Das to a rank of 4,000 horses.[2] Demonstrating his allegiance to the Mughals by attacking the Jagannath Temple, Kesho Das earned for himself a mention in the *Tuzuk-I-Jahangiri*, the autobiography of Emperor Jahangir. The following is recorded there: '*Kesho Das Maru, who is a Rajput of the province of Mairtha and is greater in loyalty than his contemporaries, I promoted to the rank of 1500.*'[3]

After Hasim Khan, Kalyan Mal, son of Todar Mal (the revenue minister of Akbar), became the subedar of Odisha (AD 1611–1617). In order to please his overlord, Emperor Jahangir, Kalyan Mal followed in the footsteps of Kesho Das Maru and invaded Khurda in 1611.

The repeated attacks on his kingdom had left Gajapati Purushottama Das vulnerable and weak. He was just about recovering from the war with Kesho Das when he had to face the invasion by Kalyan Mal. Realizing that Kalyan Mal's attack could have a very damaging impact on his kingdom, the Gajapati chose to salvage the situation by appeasing the new subedar to save his kingdom and the temple of Lord Jagannath. Before Kalyan Mal could attack, Purushottama Deb agreed for a truce and reached a compromise that warranted offering his daughter 'as a present for the service of the emperor' and his best elephant 'Seshanaga' as well as a *peshkash* of Rs 3 lakh to the Mughal emperor.[4]

In the history of the rule by the Gajapatis, this was a unique moment when two Hindus had attacked the Jagannath Temple back-to-back acting with the intention of pleasing the

Mughal emperor. It may appear from this history that Gajapati Purushottama Deb was a weak ruler who succumbed to the attacks of aggressors. However, a more charitable assessment would show that Purushottama Deb took the practical and best possible steps that he could have taken considering the circumstances and potential consequences. His actions probably prevented further damage and destruction to Lord Jagannath's temple as well as to the Khurda kingdom.

Makram Khan became the subedar of Odisha in AD 1617, and established himself in Cuttack. He too attacked Khurda like his two predecessors. The *Tuzuk-I-Jahangiri* records this invasion and also mentions that the ruler of Khurda, defeated by Makram Khan, fled to the shelter provided by the King of Rajahmundry in order to survive. It also mentions that 'the province of Khurda has come into the possession of the servants of the court. After this, it is the turn of the country of Rajmahendra. My hope in the grace of Allah is that the feet of my energy may advance farther'.[5]

The *Madala Panji* also records that Makram Khan had dislodged the Khurda Raja from his fort and occupied it for one year. It is believed that at that time the Gajapati stayed at Gadamanatri, some miles away from Puri towards Chilika Lake. However, this is disputable as the *Madala Panji* makes no reference of this. For this victory, Makram Khan was honoured by the Mughal emperor with a higher *mansab* (rank or position) with 3,000 personnel and 2,000 horses, and also with drums, a horse and a dress of honour.

Khurda was again attacked in 1621 by another subedar, Ahmed Beg Khan. This too is recorded in the *Tuzuk-I-Jahangiri*.

Facing such repeated invasions over the years made Purushottama Deb's rule as Gajapati a unique one. His reign saw the vicious attack by the wily Kesho Das, which caused great damage to the Jagannath Temple. Even the *Mahaparasad seva* (food offering to the deity) was stopped for eight months. Subsequent attacks by other subedars meant that the idols of Lord Jagannath, Balabhadra and Subhadra had to be constantly moved to keep them safe from the hands of the invaders. The priests and *sebaks* had hidden the idols in a secret place in Chilika, described as Gurubadai in the *Madala Panji*. Later, they were hidden in Gabapadara near Banpur.

In such desperately adverse circumstances, Gajapati Purushottama Deb tried to keep his kingdom from harm by making compromises, even accepting great personal humiliation and loss in order to keep peace. We have to consider his actions in view of the then prevailing hostile situation, which left him with no option but to choose the so-called feeble ways to keep his kingdom and Lord safe.

7

GAJAPATIS ON THE RUN
Turbulent Times for Both the Lords

Narasimha Deb acceded to the throne of Khurda in AD 1621. Ahmed Beg (AD 1621–1624) was the subedar of Odisha at that time. Beg is reported to have attacked Narasimha Deb nearly a year after the latter assumed the throne. In the meanwhile, in the north, Prince Shah Jahan revolted against Emperor Jahangir as he was deprived of the throne because of a conspiracy hatched by Noor Jahan, the Emperor's favourite wife who wielded immense power. Even as the Mughal emperor tried to suppress the rebellion, Shah Jahan, with the help of the Sultan of Golconda, moved towards Delhi from the south to occupy the Mughal throne. When Shah Jahan came to Odisha on his way to Bengal, Raja Narasimha Deb welcomed him and accepted his suzerainty. Shah Jahan occupied Cuttack towards the end of 1623.

As mentioned earlier, Beg was engaged in a war against Narasimha Deb around the same time. When he learnt about Shah Jahan's march towards Khurda and Narasimha Deb's support to him, he was so petrified that he withdrew his troops, abandoned the campaign against Khurda and fled to Burdwan. Mohammad Taqi, a loyal servant of Shah Jahan, was appointed as the new subedar of Odisha before Shah Jahan headed to Midnapore. The *Madala Panji* chronicles this expedition of Shah Jahan in detail.

However, Shah Jahan could not conquer Bengal and returned to the south from Rajmahal (capital city of the early 17th century Bengal, in present-day Santhal Pargana, Jharkhand), passing through Odisha in 1625. Ahmed Beg again became subedar of Odisha towards the end of 1625 and remained in the post till 1628. There was no attack either on the Khurda King or the Jagannath Temple at Puri at this time. In 1628, Odisha got a new subedar, Baqir Khan Nazim Sani, who attacked the Sun Temple at Konark. Narasimha Deb, however, managed to take the idol of the Sun God out of the temple and installed it in the Niladrimahostav Temple, inside the premises of the Jagannath Temple on 17 March 1628.[1]

With Shah Jahan's return to the south in 1625 and till the death of Narasimha Deb in 1647, there was peace. The Jagannath Temple and Khurda were spared from predatory attacks. Mutaqud Khan, who was the subedar of Odisha during AD 1628–1648, undertook the construction of the famous Lalbagh Palace at Cuttack, which then became the official residence of the Mughal subedar. From a letter of the Khan-i-Dauran to his agent at the imperial court, we come to learn that Mutaqud Khan reportedly killed Narasimha Deb. The letter states:

> I have learnt the following facts from trustworthy men; when the late Mutaqud Khan was subahdar, he slew Narsingh Dev and made his nephew Gangadhar the Raja. Balabhadra Dev, the elder brother of the slain, became Rajah after killing Gangadhar with the help of the officers of the State. When he died, Mukund Dev succeeded at the age of four only.[2]

However, it is not certain that Mutaqud Khan did indeed kill Narasimha Deb. It is widely believed that the subedar was a peace-loving person and, apart from the letter cited above, there is no record of him inflicting any personal harm on the Gajapati during the 11 years of his rule. Therefore, some historians are of the view that Mutaqud Khan cannot be held responsible for killing the

Gajapati. It appears more likely to have been a family conspiracy for succession to the throne.

Since the tenure of Narasimha Deb was peaceful, the Gajapati was able to pay attention to the repair and restoration work of the Jagannath Temple, which was in a neglected state because of frequent attacks and disturbances. To protect the temple from adverse effects of the saline sea winds, the Gajapati got the whole temple plastered with white lime. His tenure also saw great resurgence of Sanskrit and Odia literature. Salabega, a great devotional poet known for his heart-touching *bhajans* and *jananas* (devotional songs and prayers), was the most significant literary success during his tenure. Since Salabega and his devotional poems have become an integral part of the Jagannath cult with which the Gajapati tradition is so intertwined, the story of Salabega and his contributions to the culture and literature of Odisha is worth a mention here.

Salabega was the son of Mughal subedar Quli Khan, who was popularly known as Lal Beg. During the reign of Jahangir, Quli Khan was appointed as the subedar of Bihar. After death of the subedar of Bengal, he was appointed in his place in 1607. During an expedition to Puri, he came across a beautiful young Brahmin widow bathing at Danda Mukundapur (on the outskirts of Puri). Fascinated by her beauty, Lal Beg forcibly took her away and married her. Salabega was born to the couple.

In his childhood, Salabega accompanied his father in a military campaign, where he got injured in a battle. There is another account that states that Salabega suffered from an incurable ailment in his childhood. His mother, who was a Hindu, advised him to pray to Lord Jagannath, an incarnation of Lord Krishna, to cure his disease. It seems, he chanted the holy name of Lord Krishna and was miraculously cured. These details about Salabega are described in *Dardhyata Bhakti Rasamruta* by Rama Dasa, an Odia poet. His recovery from a hopeless situation became the turning point in Salabega's life. He developed great devotion towards Lord Jagannath and spent all his time in singing prayers of the Lord and led a saintly life of detachment from worldly matters.

Salabega, being the son of a Muslim, was denied entry to the Jagannath Temple, but he had deep devotion for the deity. He travelled on foot to Vrindavan, where he lived the life of an ascetic in the company of *sadhus* reciting prayers to Lord Krishna. After a year in Vrindavan, he returned to Puri longing to watch the Ratha Yatra festival of Lord Jagannath. However, he fell ill on the way. Feeling hopeless and helpless, he offered prayers to the Lord, earnestly pleading to Him to wait till his return. It was his fervent wish to see the Lord in the chariot outside the temple which was out of bounds for him. Miraculously, on the day of Bahuda Yatra or the Return Car festival, Nandighosa, the chariot of Lord Jagannath, suddenly stopped on the way and did not move until the arrival of Salabega. The Lord waited there and gave *darshan* to Salabega, His dear devotee on Bada Danda (Grand Road) near Balagandi. Salabega's wish was fulfilled!

Being a Muslim, he faced resistance and ridicule from the *pandas* (priests) of Puri, and was often at the receiving end of their hate and anger. Since the Gajapati had given a place to Salabega near the Bada Danda, the priests were especially annoyed. They went to the extent of damaging the Badachatta Matha, where Salabega was staying. When the Gajapati came to know about the treatment to Salabega, he felt very ashamed and punished the erring *pandas*. The Gajapati had immense respect and devotion for Salabega; in fact, upon the poet's death the Gajapati was reported to have attended the cremation of Salabega at Badachatta Matha. This place has now become a place of pilgrimage.[3] Every year, the chariot of Lord Jagannath on its return journey from Gundicha temple (3 km away) stops near the *samadhi* at Balagandi for a while as a mark of remembrance and love for Salabega.

Salabega signifies a great resurgence in devotional literature in Odisha. His popularity also signifies tolerance as well as acceptance of non-Hindus, particularly Muslims, in the cultural and literary heritage of the Jagannath tradition. His arrival on the scene when the Jagannath Temple was under constant attacks by Muslims and the great respect for him among the people, is a reflection of the liberal ethos of Odishan culture and tradition. Though he was a Muslim, he was deeply influenced by his Hindu mother, who initiated him into the cult of Sri Krishna as well as Lord Jagannath. For Salabega, Lord Jagannath was an incarnation of Sri Krishna. Being influenced by Vaishnava culture, he was also deeply moved by the Radha-Krishna *leelas* (divine love) and ethos. As a devotional poet, he made immense contribution to devotional culture and literature through devotional songs, namely *bhajans* and *jananas*, which he composed in various ragas and sang sitting outside the temple. Through his songs, the oral tradition was also enriched.

Salabega himself did not write down his compositions in any form. His poems were subsequently written on palm leaves by his numerous admirers who inherited the oral tradition over the years. His devotional songs had such appeal, depth and reach that he became immortal through his renditions. His songs outlived him, making him ageless and immortal; his devotional songs were timeless and left a perennial footprint, which has no parallel in devotional literature. Salabega brought people closer to God and nearer to divinity. In his work, there are elements of *shravana, kirtana, smarana, padasebana, archana, bedana, dasya, sakhya* and *atmanibedana*—the nine streams of bhakti or devotion—in ample measure.

The elemental composition and measure of these attributes in his poems are so well presented that anyone who sings or listens to Salabega's songs gets immersed in devotion. Salabega's humbleness is epitomized by his abject, unconditional surrender before the lotus feet of the Lord. The devotional spirit exhibited in his songs makes one humble by taking away the elements of ego, pride, arrogance and ignorance from oneself. The songs have a great purificatory impact on the soul, making one surrender before the Almighty.

The significance of Salabega's poems transcends their literary themes. They also present reflections on the society. During the Mughal rule, the Jagannath Temple was the target of attacks and plunder by various Muslim rulers. Lord Jagannath was considered as the presiding deity of the kingdom. Therefore, any attack on the temple was expected to destabilize the kingdom. In those turbulent times, the Gajapatis and priests of the temple used to secretly take out the idols and hide them in far-off places to save their revered deities from the *jabana* or Muslim invaders. The devoted priests of Puri considered Lord Jagannath to be a living and loving god, the caretaker of beings and their country. The frightened priests used to take the idols to distant hills and mountainous areas, and often to the islands in Chilika Lake. During Ahmed Beg's time, the deities were secretly removed from the temple. Salabega was a witness to this pitiable sight. He found the *pandas* and devotees shedding tears, weeping and sobbing uncontrollably as the Lord was being taken out from His abode. Salabega has described this in one of his finest poems which reflects the feelings and emotion of every affected and afflicted Odia. The poem *Kene gheni jauchha Jagannathanku...* runs as under:

> Where, O' Whereto
> Are you taking away the Lord?
> Whom do our eyes then feast on?
> Whose darshan shall we have?
> At the khuntia's call
> you begin your ritual journey
> of Pahandi or go for
> boating in the sacred tank.
> But now instead
> the women folk
> are wailing, the priests are
> rolling in dust
> lamenting destiny's curse on Odisha.
> Out of the sanctum sanctorum
> on an ordinary cart you left
> dust particles must be
> falling on your charming face.
> Says Salabega shame on our lives!
> where on earth would we get
> now a grain of nirmalya?[4]

Salabega represents the cultural synthesis of Odisha's history and heritage. He and his works reflect the best aspects of humanism when the Mughal subedars were pursuing an anti-Hindu agenda by attacking temples. Salabega represents an antithesis to the dogmatic approach of the invaders. His devotional poems have had such an enduring impact on the hearts and minds of people that history has withstood the attacks and made Salabega a hero through his devotional songs.

His popular and famous poem *Ahe nila saila* (O Lord of the Universe) continues to be on everyone's lips. It is the most popular prayer in Odisha. It is sung in every Odia home in the evening and on most religious occasions. It is sung every day in the Jagannath Temple. This is an intense prayer of surrender seeking the mercy of Lord Jagannath. In it, Salabega seeks the mercy of the Lord, surrendering himself before His lotus feet. Similarly, every song by Salabega ends with a personal invocation to the Lord. This unique style makes his songs profound, providing a personal devotional touch. *Ahe nila saila* is iconic and it vividly demonstrates the irrelevance of one's individual identity in terms of religious affiliation. Devotion and faith in Lord Jagannath is an inclusive culture, subsuming and assimilating different strands of thought without any distinction. And Salabega is a symbol of such a tradition. The poem '*Ahe nila saila*' reads as under:

Oh, the intoxicated powerful
elephant of Nilashaila
come and crush
the lotus forest of my anguish.
The elephant prayed million miles away
and you saved him crushing the crocodile
with your disc
Seeing Draupadi's plight
in the court of the Kurus
you saved her self-respect
by gifting million sarees.

When the wild deer moaned
in mid-forest, you redeemed
her from all woes!
When *Bibhisana* took refuge
at thy lotus-feet, you saved
him from his miserable plight!
When *Ajamila* wept showers
and prayed in the zero-hour
you lifted him to your garden!
When *Hiranya's* wrath rose high,
You did tear him, emerging
From the stony pillar!
As a Buddha, the enlightened,
you came to *Nilachala;* lifting your hands
you could render shelter to everyone.
Shelter me, treasure me, save me
Beneath the shade of your lotus feet–
Thus prays Salabega, the lowborn.[4]

In Odia society and culture, Salabega's presence is pervasive and overwhelming. Salabega epitomizes the best of Odisha's rich culture.

Gajapati Mukunda Deb I: AD 1657–1689

After Narasimha Deb was murdered, his nephew Gangadhar Deb, i.e., son of his brother Gokul Raya, was made the Raja of Khurda. Gangadhar Deb ruled for a few months. Balabhadra Deb, the elder son of the slain, became the king after killing Gangadhar Deb with the help of royal officers. In the *Madala Panji*, however, there is no reference to the relationship between Gangadhar Deb and Balabhadra Deb, but the information that is recorded mentions that Balabhadra Deb killed Gangadhar Deb and became the king. As per Mughal history, Balabhadra Deb was the elder brother of Narasingha. A reading of both Mughal history and the *Madala Panji* reveals confusion.

While the Mughal version says Balabhadra Deb is the brother of Narasimha Deb, according to *Madala Panji* he is the son of Narasimha Deb. Balabhadra Deb ruled from AD 1647–1657 and this period was not particularly peaceful. After the death of Balabhadra Deb, his son Mukunda Deb acceded to the throne of Khurda in AD 1657. This Mukunda Deb has no connection with the Mukunda Deb (AD 1560–1568) of the Chalukya dynasty, the last independent Hindu king of Odisha. The Mukunda Deb under discussion is referred to as Mukunda Deb I as per regnal practice.

Aurangzeb was the emperor at Delhi at that time. Shaista Khan was the subedar in Odisha for a brief period up to 1660. Thereafter, Khan-i-Dauran became the subedar. Mukunda Deb was a powerful king. This is known from Sir Jadunath Sarkar's *Studies in Mughal India*, described below:

> When the Khan reached Kataka, Rajah Mukunda Dev of Khurda, the leading Zamindar of the country, whose orders are obeyed by the other Zamindars of the country, whom all other Zamindars of this country worship like a god and disobedience of whose orders they regard as a great sin, waited on him with due humility accompanied by other Zamindars and Khandaits of Central Odisha.[5]

However, Khan-i-Dauran soon after becoming subedar fell ill and was confined to bed for two months. Taking this opportunity, the local zamindars created disorder. They became rebellious and caused dissatisfaction against the Mughal subedar. Khan-i-Dauran sought the help of Mukunda Deb for suppressing the rebels. Mukunda Deb, however, did not come to his help; instead, he chose to side with the rebels. After recovering from his illness, Khan-i-Dauran proceeded in a military campaign on 7 February 1661 from Cuttack to conquer the forts of the rebel zamindars. On 16 February, he arrived near the forts of Kaluparah, Mutri near Delanga, Khurdiha, Karkahi and three others, totalling seven forts that were close to each other. An assault was launched the following day. The Mughal troops faced severe attacks from the *paiks* and infantry. The zamindars of Banki (in Cuttack, on the banks of the Mahanadi), Ranapur (in Nayagarh) and other *khaandayats* (feudal militia) and *bhuyains* (ethnic group) participated in the battle. They attacked with matchlocks, arrows, swords, *sablis*, *duars*, *dhukaus*, *sintis* (local names of indigenous weapons) and other such weapons. But the Mughal army was able to prevail and finally conquered the seven forts and took control of the area.[6]

After the conquest, Khan-i-Dauran proceeded to attack the Khurda Fort, the citadel of power, on 20 February 1661. His army pitched their tents a mile away from the fort and made huge preparations for the assault. Sensing trouble, Mukunda Deb fled from the capital. The Mughal subedar took this opportunity and attacked Khurda. Khan-i-Dauran seized the fort and took away vast amounts of loot, and many were taken prisoner. According to Khan-i-Dauran, 'During the last 50 years, no other subahdar had reached these places. They were all conquered by my army and the rustics became the food of the pitiless sword.'[7] Mukunda Deb's younger brother Bhramarabara was installed as the Raja of Khurda.

The capture of Khurda and the fleeing of Mukunda Deb brought about the desired effect for the Mughal subedar. The rebel zamindars started surrendering to Khan-i-Dauran. The zamindars of Banki and Ranapur sent their loyal agents to the subedar expressing their allegiance and their willingness to pay the dues. The zamindars of Mallipada and Danpada met Khan-i-Dauran and agreed to pay annual *peshkash* (tribute). One by one all the zamindars fell in line. Mukunda Deb found himself isolated and in a difficult position. He finally met Subedar Khan-i-Dauran on 18 March 1661 and expressed regret for his actions. Thus, Mukunda Deb was reinstated to the throne of Khurda.

After this incident, Khan-i-Dauran found it strategically convenient to rein in the rest of the rebel zamindars. Lakshminarayan Bhanja, King of Kendujhar, who was a rebel, was attacked and defeated by the Mughals. The zamindar of Kanika (in Kendrapara) was also brought under control of the Mughal subedar. The Khallikote (in Berhampur) zamindar proved to be a stumbling block. However, he was attacked and he also accepted Mughal supremacy. The Madhupur zamindar was taken prisoner as he failed to pay huge arrears in the form of tribute. One after another, the remaining zamindars toed the line and surrendered to the Mughal subedar agreeing to pay the annual tribute.

The result of these actions was the restoration of Mughal imperial authority in Odisha. Khan-i-Dauran could thus justifiably boast of his military successes, which in his own words were 'unrivalled by any preceding subadhar'. He wrote in his dispatches to Emperor Aurangzeb, 'I have punished all the usurpers, oppressors, and lawless men of the province and made them obedient. The revenue is being collected by our officers. The people are enjoying peace and happiness and plying their trades.' A year later, about April 1662, he wrote, 'The province is being well administered.'[8]

Khan-i-Dauran was the subedar of Cuttack for five years after Mukunda Deb resumed the seat of Khurda. During Mukunda Deb's time, Khan-i-Dauran destroyed the famous Baladevji Temple at Kendrapada and in its place constructed a mosque. There is no information of his attacking the Jagannath Temple at Puri.[9]

Shaista Khan was made the subedar of Cuttack from AD 1680 to 1688 for the second time. He followed the anti-Hindu policy of Emperor Aurangzeb. In 1686, the famous Sarala Temple at Jhankada (Jagatsingpur) was destroyed and in its place a mosque was constructed. In the following year, many Hindu temples were destroyed in Jajpur in whose place a huge mosque was constructed. The Mughal subedar then proceeded to attack Puri. However, at Pipli, he was hit by severe lightning and returned to Cuttack. The Puri Temple was thus saved.

Mukunda Deb died in Jajpur in 1689 from smallpox. His wife, the Pattarani, jumped into the funeral pyre and ended her life.

Gajapati Dibyasingha Deb I (AD 1689–1716)

Gajapati Dibyasingha I succeeded his father Mukunda Deb in 1689. His coronation took place at Rathipore, Cuttack, near Khurda. Both Gajapati Mukunda Deb and Gajapati Dibyasingha Deb ruled during the period of Mughal emperor Aurangzeb. They both faced the brunt of Aurangzeb's anti-Hindu religious policy. Many Hindu temples were demolished and in their place mosques were built. As we have seen, during Gajapati Mukunda Deb's regime, historic temples were demolished at many places to construct mosques.

It must be mentioned here that Emperor Aurangzeb had issued a general order for demolishing Hindu temples in Bengal and Odisha. The order is reproduced here.

> To all *faujdars, thanahdars, mutasaddis*, agents of *jagirdars, kroris*, and *amlas* from Katak to Medinipur on the frontier of Odisha. The imperial Paymaster Asad Khan has sent a letter written by order of the Emperor, to say that the Emperor, learning from the newsletters of the province of Odisha that at the village of Tilkuti in Medinipur a temple has been [newly] built, has issued his august mandate for its destruction and the destruction of all temples built anywhere in this province by the...infidels. Therefore, you are commanded with extreme urgency that immediately on the receipt of this letter you should destroy the above-mentioned temples. Every idol-house built during the last 10 or 12 years, whether with brick or clay, should be demolished without delay. Also, do not allow the... Hindus and...infidels to repair their old temples. Reports of the destruction of temples should be sent to the Court under the seal of the qazis and attested by pious Shaikhs.[10]

When Aurangzeb was in Bijapur (Karnataka), he had ordered the demolition of the Jagannath Temple. Aurangzeb had entrusted his loyal employee Ekram Khan with this task. Ekram Khan, accompanied by his brother Marmast Khan Jamaullah, attacked the Puri Temple in 1698. As per the *Madala Panji*, before Ekram Khan could attack the temple, the idols were removed and hidden behind the Bimala Temple. From the southern gate the idols were taken to a place called Kokilagad on the banks of the Bhargavi River, about 15 km from Brahmagiri (Puri district). Ekram Khan, his brother and one Imam Quli entered the temple with 50 soldiers. Raja Dibyasingha Deb I broke the battlements and the two *rakhsas* idols at the *Singha Dwara* (Lion's Gate) and handed over a jewel-studded image of the Lord made of sandalwood to Ekram Khan. The *Madala Panji* mentions that Ekram Khan's brother even climbed on the *Ratna Singhasana*, the seat of the Lord.

This description in the *Madala Panji* is supported by another document called *Chakadapothi*. It mentions that Ekram Bhai Jamal and Abdullah Khan reached the temple along with Dibyasingha Deb. They broke through the Lion's Gate and entered the temple. Dibyasingha Deb handed over the idol of Jagannath to Jamal and retained with him the idols of Balabhadra and Subhadra. Ekram Khan tied the idol in a leather belt and took it to Cuttack from where it was sent to Aurangzeb.

The Mughal account depicts the situation as under:

> He (Mir Sayyid Mahmud of Bilgram) was a man held in great respect and served under Nawab Ikram in Odisha. When Aurangzev had sent orders to the Nawab to destroy the temple of Jagannatha, Raja Durup Singh Deo who had the temple under him asked the Mir to introduce him to the Nawab. The Raja promised to break the temple and to send the big idol to the Emperor. He actually did break the statue of Rakas which stood over the entrance of the temple; and also to battlements over the door. The idol which was made of sandalwood and which had two valuable jewels set in the eyes, was carried off and sent to Aurangzeb at Bijapur, where it was thrown by order on the steps of the mosque.[11]

The idol of Lord Jagannath was sent to Aurangzeb, who at that time was camping at Bijapur. The attack on the Jagannath Temple was a dreadful day in history as for the first time in the temple's history, a Mughal general managed to climb the *Ratna Singhasana*, the sacred seat of the revered Lord of Hindus. Such an act of sacrilege was unprecedented and unheard of in Odisha. It is also significant to mention that Gajapati Dibyasingha Deb I did not offer any resistance to Ekram Khan. It is believed that he made some kind of a deal with the Mughal general by which he invited the invader and broke the temple structure in their presence and handed over the idol of Jagannath (which was not the real one as that had been secretly taken to Kokilagarh, near Chilika Lake). Dibyasingha surrendered without offering any resistance, and swallowed such insult by the Mughals only to save the temple and the deity from severe damage and destruction. However, a Muslim invader climbing on the *Ratna Singhasana* left a permanent wound in the psyche of the Hindus of Odisha.

The fallout of the attack was very miserable. The *Madala Panji* has described its aftereffects. The chronicle mentions about eight major rituals and festivals that were discontinued:

1. *Chandan Yatra* (Sandalwood Yatra or journey), which is celebrated for 21 days, was stopped. The people mourned and did not celebrate any festival.
2. *Rukmani barana nitti*, which is celebrated in Vaishnava worship, was stopped.
3. The tradition of *Mahadeep alati* (great light offering) observed on every *Ekadasi* was discontinued.
4. The marriage ceremonies held inside the temple were stopped.
5. *Debasnana* (ceremonial public bath of the deities) observed on the full moon day of *Jyestha* month (May-June) was not performed on the usual *snana mandap* (bathing altar). That year, it was observed inside the temple at a location in front

of the *Ratna Singhasana*. The deities were not brought out in royal procession from the temple premises.
6. Offering of *prasad* (food offering) was done very silently without being accompanied by the ringing of temple bells and beating of drums.
7. No ceremonial Rath Yatra (Car Festival) was observed that year. The ritual of *Gundicha yatra* was observed by taking the deities to *bhogamandap* (hall) behind the *Garuda Stambha* (one of the two unique pillars in the temple; Garuda is also the vehicle of Lord Vishnu).
8. Finally, *mahaparasad seba* (56 food items offered to Lord Jagannath) was stopped. As a result, pilgrims stopped visiting the temple.

It is learnt from the *Madala Panji* that some of the temple rituals continued to be held but very quietly without the usual festivities. It is also learnt that the deities, during this period, were not in the main temple. To save them from further attacks they were moved to a place called Niladriprasad near Banpur. During this time, some inauspicious happenings took place at the Jagannath Temple at Puri.

As per the *Madala Panji* on 6 October 1694, there was a huge cyclone that swept across the coastal region causing unprecedented devastation. On that day, the *Neelachakra*, a blue wheel fixed atop the temple, broke and fell in front of the Ganapati temple and large stones fell off the temple structure. The branches of the sacred banyan tree broke. Outside the temple, houses were blown away and people lost their possessions in the cyclone and in the torrential rain that followed the cyclone. Hundreds died. Next year, there was an unprecedented famine. There was a huge shortage of food grains, causing prices to shoot up, putting them beyond people's reach (*Dasa anaka re maharaga kala dhana bharana pachisa kahana hoila, Manisha maanasha Manisha khaila*). The *Madala Panji* mentions that the famine was so serious that humans resorted to cannibalism.[12]

Aurangzeb died on 20 February 1707. After his death, Dibyasingha Deb I got together 18 Gadajat kings (rulers of independent areas that paid annual tribute to the Mughals and later to the English) and drove away the Mughals from Odisha; and the rituals and festivities recommenced at the Jagannath Temple. This is recorded in the *Madala Panji* which says that the main gate, i.e., the Lion's Gate that was closed since Ekram Khan's attack, was reopened. As per the same records, Shuja Khan or Shujaudin Muhammad Khan became the Naib Nazim of Odisha in 1706. All the rituals like offering *mahadeep alati* on *Ekadasi,* Rath Yatra, etc. were resumed. Life returned to normal at the temple. The period of uncertainty and darkness that prevailed for the previous 15 years since 1692 came to an end, and a new beginning was made for the Hindus.

We have mentioned earlier that the *Neelachakra* atop the temple got uprooted on 6 October 1694 due to a storm. Dibyasingha Deb I got a new *Neelachakra* installed on 26 January 1715, and the temple got back the *Neelachakra* after a gap of more than 20 years. As per the *Madala Panji*, a person named Dharamu Harichandan climbed the temple and managed to install it firmly. Fluttering of the flag on the *Neelachakra* atop the temple after 20 years brought immense joy to millions of devotees.

8

RAMACHANDRA DEB II
Fallen King, Unfailing Devotion

Harekrushna Deb, the younger brother of Dibyasingha Deb, acceded to the throne of Khurda in 1716 and was Gajapati for a brief period of four years. After his death, his son Gopinath Ray assumed the name of Gopinath Deb and became the Raja of Khurda in 1720. As per the *Madala Panji*, after about seven years of his reign, some officials of the king's administration conspired to remove him.

Dewan Sayed Beg, Khoja Krushna Narendra and Benu Bhramarabara conspired together, entered the palace and murdered Gopinath Deb on 26 April 1727. Having assassinated the Gajapati, Benu Bhramarabara played an influential role in installing Gopinath Deb's younger brother Keshav Ray as the Raja of Khurda. Keshav Ray assumed the name Ramachandra Deb when he ascended the throne. Taking advantage of his powerful position in the new king's administration, Benu Bhramarabara began to show his true colours. He became very ambitious, and to consolidate his position further, soon appointed his son Nilamber Harichandan as the Dewan.

At the time of Ramachandra Deb II's accession, several changes were taking place in the Mughal administration of Bengal and Odisha. Shuja-ud-Din, who was earlier the Naib Nazim of Odisha, became the subedar of Bengal and Odisha in 1727 and appointed his son Mohammed Taqi Khan as the Naib Nazim (deputy subedar) of Cuttack, entrusting the entire administration of the state to him. Taqi Khan was an incorrigible Hindu hater and more fierce than his father. He started on a mission to build mosques and dargahs throughout Odisha. Like the Kadamrasul (Qadam-E-Rasool) built by his father in Cuttack, he constructed a Kadamrasul (Qadam-E-Rasool) in Balasore. He also built a dargah in Pipli and constructed several other mosques along with many monuments at Jajpur, Remuna (in Balasore) and other places. By constructing these shrines and structures, Taqi Khan wanted to strengthen his presence in the state as well as disturb and destabilize the Khurda Raja, with an ultimate plan of attacking the famous Jagannath Temple at Puri.

The Machinations of Taqi Khan

Taqi Khan attacked Khurda as many as four times during his reign as Naib Nazim. As per the *Madala Panji* and other corroborative records, the first attack was on 2 December 1731. At the time of this attack, Bakshi (Prime Minister) Benu Bhramarabara and his son Dewan Nilamber Harichandan were in charge of Rathipur Fort, near Khurda. Unable to defend themselves from Taqi Khan's army, the Bakshi and the Dewan fled from Rathipur. The reason behind their inability to defend themselves is quite interesting.

Bakshi Benu Bhramarabara had stirred up widespread discontent among the *paiks* (soldiers) in his army by appointing his son as the Dewan, as it was widely believed that Nilamber Harichandan did not have the qualifications for that post. Taqi Khan exploited this by fomenting disobedience among the *paiks*. The Mughals penetrated into the ranks of the Bakshi's army and won them over. Thus, when Taqi Khan attacked Rathipur, the *paiks* refused to heed the Bakshi's command to fight the Mughals and did not offer any resistance to the attackers. In the history of the Khurda Gajapatis, this was the first time when the soldiers chose to side with their attackers and refused to safeguard their own territory. Such unusual conduct by the *paiks* warrants deeper historical research, which is outside the scope of this work.

Sensing how unpopular Bakshi Benu Bhramarabara and Dewan Nilamber Harichandan were and fearing internal revolt, Ramachandra Deb II appointed a new Dewan and a new Bakshi, and with them he met Taqi Khan. As per the *Madala Panji*, there was a secret understanding between Ramachandra Deb II and Taqi Khan: Taqi Khan made an unusual demand of beheading both Benu Bhramarabara and Nilamber Harichandan. Ramachandra Deb II complied with the order and sent their decapitated heads to Taqi Khan on 20 December 1731.[1] It is ironical that Ramachandra Deb II had earlier relied on the same Benu Bhramarabara, who, through a conspiracy, had made him the Raja of Khurda. As we shall see soon, Benu Bhramarabara thus became the cause and consequence of Ramachandra Deb's ascendancy to the royal seat of Khurda as well as his fall.

Although Ramachandra Deb II sacrificed Benu Bhramarabara to save his seat of power, it proved to be of no avail. Taqi Khan, being very shrewd and clever, realized that he could not trust Raja Ramachandra Deb, who did not hesitate to kill his own Bakshi and Dewan. So when Ramachandra Deb met Taqi Khan along with his new Dewan and Bakshi at Rathipur on 3 January 1732, the Mughal treacherously detained them and killed a large number of troops of the Raja of Khurda, reneging on his earlier promise of truce. The Raja became a prisoner in his own fort.

Hearing of their father's incarceration, Ramachandra Deb's eldest son Krishnarai Jena along with his brothers Mukund Kumar, Madhusudan Kumar and Bhagirathi Kumar retaliated and began an armed campaign to capture Khurda from the Mughal invader. But they were no match for Taqi Khan's forces who marched ahead and drove the Raja's sons out of Khurda, capturing the area up to Banapur. Krishnarai and his brothers moved to the south and took shelter at Athagarh of Ganjam under the Raja of Athagarh. Taqi Khan then returned to Rathipur, from where he took along Ramachandra Deb II to be detained at Barabati.

Not willing to accept defeat so easily, Bhagirathi Kumar with the help of soldiers and support from the Raja of Athagarh moved against the Mughals once more and drove them out of Puri and Khurda. He visited Lord Jagannath at the temple in Puri and offered the Lord the customary *saree*. Then he went to Khurda, where he declared himself as the Raja. On learning this, Taqi Khan prepared a massive attack on this self-appointed Raja of Khurda. In a cunning move, he brought the imprisoned Ramachandra Deb II along with him when he faced Bhagirathi Kumar, who seeing his father in the opposite camp got demoralized. Bhagirathi Kumar lost to Taqi Khan and fled to Dashapalla (Nayagarh, Odisha). However, Taqi Khan was still very apprehensive about controlling Khurda after this victory. He was aware that Bhagirathi Kumar would gather forces and would someday try to recapture Khurda. He, therefore, strategically reappointed Ramachandra Deb II as the Raja of Khurda but clipped his powers by forcing him to enter into an agreement to secure his loyalty. Taqi Khan also ensured that the Raja would be kept under house arrest at Khurda, restricting his movement. Khan then returned to Cuttack.

Before Ramachandra Deb II was reinstated in Khurda, he had been kept imprisoned in Barabati Fort for 13 months (some sources say that he was imprisoned for 18 months).[2] It was Ramachandra Deb's advisor Rajguru Param Lakshmi Mahapatra who came to his rescue at that time. The Rajguru was an intelligent and learned scholar in Sanskrit, Odia and Arabic. He translated the Sanskrit *Bhatti-kavya* (authored by 7th century poet Bhatti) into Arabic and read it out to Taqi Khan, who was very pleased with Rajguru's knowledge and particularly his Arabic translations of rare Sanskrit texts. Having gained the trust of Taqi Khan, Param Lakshmi Mahapatra utilized his proximity with Taqi Khan to negotiate the release of Ramachandra Deb II.[3] Thus, it was on the Rajguru's request that Taqi Khan released

Ramachandra Deb from prison and subsequently stationed him at Khurda as the Raja—but under his watchful eyes.

There is an interesting legend regarding the help that the Rajguru rendered to Ramachandra Deb II. While in prison, the Gajapati had vowed that whoever released him from prison would gain his gratitude and he would honour that person by giving up the throne of the Raja to him for one day a month for every month of imprisonment. He himself would do *Chamara Seva* (offering a service to the king while seated in the throne).

After his release from the Barabati Fort, Ramachandra Deb chose to stay at Rathipur instead of Khurda. One day, he called Rajguru Param Lakshmi and informed him of his personal vow. The Raja pleaded with the Rajguru to sit on the royal seat for 18 days, a day for each of the 18 months of his imprisonment. Such a vow of Ramachandra Deb II was unusual and unprecedented. Indeed it was shocking and surprising for the Rajguru, and he protested saying it would enrage the highest of the Brahmins to acquiesce to this offer.[3] However, the Gajapati did not relent and his orders were complied with. Param Lakshmi Rajguru was ushered onto the throne for one day in a month, for 18 months, totalling 18 days, and Ramachandra Deb II performed *Chamara Seva* as per his promise. Although this was supposed to be a secret, the information leaked out and became known to everyone subsequently.[4]

Gajapati, the Protector of Idols

To come back to the events we were discussing, when Ramachandra Deb II was in Khurda, he was always apprehensive of an attack on the Jagannath Temple at Puri by the Mughals. It became his mission to prevent any attack on the temple, and particularly to avoid any disrespect and damage to the idols of the deities. Thus, on his orders, his most trusted employees *Bada Parichha* Paramananda Mahapatra and *Sana Parichha* Paschimakabat Singh took the idols in a palanquin to Dobandha and from there they crossed the Chilika Lake on a boat and installed the idols in the Nairi

Harishwar Mandap at Banapur. Around this time Ramachandra Deb had also secretly gone to participate in the Gundicha festival at Puri.

Taqi Khan learned about these two events, which were in clear defiance of his orders on the restriction of the Gajapati's movements. He wanted to teach Ramachandra Deb a lesson, and so for the third time he attacked Khurda in 1733. The Gajapati left Khurda and first went to Nayagarh, then took shelter at Khandapada, and later went to Bolgarh. Sensing further trouble, the idols of Jagannath, Balabhadra and Subhadra were moved from Nairi Harishwar Mandap to the border of Khallikote at Tekkali (now in Andhra Pradesh) to ensure their safety.

The wily Taqi Khan exploited this situation: He brought Bhagirathi Kumar, the displaced son of Ramachandra Deb II, from Dashapalla (Nayagarh) and installed him as the Raja of Khurda, and stationed Mughal soldiers at Khurda to defend the newly-appointed king. Through this strategic move, Taqi Khan was successful in breaking the unity of the royal family of Khurda. Satisfied, Taqi Khan returned to Cuttack and left for Murshidabad.

However, the installation of Bhagirathi Kumar was short-lived. His taking over the throne while his father was alive was not liked by the other members of the royal family. Further, the support from Taqi Khan for his accession to the throne was resented by the people of the kingdom in general.[5] Sensing the rising unpopularity of Bhagirathi Kumar, Ramachandra Deb II returned from Bolgarh and reoccupied the throne of Khurda with the help of his loyal soldiers. His son fled to Cuttack accompanied by the Mughal troops who were stationed at Khurda. At this time Ramachandra Deb II brought back the idols of Jagannath, Balabhadra and Subhadra from Tekkali to Puri and in celebration performed the Shri Gundicha Yatra (Car Festival) on 2 July 1733.

The news of the successful holding of the Shri Gundicha Yatra enraged Taqi Khan. He attacked Khurda yet again. Anticipating yet another attack on the Puri Temple, the idols were taken first to Nairi Harishwar Mandap and from there to a place called Marada in Athagarh (Ganjam), where they were kept in a sacred place from 29 December 1733 onwards. Ramachandra Deb II hid in the forest to escape Taqi Khan's attack. With Ramachandra Deb II gone from Khurda, Taqi Khan decided to strengthen and secure his hold over the region by setting up 22 police stations from Balianta to Banapur.

Taqi Khan died in 1735 and Murshid Quli Khan II became the Naib Nazim of Cuttack. He appointed Mir Habib, his loyal and efficient employee, at Cuttack. Just like Taqi Khan, Mir Habib too attacked Khurda and occupied it. At this time, Ramachandra Deb II took shelter in a place called Rumagarh in Athagarh.

The Jagannath Temple at Marada

When the idols of the deities were removed from Puri during the fourth attack of Taqi Khan, they were taken to Marada in Athagarh, which was then under the rule of Jagannath Harichandan Jagadeva. The shifting of idols from Puri to Marada was considered as a very special and significant event. As Jagannath Harichandan Jagadeva did not fear any unexpected attacks from the Muslim rulers, he constructed a temple in a forest at Marada under instructions from Gajapati Ramachandra Deb II. Skilled workers of the village of Mathura near Athagarh worked day and night to construct this new temple and the work was finished in a record time of two months. The idols were kept safely in the new temple at Marada from 1734 to 1736.* Jagannath Harichandan Jagadeva introduced all the rituals of the Puri Jagannath

---

* For the two-and-half years the idols were not in Puri, the rituals and festivals in Jagannath Temple were stopped. Lakhs of people who used to visit Puri on pilgrimage did not come. Consequently, the Mughal government lost out on the huge revenue by way of pilgrim tax to the tune of 900,000 cowrie (a local measure of rupee). On the wise advice of Mir Habib, Murshid Quli Khan ordered for the reinstallation of the idols in the Jagannath Temple at Puri.

Temple at Marada. After the Marada Jagannath Temple was established, many other Jagannath temples came up in Ganjam.

Ramachandra Deb II's Rajguru, Param Lakshmi, in the presence of both the Gajapati and the Raja of Athagarh performed the sacred fire ceremony for the consecration of the new temple. On this occasion, Gajapati Ramachandra Deb II honoured the Raja of Athagarh with the title of 'Sarana Panjara* Mana Udharana** Viradhibirabara Bhai Sri Harichandan Jagadeva Raja Bahadur'.[6] The Gajapati addressed Harichandan Jagadeva as his brother ('Bhai Sri Harichandan Jagadeva'). He embraced the Athagarh Raja before conferring the title. This honour was an expression of deep gratitude by Ramachandra Deb II to the Raja of Athagarh for giving shelter to him in Rumagarh and also to the revered Lord Jagannath at Marada.

In recognition of the King of Athagarh's great act of magnanimity, Gajapati Ramachandra Deb II introduced a ritual according to which on *Ekadasi* days, while offering the *mahadeep alati* (great lamp offering), the *sebaks* recite *Sarani dharanaisha bhai Jagadeva Raounku sankhe purai chakrare adhuala kari rakhiba agyan heu he Manima* ('May the Lord save brother Jagadeva Rao, the king of Saranadharani, sheltering him inside the conch shell, shielding him by the disc of the Lord'), Marada in Athagarh being referred to as *Sarana Sri Khetra* or *Sarana Dharani* (the place of shelter). The Record of Rights of the Puri Temple clearly mentions this practice. It states that the name of the present king of Tekkali Sri Laxminarayan Harichandan Deb (a descendant of the Athagarh King) should be taken while offering the *mahadeep alati*.

As a gesture of gratitude, Gajapati Ramachandra Deb II had donated an area in Puri to the Raja of Athagarh, which is known as Athagadia Sahi. It is also significant to note that of the 16 pillars in the *Mukti Mandap* at the Jagannath Temple, Puri, one pillar is known as Athagarh, testifying to its historical

---

* *Sarana Panjara* means great protector or the provider of ultimate shelter.

** *Mana Udharana* implies redeemer of prestige or honour.

significance. The court pandit of the Raja of Athagarh used to be a representative at *Mukti Mandap*. When Lord Jagannath was at the Marada Temple, the famous Car Festival was celebrated there, in which Ramachandra Deb II himself performed the ritual of *chherapanhara*. This is a unique instance where a Gajapati had performed the *chherapanhara* ritual outside the Lord's permanent abode at Puri.⁶ This fact is, however, not supported by any records. After the idols were brought and restored at Puri, the seats of the deities at the Marada Temple became empty, but the empty pedestals are continued to be worshipped every day till date.

Besides conferring the title on Jagannath Harichandan Jagadeva, special privileges were granted by the Raja of Khurda to the King of Athagarh. This is known from a *Chamu Citau* (a royal letter) issued by the Raja of Khurda. A copy of the *Chamu Citau* is given below for reference. A reading and analysis of this *Chamu Citau* reveals that the same was issued in favour of King Jagannath Harichandan Jagadeva of Athagarh. It is written both in Odia and Persian scripts in black ink on a handmade paper of 11¼ inch in length and 5¾ inch in breadth. At the top of the letter, it is written in Odia in bold letters 'E Pramana'. A royal seal of oval shape with Persian characters is inserted below it. There are 12 lines in Persian script, below which 11 lines are written in Odia script. Both the 12 lines of Persian and 11 lines of Odia are written horizontally. There are six lines in Odia script written vertically which is in continuation of the former 11 lines. The letter ends with the emblem of a conch shell and is followed by the signature of the king. This letter was found by late Laxminarayan Harichandan Jagadeva, the king of Tekkali while searching his old records in the ruined palace of Athagarh Fort.*

---

* The late Laxminarayan Harichandan Jagadeva had published this letter in the Journal of K.R. Kama Oriental Institute under the title, 'Circular Issued by the Maharaja Mukundadeva of Orissa'. There appears to be an error assigning this letter to Shri Mukunda Deb, whereas it should be factually relatable to Shri Birakeshari Deb.

A *Chamu Citau* (a royal letter) issued by the Raja of Khurda in favour of King Jagannath Harichandan Jagadeva of Athagarh.

As far as the date of this letter is concerned, the same is mentioned at the end of the letter, i.e., 30th day of Karkata month of the year 4th *Anka*. Taking into account the tenure of the reigning King of Athagarh in whose favour this letter was issued, the issuer of the letter can be identified as Gajapati Birakeshari Deb (AD 1736–1793). The 30th day of Karkata in the 4th *anka* is calculated from the almanac as 30 October 1738, which is the date of issue of the letter. The letter is addressed to the Temple Superintendent of Puri (*Parichha*) and all other officials like *Suras, Mahasura, Sahara Chabhaga Bisoyee, Bhandara Mekapa, Sahara Sardara, Chautara, Tahasildar, Korakadar, Sithikarana, Nayaka* of *Balisahi, Karanas* of Charibata and to the *Bisoyee, Dandia* and policemen posted from the village Pathara to the Lokanatha's field in the market places, ferry places and highways.

The letter informs all of them that King Harichandan Jagadeva of Athagarh has a house plot in Balisahi. He is allowed to construct a house there. Further, the King of Athagarh is allowed to perform *Chamara Seba* (waving of a fan made of the tail of a yak with golden handle) before Lord Jagannath during different festive occasions, including the Car Festival and boating ceremony of the Lord. He is allowed to perform daily offerings beginning from the *Gopalaballabha bhoga* (the first morning offering) to the *Badasinghara bhoga* (the last offering of the day) including other three offerings (*bhogas*). He is also allowed to offer 56 kinds of offerings to the Lord. The officials are requested not to provide him fresh cooked food regularly from the kitchen. He is allowed to go with his torches as far as the Kalpavata (banyan tree) with all paraphernalia without any obstruction. Whoever comes on his behalf for a *darshan* is also allowed to perform offerings.

The royal letter shows special privileges were granted to King Jagannath Harichandan Jagadeva of Athagarh by Gajapati Birakeshari Deb of Khurda. The Kings of Athagarh and Khurda shared a unique relationship. The King of Athagarh always helped the Kings of Khurda, namely Ramachandra Deb and his son Birakeshari Deb, during crisis. So in acknowledgement of the help rendered by the King of Athagarh, the Raja of Khurda expressed gratitude, not only by conferring the title but also by extending the special privileges in the Puri Temple and for various services.[7]

The Conversion

Ramachandra Deb II holds a very uncommon place in the history of the Gajapatis of Odisha. It is mentioned in the *Madala Panji* that when imprisoned in the Barabati Fort, the Gajapati was attracted by the beauty of Razia, the daughter of Shuja-ud-Din. Ramachandra Deb married Razia in the presence of Taqi Khan and many other followers of Islam at Kadamrasul in Cuttack. The Gajapati was given the name Hafiz Kadir Beg.* But there is also the alternative view that Ramachandra Deb might have been forcibly converted to Islam.

While the Gajapati's marriage with Razia is not disputed as a historical fact, whether it was a forced conversion or love marriage has been a matter of speculation and debate. The marriage took place when Ramachandra Deb was imprisoned in the Barabati Fort. The part of the fort where the Gajapati was imprisoned would have been out of bounds for others; therefore, the idea of the Gajapati falling in love with the daughter of subedar seems improbable. The possibility of a meeting between them also appears to be remote. This leads to the conclusion that the marriage was

---

* Ramachandra Deb's first wife, the *Pattarani* Kalabati Devi, was from Kannauj near Ayodhya. Kalabati was very religious, ritual-bound and a disciplinarian. His second wife was Lalita Devi, a Bhagela princess from Rewa in Madhya Pradesh. With Kalabati Devi, Ramachandra Deb II had three sons: Krishnarai Jena, Mukund Kumar and Madhusudhan Kumar. From Lalita Devi he had one son, Bhagirathi Kumar. After Ramachandra Deb married Razia, *Patamahadei* Kalabati Devi left and moved to Manatrigarh, where she spent the rest of her life with her three sons. Lalita Devi stood by her husband and stayed with him along with the new rani, who was later known as Suryamani Dei (Source: Mahimohan Tripathy, *Shree Jagannath* [in Odia], Ama Odisha, p. 280).

likely a forced one.⁸ Such an inference is, however, not supported by any available records.

Whatever the case might have been, this is a special historical incident, where a Gajapati, the Thakur Raja, was converted to Islam. Despite his conversion, Ramachandra Deb neither used his Muslim name nor did he lose his loyalty and devotion to Lord Jagannath.⁹

But, the conversion of Ramachandra Deb II invited great annoyance and opposition from the Brahmins, pandits and priests in Odisha. The Gajapati was no longer allowed to visit the Jagannath Temple at Puri. Although a section of the society, including Param Lakshmi Rajguru, made an attempt in favour of Ramachandra Deb's entry into the temple again, they were effectively resisted by a large body of Hindus. The Rajguru sensed the predominant view of the society, particularly the priestly class and local population who did not approve of the Raja's entry into the temple.

The Gajapati's unflinching loyalty and devotion to Lord Jagannath remained unchanged even after he was disowned by Hindu society. After his release from the Barabati Fort until his death in 1737, Ramachandra Deb II suffered humiliation and rejection, yet he fought relentlessly for the honour and protection of the presiding deity of Odisha, Lord Jagannath. Since he was not allowed to enter the temple, the image of *Patitapabana* (Lord Jagannath as the Lord of the fallen) was installed near the main entrance of the temple so that the fallen king could have *darshan* of his beloved Lord from outside.

Razia or Suryamani Dei, the new queen of the Gajapati, had expressed her desire to visit the Jagannath Temple. According to some records, her mother was a Brahmin lady who was a devotee of Lord Jagannath. But her wish remained unfulfilled. Just like the Raja, she too was barred from entering the temple. However, with the installation of the image of *Patitapabana* at the entrance of the Jagannath Temple, Suryamani Dei could partially redeem her wish.

The ignominy heaped on Ramachandra Deb II started to become unbearable for him. He was despised and rejected by people for his conversion to another religion, and people disapproved of having a Muslim as the Thakur Raja. The Gajapati decided to relinquish the kingdom and his power, position and wealth.* He along with his Muslim queen left Puri and moved to Narsinghpur (Cuttack district) under the shelter of Raja Mandardhara Mansingh Harichandan Mahapatra.

The Gajapati and his wife stayed in a village called Lakhapada, and the Raja of Narsinghpur looked after them with great care. The Raja of Narsinghpur considered it a great personal privilege and honour to be of service to the Gajapati. However, the fallen king and queen found the benevolence and magnanimity of the Raja of Narsinghpur a burden. One day, around December 1737 (about one year 10 months after leaving Puri), they ended their lives by drinking poison together. The place where they were consigned to flames together is known as Mahasmasana. Since then, the Mahasmasana of Goradia village in Narsinghpur has gained great historical import. From that time, whenever a member of the royal family of Narsinghpur died, he was cremated at Mahasmasana. Even till date, a lamp is lit at the Mahasmasana every evening in the memory of Gajapati Ramachandra Deb II.[10]

Ramachandra Deb II Rises from the Dead

Ramachandra Deb II was resurrected nearly 150 years after his death, when the issue of recognition of the adopted infant son of

---

* As per the *Madala Panji*, Mir Habib installed Padmanava Deb, the Raja of Patia, as the Raja of Khurda by removing Ramachandra Deb II. This is not entirely correct, as there are contemporary evidences to show that even after his release and conversion, Ramachandra Deb II had functioned from Khurda as the Raja till about a year before his death. It was only after Ramachandra Deb II gave up his power that Padmanava Deb became the Khurda Raja.

Gajapati Dibyasingha Deb III (AD 1859–1887), who was convicted of murder, came up as a critical issue (see Chapters 14 and 15 for details). However, it would be appropriate to briefly discuss the issue here. The conviction and subsequent transportation of Dibyasingha Deb to the Andamans threw up a big challenge. The request of Suryamani Patamahadei (Dibyasingha Deb's mother) to recognize an infant boy who had been adopted as the Raja put the colonial government in a dilemma. The issue was taken up by eminent lawyer Madhusudan Das on behalf of Suryamani Patamahadei. F.C. Grant, the District Collector and Magistrate of Puri, did not accede to such a request. According to him, though Dibyasingha Deb had been convicted and sent to the Andamans, he was not divested of his position as Raja. He argued that the Gajapati's adopted infant son could not be recognized as a ruler when his father was still alive. He asked what would happen in the event of the release of the Raja, for which Suryamani Patamahadei had petitioned the government and was under consideration. These questions occupied the mind of Madhusudan Das, who struggled to find answers. At this crucial time, Ramachandra Deb II, the fallen king, came to the rescue of his successor.

As mentioned earlier, Ramachandra Deb II converted to Islam by marrying Razia. After the change of religion, he was deprived of the right to perform the rituals and services of Lord Jagannath. Although he continued to be a devotee of the Lord, he could not have access to the temple nor its rituals as His *sebak*. He also had to give up his throne, and came to be regarded as a *mlechha* (outcaste). Madhusudan Das decided to apply a similar logic for the disqualification of Dibyasingha Deb. Madhusudan Das told the British that the act of transporting Dibyasingha Deb across the sea to the Andamans had the effect of making him a *mlechha* (outcaste), as per the Hindu religious texts and tradition, thus rendering him ineligible to perform the services of Lord Jagannath as a *sebak*. He argued that even if the convicted Raja was released, his earlier position could not be restored. He would continue to be a *mlechha* and would not be able to perform any temple services. In this context the relevant portion of the petition of Suryamani Patamahadei drafted by Madhusudan Das is interesting, and is reproduced below:

> As a precedent, I take the liberty to bring to your notice that one of my ancestors named Rama Chandra Dev, who ascended the throne in 1660 Shakabda having been compelled to be associated with a daughter of the then Mahammedan noble was not allowed to perform the services of Jagannath or to enter the temple, and as he expressed his desire to worship the idol, the Pattitapaban Dev, a representative of Jagannath, was set up at Singhaduar (the Lion Gate of the temple) in order that the fallen Raja might be able to see and worship it from outside. The Raja having thus become disqualified to perform the religious and social ceremonies of the family, the officials of the palace brought down his daughter's son from Athagarh and installed him on the Gadi as Raja Birakishore Dev.[11]

The grounds on which Ramachandra Deb had to give up his throne became a precedent for applying the same to his successor in history, Makunda Deb, the infant adopted son of the deported Raja Dibyasingha Deb. This shows that a dead king was resurrected to save a later successor. This also shows that the dead live forever in history!

Though Ramachandra Deb II ruled for nine years, the significance of his regime lies in his commitment to protect the temple of Puri and the deities housed there. He succeeded to the throne when the Mughal dispensation was very anti-Hindu. The orthodox Naib Nazims of Cuttack were not only Hindu-haters but they also targeted the Hindu temples and, particularly the Jagannath Temple at Puri. In such a scenario, the deities were moved and hidden at different locations frequently, which invited the wrath of the Naib Nazim of Cuttack against the Raja of Khurda. As a clever strategy, Ramachandra Deb II kept the

Mughals engaged with his person and, in the process, saved the temple and the deities from their repeated assaults.

Ramachandra Deb's conversion to Islam can also be interpreted as an act of appeasement of the Mughals, which helped in saving the revered deities and temple from many more direct attacks. Thus, Ramachandra Deb II will go down in history as a Gajapati who successfully prevented attacks on the abode of the presiding deities of Odisha from hostile Muslim subedars.

9

BIRAKESHARI DEB I
Gajapati Goes Mad

With the exit of Gajapati Ramachandra Deb II from Khurda, the Mughals were gifted with an opportunity to destabilize the power of the Khurda royal family. Mir Habib, then in charge of Odisha, appointed Padmanabha Deb, the Raja of Patia, as the ruler of Khurda in place of Ramachandra Deb II.

Bhagirathi Kumar, the younger son of Ramachandra Deb II from his second queen Lalita Devi, resisted this move of the Mughals. He had already staked his claim to the Khurda throne earlier but had been defeated due to the cunning machinations of Taqi Khan. Now, as the lawful claimant to Ramachandra Deb II's throne, being the hereditary successor, he decided to fight for his right (Ramachandra Deb II had three other sons from his first wife *Patamahadei* Kalabati Devi, but after he married Razia, she moved to Manatrigarh near Khurda with her sons). Bhagirathi took the help of Raja Ghanabhanja of Gumusar (Ganjam district) and was able to win back his place as the Raja of Khurda. For the help extended to the Gajapati, Raja Ghanabhanja was conferred the title of *Khetriyabara* (highest warrior)*.

Association with the Mughals

When the Raja of Gumusar extended his military support to Bhagirathi Kumar, the other local rajas also joined in the cause of Ramachandra Deb's heir. Bolstered by this, Bhagirathi Kumar began preparations to attack Khurda, then being headed by Padmanabha Deb. However, a battle was ultimately avoided by the clever manoeuvres of Murshid Quli Khan II, the then Naib Nazim of Odisha (After Taqi Khan's death, Shuja-ud-Din, the Nazim or Governor of Bengal, Bihar and Odisha, appointed his son-in-law Murshid Quli Khan II as the Naib Nazim or Deputy Governor of Odisha). He shrewdly assessed the situation and thought it appropriate to avoid hostilities and bloodshed by appointing the right claimant to the throne.

We come to know from the *Madala Panji* that at a place called Baideswar (in Cuttack), Quli Khan applied *tika* and tied the *seropa* (turban) on the head of Bhagirathi Kumar, who henceforth came to be known as Birakeshari Deb, formally recognizing him as the Raja of Khurda. The new Raja had to pay Rs 18 lakh to Murshid Quli Khan towards arrears of pilgrim tax for the previous four years. It was at this time when Lord Jagannath was reinstalled in the temple at Puri.

However, Murshid Quli Khan's fortunes soon waned. His brother-in-law, Sarfaraz Khan, became the Naib Nazim of Bengal and Bihar in 1739. But Safaraz Khan was a weak administrator, and taking advantage of this, Alivardi Khan, who had earlier

---

* This title was used by Ghanabhanja and his successors as an emblem and status of their pride and honour. Historical records also show that Ghanabhanja, as a mark of respect for the title he had been bestowed, had donated a Brahmin *sasana* called Khetriyabarapur. This shows how loyal and respectful local kings were of the Gajapati and in what high esteem they held any title the Gajapati bestowed on them.

been the Naib Nazim in Patna, attacked and killed him, thereby assuming the title of Naib Nazim of Bengal and Bihar. This caused fierce enmity between Murshid Quli Khan II and Alivardi Khan, as the former did not accept the latter as the Nazim. In a fight between them at Phulwari (near Balasore), Murshid Quli Khan II was defeated and had to leave for Machilipatnam (Andhra).

At this difficult time of Murshid Quli Khan II, the Gajapati Birakeshari Deb came to his help. The Gajapati directed his commander (*senapati*) Murad Khan to safely escort Murshid Quli Khan's wife and daughter, who were at the Barabati Fort, to Machilipatnam where the defeated Nawab had fled.[1]

After his victory at Phulwari, Alivardi Khan came to Cuttack and took over all the wealth of Murshid Quli Khan II stored there. He stayed in Cuttack for one month, after which he left for Bengal putting his nephew Sayed Ahmed Khan in charge along with a contingent of 3,000 cavalry and 4,000 infantry.[2] As soon as Alivardi Khan left Cuttack, the supporters and sympathizers of Murshid Quli Khan II became very active to undermine Sayed Ahmed Khan. The Khurda Raja again entrusted his commander Murad Khan to get in touch with Murshid Quli Khan's son-in-law in order to prepare for dislodging Sayed Ahmed Khan. But as we will see, the time of the Mughals had come to an end in Odisha and a new power would come to occupy the state—the Marathas.

The Marathas in Odisha

To avenge the defeat of Murshid Quli Khan II, his confidant Mir Habib conspired against the Nawab of Bengal Alivardi Khan and took the help of the Marathas under King Raghuji Bhonsle of Nagpur. Bhonsle, in turn, saw this as an opportunity to bring Odisha under his control and hence agreed to help Mir Habib. The Maratha force under the command of Mir Habib captured Cuttack in 1742. From 1742 to 1751, intermittent wars continued to be fought between the Marathas and Alivardi Khan.

The Nawab of Bengal was almost 75 years old by this time and was suffering from various physical ailments. He was tired of the wars and wanted to rest; his own people who were much troubled by constant conflict also desired peace. On the other side, the Marathas too wanted an end to the hostilities. With both parties being inclined towards peace, Mir Jafar (brother-in-law) on behalf of Nawab Alivardi Khan and Mirza Saleh (nephew) on behalf of Mir Habib and the Marathas carried out the detailed negotiations to sign a treaty, which was finalized in 1751.

According to the agreement, Mir Habib came to rule over Odisha on behalf of Nawab Alivardi Khan. He had to pay the arrears for having engaged Raghuji Bhonsle's troops and also agreed to pay Rs 12 lakh annually as *chauth* (revenue) to the Maratha King on the condition that the Marathas would not intervene in the dominions of Alivardi Khan. River 'Sonamukia', now known as Subarnarekha River, formed the demarcating line between the boundaries of Odisha and Bengal. As is evident, this treaty was a triangular compromise between Raghuji Bhonsle, Mir Habib and Alivardi: Raghuji entered into it for money, Mir Habib for honour and revenge, and Alivardi for rest but mindful of retaining his nominal lordship over Odisha.[3]

During the Maratha occupation of Odisha, not much is known about Gajapati Birakeshari Deb. We do know that he initially supported Murshid Quli Khan II and waged a war against Alivardi Khan. Since relations between Mir Habib and Birakeshari Deb were good, it is inferred that Birakeshari Deb must have supported the Marathas, who were allies of Mir Habib. The Gajapati himself would soon have occasion to seek the assistance of the Marathas.

After the hostilities with the Mughals came to an end, Sheo Bhatt Sathe was appointed Governor of Odisha by Raghuji Bhonsle. It was during his time that a pretender to the Gajapati title reared its head. Jagannath Narayan Deb, the Raja of Paralakhemundi (Gajapati district) was a powerful ruler and he refused to acknowledge the suzerainty of the Raja of Khurda, even insisting on using the title of Gajapati. He claimed the title belonged to him as a matter of right and hereditary privilege as he maintained that he was the direct descendant of the Gangavansh rulers (for more details, see Chapter 17).

Taking advantage of a weakened Birakeshari Deb due to the Mughal–Maratha warfare, Jagannath Narayan Deb invaded Khurda and defeated the Gajapati. Birakeshari Deb in his distress sought the help of Maratha Governor Sheo Bhatt Sathe to raise an army to fight Narayan Deb. Birakeshari Deb assured the Marathas that he would pay all the expenses incurred in the battle. On such assurance, the Marathas came to his help and the Raja of Paralakhemundi was driven out. However, Birakeshari Deb was unable to pay the Marathas the money he had promised. For his inability to pay the sum of Rs 1 lakh towards war expenses, Sheo Bhatt confiscated the parganas of Lembai, Rahanga, Chabiskud and Serai from the Gajapati. Additionally, 14 Gadajat (feudatory) states, which were under the control of Khurda, were made independent. This led to the dismemberment of the territory of Khurda, but more importantly the loss of the prized possession of Puri. This was the last and biggest blow to the Raja of Khurda.

The occupation of Puri and making free the feudatory states from the control of the Khurda Raja was a wilful act by the Marathas to destroy the foundation of the Khurda kingdom. In this connection, the detailed insight provided by Thomas Motte in his travel account in 1776 is worth referring to. It states:

> When Ragoojee entered Orissa at the instigation of Meer Hubeeb who had fled disgusted from Alliverdi Khan's service in 1738, he found these parts divided into small Zameendaries, dependent on the Rajah of Pooree, at whose capital is the famous temple of Jaggernaut near Point Palmeras. This prince was regarded by his subjects in a religious light also, and appeared formidable to the Marhattas, who, apprehensive lest he might seize a favourable opportunity to cut off the communication between Nagpoor and Cuttac, resolved to reduce his power by dividing it. He made the petty Zemeendars

independent of him, and formed the Chuclas* of Dinkanol, Bonkey, Nersingpoor, Tigorea, Tolchair, Cundea Parra, Duspulla, Hindole, Ungool and Boad.[4]

As a result of this dismemberment of the Khurda territory, the management of the Jagannath Temple at Puri—that was enjoyed by the Khurda Raja from very ancient times—was taken away from the Gajapati's hands and placed under the Maratha government. The Marathas were particularly interested in the Puri Temple as the pilgrim tax was a big source of revenue for them. In a humiliating situation, the Khurda Raja was only allowed a pension. This can be considered an important turning point in the history of the Rajas of Khurda. It set in motion the decline and degradation of the institution of the Raja of Khurda. The loss of the four parganas, and more than that of the Jagannath Temple, dealt a great emotional blow to the Gajapati. Relinquishing control over the temple meant an ultimate distancing and dissociation from the temple and the deity. The very source of the Khurda Raja's existence and authority slipped away.

Birakeshari Deb made attempts to regain Khurda after this but did not succeed. Even his attempts to take help from the chief of Ganjam failed.[5] Driven by defeat and frustration, Birakeshari Deb became mad and allegedly killed four of his sons. The Marathas captured the mad Gajapati and imprisoned him at the Barabati Fort. His four-year-old grandson Dibyasingha Deb was made the Raja of Khurda in 1781. After spending nearly 13 years in prison, Birakeshari Deb died in 1793.

Mystery of Madness?

Gajapati Birakeshari Deb's descent into madness is shrouded in mystery; and even more mysterious and inexplicable was the

---

* Chucla means division. The terms used are for Dhenkanal, Banki, Narsingpur, Tigiria, Talcher, Khandpara, Daspalla, Hindol, Angul and Baud.

alleged killing of his own sons. A close scrutiny of the historical facts leads us to realize that the incident of filicide conceals more than it conveys. It is not a simple fact which can be accepted at face value, nor can it be ascertained from what is mentioned, or not mentioned, in the *Madala Panji*. As we have already seen on multiple occasions, the *Madala Panji* records all significant events in the history of the Gajapatis. It is strange that although the *Panji* mentions in brief the insanity of Birakeshari Deb, it does not mention anything regarding the Gajapati killing his own sons. Such an omission of a significant historical incident pertaining to the Gajapati is unusual. Was this a deliberate omission? That seems quite puzzling.*

In the absence of firm evidence to support any claim regarding the murder of his sons by the Gajapati, several theories may be adduced. In fact, it is equally plausible to conjecture that the death of the four sons of Birakeshari Deb had something to do with succession intrigues or was part of a bigger political conspiracy. We will explore some of the possibilities here.

We must recall from the previous chapter that Gajapati Birakeshari Deb (then known as Bhagirathi Kumar) had shown great courage by raising an army to defend Khurda and his father's honour when Ramchandra Deb II was taken prisoner by Taqi Khan. At that time, Taqi Khan had brought Ramchandra Deb with him to the battle for a face-to-face encounter to demoralize the young Birakeshari Deb. The ploy had worked and seeing his father in the opposite camp Birakeshari Deb lost the will to fight as he did not want to offend his father with bloodshed. It is inconceivable that such a sensitive man, who respected his father so much, would later kill his four sons.

---

*The *Madala Panji* has not omitted mentioning several other murders. For example, it records the killing of two minor sons of Prataprudra by Govinda Vidyadhara. It also mentions many other incidents of murder, greed and treachery. So, the *Madala Panji*'s reference to only the Gajapati's madness and not the murder of his sons makes us think that there is more to the incident.

Can a fight for the succession to the Khurda throne explain the murder of Birakeshari Deb's four sons? As we have seen, Bhagirathi Kumar, the son of the younger Rani of Ramachandra Deb II, Lalita Devi, ascended to his father's position. However, Ramachandra Deb's first wife, *Pattamahadei* Kalabati Devi, was the principal queen and she had three sons: Krishnarai Jena, Mukund Kumar and Madhusudan Kumar. We assume that the recognition of Bhagirathi Kumar, first by Taqi Khan as the replacement of his father and then by Mir Habib to replace Padmanabha Deb, created discord and division in the royal family over succession to the throne. As a result, the claim of Krishnarai Jena, the eldest son by the first wife of Ramchandra Deb—who should have ascended the throne by the law of primogeniture—was ignored. Although purely conjectural, can we suppose that this had some bearing on the killing of Birakeshari Deb's descendants? Family feud, revenge and killing forming part of the game of conspiracy and succession cannot be ruled out.

A possible conspiracy by the Marathas and the English in the incident cannot be ruled out either. By the late 18th century, the British had already established their supremacy over Bengal and Madras. However, the approach from Bengal to Madras through the land route lay in the territory controlled by the Marathas and other anti-British kingdoms. Moreover, the Marathas under the Raja of Nagpur, who controlled Odisha, had joined an anti-British confederacy, creating obstacles in the path of British domination. For any passage through Odisha, the Raja of Nagpur demanded revenue or *chauth* from the British in Bengal.

It was in this situation that Warren Hastings, the Governor General of Bengal, desired that the Raja of Nagpur withdraw from the anti-British confederacy by threatening him with the use of force. The Raja of Nagpur was not prepared to risk a war with the British for the cause of his allies nor was he ready to give up the lure of money through the imposition of *chauth*. After protracted negotiations, a settlement was reached: Rs 13 lakh was advanced by the British to Rajaram Pandit, the Maratha Governor of Odisha who served under the Raja of Nagpur. He was also given a loan of Rs 10 lakh. On the other hand, the English were ensured the most sought-after access through Odisha to the south.⁶

While these changes were taking place, the feudatory kings and large zamindars in the region seemed to be more inclined towards supporting the British over the Marathas. Birakeshari Deb's silence at this time was a cause for worry for the Maratha Governor. The Gajapati was already in an adversarial relationship with the Marathas after losing the four important parganas and the Jagannath Temple to them. Therefore, we can speculate that there may have been a possible conspiracy and collaboration between the Marathas and the British to get rid of Birakeshari Deb. Imprisoning the mad Gajapati in 1781 on the trumped-up charge of killing his own sons would have benefitted the Maratha–British coalition. To avoid any further unrest due to the imprisonment or death of Birakeshari Deb, the Marathas recognized the child Dibyasingha Deb, the grandson of Birakeshari Deb, as his successor and agreed to the payment of the annual tribute of Rs 10,000 by him to Marathas (in 1781).⁷

It is significant to mention here that with the accession of Dibyasingha Deb, a new *anka* (regnal year) was not introduced, although it was an established convention to do so whenever a new Gajapati assumed power. The *anka* of Birakeshari Deb continued till his death in 1793. By anointing the four-year-old Dibyasingha Deb as the Gajapati, the Marathas along with the English were successful in checkmating a possible collaboration between the zamindars, the Gadajat kings and the *paiks* in support of Birakeshari Deb to avenge his abrupt loss of power and the loss of privilege of being the custodian of the Jagannath Temple.

Birakeshari Deb was also an outstanding man of letters who authored great literary works.* During his regime, there was a

---

* Although the Gajapati being a literary man does not prove or disprove his guilt, the point we are making here is that in our estimation Birakeshari Deb was a well-rounded man. It is unlikely that he changed so drastically that he ended up killing his own flesh and blood.

discernible patronisation of both Odia and Sanskrit literature. Some of the outstanding works during his time were *Baishnovamruta Sarodhara* by Kabi Dayalu Das and *Suchitra Ramayan* by Kabi Banamali Das. *Prema Tarangini* and *Jugala Rasamruta Lahari* were works of exceptional merit by Kabi Sadananda*, and he was honoured with the title of 'Kabi Surya Bramha' by Birakeshari Deb for his monumental work *Prema Tarangini*. With the patronage of Birakeshari Deb, Kabi Pitambar Das translated *Nrusingha Purana* into Odia in seven volumes. Kabi Ramadas's work *Dardhyata Bhakti Rasamrita* (Aesthetic bliss of firm faith in God), written during Birakeshari Deb's time, continues to remain as popular today as the epic *Bhagabata* of Jagannath Das. *Srikrushnalilamruta* by Kabi Laxman Misra, *Sabdabrahmagita* by Kabi Daya Das, and *Bichitrabharat* by Kabi Bisambar Das are some major works written with Birakeshari Deb's active patronage. The book *Bichitrabharat* addresses the Gajapati as *Lakhye rajara mauda mani* (a jewel among hundred thousand kings).

Some other great poets emerged and flourished during Birakeshari Deb's reign and made significant contribution to Odia literature. Brajanath Badajena wrote a number of books at this time, with *Samarataranga*, *Gundicabijaya*, *Ambikabilasa* and *Caturabinoda* (a monumental work) being some of his great works. Abhimanyu Samanta Singhara is considered as one of the greatest Odia poets. His celebrated work *Bidagdha Chintamani* is a jewel in the treasure of Odia literature. He wrote most of his outstanding works during the last days of Birakeshari Deb's reign. Banamali Das was a devotee of Goswami Sri Chaitanya Mahaprabhu, and earned fame because of the Gajapati's patronage. He wrote 22 poems for Gajapati Birakeshari Deb and was honoured with 22 *battis* (a unit of measurement) of land.

Among the Sanskrit poets, Chayani Chandrasekhar Rajguru wrote *Madhura Nirudha Natakam*, a classical play in Sanskrit,

---

*He has written several other books such as *Mohanalata*, *Prema Kalpalata*, *Nama Chintamani* and *Stuti Chintamani*. His work *Jugala Rasamruta Lahari* describes the eternal love between Radha and Krishna.

and was held in high esteem by the learned scholars. Kavibhusan Govinda Samantaray (who belonged to the family of Kavichandra Biswanath Samantaray, honoured by Emperor Akbar for his erudite scholarship and learning) is known for his work *Surisarbasva*. He also wrote a play called *Samrudha Madhava*. Basudev Rath Somayaji, a famous scholar, wrote *Ganavansanucharitam* which gives significant literary and historical insights. The promotion of literature and language during Birakeshari Deb's time was so extensive that it would require a separate discussion to do justice to the same. It is worth noting that the growth and development of literature and the extent of patronage by Birakeshari Deb probably had no equal in the history of Odisha.

Birakeshari Deb spent nearly 13 years in the prison of the Barabati Fort. This was the saddest part of his life. He wrote some outstanding poems expressing his intense feelings. Some of his poems deeply reflect his pathos and helplessness. In one of his poems, *Patita Pabana Bana* (the holy flag atop the Neelachakra on the Jagannath Temple), the Gajapati submits that he has been swept away and was in need of a boat to take him ashore. He expressed his indignation over Lord Jagannath for not listening to his prayers and predicament. He, however, does not give up hope and surrenders before the lotus feet of Lord Jagannath. The translated version of this poem written by the Gajapati is produced as under:

The Destitute-Saviour Banner
(Patita Pabana Bana)

> *For what other occasion then*
> *your destitute-saviour banner!*
> *I am swept away*
> *in the current of samsara (worldliness).*
> *Send a boat to take me ashore.*
>
> *You had planted a tree*
> *and now you are cutting its roots.*

*O' primeval beginning,
you will only earn a bad name
in all the three worlds.*

*Your ears are alert to the anguished calls
from far far away;
it is my cruel destiny that
you don't listen while I'm near at hand.*

*Million miles away the elephant prayed
and you sent your disc to save him.
As the stars burn as lamps in the sky
your evening arati is performed.
The garlands of dayana extend
right down to your lotus feet*

*The yogis meditate on you
deep inside their hearts.
To obtain a place
at your sacred feet
is Birakeshari's only hope.*[8]

There is another poem written by Birakeshari Deb titled *'Dukha Nasana He'* (O' Destroyer of Sorrows). This is a fine rendition where the Gajapati is pleading before Lord Jagannath as the ultimate saviour to remove his sorrows. He complains to the Lord: 'Do you ever listen to the entreaties of the deprived?' The translated version of the poem is presented as under:

*O' destroyer of sorrows,
happiness never came my way
even for a day.
With each passing moment
my sorrow grows
like lightning in rain-clouds.*

O' saviour of orphans
the Lord of the Blue Mountain
O' Laxmi's spouse
you do not rescue this soul
adrift in the ocean of samsara.

O' Hari I can't bear
the anguish raging inside of me,
The remover of anxieties
you never showered your mercy on me.

You are so cruel
towards this sorrow-engulfed soul,
do you ever listen
to the entreaties of the deprived?

Shame on my fate.
With a Lord like you
I suffer lack of food and clothes
Says Maharaja Birakeshari,
let my heart cling
to your lotus feet.[9]

Considering all the information presented in this chapter, we find that Birakeshari Deb was a Gajapati who was not only a ruler but also a poet and a passionate patron and promoter of literature. He was a great devotee of Lord Jagannath but also a helpless king caught in the political turbulence of his time. In spite of being a man of many talents, he is also thought to have gone mad and killed his sons. What such a combination of contradictory attributes points to is for the readers to assess and form their inferences. We think that Birakeshari Deb ultimately became a victim of history. The missing link explaining his act of filicide will continue to haunt historians till, and if ever, the mystery is revealed.

10

MUKUNDA DEB II

The Fall of the Last Pillar

The conquest of Odisha was politically and strategically significant for the East India Company. The English occupied Bengal by winning the Battle of Plassey in 1757. In 1765, the Dewani of Bengal, Bihar and Odisha was granted to the British. On 12 November 1766, Northern Sarkars* under the occupation of the Nizam of Hyderabad were transferred to the British. Ganjam was part of the Northern Sarkars under Madras Presidency. Therefore, from Balasore to Chilika Lake, three districts—Balasore, Cuttack and Puri—became locationally and strategically important for the East India Company. Without access and occupation of this area, it was difficult to connect Bengal with Madras. Since this area was under the control of the Marathas, the British tried their best to conciliate with them to get possession of Odisha. Finally, Lord Richard Wellesley decided to take on the Marathas head-on to occupy this region.

---

* The Northern Sarkars (also spelt Circars) corresponded roughly to several districts of present-day Andhra Pradesh, Odisha and Telengana.

After Lord Cornwallis failed to acquire Odisha from the Marathas through diplomacy, Lord Wellesley, after becoming the Governor General of India, calibrated the policy of annexation by following negotiation, conciliation and use of force. On 27 June 1803, the Governor General wrote to his brother and his military adviser, Arthur Wellesley:

> From the Raja of Berar I wish to acquire the whole province of Cuttack so as to unite the Northern Circars by a continued line of sea coast with Bengal. This cession including Balasore, etc. to be made either absolutely or upon payment of a moderate rent or a security for a subsidiary force to be introduced into the dominions of the Raja of Berar.

He instructed Arthur that in the event of a war with the Raja of Berar, this object could be easily achieved and that he should not make peace with the Raja unless Odisha was secured.[1]

The Governor General-in-Council reported on 1 August 1803 to the Secret Committee of the Court of Directors that all arrangements were ready for the occupation of Cuttack. The report explained that by occupying Cuttack in Odisha, an effectual blow would be struck against the Raja of Berar's resources. It mentioned that the occupation of the Cuttack province could be a valuable addition to the Company's revenue and a strong barrier would be added to the frontier of Bengal against predatory incursions; uninterrupted connection could also be established between Bengal and the territories of Fort St. George.[2]

The plan of invasion included joint operation of forces from four directions: Ganjam, Kedigree, Jaleswar and Midnapur. The occupation of the maritime district of Cuttack formed the principal part of a general plan of attack against the confederations.[3]

The occupation of Odisha was conceived of and executed with meticulous planning. By 1803, the British were very familiar with the geography of the state. The survey of Odisha by Portsmouth under James Rennell* and Blunt had given the British a sound knowledge of roads, routes, location, topography and climate. They had complete information about the influential zamindars, chiefs, movement of Marathas and their activities with a vast network of intelligence. The British planned the movement of their forces from the four directions under the command of four officers.

The most important and sensitive part of the operation was led by Col Campbell from Ganjam. Campbell was from His Majesty's 74th regiment, commanding the northern division of the army of Fort St. George. He was entrusted with the task of conquering the Barabati Fort at Cuttack, the Maratha stronghold, by proceeding from Ganjam. In the very initial days of the campaign, Campbell fell ill at Ganjam and was replaced by Lt Col Harcourt. Harcourt acted under the instruction of Lord Wellesley. John Melville, who was appointed the Civil Commissioner of Cuttack, accompanied Harcourt.[4]

As we have seen, the Odisha region was under the control of the Marathas since 1751, posing numerous challenges to the aspirations the British nurtured. But they also feared that the dislodgement of the Marathas would prove to be a sensitive issue prone to possible revolts by the local population. It could be potentially dangerous to wage a war against the Marathas as that could unite the Hindu population of Odisha in support of the Hindu Marathas. The British were worried that the Raja of Khurda might support the Marathas; in that case, with a big following among the population and a historical connection to Lord Jagannath, the Raja would prove to be a thorn in the East India Company's designs. Hence, in spite of their superior military

---

* James Rennell (1742-1830) was an English geographer, historian and a pioneer of oceanography. He is credited with constructing the first nearly accurate map of India. He published *A Bengal Atlas* in 1779. Rennell became an expert surveyor while serving in the Royal Navy (1756–63). He then served as Surveyor General of Bengal (1764–77) and of Bihar and Odisha (1767–77).

advantage, the East India Company thought it prudent to explore diplomatic channels and other initiatives to achieve their objective of conquering Odisha.

Gajapati Birakeshari Deb died in 1793. As discussed in the last chapter, Dibyasingha Deb was made king in 1780 although the *anka* continued in the name of his grandfather Birakeshari Deb till 1793. After Dibyasingha Deb's death in 1798, his minor son Mukunda Deb II succeeded him. In Mukunda Deb II's reign, three significant people played decisive roles: Jayee Rajguru, who was the Rajguru (royal preceptor); General Baxi Jagabandhu Bidyadhar; and Dewan Harihara Bhramarabar Ray, a close associate of Baxi and the Dewan (revenue minister) of the Khurda Raja. Since Mukunda Deb II was a minor, Jayee Rajguru played the roles of the guardian, advisor and regent of the Gajapati.

Jayee Rajguru was a very intelligent and erudite man, a visionary and a shrewd strategist, skilled in war and military planning. He had overwhelming influence in the decision-making process of the Raja of Khurda. He shifted the Raja in 1802 to the Balighar Palace at Puri while the Dewan and the General continued to be stationed at Khurda.[5] This meant that effectively, Jayee Rajguru became the centre of power and was in charge of the administration. Thus it came to be that at a very defining and delicate moment in Odisha's history, Jayee Rajguru played a very important and decisive role.

Jayee Rajguru was born on 29 October 1739 at Bira Harekrushnapur near Puri town. His real name was Jayakrushna Mahapatra Rajguru but he was popularly known as Jayee Rajguru. He belonged to a renowned learned family and mastered various branches of education and learning such as the *vedas*, *shastras*, *vyakarana*, *jyotish vidya*, *sangeet vidya*, *tantra shastra*, *mantra shastra*, *darshan shastra*, *tarka*, *nyaya*, etc.[6] Along with his pursuit of knowledge he trained himself in martial arts and was adept in horse riding.

Jayee Rajguru organized the local youth and imparted training to them in *akhadas* (local gymnasium) in sword fighting, wrestling and horse riding. He aimed at creating a strong local force for the region's defence. He remained a bachelor all his life and served the Gajapati as a trusted and loyal servant. Gajapati Dibyasingha Deb had appointed him as Rajguru in 1780. After Dibyasingha Deb's death, he continued to occupy the same position and became a trusted advisor to Gajapati Mukunda Deb II.

After the death of Dibyasingha Deb, there was a conflict for succession to the throne of Khurda between Mukunda Deb (son of Dibyasingha Deb) and Shyam Sundar Deb (son of Birakeshari Deb). Shyam Sundar Deb was living in the south, where he obtained help from the officers of the East India Company and planned to occupy Khurda by force. As it was crucial for the British to occupy Khurda, the British had planned a clever strategy of using Shyam Sundar Deb to occupy the region without directly getting involved in the fight. But this did not fructify due to stiff resistance from Jayee Rajguru and the Marathas. Sadashiv Rao, the Maratha subedar, supported Mukunda Deb and lodged a strong protest against the British alleging undue interference in the affairs of Odisha. This paved the way for the infant Mukunda Deb to ascend the throne of Khurda.[7]

Col Harcourt, stationed at Ganjam, had to cross Khurda to reach Cuttack for its ultimate takeover in 1803. He sent a personal letter to Baxi, seeking permission for a safe passage through Banapur (situated between Ganjam and Khurda) and Khurda to reach Cuttack. Baxi sent his personal messenger Param Guru Pandit to Harcourt declining permission for such a passage through Khurda. Harcourt, however, prevailed upon Param Guru Pandit, bribed him, won him over and collected a lot of confidential information about the Khurda state, the Raja, the General, the Dewan, the Rajguru and temple priests. After analysing this information, he thought it was safe and convenient to approach for a passage through Puri.

Harcourt and J. Melville were concerned about a potential alliance between the Raja of Khurda and the Maratha forces. This was the biggest impediment in their plan to snatch Cuttack from the Marathas. Harcourt sent a *vakil* (lawyer or legal officer) to Mukunda Deb II seeking permission for a safe passage for East

India Company troops through his kingdom. He also sought the Gajapati's acknowledgement of the supremacy and sovereignty of the British instead of the Marathas. Harcourt said he wanted to move stores, baggage and artillery troops to neutralize any possible attack on them by the Marathas. As compensation, he offered Rs 1 lakh to the Raja.

However, Jayee Rajguru could comprehend the ulterior motives of Harcourt and a possible danger to the kingdom from the British. He warned Mukunda Deb II of the follies of entering into an alliance with the East India Company's representative and opposed granting the British troops a safe passage through Khurda.

There were, however, several factors which weighed in favour of the Company's proposal. The Raja thought this was an opportune moment to provide support to the Company's forces as it would put him in an advantageous position from which he could make some demands on the British when they wrested power from the Marathas. For instance, the Gajapati was thinking of the four parganas—Rahanga, Lembai, Serai and Chabiskud—to which the Rajas of Khurda had lost claim and had surrendered to the Marathas. The recovery of these valuable parganas from the British was of paramount importance to the Raja. The British request for safe passage was considered a means to attain this purpose.

Therefore, Mukunda Deb II responded to Harcourt's request and sent his *vakil* to the Englishman in Ganjam for further negotiation. The *vakil* agreed to Harcourt's proposal on the condition that the parganas taken over by the Marathas would be restored to the Raja. Harcourt and the Magistrate of Ganjam in their anxiety to gain support of the Gajapati agreed to this in addition to the Rs 1 lakh they had already promised to pay to the Gajapati after conquering Cuttack.[8]

The British government wanted to play safe and cautious because they feared that the Rajguru could not be trusted. They also knew that the Rajguru had a great appeal and hold over the Puri priests. The Brahmanical influence over the Jagannath Temple and society was immense and decisive. So, to weaken the

Rajguru's grip, they obtained a religious approval in favour of British occupation of Puri. For this, the support and concurrence of the Puri priests was considered very vital.

Lord Wellesley, the Governor General of India, got an appeal written by Jagannath Tarka Panchanan of Triveni—the oldest and most eminent of pundits in Bengal—to the priests and Brahmins of Jagannath Temple. Panchanan[*] was an outstanding scholar and authority on religious texts and commanded great respect from the highest Hindu nobles and the community. Panchanan, who was held in high esteem by the Puri priests, appealed to them to place the temple and themselves under British protection. The English abstract with which Melville and Campbell were furnished is as follows:

> The Pundit states from the knowledge which he possesses of the character of the English, he is enabled to assure Ram Chund & Co.[9] that they need not be afraid to form a connection with the British Government, which is distinguished for its peculiar benevolence to its subjects. Thus satisfied of this truth themselves, they must exert all their powers of persuasion to inspire the respectable characters in that quarter with the same degree of confidence. That it is impossible adequately to express his sense of the excellencies which characterize the disposition of the English; and that the British Government not only permits the Hindoos to enjoy the free exercise of their religion, but manifests the greatest degree of benevolence, favour

---

[*] Panchanan was born in 1695. He lived for nearly 111 years and died in 1806. He was known for his remarkable memory and was a great logician. He had unparalleled knowledge of Hindu law. Panchanan was known to have taught Sanskrit to Robert Clive. He assisted William Jones to compile *Vivadabhangarnava* (literally 'a break wave on the ocean of disputes). He also helped William Jones to gain a deeper understanding of Hindu law. Incidentally, William Jones later became the first Chief Justice of Bengal and was the founder of Asiatic Society. His book on Hindu Law compiled in 1796 was translated and extensively annotated by H.T. Colebrooke.

and indulgence towards them, and all persons of whatever persuasion, rank, or condition in life.

To create a psychological impact on the people, Melville circulated a rumour through a *munshi*, Sayed Rehmutullah, that the Maratha chief had already delivered the empire to British in writing. It had the desired effect on the attitude of feudatory chiefs, who were being pressurized by the Marathas to pay exorbitantly high tax. Feudatory kings felt relieved over the reported exit of the Marathas because they felt they would get a reprieve from their tyranny of taxation. As a matter of fact, to secure the support of Gadajat kings, the Marathas had announced an exemption of tax for one year on such kings who joined them in their fight against the British. This ploy did not work. Except Athagarh, no other king supported the Marathas.[10]

Lt Col Campbell circulated a news obtained from a Brahmin predicting that the British government would be the guardian of the Jagannath Temple and that this was the wish of Lord Jagannath. The British communicated this 'divine message' to numerous chiefs and zamindars of Odisha to encourage them to submit to British authorities.[11] Harcourt succeeded Campbell who suddenly fell sick.

On 14 September 1803, Harcourt reached Manikpatna, a few miles from Puri, and wrote to the priests of the Jagannath Temple to provide the British their assurance and comfort. Harcourt writes that the priests 'appear to consider they are being placed under the protection of British Government as blessings of the Providence'.[12] Once Harcourt had established a direct connection with the priests, Brahmins and other officials of the temple, the march to Puri became smooth and he occupied Puri four days later. There was no resistance from any quarter. The people were conciliated as the priests and Brahmins had been taken into confidence. Major Fletcher was stationed at Puri while Harcourt continued his expedition to occupy Cuttack.

This unusual friendly response by various sections of the society in Puri appears intriguing. It almost appeared that the takeover by the East India Company was actually welcomed. Thus, the British apprehension of a possible alliance between the Raja of Khurda and the Marathas proved to be unfounded. Further, the public, and particularly the priests, Brahmins and temple officials, found an opportune moment to end the Maratha tyranny. They thought this was a good opportunity to bring the Maratha control over temple affairs to an end by replacing it with a benevolent British regime. All these considerations paved the way for the East India Company. Harcourt finally occupied the Fort of Barabati with very little use of force and by adopting devious means of winning over the Marathas.* The fort passed into the hands of the British on 14 October 1803.

The British Betrayal

After the occupation of Cuttack, the Raja of Khurda expected the four parganas that had come under British control to be restored to him as promised. However, this did not happen. Additionally, the Raja did not receive the balance of the Rs 1 lakh he was promised. On being instructed by Mukunda Deb II, Jayee Rajguru proceeded to Cuttack in March 1804 with 2,000 armed men. He met Harcourt and submitted a petition requesting the restoration of the four parganas and urging him to pay the balance monetary amount. He further desired a reduction in the annual *peskas* to the British.

Harcourt agreed to pay Rs 20,000 to the Rajguru claiming the balance would be paid at a future date. Regarding the restoration of the four parganas, Harcourt refused outright stating, 'Not a span of land will be given.'[13] The British were aware that such a promise had been agreed to. Toynbee wrote, 'When we took the province in 1803, the Rajah passively espoused our cause and tendered his allegiance to the British Government, doubtless in the hope that

---

* The British bribed the Marathas. They paid the corrupt Maratha officers heavily. Two principal officers were offered Rs 2 lakh each for agreeing to a peaceful surrender.

these parganas would be restored to him.'[14] He also rejected any reduction in the annual *peskas*.

The Rajguru returned extremely annoyed and disappointed. The dream of restoration of the four parganas, which were taken away by the Marathas during the reign of Mukunda Deb II's grandfather, was shattered. The Raja felt betrayed. It was a case of treachery by the British. In fact, it was the support of the locals that had made conquering the Marathas easier. But having faced no resistance, the British became emboldened to renege from their promise.

The young Mukunda Deb II, still a minor, did not understand the politics of this volte-face. The shrewd and intelligent Rajguru had an inkling of the true colours of the foreigners and hence had been unwilling to grant them any safe passage. Now, he was proved right. So clear was the Rajguru's stand that Harcourt and local East India company officials felt that the Khurda Raja himself was not inimical to them but the Rajguru was. He controlled everything and everybody at Khurda. The British, therefore, had engaged their strategic acumen and deceitfully achieved the consent of the Raja of Khurda to keep the powerful Rajguru at bay.

After the disappointed Rajguru returned to Khurda, he informed the Raja that Harcourt was not only unwilling to give up the four parganas but also had the intention of taking from the Raja whatever hereditary country remained in his possession. This enraged Raja Mukunda Deb II, who was shocked by such conduct. He developed a hostile attitude towards the British government.

In the meanwhile, Mukunda Deb II suffered another humiliation. The British wanted all the tributary Rajas of Odisha to sign an agreement with them accepting the sovereignty of the British. All of them signed except the Raja of Khurda. Mukunda Deb II kept delaying the signing under various pretexts. The British Commissioner at Cuttack sent Govind Ray, the *kanungo* (a revenue officer), and requested the Raja to hand over the signed agreement to him. The Raja was informed that Rs 50,000 had been kept in his name and he would get the money only if he removed his 'evil advisor'. He was asked to return the papers in case he did not sign them, with the warning that he would incur the displeasure of the British government over such an attitude.[15]

The 'evil advisor' referred to here was none else than Jayee Rajguru. The British thought that out of greed and fear, the Raja would sign the treaty and accept the money. But, the Rajguru did not allow the Raja to acquiesce to such terms. This intransigent attitude of the Khurda ruler further hardened the stand of the British. The British Commissioner again wrote to Mukunda Deb II on 20 February 1804 and warned the king that he was under ill-advice. He was asked to send Jayee Rajguru to Cuttack with the assurance that the royal preceptor would not be treated badly.

Mukunda Deb II did not respond to this letter and further delayed signing the agreement. The Commissioner finally sent a special officer to the Raja warning him of the 'impropriety of his conduct' and 'danger of its continuance'. The messenger was given a time of 48 hours, after which he was instructed to return in the event the Raja continued to withhold his signature and did not accept the terms. Faced with severe pressure, Mukunda Deb II accepted the agreement; however, he did include the observation that 'he made peace with English'. This was construed as an arrogant and impertinent act on the part of the Raja of Khurda towards the British.[16]

With the tussle for power continuing between the British and Mukunda Deb II, several unpleasant situations arose. For instance, the Raja of Khurda wanted to establish his right over the Jagannath Temple, which the British rulers were not prepared to allow. The Raja claimed a *nuzur* (gift of money) from the temple as a customary practice every year on the *Sunia* day (the beginning of New Year or the New *Anka)*. This put the British government in a dilemma as they did not want to allow this. Reluctantly, the British agreed to the Raja's demand. Murar Pandit, the custodian of the temple, was directed to pay nine gold *mohurs* (gold coins) and Rs 10 to Mukunda Deb II.[17]

In another situation, the Dewan of Raja Mukunda Deb II wrote to Murar Pandit threatening him with punishment for oppressing the Odiya Brahmins working with him. The Raja wanted to exercise his authority as an arbitrator in temple conflicts. But this was challenged by the East India Company administration, who refused to recognize the Gajapati's authority over the temple functions.[18]

The thought of regaining the four lost parganas remained supreme in the mind of Mukunda Deb II. With a view to repossessing these lands, he initiated a secret dialogue with the Raja of Berar and sought his help against the British. On the other hand, Raghuji Bhonsle of Nagpur deputed Antaji Naik, his man of confidence, to plan for a possible alliance with the Raja of Khurda and attack the British. Antaji Naik had extensive consultations with Jayee Rajguru before meeting the Raja. He informed Raghuji Bhonsle that the Khurda Raja desired to hire 1,000 horses for which he would defray the expenses. Naik also informed Bhonsle that they had found the 'lucky hour' to attack and that the other tributary kings would join in the assault.

The correspondence was intercepted by the British, and Antaji Naik was captured by them. Naik disclosed his detailed discussions and plan finalized with Jayee Rajguru. The British officials were very vexed by this development and decided to teach the Rajguru a lesson.

In the meantime, the Raja of Khurda engaged Sambhu Bharati, an influential *gosain* and a religious mendicant, to reach out to the other tributary chiefs to unite them against the British. The Rajas of Kujang and Kanika accepted the invitation. Harcourt realized that this alliance could prove to be dangerous to the British. His first endeavour was to attempt to bring the Khurda Raja to his senses by conciliatory measures but this did not yield any success. Harcourt observed, 'Our moderation has been construed into weaknesses, our silence into ignorance and our endeavours to conciliate into apprehension and fear.'[19]

Harcourt wanted to put the Raja of Khurda under test by imposing conditions on his conduct. In a communication to the higher officials of the British government, he wrote, 'I do think the Raja of Khurda must be exterminated. It is my intention to demand the immediate dismissal of his troops and destruction of his barriers; that he should give up his correspondence with any persons dissatisfied with the British Government.'[20]

But Governor General Wellesley was cautious and did not agree immediately. He advised Harcourt to try again to bring the Raja to his senses without using force. As a precaution and also to send a warning to the Khurda Raja, Harcourt arrested and imprisoned Sambhu Bharati, the king's emissary. Harcourt wanted the removal of the Rajguru from his office, who the British believed was the root cause of Raja's hostility towards them. To convey this message, Harcourt deputed Captain Blunt with the mission. A messenger was sent to the Raja in advance informing him that he was to receive Blunt.

Although the Raja agreed initially, he changed his mind the next day and told the messenger that he won't meet Blunt. On the messenger's insistence, the Rajguru yielded and said he would obtain the requisite letter from the Raja. In this process, the messenger was made to wait for 14 days. Even after that, the required letter did not materialize and the meeting was turned down. The messenger's attempt to meet the Raja proved futile forcing him to return to Cuttack. To ensure his own safety, the Raja took several measures such as preventing the movement and communication in his territory: he placed guards on the banks of Mahanadi River and instructed them not to allow entry to anyone belonging to the English ranks.

The Rajguru went to Puri to take the necessary steps to protect the Jagannath Temple from the clutches of foreign invaders in case of a war. He convened a meeting of *sahinayaks* (headmen of different localities) and organised them for protecting the temple and fighting the foreigners. The task of temple protection was entrusted to Patajoshi Mahapatra, the *Chatisniyoga* leader who took upon the responsibility with the help of *sahinayaks*. All strategic points were reinforced with local troops. The Rajguru also enlisted the support of Dalabeheras, Samantarays and Bisois from different areas. He planned a war strategy in consultation with important people.[21]

The British wanted to ensure there was no untoward upheaval after their occupation. They followed a policy of appeasement to ensure a calm and tranquil situation, which would help them consolidate their regime. For that purpose, the British took a selective and opportunist approach. One measure was to secure the continued support of priests, mahantas and Brahmins in the region.

In 1803, Harcourt procured a written declaration from the mahantas and santhas of Puri written in Sanskrit on a country-made paper which was treated with gold wash. The signatories in this document included Krishna Chandra Mahapatra, *Chattisaniyoga Nayak*, who signed in Odia; Guruji Indarlalji (Rajasthani); Chetan Das Mahanta of Bada Akhada Math, (Devanagari); Gayaramji (Devanagari); Ratna Nrusinghachari Swami (Kanada); Mahanta Soumajya (Devanagari); Santh Ramasevak Das (Devanagari); Mahanta Sriramdasji (Devanagari); Sri Krushnachandra Deb Goswamy (Bengali); Sri Gopinath Deb Goswamy (Maithili); Adhikari Narayan Das (Devanagari); Mahanta Tejram Dasji (Devanagari); Tirumala Venkatachari (Telugu); Gurumukhdas Mahanta of Jagannath Ballav Math (Devanagari) and Jagannath Rajguru (Devanagari).[22] The English translation of this letter can be found in Appendix 1.

This historical document written to Governor General Wellesley addresses him in glorious terms – 'Illustrious God, the Sovereign of the Universe, be our refuge' and 'the unrivalled sun that has caused to bloom the lotus that the English race is; and who has besides taken the vow of protecting the gods, the Brahmanas and the Vaishnavas'. In an unprecedented praise and support of the Governor General, the document declares, 'We, the people of the holy city are ever engaged in pronouncing our benediction and we wish to send our felicitations to your lordship. Further, we cherish but this desire that your authority over this holy city may continue in this way forever.' Highlighting the protection provided to the people, the document pointed out that in the earlier regime people met 'obstruction even in the smallest matter'. The signatories prayed that the supremacy of the English power may last forever. The document further mentions, 'we your well-wishers, being rid of all fear (worries) under your rule may ever remain engaged in the service of the Sovereign of the Universe.'

This outreach of the British and the securing of such proclamation or declaration from the mahantas of various *mathas* and *sansthas*, including the Jagannath Rajguru, was a strategic move though significantly annoying and humiliating for the Raja of Khurda.

Jayee Rajguru, the first crusader of anti-colonialism

The continuing hostilities between the British and the Raja of Khurda were reaching a flash point. On the one hand, Harcourt was trying to wage a war against him, but on the other hand Raja Mukunda Deb II, feeling cheated, humiliated and harassed, was trying to assert his rights. In March 1804, Mukunda Deb II sent a *parwana* (order) to Murar Pandit, the custodian of the Jagannath Temple as well as the *tahsildar* of Cabiskud, to supply 2,000 coolies and carpenters to build the cars of Lord Jagannath for the upcoming Car Festival. The Raja threatened that he would get them by force if they were not voluntarily supplied.

In July 1804, Mukunda Deb II, to assert his rights in one of the four parganas the British were to return to him, appointed a *moquaddam* to collect rent from Batagaon, a village near Pipli. The East India Company reacted to this appointment violently and treated it as an 'act of presumption and unprovoked aggression' as they considered the village to be under the control and authority of the administration of the East India Company being in a *Mughalbandi* area. The British treated the act of the *moquaddam*'s appointment as a transgression of authority by the Khurda Raja.

Unmoved by the Company's adverse reaction, a few months later, the Raja sent his men to collect revenue from the villages of Barpada, Matiapada and Kharad. He also sent a letter to Murar

Pandit demanding sheep and goats from the parganas of Rahanga, Serai and Chabiskud. When Murar Pandit did not comply with the orders, Mukunda Deb raided some villages near Pipli in October 1804 and took away 144 heads of cattle.

The British viewed these as hostile acts of defiance. Harcourt wanted to settle the matter once and for all. A proclamation was issued on 7 December 1804 by the British Commissioner declaring expulsion of the 'late Rebellious Tributary Gurjat Raja of Khoorda from the Territories of Khoorda by the British troops and the annexation of that country to the Territories of the Honourable Company in the province of Cuttack'.[23] In another proclamation on the same day, addressed to the British subjects, zamindars and *sarbakaras* (rent collectors), the Commissioner declared all debts contracted by the Raja as illegal.

A communication to Charles Grome, the Collector of the district, on 15 December 1804 conveyed that 'the Board directs you will adopt every requisite means for the promulgation of the proclamation within the district of Jaggernath and that you will direct copies of these to be hung up in the most public places'.[24] Murar Pandit, the head priest of the Jagannath Temple, was directed not to take the name of Mukunda Deb II at the time of prayer to Lord Jagannath as he was declared an 'enemy of the British Government'.[25]

The British reached out to zamindars and *khandayats* (men belonging to the warrior class) owing allegiance to the Khurda Raja and told them not to extend any help or cooperation to him. With matters coming to such a pass, Mukunda Deb II was ready to try his strength against the British. Elaborate preparations were made by the Rajguru.

When the guards were posted near the Delanga village, the British retaliated. Their plan was to break the Raja's defence in that village. Harcourt, who was joined by Capt. John Hickland from Pipli with adequate forces and ammunition, marched to Delanga and made sudden attacks, and routed the Raja's army. When the British forces were returning to Pipli, they met with resistance from a 700-strong cavalry. Here the local *paiks* fought valiantly and the British soldiers were defeated.

To manage the situation, the British brought in additional forces under the command of Maj. Fletcher. Harcourt moved another contingent from Cuttack as the Khurda Raja's forces were in occupation of *Mughalbandi* areas.* With the arrival of Harcourt's forces, the Raja's troops moved back towards Khurda, chased by the British. Though the Raja's army fought with courage and determination, superior skill, knowledge of artillery warfare, fresh reinforcements and better coordination helped the British to succeed.

A proclamation was issued that whoever promoted British interest would be suitably rewarded. Shaikh Wyoz Muhammad, a native of Cuttack, offered his services to the British with a contingent. He was placed in charge of artillery and was directed to attack the Fort of Banpur. There he captured four of the Raja's brothers and a son of his. Maj. Fletcher was ordered to attack the outer fort with 120 men from the Madras European regiment and two flank companies of the 2nd battalion of the 7th Bengal Native Infantry, together with a six-pounder and along with artillery men and gunners.

Sensing defeat and adverse consequences, the Raja escaped with his Dewan and other principal officers. He hid in the jungle and sent a *vakil* to Harcourt requesting for an audience. But the *vakil* was made a prisoner. Then the Raja sent his Dewan but he too was imprisoned. A servant of the Company, Fateh Muhammad, was engaged by the Raja to reach out to Harcourt. Having been granted an audience finally, the Raja was returning after meeting Harcourt when he was arrested by a small detachment of Company forces on the night of 3 January 1805 and was sent as a prisoner to Cuttack. Fateh Muhammad was awarded Rs 3,000 for 'helping' in arresting Mukunda Deb II.

---

*The province was divided into two categories of areas: *Mughalbandi* areas comprised plain and open part of the country in possession of the government as the royal domain. The Gadajat areas were held by tributary chieftains; they were hilly and distant areas under independent chieftains with annual fixed tribute.

After this, Harcourt came down heavily on others who had collaborated or sympathised with the Raja of Khurda against the British, including rulers of some tributary states. Harcourt was particularly harsh on the Rajas of Kujang and Kanika. The imprisoned Raja of Khurda was removed to the Fort of Midnapore in Bengal to prevent unrest in Odisha. His country was entrusted to the charge of the judge and magistrate of Cuttack.[26]

When Harcourt wrote to the British government about his measures, he said he expected his actions would effectively prevent the occurrence of similar difficulties with other rulers in future. The Rajguru was declared a traitor, captured and brought before Harcourt. Harcourt asked him if he caused the disturbances himself or if he acted at the instigation of the Raja. The Rajguru declared, 'I caused the disturbance. The Raja was a child and what was done was done by me.'[27]

The Rajguru had fought the British. His conduct provides an insight into his strong character. Although he was aware of the superior military strength of the British, he did not succumb or surrender to them and held on to his convictions till the end without making any compromises. Further, he showed great courage and strength of character by owning up the entire responsibility of the rebellion in the presence of Harcourt. He was awarded capital punishment for waging war against the British government. The Rajguru did not appeal for mercy and fearlessly told the court which sentenced him that fighting for freedom of one's own motherland was never a crime. He was put to death on 6 December 1806 in a very brutal manner. His legs were tied to two different branches of a tree and the branches pulled apart splitting his body into two. Thus was martyred a great freedom fighter and warrior.

Raja's Petition for Release

Gajapati Mukunda Deb II came of age when he was imprisoned at the Midnapore Fort. By this time, the young man was severely mentally disturbed as he was frustrated and depressed. He made a petition to the Governor General seeking his release. Knowing Harcourt's animosity towards the Rajguru, Mukunda Deb II tried to secure his release by shifting all blame for the rebellion on the Rajguru, who by then had been executed.

The Raja's petition pointed out that the Rajguru was solely responsible for directing the affairs of the country. Only the Rajguru was to blame for his defiance. The Gajapati mentioned the incident where the Rajguru went to Cuttack to remind Harcourt about the return of the four parganas as promised by the British colonel. The Raja also referred to the Rajguru's warning to not to form any alliance with the Company's forces.

The Gajapati mentioned that he had told the Rajguru to dismiss the troops in his service as per a *quirarnama* which he had signed with Harcourt. However, since the Rajguru was displeased with the response of Harcourt, he told the Raja that he distributed the money received from Harcourt among the troops. The Raja pleaded his innocence and begged compassion, praying for release from prison.[28] His strategy of gaining British sympathy worked. The translated version of the petition of Gajapati Mukunda Deb II, available in state records, can be seen in Appendix 2.

On 5 March 1807, George Dowdeswell, Secretary to the British government, informed the Magistrate of Midnapore the decision of the Governor General to release the Khurda Raja from confinement. Additionally, the government decided to pay the Raja an allowance equal to *mallikana* or 1/10 of the revenues of his estate. The government also decided to invest him with the internal management of the Jagannath Temple.[29]

After his release, Gajapati Mukunda Deb II was not allowed to reside at Khurda. He was shifted to Puri and his estate was forfeited. With this, the Raja of Khurda became the Raja of Puri—'A king without any kingdom'. 'Gajapati' became a mere title, an inherited legacy of the past.

Later, the Raja made a representation to the government for the restoration of his estate and for making a permanent settlement of his lands. He also offered *Saddar Jumma* (an annual land revenue fixed to be given to government) of Khurda at Rs 30,000. But this proposal was not accepted by the government.[30]

Though the release order stipulated the government's intention to invest him with the internal management of the Jagannath Temple, this did not happen immediately. The Raja was disappointed. He had expected the Christian government to dissociate itself from the temple management and to vest it solely in him. It was only much later, by the Regulations of 1810 that the government finally decided to appoint the Raja as superintendent of the temple. His power was, however, severely curtailed. By a regulation, the government reserved the right to axe the Raja and his successors from the superintendence of the temple on account of misconduct or incapability.

From then on, the life of Gajapati was not smooth. The British government started humiliating the Raja even for minor things. In 1812, Mahadev Mekap, the master of the wardrobe of Lord Jagannath, died and his son Dhundi Mekap succeeded him as a hereditary practice. Since it was difficult for him to execute his duties alone, the Raja appointed three deputies under Dhundi Mekap.

The Raja used to occasionally operate the *bhandar* (stores) but the store keys were kept with Dhundi Mekap. In September 1813, an inventory of articles was taken and some articles were found missing. The Collector of pilgrim taxes, who made enquiries, accused the Raja of theft. The Raja pleaded his innocence but that was not accepted. The matter went for appeal to the Calcutta Court of Circuit. E. Wadson, the judge, did not approve of the action of Collector. When the matter was referred to the government, it held that the Collector of pilgrim tax had no right to interfere in this matter.

Paika Bidroha, the Rebellion by Baxi

While Mukunda Deb II was not allowed to visit Khurda, the erstwhile seat of power, royal officials continued to stay there. The misery of the common people increased manifold. This resulted in the great Paika Bidroha (Paika Rebellion) of 1817, the first war of independence against the British rule, led by Baxi Jagabandhu Bidyadhar Mahapatra, who was the *bakshi* or commander-in-chief of the Khurda Raja.

The causes behind the rebellion were numerous, the principal being the government reclaiming ownership of hereditary 'Paikana' lands, which the *paiks* were enjoying rent-free from time immemorial. The government decision hit them hard and caused discontent and hatred, leading to a widespread rebellion against the British.

Though it is titled as the Paika Rebellion, the insurrection had the support and participation of various sections of society and was not limited to *paiks*. The rent-free lands were subsequently reassessed and the zamindars who came into the possession of the land through auctions, rack-rented them to realize the enhanced *jumma* (revenue tax). Frequent settlement and reassessment of land resulted in the onerous burden on farmers. Further, the lands that were auctioned were cornered by speculative strangers in Calcutta. The policy caused mass dispossession and displacement of cultivators, leading to the general population being reduced to extreme poverty.

Baxi was also divested of his ancestral estate known as Bakshi Bada from the estate of Kila Rorang. The Ewer report states, 'The primary source of the deplorable occurrences of 1817 was undeniably the dispossession of Jugabandhoo from the estate of Kila Rorang.' A discussion on the causes and consequences of the Paika Rebellion is out of the scope of this book. What is pertinent to note here is the role of the Gajapati, the Raja of Khurda, in the rebellion with particular reference to his relationship with Baxi Jagabandhu.

When the rebellion was gaining momentum, the role and participation of the Raja of Khurda assumed pivotal and potential importance. The Gajapati was still held in high esteem and revered by the general people as well as most of the feudatory states. As a strategic initiative that would grant the rebellion a great deal of legitimacy and support. Baxi wanted to secure the active support and participation of the Raja. He had already been successful in enlisting the support of various sections of the population from different places in Puri and Cuttack, including a number of feudatory states and local zamindars. Even the priests of the Puri Temple supported Baxi. These were the same people whose support was enlisted by the British at the time of their occupation in 1803. The British were aware of what Baxi was planning and they wanted to prevent the imminent collaboration between the Raja of Khurda and Baxi. So, the Governor General ordered the removal of the Raja of Khurda from Puri. It also appears from the records that Baxi did not get the active support of Mukunda Deb II.[31]

In a delicate and secret operation, Captain Le Fevre arrested Raja Mukunda Deb II on 18 April 1817. The Gajapati was brought as a prisoner to the Barabati Fort on 11 May 1817. Baxi's outreach to Raja failed. In this way, the British were successful in isolating the Raja so that he could not lend any support to the uprising.

On Paika Rebellion, two letters assume significance. Mukunda Deb II submitted a petition to the British pleading his innocence. He recounted how Baxi tried to persuade him to rise against the foreigners, 'the Lords of Hindustan', but how the Raja refused to follow 'a course of wickedness' against the English who had conferred many benefits on him.[32]

The second letter is a petition which Baxi Jagabandhu and Krushna Chandra Ray (the Dewan) jointly submitted to Melville, the Joint Magistrate of Puri in April 1819, explaining why they took up arms against the government. A translated version of this letter titled the 'Ooriya Chhitao' was sent by A. Sterling, Secretary to the Commissioner of Odisha, to W.B. Bayley, Chief Secretary to the government, with a covering letter. This letter is of historical significance as it brings out certain critical facts. This is presented as follows:[33]

> Jugbundoo Bownerber Raee Bukshee of Orissa and Dewan Kishen Chender Bownerber Raee offer their salutations to the English gentlemen and beg to represent as follows:

It is now 14 years since the Province of Cuttack was conquered by the British arms. At that period Maharajah Mukoond Deo who was quite a youth was urged on by the evil counsels of Jey Raye Gooroo, contrary to our earnest advice and remonstrances, to oppose the establishment of the British authority. He was accordingly taken prisoner and sent to Midnapore. Major Fletcher was then appointed to the charge of Khurdah. We from the beginning waited on that Officer. We gave in Derkhausts specifying all the lands which ourselves and our ancestors from time immemorial had been permitted to hold rent free under the heads of written Muhutteran Khereedgee and Jageer, both in Khoorda and in the 4 pergannahs (viz. Limbaee, Rahung, Seraeen and Choubeescood) and we particularly urged our claims to the possession of Bukshee-Bar and Deewan Bar (valuable Mehals now annexed to Rahung). Major Fletcher however utterly disregarded our claims and resumed every particle of our lands, leaving us not a Bukhra nor a Bigha of ground.

When the Maharaja was brought back from Midnapore and settled at Pooree with a fixed allowance for his maintenance, we ventured to represent our cases also to the authorities of Cuttack stating that we were entirely destitute of the means of supporting our families and dependents amounting to upwards of 500 souls and that if they would but give possession of our lands, we would agree to pay such revenue for them as it might be thought equitable to fix on a fair consideration of our cases, notwithstanding that we had enjoyed them as rent free Jageers obtained by our ancestors many generations back under grants from the Maharajah and the Soobahdars of the Province.

Such was our ill fortune however that this request also was disregarded and further the Khoodkast Zemindaree of Killa Rorung which the Emperor of Delhi had conferred on the ancestors of one of us (the Bukshee) which his family has always held and which he himself was allowed to engage for under the British Government during 3 successive years was taken away from him. Year after year he petitioned the local authorities for redress but in vain. He became in consequence reduced to a state of beggary and compelled to depend for his subsistence on the bounty of certain Zemindars.

The Dewan also was brought into a similar condition being dispossessed of Garh Chittri and other places ages since granted by the Rajahs to his family, allowed food and clothing; what had we done that we should be so degraded and impoverished? Under the same Government also how many Zemindars and Rajahs who have offended have not been pardoned and restored to their country and Estates? But Rajah Mukoond Deo for an offence against the State committed in his youth at the sole instigation of a wicked and designing Minister was for nearly 14 years kept out of Khoorda and that country, the Guddee of Orissa, the seat of its ancient sovereigns abandoned to ruin and devastations.

Had the Maharajah been placed in authority over his country according to former usage a population of 3,00,000 souls would have prospered and been happy but from the Guddee being vacant they have perished. From Darootheng to Chuttergarh (or from the N.E to S.W extremity of Khoorda) the whole country was let out to farmers; where there were resources of 5 Rs. these farmers demanded payment of 15; salt rose from 1 pun to 5. Such was the deplorable state of the ryots that they were obliged to subsist on herbs and water and scarcely one amongst them had a vessel left to drink his water out of it; yet notwithstanding the extremity of wretchedness no one took any notice of their condition. At length the people of the country came to us, who were destitute and impoverished like themselves, in a body and said 'we and you and Maharajah have sunk to the lowest stage of misery; this is now our plan; let us retire to the jungle and fix our abode there; the lands will then become waste and no revenue be collected. It is possible that on seeing this the English may be induced to take our condition into consideration.'

Confirmably with this scheme the people of Khoorda retired into the jungles but the British Authorities instead of viewing their conduct in the light that was expected and sending a

Vakeel, drew forth their armies and began slaughtering and devastating the country. At length from the good fortune of Sree Ramchandra Deo[34] and for the benefit of us, of the Maharajah and of the people of Khoorda the present rulers have visited the Province. Let our case now be taken fully into consideration and each man reinstated in his just rights. Let Maharajah Ramchandra Deo be placed on the Guddee of Khoorda, we restored to our ancient possessions and former condition and the people of Khoorda to a state of happiness and prosperity. Then, should any one hereafter commit crimes against Government we will undertake to destroy him with the sword and let this offence of Bukshee Jugbundoo Bhownerber Raee be pardoned.

The government appointed a commission consisting of G. Martindell and W. Ewer to enquire into the causes of the rebellion. Ewer, Commissioner of Enquiry, concluded 'that the last Rajah of Khoorda ever favoured the designs of his rebellious servants or was even previously acquainted with them, not a particle of evidence is available'.[35]

As far as Baxi was concerned, we find that his loyalty and confidence was supreme. Baxi was attempting to reach out to the ideological nerve centre by approaching the Raja in Puri. Although the movement never entered the realm of the Jagannath Temple in Puri nor did it acquire the Gajapati's leadership, it did gain a certain measure of legitimacy by a tacit acknowledgement of the dominance of the temple-state nexus. It is also significant to note the continued faith and loyalty of Baxi to the Gajapatis as expressed in his faith that Raja Ramchandra Deb III, the successor to Mukunda Deb II, would herald a regime where 'their ancient possessions and former condition would be restored and people of Khurda would achieve the state of happiness and prosperity'.

The Ewer report, however, made scathing observations about the role of Baxi in the rebellion. An award was declared by the government for his arrest. But Baxi was successful in evading arrest, till finally, he responded to a call of amnesty and surrendered.

The Paika Rebellion of 1817 signifies the earliest popular landmark event in freedom struggle in India. It may be mentioned that Odisha Chief Minister Naveen Patnaik had taken up the historical issue with the Centre, urged that it should recognise 'Paika Bidroha' as the First War of Independence against the British rule as it took place four decades before the 1857 Sepoy Mutiny, which has so far been regarded as the first war of Indian Independence. Responding to this, 'Paika Bidroha will find a place as the First War of Independence against the British Rule in the history books. The students should learn factual history of 1817'—were the words of the then Union Minister of Education (*The Economic Times*, 23 October 2017).

The conduct of Mukunda Deb II throughout the turbulent period when the British took over Odisha appears to be intriguing and shrouded in mystery. All we know for sure is that for his first arrest in 1804 the Raja blamed the Rajguru and for his second arrest in 1817 he held Baxi responsible.

The role of Baxi in 1803, when the East India Company captured Puri and then the rest of Odisha, has drawn the attention of scholars and researchers. The Rajguru alone was found to be guiding and advising Raja Mukunda Deb II and played a dominant role at that time. What role did Baxi as the commander-in-chief or general play at that crucial juncture in Odisha's history when the English came face to face with the Raja of Khurda at Puri?

The way in which events came to pass provides an indication of the fraught relationship between the Rajguru and Baxi. The joint letter of Baxi and Krushna Chandra Ray delivered to Melville gives us sufficient indication of a strained relationship. Baxi mentions in the letter that when Maharaja Mukunda Deb II was a youth, the king opposed British authority upon the 'evil counsels of Jey Raye Gooroo', which was 'contrary to [his] earnest advice and remonstrances'. This strengthens the supposition that opposing the British authority was a decision solely taken by the Rajguru which Raja Mukunda Deb II was forced to accept. Baxi further writes that Raja Mukunda Deb II committed an offence against the state in his youth at the instigation of 'a wicked and designing Minister (Rajguru)'.

The circumstances we have explored in this chapter clearly convey a situation where Jayee Rajguru and Baxi Jagabandhu, the two pillars of Gajapati Mukunda Deb II's government, were acting without agreement when the ruler was in a helpless state. Under these circumstances, the British had an upper hand in undermining the Raja's regime. Madhusudan Bipra, a contemporary author, mentions in his Odia book *Phiringi Kali Bharat* that had the Rajguru, Baxi and Dewan Harihara Brahmarbar Ray been active in their respective roles and given collective and collaborative advice to Mukunda Deb II, the path of history could have been different.[36]

Mukunda Deb breathed his last on 30 November 1817 in a prison cell at Barabati. Ewer informed the news to the Government of Bengal on 1 December. On 5 December, the young son of Mukunda Deb, Sri Ramchandra Deb III, was released from prison and allowed to perform the funeral rites of his father. The young Raja had requested the British government for an advance of Rs 10,000.

The Commissioner of Cuttack observed while approving the sanction that 'the money thus granted is to be considered an advance on account of the Rajah's *malikanha* as proprietor of the Khoorda Estate and will be deducted from the amount of 24,000 rupees which the Rajah of Khoordah is at present entitled to receive annually, in that capacity'. As there was a delay in receiving the amount, young Ramchandra Deb borrowed it from a *mahajan* (moneylender) and performed the funeral ceremony.

The act of borrowing money to meet the funeral expenses of the father reveals the financial condition of the Gajapatis after the British took over. This also shows British insensitivity in not acting promptly for such disbursement and pointed to an absence of a humanitarian approach to the Raja in his hour of personal grief.

Subsequently, the widowed Rani made a representation to the British government regarding the grant of an allowance to her and her son. She desired that 'Khelat' of Khurda be conferred on her son. The Commissioner of Cuttack, while recommending a grant of Rs 1,250, observed on the second plea: 'None of the Tributary chiefs claim such a distinction and we cannot therefore recommend that it be granted to the Head of a family which the Government has thought proper to degrade from that rank.'[37]

The young Raja then wrote another petition requesting that Rs 10,000 advanced to him be treated as a donation and the annual stipend of Rs 24,000 allowed to his late father for household expenses be continued in his favour. He pleaded:

> Taking into your consideration the honour and reputation with which my ancestors were regarded by the Hon'ble Company be pleased to grant me the token of Investiture of the Rank and Title of Maharaja (Khilaut-i-Maharajagie), agreeably to the ancient custom of our family, that I may succeed to the honours of my family conformably to the customs of my predecessors, and enjoying the protection of the Hon'ble Company at my residence at Purusottam.[38]

The Commissioner was of the opinion that a gift of the sum in question would be a misplaced act of liberality and munificence 'as there were heavy arrears outstanding against late Mukunda Deb from the pargana Lembai which had been made *khas*. The second request was granted. As regards the third request, the Commissioner observed that it was neither necessary nor expedient to confer on Raja Ramchandra Deb, the Khelat of Maharajgee.'[39]

The British followed an antagonist policy in depriving the Raja of the title and honour while restricting his role to being the superintendent of the Jagannath Temple. In the British estimate, the position of the superintendent given to the Raja was a political imperative and religious necessity to maintain an apparent distance and dissociation from interfering with the religious affairs of the temple. However, conferring a political title had a political significance and was out of question. In October 1848, the Raja again requested for the restoration of power and rank to him. This was again turned down.[40]

11

THE FORT OF BARABATI
The Pride and the Prison

The history of Odisha is incomplete without the history of Barabati. Kataka (now known as Cuttack) was the capital of Odisha and the citadel of power of the Odishan Empire. While Puri, the abode of Shri Jagannath, was the religious and spiritual epicentre of the state, Cuttack was the political, commercial and imperial capital with the seat of power.

There are different views on the foundation date of Cuttack. Relying on historical evidences, S.N. Rajguru opines that Yayatinagar was built by Yayati I in AD 950, which was renamed Varanasi Kataka.[1] Sterling, while writing the accounts of Cuttack in 1822, relies on the *Madala Panji* and writes:

> Raja Nrupa Keshari, a martial and ambitious prince, who was always fighting with his neighbours, is said to have first planted a city on the site of modern Cuttack in 989 AD. The reign of Markat Kesari was distinguished for the construction of a stone revetment or embankment faced with the material (probably the ancient one of which the remains are yet to be seen) to protect the new capital from inundation in 1006 AD.[2]

Persian writer Sayed Aulad Haider Fouqee Bilgrami, in his monumental work *Tarikh-i-Jadid-i-Subah-Orissa*, records that Cuttack was the capital of Odisha for the last 1000 years and states that 'Raja Nrupa Keshari founded Cuttack in AD 950'.[3]

In the absence of adequate historical records, the date of the foundation of the city has become a subject of intense debate and interpretation giving rise to many conjectures. While historians differ on the date, it would be naïve and difficult to accept that Cuttack did not exist before the dates on which they differ and debate. Ascertaining the date of establishment of the city is not the subject matter of the present work.

There, however, seems to be a predominant view recognizing AD 989 as the year of the foundation of the capital at Kataka. This has been accepted as the year of establishment of the capital town by a number of historians working on the history of Kataka. Based upon such findings, the Millennium Celebration Committee decided to celebrate 1000 years of Cuttack city in 1989. From the time of Nrupa Keshari onwards, the city of Cuttack remained a pivotal centre of Kalinga and in spite of weathering many political storms, turmoil, prosperity and adversity, foreign attacks and domination, Cuttack has never lost its position as a political stronghold of Odisha.

Looking Back

Anantavarman Chodagangadeva (AD 1078–1150) founded the Kalinga Empire at a critical juncture when the northern part of the empire was facing continued Mohammedan invasion. Chodagangadeva, who ruled for 72 years, not only founded a vast empire but also a strong and prosperous one.

Eminent historian M.N. Das, in his famous work *Glimpses of Kalingan History* while writing about the long rule of Chodogangadeva, comments:

> Chodaganga Deb ruled for seventy-two years. Such a long reign of almost three quarters of a century is rare in the annals of

kings. For an efficient monarch like Chodaganga, such a long period of royal authority was destined to cover itself with far-reaching conquests and administrative reforms. History records innumerable conquerors who conquered but could not rule, and their conquests melted away with their death as they could not give effective administration during their short span of military career and when they aimed at giving administration after hectic days of militarism, death dropped its icy curtain over their brilliant careers. Chodaganga was perhaps a favored child of history who conquered and lived long to see his conquests duly organized and effectively administered.[4]

Chodagangadeva's original capital was at Kalinganagar, whose other name was Mukhalingam, in the Srikakulam district of present-day Andhra Pradesh. After he occupied Odisha in AD 1128, Chodagangadeva shifted his capital to Cuttack. From this new capital, the Gangas ruled for 14 generations with dignity, valour and glory. They later became integrated with Odias, removing permanently their 'outsider' tag. Chodagangadeva occupied the *Pancha katakas* (five fortified towns)—Jajpur, Amravati, Choudwar, Varanasi Kataka and Sarangagarh—which because of their strategic locations formed a chain in a military grid, each closely linked to the other.[5] These five forts find mention in the *Madala Panji*.

Forts—Types and Tradition

Odisha has a long tradition of building temples and forts. According to Manu, a king has to resort to a fort for his safe settlement. The *Shastra* describes forts to be of six types:

1. *Dhanvadurga* (protected by a desert)
2. *Jaladurga* (protected by a stream of water)
3. *Vrksadurga* (protected by trees)
4. *Nrdurga* (formed by an encampment of armed men)
5. *Giridurga* (protected by hills) and
6. *Mahidurga* (built of stones)

Of these six, *Giridurga* is said to be the best because a hill fort is distinguished by many a superior quality. The next best is the fort protected by a stream of water. If the king stays in such a fort, foes cannot easily attack him. Though Kalinganagar (Mukhalingam) had hill forts, the Fort in Cuttack was protected by water.

The capital was shifted to Cuttack for strategic reasons—to be the centre of the expanded empire and to obtain the acceptance and legitimacy of the Odia people by being close to the subjects. The natural geography of Cuttack is formed by a natural stream and water of Chitrotpala (modern-day Mahanadi) and her branch Kathjori. As per the *Smritis*, a fort protected by furious crocodiles in the water deters enemies from interfering. Accordingly, the Fort of Barabati was surrounded by the great *garakhais* (a circle of water body) around it, acting as a shield.

Kautilya's *Arthashastra* is considered to be one of the most important texts on fortification. He considered forts as one of the seven most important constituent elements of a state. Emphasizing the importance of forts, he says, 'For it is in the fort that the treasury and the army are safely kept and it is from the fort that secret war (intrigue), control over one's partisans, the upkeep of the army, the reception of allies and the driving out of enemies are successfully practiced. In the absence of forts, there is no destruction.'[6]

On the question of location, Kautilya classified forts under four broad heads:

1. *Parvata* (hill fort—located on a rocky bed or built in the midst of encircling hill ranges)
2. *Audaka* (water fort—situated on an island of a river or on a plain)
3. *Dhanavana* (desert fort—situated either in a desert or in a wild tract devoid of natural facilities)
4. *Vana Durga* (forest forts—in the midst of a forest encompassed by thickly set tall trees)

Kautilya gives more stress on the hill fort, which is the most unassailable and is more advantageous than any other variety. He justifies this by explaining:

> Of two fortified kings, one who has his forts on a plain is more easily reduced than the other owning a fort in the centre of a river, for a fort in a plain can be easily assailed, destroyed or captured along with the enemy in it, whereas fort surrounded by a river requires twice as much effort to capture, and supplies the enemy with water and other necessaries of life. Again, of two kings, one owning a fort surrounded by a river, and another having mountainous fortifications, seizing the former's land is better, for a fort in the centre of a river can be assailed by a bridge formed of elephants made to stand in a row in the river, or by wooden bridges, or by means of boats; and the river will not always be deep and can be emptied of its water, whereas a fort on a mountain is of a self-defensive nature, and not easy to besiege or to ascend; and where if one portion of the army defending it through the other portions can escape unhurt, and such a fort is of immense service, as it efforts facilities, to throw down heaps of stone and trees over the enemy.[7]

Situated in a strategic geographic position on the bifurcation of river Mahanadi, which along with its tributary Kathajodi, provided natural protection, Cuttack was considered as an ideal place for a fortified capital. The geographical situation of Cuttack is such that it served as the only narrow strip of the land route of the country; as such people coming from the north to south or from the south to north had no other alternative but to cross the Mahanadi at or near Cuttack. The hill range to the west and wide rivers to the east of Cuttack exclude all possibility of the alignment of the highway from north to south and it seems that the Nanda and Maurya kings of Magadha had to cross the Mahanadi at or near Cuttack. The same route was traversed by Kharvela at the time of his Magadha campaign. Neither the Dhauli rock edict of Ashoka nor the rock inscription of Kharvela mentions any highway from Kalinga or

Odisha to Magadha. The route of communication from central India lay through the valley of the Mahanadi and terminated at Cuttack.[8]

In the history of the ancient fortified cities and towns of India, Cuttack, due to its strategic location, must have flourished as a fortified town from ancient times—in fact, much before the recorded history in AD 989. Its military significance can be well understood from the connotation of the word 'Kataka', which means military camp and the fort or capital or the seat of the government protected by the army.

The history of Barabati is the history of Cuttack, the capital of the Odishan Empire over the ages. The notable events of the Odishan history are interwoven and centred round this citadel. Ever since the Gajapati emperors assumed the title of 'Nabakoti Karnata Kalabargeswar' spreading their empire from Ganga to Kaveri, Barabati, the seat of administration of such vast empire from the reign of the Gangas and the Suryavanshis, occupied a pivotal position. Forts played a very important part in the expansion and protection of a territory. Forts have been erected and used by kings to defend their territory from enemy invasions, and on the other hand conquests have been launched from forts.

In the 16th century, Abu'l Fazl, the minister in Akbar's court, during his travel to Odisha mentioned that Odisha was full of forts and each of the five *sarkars* (divisions)—Jaleswar, Bhadrak, Cuttack, Kalinga Dandapat and Rajahmundry—had forts with well-garrisoned and trained armies. Abu'l Fazl mentions a list of 72 forts in Jaleswar, Bhadrak and Cuttack *sarkars*. There is a mention of 129 forts possessed by the Gajapatis of Odisha in the *Ain-i-Akbari*.[9]

Although Cuttack had been the capital of the Gangas since the time of Chodagangadeva, it got a facelift and was rejuvenated during the time of Anangabhimadeva III (AD 1211–1238). He built a new town called Varanasi Kataka on the left bank of Mahanadi, opposite Chaudwar. Subsequently, he transferred the headquarters from Abhinava Yajatinagara (Chaudwara-Kataka) to Abhinava

Baranasi Kataka. This has been recorded in the *Madala Panji* as follows:[10]

> Anangabhimadeva – This king used to reside at the town called Chaudwar Kataka. While he was residing there, one day, the king crossed the Mahanadi and on the southern bank of it in the vicinity of Bisweswara Siva situated in the village Barabati in the Kodinda Dandapata, he saw that a heron killed a hawk. The king was astonished at this unusual event and laid the foundation of a Kataka in the Barabati village, and after building the palace and making it a Kataka, called the place as the Baranasi Kataka and left Chaudwar Kataka.

Sterling refers to this episode and writes,

> He (Raja Anagabhim Deo) resided during the early part of his reign in the Nour or Palace called Chaudwar at Jajapur, but was induced by some omen to build a magnificent palace on the site of Fort Barabati, adjoining the town of Cuttack, where he afterwards held his Court chiefly. The construction of the present castle of that name should in all probability be referred to this period, though a later date is generally assigned to it.[11]

It is seen from the Nagari Copper plate of Anangabhimadeva issued from Abhinava Kataka that he resided in the Fort of Barabati. The next rulers of the Ganga dynasty stayed in this fort and made further improvements to Kataka city.

Narasimhadeva, the greatest warrior and builder of the Ganga dynasty, started his war procession against Humayun Shah of Bahmani Sultanate and returned victorious amidst joy and pomp. In order to stop the constant attacks of the Muslims of Bengal, he erected the famous Fort of Raibania near Jaleswar on the border of present-day Odisha and crushed the Muslims on the bank of Hooghly River. As a sign of victory, he built the renowned Sun Temple at Konark.

Sterling, in praise of the valour of Narasimhadeva, has said, 'The boldness and enterprise of the Odishan monarchs in those days may surprise us when we consider the situation of Kola in the heart of Central India beyond Kalberga and Bedar.'[12] The Barabati Fort played a decisive role in the self-defence and protection of the Gajapatis, essential for their victory or conquest.

Gajapati Purusottama Deb after his Kanchi expedition brought the image of Sakhigopala from Kanchi and installed it within the Fort at Barabati. Shri Chaitanya visited the temple of Sakhigopala within the fort in 1510. The image of Sakhigopala was taken away from the fort before General Kalapahad (1568) destroyed this temple. The image was installed at different places in different times before finally being installed at Satyabadi near Puri by a Maratha saint, Baba Brahmachari.

Mukunda Deb, the last independent monarch of Odisha, rebuilt the defensive walls of the fort and erected a nine-storied palace. Since then the Fort of Barabati was popularly known as the palace of Mukunda Deb. He is recorded as the greatest builder and warrior of his time. His sway extended to Tribeni Ghat on the Hooghly River where he built a temple and bathing steps. During his reign, the invasion of Muslims from the north began to grow in frequency. To oppose the inroads of the Afghan King of Bengal Sulamania Gurzani (Sulaiman Khan Karrani), he built a strong fort at a strategic location in the northern frontier of Odisha. The Raibania Fort of Narasimhadeva, backed by an impenetrable forest, was at a commanding position in the northern frontier. To provide greater strength on the northern side, he built the Deulgaon Fort, seven miles west of Raibania. Evidence shows that it contained chlorite stone figures of Jagannatha and Balarama, The fort has been demolished and on its ruins now stands a high school. Mukunda Deb followed a well-calibrated war strategy and built a strong line of defence at the frontier of his state. The contribution of this monarch in maintaining the prestige of Odias and the independence of the Odishan Empire will forever be remembered.

Unfortunately, details of the other forts as a line of defence constructed by Mukunda Deb are not available. However, it may be pertinent to mention here that the Barabati Fort as the capital of Odishan Empire was by far the strongest and the finest of all the citadels erected during the period.

The death of Gajapati Mukunda Deb in 1568 created a conducive condition for the Sultan of Bengal to attack Odisha. General Kalapahad attacked and plundered the Jagannath Temple and unleashed a reign of terror among the common people. This was the time when the Barabati Fort was attacked and the Odishan Empire was taken over with the death of Mukunda. Al-Badaoni, a contemporary of Akbar, in his work *Muntakhab-ut-Tawarikh,* has mentioned about establishing control of Islam over Puri as:[13] 'He (Sulaiman) had conquered the fort of Katak Banaras, the mine of unbelief, and made Jagannath a home of Islam.'

Abu'l Fazl visited the fort with Mansingh in 1592 and described it in the following manner:

> Katak (Cuttack) – the city has a stone fort situated at the bifurcation of two rivers, the Mahanadi, held in high veneration by the Hindus, and the Kathjuri. It is the residence of Governor and contains some fine buildings. For five or six Kos round the fort during the rains, the country is under water. Raja Mukunda Deb built a palace here nine-stories in height, the first storey was taken up for the elephants and the stables; the second was occupied by the artillery and the guards and quarters for attendants; the third by the patrol and gatekeepers; the fourth by the workshops; the fifth by the kitchen and the sixth contained the public reception rooms; the seventh the private apartments; the eighth, the woman's apartments; and the ninth, the sleeping chamber of the Governor. To the south is a very ancient temple.[14]

Two English merchants, William Bruton and R. Cartwright, who visited the fort 63 years after the death of Mukunda Deb, were surprised at the splendour of the fort and described it as the Court of Malcandy. Abu'l Fazl refers to the nine-storied structures of the fort whereas the English merchants describe it as having nine courts.

During the Afghan and Maratha reigns, the Fort of Barabati was the seat of administration. Raja Ramachandra Deb of Khurda was imprisoned in this fort by Taqi Khan in AD 1732. In 1742, Bhaskar Pandit, the leader of the Marathas, attacked the fort and in 1745 Raghuji Bhonsle occupied it. Thus by 1751 the fort and Cuttack came entirely under the occupation of the Marathas. T. Motte, a European traveller, visited Cuttack in 1766 on his way to Sambalpur and described the Barabati Fort thus:

> Cuttack is not fortified now, but on the side next the Maha Nuddee is a citadel, called Barahbattee, because it is said to contain 12 battees, or 240 biggahs of land. But this must be understood not only of the fort itself, but of the official fleet annexed to the command; for the fort itself did not appear to me above 800 yards in circumference. It is square with a small bastion at three angles; at the fourth, to the N.W. a very large one, evidently the improvement of an European engineer, to counteract lofty mosque, which commands that quarter of the fort; the ditch is 20 yards wide; and 7' deep, lined with stone, and a perfect square without; for the bastions having been added since the fort was built there are no projections in the ditch to answer the projections of the bastion. The works are formed of two stone walls, each 18 inches thick, built perpendicular two feet from each other, which distance is filled up with rubbish. The entrance is defended by three gateways, so strong, it would be impossible to force them if they were manned by brave fellows, for the passage between them is narrow and winding with a stone wall on each side, thirty feet perpendicular, from the top of which, if they were to let large stones fall, every man in the passage must be crushed. The fort is, however, too small to make a long defence against a European enemy.[15]

Sterling, who was present at Cuttack in 1818, described the condition of the fort.

> Its square slopping towers or bastions, and general style, bespeak clearly a Hindu origin. The Mohammedan or Marhatta Governors added a round bastion at the N.W. angle, and constructed the great arched gateway in the eastern face, which alterations are alluded to in a Persian inscription, giving for the date of the repairs and additions according to the rules of the Abjed, the fourth fort has double walls built of stone, the inner of which enclose a rectangular area measuring 2,150 by 1,800 feet. The entrance lies through a grand gateway on the east, flanked by two lofty square towers, having the sides inclining inwards, from the base to the summit. A noble ditch faced with masonry surrounds the whole measuring in the broadest part two hundred and twenty feet across. From the centre of the fort rises a huge square bastion or cavalier supporting a flagstaff. This feature, combined with the loftiness of the battlements on the river face, give to that edifice an imposing, castellated appearance, so much so that the whole when seen from the opposite bank of the Mahanadi, presented to the imagination of Mr T. Motte, who travelled through the province in 1767 A.D., some resemblance to the west side of Windsor Castle. No traces of the famous palace of Raja Mukund Deo nine-storeys in height, mentioned in the Ayin Acberi, are to be found within the walls of fort Barabati, but the fragments of sculptured cornices, and which have been dug up at different times, and more especially a massive candelabra, or pillar furnished with branches for holding lights, formed of the fine grey indurated chlorite or pot stone, are probably the remains of some marge and splendid edifice.[16]

In September 1803, the British army reached the Barabati Fort. However, the Maratha armies stationed in the fort were neither ready for the unexpected battle nor had any opportunity to get military help from the feudal lords of Odisha. So, the British army under the commandership of Col Harcourt and Lt Col Celton bombarded the fort and entered without resistance.

The attack on and ingress into the Barabati Fort on the night of 12 September 1803 has been vividly described in *Military History of Kalinga*. It reads as under:

> On the night of the 12th, a spot was fixed for a 12-pounder battery, distant about 500 yards from the outer gate of the fort. This battery was completed on the night of the 13th and 12-pounder placed in it, together with two howitzers and two 6-pounders, the whole of which opened their fire on the morning of the 14th. By eleven o'clock in the forenoon most of the defences in the south face of the fort, against which our fire was directed, were taken off, the enemy's gun silenced and every appearance promised success: upon which I directed Lieutenant Colonel Celton to advance with one 6-pounder, and a party of artillery-men, two hundred Europeans from His Majesty's 22nd, and the Madras European regiment, and four hundred sepoys from the 29th Bengal, and the 9th and 10th regiments of Madras native infantry. The party had to pass over a narrow bridge and under very heavy, but ill-directed fire of musketry from the fort, to which they were exposed for forty minutes. They at length succeeded in the blowing open the wicket (the remaining part of the gate had been fortified with thick masses of stone). Having accomplished it, the party entered singly and although they met with considerable resistance while entering the fort, and passing two other gates, the British troops were soon victorious.[17]

The total casualties sustained by the British troops were 5 killed and 29 wounded. It is curious that no mention is made of the casualties sustained by the Marathas or of the leader or leaders who resisted the British troops' advance. There is no doubt that measures adopted by the British to induce and bribe the servants of the Maratha government in Odisha to desert their master must have produced the desired effects or else it will be difficult to explain the mysterious circumstances connected with the enemy and finally the surrender of the Fort of Barabati after slight resistance. It is noteworthy that none of the notable civil officers of the Maratha government in Odisha, such as Banuji, Harivamsa Ray and Moro Pandit, have ever found mention in the British records describing their exploits. Only Balaji Kumar, the commander-in-chief, has become an exception and therefore he seems to have remained true to his master's cause.[18]

Great damage was caused to the Barabati Fort after the British took it into their possession. It was deplorable. The fort was ultimately used as a prison to hold illustrious kings and nobles of this land. In 1803, the Raja of Kujang was kept under confinement in this fort. In 1818, the Raja of Khurda, Mukunda Deb, and his son were imprisoned. In 1819, four persons (two belonging to the family of the Raja of Surguja) were kept as prisoners in this fort. After the release of the Surguja prisoners, the fort was abandoned.

In AD 1828, Commissioner Thomas Packenham suggested that the stones from the Barabati Fort might be useful for repair of revetments and public roads. Packenham's suggestions were accepted and he was instructed that the stones should be sold to affluent men of the town. It is known from the letters (in 1829) addressed to Packenham that the price of a hundred stones of all sizes varied from Rs 5 to Rs 6. Even the walls of the fort were dismantled and the stones sold. Thus, the demolition of the fort was accelerated since AD 1829.

The stones were used for constructing a lighthouse at False Point. Stone fragments were used for building the Cantonment Road in Cuttack. On 21 September 1829, J.A. Schultz, the Superintendent of Embankments, wrote to G. Stockwell, Commissioner of Revenue, Cuttack, suggesting a search for the hidden treasures in the fort. Nothing is known from government records regarding the result of Schultz's exploration. But according to an Odiya book (*Katak, the Capital*) written in 1896, an English officer during the treasure hunt excavated several places in the fort and unearthed a temple containing a number of images and a well.

In 1855, the revetment was damaged in several places by a high flood. Lieutenant John Harris repaired it by using the stones of Barabati. District Magistrate R.N. Shore obtained the sanction order from the lieutenant governor to stop further destruction of the fort. 'The injury done to the old fort,' Odisha Commissioner G. F. Cockburn observed, 'is irreparable and it is a most discreditable circumstance that one of the finest remains of antiquity in the province of Odisha should have been destroyed in the way it has been for the sake of stones for the use of road and other public works.'

Even after this, Harris not only removed the stones from the fort for the embankment but he suggested to the government that valuable material worth thousands of rupees might be obtained by excavating the buildings within the fort. This was forwarded to the Lieutenant Governor of Odisha. The Secretary to the Lieutenant Governor replied on 13 May 1857 that His Honour had authorized the systematic excavation of the Barabati Fort, under the supervision of the Embankment Department with the conditions that 'any evacuation in the course of these operations are to be filled up with as little delay as possible with earth and sand that the stone revetments (of the fort) the gateway and the mosque within the fort are on no account to be in any way injured.' Obtaining this sanction order, John Macmillan, the Superintendent of the Central Embankments Department, demolished and removed the remains of the walls of the fort.

During the 1857 Mutiny, a magazine was constructed out of the stones of Barabati within the fort. According to G. Toynbee, the Public Works Department in 1873 converted this fine building into an unsightly series of earthen mounds and the ground within the moat into 'a wilderness of stone pits.'[19] A hospital was erected out of the stones of the walls.[20] Thus, it has been conclusively established that this magnificent edifice was defiled and demolished only during the British rule. This fort was a pride for the Gangas, the Suryavanshis and the Bhois up to 1568; thereafter it was used by the Mughals as well as the Marathas. They had carefully maintained, repaired and even rebuilt the fort. The British were the exception to this tradition.

Among the high-profile prisoners once held in the Barabati Fort were Gajapati Ramachandra Deb II (AD 1727–1736), Gajapati Birakeshari Deb I (AD 1736-1793) and Gajapati Mukunda Deb II (AD 1798–1817).

As we have seen earlier, it was while he was held at Barabati that Gajapati Ramachandra Deb was forced to convert to Islam. It was also here that he was married to Razia. As a result of his conversion, the Gajapati was rejected by the people of Odisha, who could not accept a Muslim Thakur Raja.

While in prison for allegedly murdering his sons, Gajapati Birakeshari Deb wrote some heart-rending poems (see Chapter 9 for details), which deeply reflect his pathos and helplessness.

Gajapati Mukunda Deb, the last Raja of Khurda, was held at Barabati before being taken to Midnapore jail. He was arrested by the British to isolate him from his people who could have banded around their leader and posed a threat to the British administration. The arrest was most shocking to the young infant Raja. While in prison, Mukunda Deb wrote an emotional poem. The poem, translated into English, reads as under:

O Jagannath, you dwell in Niladri
Since I am imprisoned in Cuttack
My days simply don't end
I yearn for you every moment.

Babu Chintamani unwittingly
brought Ramachandra in
The courtier betrayed the king
and imprisoned him in Barabati.

I wandered in Chakamba and Bikasai
and among hills and forests,
I didn't get a glimpse of your beautiful face
since I remained incarcerated in Cuttack.

Harihara, my well wisher, be kind to me,
take out the sword from the closet;
O Lord Jagannath!
Drive away the enemies of Odisha.

I am helpless, I pray to you
Why don't you answer my prayers?
I take refuge at your divine feet
You are the lion of Odisha.

The poem of the imprisoned Gajapati presents his emotional appeal to Lord Jagannath, the presiding deity, to give him strength and the sword to save the people and holy land from the British.

Gajapati Mukunda Deb was arrested again in 1817. This was when the *Paika* Rebellion under the leadership of Baxi Jagabandhu against the British was gaining momentum. The British wanted to prevent Mukunda Deb from collaborating with Baxi and so arrested him along with his infant son Jagannath Jenamani (who later became Gajapati Ramachandra Deb III) bringing them to the Barabati Fort in May 1817. Mukunda Deb died in prison on 30 November 1817 at a very young age. His infant son was declared his successor and his coronation took place in the prison.

The Barabati Fort has been both a pride and a prison of the Gajapatis. Col Harcourt will go down in history both as a traitor and a destroyer—traitor because he cheated Mukunda Deb by going back on his promise to return the lost territories of the Raja of Khurda to him (see Chapter 10); destroyer because he invaded the Barabati Fort along with Col Celton and bombarded it, destroying the fort's southern side, on 14 September 1803. This led to the eventual conquest of Cuttack, the capital of Odisha, and the foundation of the British rule in the region. The conquest of this fort laid the foundation of its decay and ultimate demise. The British followed a conscious policy of wiping out this monument of pride and symbol of power to break the spirit of the local population. The fort was demolished and its stones were sold and used elsewhere to obliterate its legacy, leaving skeletal remains of the ruin as a silent witness of a great heritage.

The Fort of Barabati which now lies in ruins has lost its glory and splendour over the ages. The fort changed its character from being the centre of power, residence of the royal kings or the governor to a prison and finally became an abandoned, demolished structure, vanquished and obliterated, the last remnant standing as a weeping witness of a lost legacy.

12

DIBYASINGHA DEB III
Crown to Conviction

After the death of Mukunda Deb II in 1817, Ramachandra Deb III (AD 1817–1854) became the Raja of Puri. As already mentioned earlier, his coronation took place at the Barabati Fort. The Collectorate was shifted from Puri to Cuttack in 1816. A Commissionerate was created there as per the 1818 Regulation. In 1820, Odisha was divided into three districts—Cuttack, Puri and Balasore. They remained a part of the Bengal Presidency till 1912 and later the Odisha Division came under the Bihar–Odisha province.

On 20 April 1840, the famous Act X of 1840 was passed, which finally abolished the British taxation of pilgrims. According to this Act, the raja—the superintendent—was entrusted with the supervision of the temple, internal funds, management of the temple affairs, and control over pujaris, officers and servants. Two important developments took place during this time:

(1) During 1843–1858, a lot of land, particularly *sataishi hazari mahal*,* was kept under the management of the Raja, the temple superintendent, and the money from the land revenue proceeds was used to meet the expenses of the rites and rituals of the deities and their services.

(2) *Ekharajat mahal* was handed over to the Puri Raja in 1863 as he was the superintendent of the temple in order to provide for a separate policing system of the temple.

After the death of Ramachandra Deb III, Birakeshari Deb II became the Raja of Puri. Birakeshari Deb II suffered an untimely death on 11 December 1859. As he was childless, a few hours before passing away, he adopted a four-year-old boy, the second son of the Raja of Kimedy (Paralakhemundi), as his successor and named him Dibyasingha Deb. Birakeshari Deb also made a will, by virtue of which his wife Suryamani Patamahadei became the guardian of all his property. The Raja's will empowered her to conduct the affairs of the Jagannath Temple as long as the adopted son remained a minor. The will mentioned that she would be authorized to adopt another son in the event of an untimely demise of the adopted son.

The dowager Rani Suryamani Patamahadei obtained a certificate from the Civil Court appointing her as the guardian of the minor and his estates under Act XI of 1858. In the meanwhile, alleging problems in the Rani's administration, the Raja of Kimedy also applied to the government seeking to be allowed to take charge of the minor's estate on the grounds that he was the minor's biological father and, therefore, had the claim to be his guardian.

Against the contending claims of Suryamani Patamahadei and the Raja of Kimedy, the relevant excerpts from the Commissioner's Report read as follows:[1]

---

* The Marathas donated some land to the temple which yielded revenue of Rs 27,000. In the course of time this *mahal* was termed as *Sataishi hazari mahal*. In 1843, the British government transferred this *mahal* consisting of 90 villages in the name of raja.

Since then it came to my knowledge that the Ranee had fallen into the hands of bad advisers, the child was neglected, and that the property was being wasted. Information was given to the Raja of Kimedy, who was alarmed at the news which he received. He came to Pooree to enquire into the matter. Being thoroughly disgusted of the Ranee's misconduct and mismanagement, he is about to petition to the Civil Court to revoke the certificate and to restore to him his child.

I apprehend that the Civil Court will not have the power to grant his request or in any way to interfere with the Ranee.

The Commissioner further observed:

It appears to me in every point of view, that it is desirable and indeed necessary that the Collector should take charge of the minor under the Court of Wards. Without entering into details, I must say that I believe that the Ranee is wholly unfit to retain the charge of the boy, the sooner he is removed from her care, the better.

He also observed, 'It cannot be however denied that considerable embarrassment will result from the assumption of the charge of the minor's property in consequence of the superintendence of the Temple being vested in the head of the family.' He went on to say, 'It will be easy on the other hand to make over the duty with adequate security to the Rajah of Kimedy or some other qualified member of the Hindoo community but the objection will always remain that Government in its capacity of Court of Wards is in (sic) the last resort the real manager of the Temple.' According to him, 'We have therefore a choice of evils. Of the least will, I think, be to leave the Temple and its lands with the Ranee and if she neglects or abuses her trust, the Rajah of Kimedy or any other member of the Hindoo community can, I presume, replace her according to Act XX of 1863.'

The government, however, did not want to change the existing arrangement. Therefore, the proposal of appointing the Court of

Wards was rejected. Suryamani Patamahadei was finally accepted and acknowledged as the guardian of the minor and it was agreed that she would look after the estate of the minor as well as the affairs of the temple.

The childhood of Dibyasingha Deb was quite eventful. He was adopted at the tender age of four and moved to the house of the Puri Raja. The Raja of Kimedy was not allowed to meet him due to apprehensions about his possible interference and influence over the child as well as the affairs of the Puri Raja's family. Due to this forced separation, the child would cry most of the time. The rani tried her best to discipline the boy but had to give up finally as he proved to be too stubborn for her to manage.

As a result, the child grew up surrounded by servants employed in the palace. It was noticed that he had become aggressive, misbehaved with people and used vulgar language. In spite of the restrictions placed on him to limit his movements within the palace, he started going out and fell into the company of dubious characters in the town. Although all arrangements were in place for his education, he showed little interest, refusing to study. He even misbehaved with the palace teacher. With bad company came bad habits such as addiction to opium and other intoxicating materials. Deprived of a regular childhood, he gradually descended into bad habits, terrible manners and evil tendencies.

The most unfortunate calamity that happened during his regime was the infamous famine of 1866, which is called *Na'anka Durbhikhya*, i.e., the famine during 9th *anka* as this catastrophic famine occurred during the 9th regnal year of Raja Dibyasingha Deb (AD 1862–1877).

Natural calamities like famine, flood and cyclones have been perennial companions of Odisha. The unprecedented and catastrophic famine of 1866 in which one-third of the population starved to death became a turning point in the region's history. It exposed the serious lapses and weaknesses of the colonial administration in Odisha and at the same time spurred the social consciousness of the people. The Famine Commission was established with Justice George Campbell as president and H.L. Dampier and Col W.E. Morton as members to enquire into the famine. The Commission submitted its report in 1867.

The famine gave rise to a new collective consciousness and awoke the nascent middle class with the development of printing press and formation of public associations. There was a resurgence of public opinion highlighting the lethargy and apathy of the colonial administration. The founding of Cuttack Printing Press in 1866 followed by Utkal Printing Company in Balasore and the emergence of *Utkal Dipika* at Cuttack by Gourisankar Ray in 1866 were the immediate outcomes of the post-famine consciousness and became a vehicle of ventilation of the voice of the people.[2]

Sri Pyarimohan Acharya, who witnessed the famine, in his celebrated work *Odishara Itihasa* published in 1879, has given a first-hand account of the famine:

> One feels stunned when one remembers the shocking events that took place at that time. It is impossible to give a faithful picture of the horrors of the famine that came accompanied by death itself. The towns were filled with sorrowful shrieks of thousands of men, women and children who had been reduced to mere skeletons. The crematory grounds near the towns and villages were full of innumerable dead bodies and upon them vultures and jackals feasted to their hearts' content. Men and women forsook their natural instincts owing to the unbearable pangs of hunger. Parents cast away their starving children before wild animals to be devoured by them. Some even ate the dead bodies of their own children like demons. Social evils such as murder, suicide etc. became a very common thing at the time. Some people tried to live upon wild shrubs and inedible materials.[3]

Ananta Das, a victim of the famine, who embraced Christianity subsequently, has vividly described the famine that he experienced, in his autobiography titled *Ananta Dasanka atma jibani*.[4]

Dibyasingha Deb came of age in 1874 and took over the reins of administration from his adoptive mother. He also became the superintendent of the Jagannath Temple. With this, bad times gripped the institution. Inauspicious and dangerous events started occurring one after another. For example, during the Car Festival of 1875, three large stone slabs fell from a height of 40 feet inside the temple. This caused large cracks in the temple walls. This was considered an ominous sign. The idols were shifted to *Anasara pindhi*—the floor in between the Kalahata door and the inner wooden crossbar—and the Raja wrote a letter to the British collector on 18 October 1875 requesting repair work to be undertaken by a Hindu engineer. One Purna Chandra Sarkar was engaged for this purpose, who reported that the accident was caused due to lightning. The repair works were completed in March 1876.

Around this time, the Raja became very unpopular among the *sebaks* due to the mismanagement of temple affairs and lack of transparency in maintaining accounts. The Raja had brought to the notice of the government that the income from the temple was insufficient to meet various expenses pertaining to its upkeep. He mentioned that he was spending Rs 15,000 annually from his own pocket to meet the deficit. In the absence of any positive response from the British government, he started adopting various means to recoup the deficit, which brought him into conflict with the *sebaks*.

In a rare happening, the servitors and priests of the temple resorted to publicly criticizing and complaining against the Raja of Puri. They dubbed the ruler an enemy. The servitors sent a petition to Commissioner T.E. Ravenshaw complaining against the 'mismanagement of the affairs of the Temple by the Raja of Puri'.[5] They alleged that the Raja was charging money from pilgrims for attending certain ceremonies of the temple such as binding *dhwaja* (flags) on the wheel at the top of the temple.

It was also alleged that the Raja had resorted to accepting bribes to appoint various persons to several positions in the temple, which were exclusively hereditarily reserved for *sebaks*.

Such appointments led to fights between the existing *sebaks* and the newly appointed *sebaks* resulting in serious irregularities in the *puja* rituals in the temple. The complaint alleged that huge sums were collected from offerings by the pilgrims on the throne of Jagannath in the form of money or gold *mohurs* (coins), but no accounts were maintained of such income.

There were also charges of misappropriation of money and valuable ornaments offered to the deities. The Raja was even accused of allowing adulteration in the preparation of *bhog* offered to the deities, thus compromising the purity and quality of the food offerings. The *sebaks* complained about the reduction of *khei* (the portion of the *bhog*) they were entitled to. The *sebaks* wrote, 'The Raja is a mere puppet and tool of oppression in the hands of low, ignorant and menial servants.' In the petition, they blamed the Raja for 'utter inefficiency and mismanagement' and added that 'the government may reconsider the matter of superintendence of the Temple being continued to be vested in the Raja'. It is clear from this petition that the *sebaks* looked upon the British government as saviours of the temple from ruin.

But in 1876, the government repealed Section 4 of Act 10 of 1840[6] and transferred full control of the temple affairs to the superintendent (in this case Dibyasingha Deb). Therefore, Commissioner Ravenshaw refused to interfere. In his order dated 5 August 1876, he observed, 'This is not a matter in which this office can interfere. The Raja is responsible for the proper management of the Temple which is infested (*sic*) by the *Sewuks* or attendants who set the Rajah's authority at defiance.'

Another misfortune arose for the Raja in February 1877. The Jagannath Temple witnessed a huge rush of pilgrims for Dola Purnima and Govinda Dwadashi, two important festivals celebrated at the Temple. A massive stampede occurred at the Lion Gate and 11 people were crushed to death. The Commissioner conducted an enquiry into this tragedy and submitted a report to the government on 23 April 1877 'upon the lamentable loss of life in the Puri Temple'.

The report was submitted to Ashley Eden, the Lieutenant Governor of Bengal. The opinion of the Lieutenant Governor was conveyed to the Commissioner by the Secretary to the government who wrote, 'Mr Eden notices that you acquit the local civil officers of all blame though they cannot be held entirely free from blame on the ground of want of foresight and of unpreparedness.' But he admitted that 'they exerted themselves to the utmost for which they deserve commendation. It is only to be regretted that from insufficient means of controlling the internal arrangements of the Temple, they were unable to prevent the loss of life.'[7]

The communication mentioned, 'The responsibility for failure rests mainly, in your opinion, with the Rajah of Pooree, and the Lieutenant Governor concurs with his view. He is the Superintendent of the Temple and has sole authority and control over the internal arrangements.'

Regarding the accident, the communication elaborated:

> To him it must have been known that the two festivals coming in close proximity to each other, would bring together a most unusual concourse of pilgrims, for even if the Oriya Pundits were not prepared to recognize in the day all the conditions that go to make up a true Govind Dvadasi, yet it was known to the Hindoos generally and to him necessarily as the Head of the Hindoo community at Pooree that throughout Hindoostan the festival would be observed and consequently that pilgrims from a distance would come in unusual numbers to the shrine of Juggernath yet notwithstanding this knowledge and this responsibility the Rajah simply did nothing.
>
> He closed the doors on the Temple on the 19th February but only on the 21st did he send to the Magistrate any information that an unusual concourse was probable. The Magistrate was out in the district, which however at such a time should not have been the case. Not until his return with the Superintendent of Police on the 23rd did he learn that the gates had been closed for days and that there was an enormous gathering of highly excited pilgrims in the town.

On that very day, the Joint Magistrate with forty Policemen had gone down on the Rajah's requisition and had opened the gates, but finding that with such a small body of Police it was impossible to keep order and after being knocked down and severely handled in the throng himself, he had found it necessary to close the gates.

The Rajah's people on this occasion were not present and gave no assistance and there can be little doubt that from the beginning and throughout the difficulties of subsequent days the Rajah, finding that proper arrangements would cost money, labour and responsibility, endeavored (sic) to throw the whole duty on the Magistrate.

The first serious accident occurred on the 24th February. On that day at noon, there being a force of 100 Policemen ready, the Hindoo Deputy Collector went to the Rajah to ask that the gates might be opened. The Rajah excused himself on the ground that the sacred food must be prepared with the gates shut and would not be ready till the afternoon. As a matter of fact it appears that the rajah had made no preparations at all. There seems to have been a real necessity for opening the gates and allowing the pilgrims in to the Temple.

The multitude was excited and there was every danger of a disastrous tumult. Armstrong, the Magistrate, accordingly determined to open the gates at midnight, when he thought that the throng would be lessened but it appears that it was an important object with the pilgrims to see the idol on that particular night before the bathing and the special and auspicious time for bathing was just before the sunrise.

The pilgrims rushed into the temple with the most excitement when two persons were crushed to death. The doors were instantly closed.

The events of the 25th, the day of Dol Jattra, was almost repetition of those of the 24th, save that they were more disastrous, nine persons being killed, by the crash that followed the opening of the gates. Here again the crash increased by the Rajah keeping the gates shut for some hours under the pretense (*sic*) of preparing sacred food, while the numbers waiting to enter the Temple were increasing and becoming more impatient.

The Secretary to the government wrote to the Commissioner on the conduct of the Raja, whose neglect and lack of control over his subordinates in the immediate charge of the temple resulted in the disaster. The Lieutenant Governor agreed with the suggestion of the Commissioner that the *sannad* and *khillat* (vestment of honour or title) which were due to be conferred upon him should be temporarily withheld until the Raja submitted a scheme in consultation with a 'Committee of Hindoo gentlemen' for regulating the visits of large bodies of pilgrims to prevent recurrence of such incidents.

Raja Dibyasingha Deb did not like the idea of this committee as he feared that it might cause him 'loss of power and influence'. The committee could not progress with its work in the face of the lack of cooperation from the Raja. Not receiving any help from the Gajapati, Armstrong, the District Magistrate, asked Mohunt Narain Das and Tarakanta Vidyasagar to frame draft rules as they were 'well acquainted with the Temple and all that goes on within.'[8]

After this the British government followed a deliberate policy of humiliating Dibyasingha Deb. The following incident proves this. By virtue of having a dual status—Thakur Raja and Raja of Khurda—the Gajapati was always accorded a special status of respect and reverence. He was given precedence over other feudatory or Gadajat chiefs of Odisha. Lieutenant Governor Sir Richard Temple presided over the darbar held at Cuttack in 1874 to grant *sannad* to the Gadajat kings.

At the darbar, Dibyasingha Deb was present but his chair was numbered 27. He was placed at the head of zamindars but below the chiefs or Gadajat kings. This seating arrangement was not in line with conventional practice and was very insulting for the Gajapati. This caused dissatisfaction and discomfort not only to Dibyasingha Deb but also to other feudatory chiefs. The other kings were almost as much hurt as their quondam superior, and, in deference to their wishes, chair no. 27 was brought to the head of the row, but placed a little in the rear. The Raja deliberately disregarded this arrangement, and his chair was then placed at such a distance as to make it to the top of the second row.

The young Gajapati rose and demanded permission to leave the darbar. On being refused, he waited silently and sullenly until the ceremony was over and then went off to Puri without taking leave. A few days later, the Commissioner announced that although the government had decided to confer the title of 'Maharaja' on the Puri Raja, the proposal had been dropped as the chief 'had left so discourteously' from the darbar.[9] It becomes amply clear that this was a ploy and an intentional act on the part of the British government to harass and demean the young Gajapati.

In the meanwhile, with the introduction of the Royal Titles Act 1876,* an Act of the Parliament of the United Kingdom, Queen Victoria (and subsequent monarchs) was officially recognized as the 'Empress of India'. The queen assumed this title in 1876, under the encouragement of Prime Minister Benjamin Disraeli. Subsequent to this, the Prince of Wales held a darbar in Calcutta in 1876. The Raja of Puri along with his chief advisor Pandit Tarakanta Vidyasagar went to Calcutta to attend the darbar. Here too the Gajapati was humiliated regarding his seating arrangement. At the darbar, in the hierarchical order of the attending rajas, the Raja of Puri was assigned the 31st place. As was expected, the Raja felt extremely offended.

On 1 January 1878, a darbar was held in Puri to mark the completion of one year of Queen Victoria assuming the title of Empress of India. A temporary structure was erected on the main grand road. Two decorated chairs, one meant for the Collector and another for the Raja, were placed and the darbar began with

---

* The long title of the Act is 'An Act to enable Her Most Gracious Majesty to make an addition to the Royal Style and Titles appertaining to the Imperial Crown of the United Kingdom and its Dependencies'. It was repealed by the Indian Independence Act of 1947 when the country became free of its colonial masters.

a ceremonial gun salute. A letter of felicitation was read out with people chanting the victory of Queen Victoria, and pundits recited shlokas invoking God's blessings for the empress. The darbar went off smoothly but one chair lay vacant throughout as the Raja did not turn up. This action was not looked upon kindly by the government.[10]

Homicidal Raja

As mentioned earlier, the draft rules regulating the visit of large bodies of pilgrims into the temple suggested the appointment of a Hindu manager for the temple, preferably a retired officer. Before the draft rules could be considered by the Magistrate, a grave situation unfolded leading to the arrest and conviction of Raja Dibyasingha Deb on charges of homicide.

The government of India had accepted the suggestion of the government of Bengal and postponed the presentation of *sannad* of 'Maharaja' to Dibyasingha Deb till 1877. But by 1878, he had received the sentence of transportation for life. After the conviction, the British government decided to cancel the conferring of the title. In this unprecedented tragic case, Dibyasingha Deb reduced himself to the lowly position of a convict from the exalted status of the Gajapati Maharaja of Puri.

Let us now look at the events that led to this unusual situation.

A *sadhu* (monk) by the name of Siba Das was staying in a *matha* (religious institution) at Damodarpur, 6 miles from Puri. He was a very religious man and was held in high esteem by the local people. He enjoyed a large following of disciples and earned the reputation of possessing supernatural powers of healing and curing people of various ailments. Suryamani Patamahadei was one of his followers and trusted him greatly.

The dowager Rani called him to the palace and requested him to cure Dibyasingha Deb, who was suspected to have lost his senses. The Raja often behaved cruelly, beating his servants with heavy sticks. This behaviour worried the Rani and she suspected the Gajapati of suffering from a mental illness. This was not the first time that she had approached Siba Das for help. On an earlier occasion, the monk had given the Rani some ash and asked her to give it to Dibyasingha Deb. The Puri King, however, refused to take the ash. Somehow, the servants of Dibyasingha Deb made him believe that the Rani was planning to poison him. Not deterred by this earlier incident, the Rani still believed that Siba Das would be able to cure the Raja.

Dibyasingha Deb harboured an aversion towards Siba Das. Once, the *sadhu* had insulted him by calling him a derogatory term *telenga* ('being no scion of the true stock') and commenting that opium had robbed him of all senses. This had angered and annoyed the Raja. So when news reached Dibyasingha that the Rani had again consulted Siba Das to treat him for lunacy, he was very upset and decided to teach the *sadhu* a lesson.

On 23 February 1878, the Raja sent his servant Gopi Singh and *sejiapat* (a category of servant) Maharatha to Damodarpur with a message that the *sadhu* was required to visit the palace to treat someone who had fallen sick. The *sadhu* was to attend to the patient and prescribe medicine for his recovery. On receiving the summons, the *sadhu* left for the palace with three disciples—Patita Nayak, Balakrushna Mishra and Nidhi Mishra. Another disciple, Nila Behera, joined them on their way at Janakadeipur.

From details that emerged later during the investigation into his death, during the journey Siba Das was wearing a dhoti with a towel thrown on his shoulder. He had a bead necklace around his neck. He and his disciples stopped for a while on the way and had bhang and smoked ganja. They also met the head constable of the Puri police station, Giridharilal Das. By the time the *sadhu* reached the palace with his disciples, it was dark. Once there, only the *sadhu* was allowed to go inside the palace while his four disciples remained outside the gate.

Siba Das was led to the gymnasium where the Raja practised wrestling. The door was closed behind the *sadhu* so that he could not escape. The Raja and nine other persons were waiting there.

When Dibyasingha's eyes fell on Siba Das, he went wild with rage and hit him on the head with a heavy stick, directing others 'to kill the bastard'. When the others encircled him, Siba Das, a healthy and strongly built person, resisted. He tried to flee but could not. He tried to jump over the wall but failed. He was showered with powerful blows from the Raja and his minions. Siba Das fell on the ground.

Two scavengers, Bana Naik and Ganesh Naik, took ordure from a pot and thrust it into the *sadhu's* mouth. As Siba Das resisted, more such stuffing went on with greater force. Ultimately, Siba Das was completely overpowered, but that only meant that the intensity of the torture increased.

The Raja's servants inserted an iron wire into his genitals and poured quicklime on them. He was bound and gagged in order to silence him. Forty pieces of cork were forced into his rectum, one after another by forcing them through the anus. He was suffering from elephantiasis of the scrotum which was roasted with a fire torch. His whole body was discoloured with fire marks. His screams with the increasing torture inflicted by the King's accomplices accelerated the anger and fury of Dibyasingha Deb. After four hours of sustained torture, the *sadhu* stopped screaming—he had become unconscious. There was no body movement. Assuming that the *sadhu* was dead, the servants dragged the body and threw it into a drain outside the palace.

When Siba Das gained consciousness around midnight, he dragged himself, crawled and made his way with difficulty and severe pain to the Lion Gate not far from the Raja's palace. He was naked and his body was full of wounds, swellings and burn injuries, with blood oozing from many areas. Breathless, he shouted for his disciples: 'Oh Nila! Oh Patita! Come quickly to me. I am dying.'

Hearing his screams, his disciples, who were dozing near the gate, ran to him. They were shocked to see their guru in such a pitiable condition. As he begged for water, Patita got some and helped him drink it. One of them rushed to the police station, where Giridharilal Das, the head constable, was present. He arranged for the *sadhu* to be taken to the hospital immediately. Nasiram Goshal, a doctor, rushed to the hospital in the dead of the night and examined the *sadhu*. He almost lost all hope of the *sadhu* surviving after seeing his condition. He was able to take out about 32 pieces of corks from his rectum. It was with a good dose of opium that Siba Das's pain could be controlled.

District Magistrate Armstrong received the news of the heinous crime in the morning. He rushed to the hospital. Superintendent of police Mahanand Gupta and Deputy Magistrate Nabin Chandra Sen joined him. Siba Das was writhing in pain, although he had been heavily drugged with opium to reduce his suffering, and was in no condition to make a statement. The pain and the opium made Siba Das incoherent. Nonetheless, Armstrong sat down to make note of his declaration.

Siba Das managed to say that the Raja and his servants had done this to him. Armstrong directed the Deputy Magistrate to conduct an enquiry in the palace where the crime allegedly took place. The Deputy Magistrate found blood and faeces on the floor of the gymnasium and the place bore marks of a violent struggle. Siba Das's necklace was found lying near the palace. A report along with all the evidence was submitted to the Collector. After a preliminary investigation, backed by evidence, the police concluded that Siba Das had been brutally assaulted inside the palace.

When Siba Das was at the hospital, a large number of disciples used to gather every day to see him. While undergoing great suffering due to the painful procedure of his treatment, the *sadhu* developed symptoms of tetanus. At this time, 15 servants of the palace were brought before him for identification. He identified nine of them: Surajan Upadhya, Gopi Routra, Daitani Singh, Gopal Das, Narayan Bahinipati, Baji Santra, Arjun Singh, Ganesh Naik and Bana Naik. On the order of the Magistrate, Dibyasingha Deb and nine of his servants were arrested.

Armstrong submitted a report to Commissioner Ravenshaw but the Commissioner was not satisfied with the police report. He thought the investigation did not present the full picture.

Ravenshaw found the entire episode to be unbelievable and incredible. He wanted the motive behind the Raja's ghastly deed to be properly investigated. Armstrong was now at odds with his senior. In his report to the Commissioner on 6 March, Armstrong remarked that it was not necessary for the prosecution to assign motives for the action of criminals. According to him, it was well known that 'persons whose guiding rule of life is not common sense often act from motives which to wise men appear absurd and insufficient'.[11]

In a further report to the Commissioner on 9 March, based on the civil surgeon's letter, Armstrong informed, 'The patient Shiva Das has symptoms of tetanus accessing to terrible scorching and the mortifying sores arising there from. There is little hope of his recovery. The case, therefore, is beginning to assume the appearance of a case of murder and it is no longer safe to allow any of the prisoners to be at large.'[12]

Siba Das succumbed to his injuries on 10 March.

On 11 March, the case came up for trial before Armstrong's court. During the trial, the defence refused to cross-examine the witnesses and did not say anything in self-defence. It was clear that they had planned to do this keeping in view the trial in the Sessions Court, where they were expecting to fight better. On the basis of evidence collected by police, Armstrong charged the Gajapati and his nine servants with murder under Section 302 of the IPC and forwarded them to the Sessions Court.

The Trial

The trial in the Sessions Court at Cuttack started on 26 March 1878 and was presided over by Judge Dickens. The trial proceedings attracted massive attention. John Beames in his memoir writes, 'Immense excitement was aroused all over Orissa and crowds assembled round the court every day during the trial.'[13] The court was packed with people and those who could not get in waited outside the jail to catch a glimpse of the Gajapati of Puri.

Nearly 5,000 people gathered around the court. Many chanted *Hori Bol* praying for the Raja. Many sat day and night in the court verandahs without returning to their homes.

Utkal Dipika reported that one well in the court premises almost dried up as the huge crowds used the water for drinking and even for bathing for days together.[14] Many people were seen silently standing and praying for the release of the Raja. The scenes demonstrated 'no end to Oriya loyalty to royalty'.[15] This display of reverence was to none but Gajapati Dibyasingha Deb, the Raja of Puri and *Adyasebak* of Lord Jagannath. Most people did not seem to care that the Raja was a convict in a murder case.

When the trial began, the first to give evidence was the compounder of the Puri hospital. He testified the following: 'I was present when Siba Das was brought to the hospital. Thirty three corks were removed from his rectum. Next day five more corks were removed after administering digestive medicine. Later, the *sadhu* died.'

The second witness was Mr Beck, the road cess engineer, who presented a location map of the occurrence of the crime. Sub-inspector Rama Rao, who came next, said that lime water was coming out from the private parts of the *sadhu*, and that his body bore marks of brutal torture. Smell of ordure came from his mouth. Gopi Singh, who had accompanied the *sadhu* to the palace, recalled that Siba Das was screaming and calling out for help around midnight saying he was dying. He along with the *sadhu*'s disciples found Siba Das lying naked on the ground in immense pain and begging for water. Nila rushed to call Giridhari Babu from the police station.* Next came Nila Behera and Patita Nayak as witnesses.

The depositions of Nidhi Mishra and Balakrushna Mishra were recorded on 28 March. The same day, constables Narayan Mohanty and Darhan Singh stated that they heard the *sadhu*

---

* Gopi Singh then went on to say, 'I am a child. I cannot say anything more.' At that point the judge intervened saying, 'You are 32 years old. You are saying you are a child. When will you grow up?'

shouting for water when they were on their rounds at the palace. Head constable Giridharilal Das on 29 March confirmed that he took the *sadhu* to the hospital. Krupasindhu Das, a Sub-Inspector, also recorded his statement.

Nasiram Ghosal, the doctor who treated Siba Das, narrated on 30 March the state of the *sadhu's* health and the nature of his injuries. He said there were burn marks and also swellings due to beatings all over the body. Cork pieces and blood were coming out of his rectum. On the first day of treatment, 33 pieces of cork were removed from his rectum. His scrotum had swollen. His pulse rate was low and he was reeling under acute pain. When asked, the *sadhu* replied, 'Raja has inflicted this pain on me.' Later he succumbed to tetanus. Dr Ghosal conducted the post-mortem in the presence of Mahanta Narayan Das. Dr B.N. Gupta, Civil Surgeon of Puri, was in agreement with Dr Ghosal.

It was then the turn of barrister Evans, who had appeared for Dibyasingha Deb. It was his first appearance in Odisha. He used to charge Rs 1,000 per appearance besides travel expenses. He argued for three-and-a-half hours to prove the innocence of the Raja. He claimed initially that the Raja was an honourable person and he could not or would not have caused the disrobing of the *sadhu*. Countering the witnesses, he stated that the claims of low-caste persons stripping the *sadhu* and putting human excreta into his mouth were imaginary and incorrect because such persons would not have been allowed to enter the palace premises as it was believed that the palace would become impure.

Evans argued that putting ordure into the mouth of the *sadhu* was a false accusation. How was it that the odour was coming from his mouth even after washing it and drinking water, he asked. He argued that claims of putting corks into the rectum were also imaginary and motivated. He explained that in order to push corks into his rectum, the *sadhu* would be required to lie facing downwards. Without such a posture it was impossible to insert corks into the rectum. In such a posture, how could he see the persons who allegedly executed such an act? Further, when he was suffering from so much pain, how could he remember the names of such people?

Quoting a case in Punjab to support his statement, Evans argued that complainants often took the names of people with whom they had enmity to take revenge. He added that the Raja's Dewan and other employees had already deposed that Dibyasingha Deb was holding *katcheri* at the palace till 11 p.m. that day. The barrister mentioned that there was never any instance of the Raja beating anyone. Regarding police witnesses, Evans insisted their statements were motivated and improper and said the Lieutenant Governor had condemned the police action.[16]

After prolonged arguments by barrister Evans, Nabin Chandra Sen, the Deputy Collector of Puri, deposed on behalf of Siba Das. He said the Raja had been proved guilty. When the deceased was tortured for four hours, *mashaals* (firelight) were burning and there was light around. Hence there was no difficulty in seeing and identifying the accused who were torturing him. Siba Das was a *bairagi* (a saintly man detached from family life) and not a person who would tell a lie. He added that there were innumerable instances of Hindus inflicting pain on others by engaging low-caste persons. He pointed out that since the Raja was a honourable man, there was no difficulty for many people to appear as witnesses in his support.[17]

After arguments and counter-arguments, the judge took the views of the assessors, Kali Mohan Ghosal and Babu Bihari Lal Pandit. In those days assessors were employed in the court to assist European judges. Both the assessors told the court that the Raja and the other accused were innocent as killing by causing pain had not been established and proven.[18]

11 March 1878. Judgement Day! About 25 constables had taken up position when the judge reached the court at 11 a.m. A Magistrate accompanied him. The courtroom was packed; there was not an inch for anyone to move. An uneasy calm and anxiety was palpable in the courtroom. The accused were presented before the court. Dibyasingha Deb and the other co-accused were asked

to stand. The Raja was not allowed to take a seat. This was taken as a bad sign and led to anxious speculation about the verdict.

Finally, the judge delivered the historic judgment in a handwritten order of 34 pages. He divided his order into three parts: commission of crime, place of crime and doctor's deposition. The judge held the Raja and four of his servants guilty of murder and sentenced them with transportation for life. The four servants were Sarjan Upadhya, Narayan Bahinipati, Gopi Routra and Gopal Das. The other five were acquitted for lack of evidence. The guilty were immediately frisked away and taken to the Cuttack jail.

The verdict was an unprecedented event. For the first time in Odisha, the Raja of Puri was convicted of a crime and sentenced with transportation for life. This extraordinary punishment was and continues to be a black spot in the history of the Gajapati tradition.

The court verdict spread like wildfire. Everyone, old and young, was shocked. They could not even imagine such an outcome, let alone accept it. A sense of disbelief, disquiet and pain engulfed the whole of Cuttack. The news quickly started spreading to other parts of the state.

Since the Gajapati is revered as the first servant of Lord Jagannath and treated as 'Chalanti Vishnu', people were overcome by a sense of revolt and indignation over the judgment. They felt a sense of hurt and humiliation. The ruling was seen not only as an insult to the Gajapati but also as blow to Lord Jagannath.

For the first time, this shook the confidence and belief of the people in the invincibility of the Gajapati. In spite of the tumultuous history through the Hindu, Mughal, Afghan and Maratha periods and occupation by East India Company since 1803, the people had always held the Gajapati in high esteem for his intimate association with the Jagannath Temple. He was revered as Vishnu incarnate. His conviction left them shocked and surprised, stunned into a sense of disbelief.

The verdict had widespread impact. The conviction of the Gajapati shifted the focus from the crime and brought him great sympathy. 'King can do no wrong' became the dominant sentiment. The people could under no circumstance accept the very rare and unusual conviction. How could the Gajapati, the Thakur Raja of Puri, be held guilty?

The speed at which the trial was conducted and verdict passed appeared very unusual. The incident with Siba Das occurred in February; the case was filed in March; the trial began in March itself; and the judgment came in April. After the judgment, an appeal was submitted to the Calcutta High Court, which passed its verdict in the same month (details later). In this case, the administration of justice was unusually fast and this became a subject of discussion and speculation.

The fast-tracking of the case was on account of the involvement of a very important person—the Raja of Puri. The conviction provided a leverage and advantage to the ruling British administrators at Puri and Cuttack at the level of Collector and Commissioner who were extremely critical of the functioning of the Raja and were anxious to repeal Act X of 1840, which related to the administration of the Jagannath Temple. The record of available correspondence demonstrates the approach and adverse attitude of the local bureaucracy against the Gajapati. Therefore, it is very possible that they took undue interest in establishing the case, expediting the trial and proving the Gajapati guilty. The order of conviction handed the British a much desired outcome and created a political opportunity for them. It was believed that by convicting the Raja, the British wanted to convey their superiority and even make possible inroads into the affairs of the Jagannath Temple.

The undue interest and haste shown by District Magistrate Armstrong reflected a motive to somehow put the Gajapati in a fix. It also pointed to a well-thought-out plan of conspiracy to justify a predetermined action. Initially, the Raja of Puri and his accomplices were charged with offence under Section 326 of the IPC for voluntarily causing grievous hurt by dangerous weapons or means to cause death. When Siba Das died on 10 March, Armstrong changed the charge to one of committing murder under Section

302. As the *sadhu* died of tetanus a few days after injuries were caused to him, it is highly debatable whether it was appropriate to charge the Gajapati with murder. Armstrong's change of stance resulted in a sentence for the Gajapati that was viewed as too harsh and disproportionate to the alleged offence.

Nabin Chandra Sen, the Deputy Magistrate of Puri, was leading the prosecution. Collector Armstrong was very happy with Sen's efforts. Armstrong had warned him not to move alone or too soon from Cuttack for the fear of being attacked by people. Sen was very keen to return to Puri after the case because he had left his newborn baby there. He returned escorted by police guards and then called on Armstrong, who embraced him and thanked him for his efforts.

Armstrong was very averse to the argument of the defence that the title 'Raja' signified a venerable institution and that the Raja of Puri was very honourable. He appreciated Sen for his argument against holding the Raja of Puri as a good man just because of his position. Armstrong took out a small note and handed it over to Sen. It read:[19]

> The history of Orissa has always been stained with blood, when Raja Prataprudra died, his commander-in-Chief, Gobinda Bidyadhar, murdered the Raja's two minor sons and ascended the throne. He founded the Bhoi dynasty. Gobinda Bidyadhar's son, Chakrapratap, was poisoned by his son Narasingh, who captured the throne. Mukund Harichandan entered the palace riding a palanquin and disguised as a woman, and assassinated Narasingh. Mukund became king and founded the Chalukya dynasty. He lost his life in a battle with the Muslim invaders of Orissa. Ramachandra, who was the son of Gobinda Bidyadhar's general, murdered the Saura tribal sardar of Khurda and became king. This is how the line of the kings of Khurda began, who are now called the rajas of Puri.

Sen went through the note but mentioned that evidence against the character of the accused or that of his ancestors was not admissible in a court of law. Armstrong was annoyed and disheartened by this remark. He told Sen to go through the verdict of the Sessions Court judge again and find new arguments to uphold the Raja's guilt at the time of appeal at the Calcutta High Court. Armstrong had by then decided that if the Raja of Puri appealed against the verdict, Sen would go to Calcutta and prosecute the case for the government.

Utkal Dipika had extensively covered the case. It followed a cautious approach in not commenting on the Sessions Court judgment as it was to be appealed before the High Court. It projected the widespread feelings of pain and sorrow of the people at the unbelievable judgment holding their venerated Raja as guilty.[20] *Utkal Dipika* published a poem, 'Puri Raninkara Rodana' (The Lament of the Queen of Puri) on 20 April 1878. The poem was an expression of the deep sorrow of the Rani over her husband's conviction and transportation to what was then known as 'Kaala Pani Jail'.[21] The poem, translated in English, reads as under:

Today in the king's palace,
like a madwoman
lives the chief queen of Puri.

Lying on the floor she cries frantically
the beautiful woman she is
completely shattered now.

Her child tugs at her sari end and asks,
'Why are you crying, ma?'
She doesn't look at the little prince,
she keeps shedding tears with a heavy heart.

It's as if some cruel hunter's sharp arrow pierced her soul
she's terrified, she's deeply perturbed
and she wails inconsolably.

Is this true my revered husband,
your reputation has been sullied,
you now suffer such insurmountable hardship.

You are my sweetheart,
you are inside a prison in your youth
why the callous breath still flows through this helpless woman?

Almighty God what's your wish
why torment me this way?
you floated me in a wave of joy
and then threw me in a well of despondency.

By your blessings
I was married to my beloved man
away from him, I live in gloom
why should I live on?

The sorrow that's impending
like a dark night,
will there ever be a bright morning
while I am still alive?

I pray to you earnestly
Take away my grief
for a woman like me, you are the only hope
you are always welcome!

Those who still yearn for happiness
and wish good luck
would be afraid of you
I only desire to die.

O Lord of the universe, the redeemer of the fallen
annihilate my life
let me be free so that my spirit may roam
where my husband is.

O Lord of the universe,
let me offer another prayer at your feet
blessed by you
let my son become a worthy warrior.

The Raja moved the Calcutta High Court against the Sessions Court judgment. The full bench of the High Court was headed by Sir Richard Garth, Chief Justice, along with two other judges, Sir Jackson and Sir Anshley. The Raja was again defended by barrister Evans, who was assisted by barristers Branson and Manmohan Ghosh. The government was represented by Advocate General G.C. Paul. The hearing commenced on 6 May. Branson argued for the first two days. On the third day, Evans presented his case. The same day, Manmohan Ghosh began his argument and completed it the next day. The Advocate General countered the arguments. The judges gave their verdict on 13 May; they agreed with the Sessions Court, upholding the sentence of Raja Dibyasingha Deb along with two of his servants, Sarjan Upadhya and Narayan Bahinipati. However, the High Court acquitted Gopal Das and Gopi Routra.

Raja Dibyasingha Deb was to be brought to Calcutta before his deportation to the Andamans. But the government feared that riots might break out. Therefore, all arrangements were made with utmost secrecy. Raja Dibyasingha Deb was transported from the jail in a horse carriage in the dark, much before sunrise, and taken to a place called Jobra. He was then ferried to a lighthouse and from where he was taken on a ship to Calcutta and lodged in the Presidency Jail. On 4 September 1878, he was sent to the Andaman Islands aboard a ship. His legs had to be fettered during the voyage as he behaved like a mad man.

The controversial sentence was a predetermined British action of proving a point. The British knew that the Puri Raja, unlike other kings, didn't have the power and paraphernalia of an army or territorial authority. They found him a weak spot to convey a strong point. The crucial issue was the expediency and necessity of the sentence of transportation. Not in all cases of even more heinous crimes was such a sentence given. The reframing of charge and awarding such a sentence in unprecedented haste conveys more to it than it meets the eye.

In an earlier case, feudatory king of Banki, Jagannath Harichandan, was convicted of committing heinous murders of people, including innocent women and infant children, in a dispute over the throne of Banki. Commissioner A.J.M. Mills conducted the murder trial. In a verdict of 21 pages, he held the king guilty and ordered extermination of the Raja of Banki for life at Cuttack. The judgment was delivered on 2 January 1840. The point to note is that for a more heinous foolproof crime, the sentence of extermination was not one of transportation. In Puri Raja's case, the British sense of justice appeared different for obvious reasons.

The verdict and the punishment was a topic of intense discussion among people all over Odisha. It hurt their sentiments so much that it influenced their religious and social feelings for quite some time. But the immediate impact of the Gajapati's incarceration was felt during the Rath Yatra (Car Festival) of 1878. On 13 July 1878, *Utkal Dipika* reported that the attendance that year was the lowest ever—only about one-third of the average of previous years. It said the low attendance was mainly because of the conviction of Dibyasingha Deb. Many believed that Lord Jagannath had also gone with the Raja and that there was no purpose left in attending the Rath Yatra. Some felt that it served no purpose in going to Puri for the *darshan* of Lord Jagannath when the Lord could not exert his power to save his own Raja.[22]

The conviction of Gajapati Dibyasingha Deb was controversial. There were reactions from various quarters of society. Even in later stages, this issue has been examined and commented by writers and the public. Well-known writer Godabarisha Mishra in his novel *Nirbasita* was very critical of the sentence. Another novel, *Nirbasita Gajapati* of Bikram Das, described the saga almost like a fiction. Both the writers took the view that the Gajapati was a victim of British injustice and was not guilty.

Without getting into the factual accuracy of the contents of the novels, such views reflected the dominant society's reaction.

Kunja Bihari Das, a great writer and an author of the celebrated work *Study of Orissa's Folklore* (1953), in one of his poems titled 'Maharajanaka Kalapani', criticised the judgment and wondered whom would the people look upon when their 'Chalanti Vishnu' goes away. The poet argued that the unjust conviction meant that bad days were knocking on the door.[23]

Many petitions, applications and appeals were made to the British government for the release of the Raja.

The Raja of Kimedy, the biological father of Dibyasingha Deb, urged the British Parliament to free his son. He incurred huge expenses in doing so but his efforts did not yield any result.[24]

On 5 January 1887, a petition signed by 1,500 Rajas, zamindars and important personalities was sent to the Lieutenant Governor appealing him to pardon the Raja on the occasion of the golden jubilee year of the reign of Queen Victoria, the Empress of India. After a few days, on 15 January 1887, Sudhal Deb, the Raja of Bamanda, wrote a similar petition. He said it was a tradition to set a few prisoners free on certain special occasions and permit a few deported prisoners to return home. He claimed that the joy of every Indian 'will know no bounds if our Governor General graciously orders the release of the former Raja of Pooree'.[25]

On the occasion of the golden jubilee, the Viceroy of India released 23,007 criminals and 298 civil prisoners from various jails in British India, including the Kala Pani in the Andamans, in February 1887 as 'a means most acceptable to native sentiment'. Raja Dibyasingha Deb was not. In spite of so many appeals, the British government did not relent.[26]

The banished Raja Dibyasingha Deb died of tuberculosis on 25 August 1887 in the Andamans.

13

RANI SURYAMANI PATAMAHADEI
Woman Extraordinaire

Rani Suryamani Patamahadei occupies a special place of distinction in the Gajapati history of Odisha. Born in 1818, she was the daughter of Raja Daityari Singh, the King of Sonepur. An intelligent child, she was fond of hunting and archery. She was said to be brave even when as a young girl.

Once, the young Suryamani and her family were travelling to Puri, at the invitation of the Puri Raja, to witness the Nabakalebara festival. On the way, they stopped at night to rest when Suryamani noticed a crocodile coming dangerously close to their camp, putting her family in imminent danger. She killed the crocodile by shooting from a pistol, and then cut it into pieces with a sword. The crocodile's blood was dripping from her sword.

The word of the girl's bravery reached Raja Ramachandra Deb III (AD 1817–1854). He appreciated her spirit and beauty and decided to get his son, Birakeshari Deb, married to her. She was then 12 years old. Birakeshari Deb became the Gajapati and superintendent of the temple at Puri in 1854 upon his father's death. However, due to his frail health he remained bedridden for about four years and met with an untimely death in 1859.

As he was childless Birakeshari adopted a son a few hours before passing away. The child later came to be known as Dibyasingha Deb (see Chapter 12 for details). Thus, at a young age, Rani Suryamani Patamahadei became a widow and the guardian of her adopted infant son as well as the superintendent of the Puri Jagannath Temple.

As we have seen, she remained the superintendent of the temple till Dibyasingha Deb came of age and took over the supervision of the temple affairs for a brief period till he was incarcerated by the British Government on the charge of murder. At this time, Rani Suryamani again became the guardian of Mukunda Deb, the minor son of Dibyasingha Deb. Overall, she was at the helm of affairs of Puri for 34 long years, as the guardian, first of her son Dibyasingha Deb and later of her grandson Mukunda Deb. During this period, she faced numerous challenges, which she fought bravely and intelligently to save not only the honour and prestige of the Gajapati Maharajas of Odisha but also the pride of the presiding deity of the state, Lord Jagannath. Her able leadership proved that she truly was a woman of substance.

Vacuum in the wake of deportation

The deportation of Raja Dibyasingha Deb to the Andamans created a vacuum in the organization of temple administration. This provided a great opportunity for the local British bureaucracy to push their agenda and undermine the importance of the Raja of Puri. Joseph Armstrong, the Collector of Puri, was very critical of Raja Dibyasingha Deb's conduct and sought to use his conviction as an occasion to remove his family from power in the region. He submitted a report:

> He [Dibyasingh Deb] has by his own act disabled himself from performing his part of the contract. He was placed in charge in order that he might satisfy the Hindoo community by a decent and orderly management of the affairs of the Temple. Since

1876, he neglected his duties and now he stands convicted of a criminal offence for which he was convicted to transportation beyond the sea. This agreement in my opinion is at an end.

With regard to the infant son of the convicted Raja, he observed: 'But it may be said that his son has full rights under that agreement and must succeed to his father's place. This question is of a difficult nature. In my opinion, as matter stands, no claim can be maintained on behalf of the infant to the property and rights of management.' Armstrong went on: 'The misconduct of the nature mentioned above on the part of the head of the family involves all members in its consequences. This is clearly in the spirit of law which attached forfeiture of property as a penalty to certain offences.'

He felt 'that the landed property given to the Rajah to enable him to carry on the services of the Temple is now entirely at the disposal of Government. The Act X of 1840 is now a dead letter and that no further legislation of any kind is necessary in any event'. He wrote that the proper course would be to bring the minor and the property under the Court of Wards.[1] This report from Collector Armstrong was sent to the Commissioner, who forwarded it to higher authorities.

A. Mackenzie, Secretary to the Government of Bengal, communicated the views of Lieutenant Governor Sir Ashley Eden, who opined that the proposed rules be kept in abeyance until a decision regarding future management of the temple was taken. The Lieutenant Governor also communicated his acceptance of the Commissioner's recommendation that the estate should not be brought into the Court of Wards and that the Dowager Rani should manage the estate during the minority of Raja Dibyasingha Deb's son. Thus, after conviction of Gajapati Dibyasingha Deb in 1878, Rani Suryamani Patamahadei became the *Mahafez* (custodian) of the Jagannath Temple and of the family property on behalf of the Raja's minor son Jagannath Jenamani (later changed to Mukunda Deb).[2]

In July 1879, Rani Suryamani made an application to the District Judge of Cuttack on behalf of Jagannath Jenamani for a certificate under Act XL of 1858 designating her as the custodian of the child and the temple as the father of the minor was undergoing life sentence at the Andamans. The Rani's pleader argued that 'owing to the Raja's offence and punishment inflicted, he has suffered such degradation as would under Hindu law cause forfeiture, and vest the whole of the estate in the minor'.

On 12 August 1879, the District Judge granted the application. He observed:

> Unless someone is appointed to act for the minor, his interest is wholly unprotected and the whole property will be sacrificed. There can be no doubt that if the minor was of age, he could have, during his father's banishment from the country under a sentence of transportation, exercised all the necessary powers of management as regard the family property. There being no male member to exercise this power there seems no reason why the minor should not exercise it through a person appointed to act in his behalf. On these grounds, I grant the certificate of administration asked for. This order does not of course in any way affect the right of superintendence of the temple of Juggernath, which is regulated by Act X of 1840.

The order made no reference to the contention that the convicted Raja had lost his rights in his family estate. The District Judge also made it clear that Dibyasingha Deb continued to enjoy his right as the superintendent of the temple.

Regarding the future management of the Jagannath Temple, the Secretary of the Board of Revenue wrote to the Commissioner of Odisha on 15 December 1879 seeking a draft bill. The Commissioner sent the draft Pooree Temple Bill, 1880* containing

---

* It was in 1880 when Lord Ripon became the Governor General of India after Lord Lytton resigned.

23 sections and mentioned that local feeling was strongly in favour of continuation of management in the hands of the Raja of Puri and his family. Keeping in view these sentiments, the Commissioner proposed a committee to run the temple affairs and suggested the Raja of Puri to continue as the Superintendent of the Temple and the Chairman of the committee when he was not incapacitated.

The committee would have a maximum of 10 members. The Commissioner also suggested the appointment of a Deputy Superintendent in the event the Raja was incapacitated and there was no one in his family to take his place. The suggested Deputy Superintendent was to be appointed by the government and the subsequent appointment was to be made by the committee, which had to be approved by the government. It also provided that the Deputy Superintendent would act as an executive officer to maintain accounts and he could only be removed by a civil court.

In a letter dated 11 July 1881, the Secretary to the Government of India suggested to the Government of Bengal to institute a suit for the purpose of appointing trustees to administer the endowment of the Jagannath Temple. The Board of Revenue met on 20 July to 'consider [if] the management of the Temple of Jagannath might be carried out by institution of a suit u/s 539 of the Code of Civil Procedure'. The views of Advocate General G.G. Paul, Legal Remembrancer T. T. Allen and Standing Counsel W. C. Banerjee were sought.

The Advocate General opined that an endowment like that of the Jagannath Temple was not a trust created for public charitable purposes under the meaning of Section 539 of Act X of 1877. Allen held the same view and said the Temple of Jagannath did not come within the scope of the Section. Banerjee felt that so long as Act X of 1840 remained unrepelled, it was impossible for the court to make an order. He added that the present law distinctly declared that the superintendence of the temple, the management of the endowments and the control over the temple officers and servants should vest in the Raja of Khurda for the time being. So long this was the law, the court could not sanction a scheme which should vest the superintendence in any person other than the Raja or even in any person conjointly with him.

In view of the above, the Secretary of the Board of Revenue, in a dispatch to the Secretary to the Government of Bengal on 29 August 1881, wrote, 'It would be useless to apply to Court u/s 539'. He communicated the views of the Board as under:

> It, therefore, appears to the Board that the desired reform cannot be carried out into effect unless recourse is had to legislation. It would perhaps be possible to amend Act X of 1840, instead of repealing it. A single section might be added, giving the Local Government power to suspend the operation of Section 2 of the Act, and to vest the superintendence of the Temple and the management of the endowments, in such persons or body of persons, other than the Rajah of Khoordah.

Accordingly, the Board of Revenue was of the view that it was better to legislate by replacing Act X of 1840 than leaving the matter of 'present state of anarchy and disorder.'[3]

Temple Management by Committee of Trustees

The proposed management of the temple by a committee of trustees, depriving the Raja of Puri from exercising his authority as Superintendent by repealing Act X of 1840, wounded the religious sentiments of the people. It was considered an insult to the Raja of Puri and to Hinduism too. This led to a volley of protests. A memorial by Govind Parichha and other *sebaks* of the temple was sent to the Collector of Puri on 6 July 1882. They pointed out that the *sebas* and *pujas* of the Jagannath Temple were conducted from time immemorial by the Raja of Puri. They raised serious apprehensions regarding the 10 trustees proposed to be appointed for conducting temple affairs. The *sebaks* mentioned that it would be unjust to deprive the Raja of Puri of the privilege of temple management for no fault on his part.

Rani Suryamani Patamahadei strongly petitioned the Lieutenant Governor on 18 July on behalf of the minor Raja against the government's proposal. She pointed out that she was 'conducting *Sebas* and *Pujas* just as they were performed by our former dynasties. None of the Hindus of Bharatbarsha has raised any objection towards our management. None can understand why under these circumstances the Temple management is to be taken away from our family'.

She added:

It will be clear on a reference to the Hindoo community at large, how painful and obstructive to the cause of Hindoo religion will be the interference of the British Government with the management of the honoured *Sebas* and *Pujas*. Specially the opinion of all Pundits and Bairagees of Bharatbarsha should be taken before any action or interference is taken on this matter.

She prayed that the minor Raja should not be deprived of his status of the Superintendent of the Jagannath Temple.

The mahant of Emar Math submitted an appeal on behalf of the mahants of Puri. The representation stated: 'The Temple had been well managed during the minority of Rajah. Under the circumstances, if the management of the holy Temple be (is) taken away from the Raj family of Pooree and entrusted to a Committee, the whole Hindoo community will be aggrieved and the dignity of the Pooree Raj family will be lowered.'

The *sebaks* of the Jagannath Temple told the Commissioner that the superintendence of the holy temple had been vested from a very long time with the ruling family of Puri. The Maharaja had been voluntarily performing the duties in connection with the *sebas* and *pujas* of Jagannath. The Jagannath Temple was well managed by Rani Suryamani Patamahadei. They warned that if the Raja's family was deprived of the management, it would be degrading and painful to the feelings of the Hindu public at large.

They further stated:

The Maharaja of Pooree is the most respectable person among the Hindoos of India. Though there are wealthier Rajas in Hindusthan, none is held by the Hindoos with equal veneration and therefore the petitioners (Brahmin servants of the Temple of Juggernath) do not feel it a degradation to conduct the *Sebas* and *Puja* under his guidance. But they feel it degradation to their honour and position to be guided by a body of men.[4]

They further pointed out that it would be impossible for the members of the committee to be present and supervise the works and services on a daily basis. By excluding the Puri Raja from the management, 'the *Sebas* and *Pujas* of Lord Jagannath will suffer and consequently the cause of Hindu religion will incur a loss'.[5]

Gopinath Misra and other pundits of Puri and of 16 *sasanas* (Brahmin villages) submitted a petition on 22 July. They referred to the *Niladri Mahodaya* and *Kshetra Mahatmyam*,* as per which 'the *Sebas* and *Pujas* of Jagannath cannot be performed in absence and without orders of the Raja of Puri. If anyone other than the Raja is entrusted with the Temple management, it would be derogatory to the Hindoo public at large'.

The District Judge of Cuttack on 14 December granted the application of the Dowager Rani to administer the estate of her minor grandson Mukunda Deb. He observed: 'The minor having been since named Raja Mukunda Deb according to the custom of his family, his guardian Rani Suryamani Patamahadei's application for the substitution of the name of Raja Mukunda Deb in lieu of Jagannath Jenamani is granted for the protection of the minor's interests in the management of his estate and in the conduct of suits.'

F.C. Grant, the District Magistrate and Collector of Puri, however, did not agree with the order and observations of the District Judge. He raised three issues before the Commissioner:

---

* These are religious texts that prescribe temple rituals, mode of their observance and other religious aspects connected with them.

(a) How could anyone administer the estate of Jagannath Jenamani, for the estate belonged to his father who was still alive?

(b) How could Jagannath Jenamani be styled Raja Mukunda Deb during the lifetime of his father?

(c) The title of 'Raja' was not recognized by the British Government as belonging to the Puri royal family.* Therefore, the government might not like to confer the withheld title on Jagannath Jenamani.

In view of this, the Collector declined to proceed with the case, holding that the title of 'Raja' had not been conferred or recognized by the government. Further, Grant held that the title of 'Raja' could not be conferred upon the son while the father was alive as per the family custom. He held that the estate belonged to the father and not to the son.

The Commissioner, however, held that 'although the title of Raja has not been formally conferred by the Government, the same has been assumed by the Raja of Puri or Khurda and has been used in the official papers from time to time'. He agreed with the Collector's view that the title of Raja during the lifetime of the exiled father would not be justified for official usage by the son. He, however, advised the Collector to allow the change of the name Jagannath Jenamani to Raja Makunda Deb to avoid the suits from being barred.

Rani Suryamani Patamahadei submitted two petitions to the Collector on 12 July and 30 July 1883. These were given in response to the *parwana* (notice) issued by the Collector (No. 329 of 26 June 1883) to produce evidence in support of her petitions praying that her grandson's name and title of Raja be conferred by the government. These petitions are historical documents of much

---

*In 1877, the government was about to confer the title of raja on Dibyasingha Deb but this honour was withheld. See Chapter 12 for more details.

significance. The translated version of the first petition from 12 July 1883 as originally available on record is produced here:[6]

> That your petitioner has been called upon in your Perwana No.329 of 26th June 83 to produce evidence before you in support of her petition praying that her grandson's name and title of Raja Makund Deb can be confirmed by Govt. She therefore begs leave to state as follows.
>
> That the Rajas of her (Bhoi) family having ascended the throne of Gajapati dynasty are well known to be hereditary Rajas. This fact is admitted by Orissa Histories and will be manifest from the genealogy of her family. In Sakabda 1503 Raja Ramchandra Deb, the founder of the Bhoi dynasty, ascended the throne and from that time till Sakabda 1736 i.e. till the beginning of the British Supremacy, the Rajas of the said Bhoi family were independent Rajas of Khorda and had to be titled as Maharaja and the era called ankas had to be reckoned from the date of their reign. Again from Sakabda 1737 i.e. from the accession of the British Raj in 1803 till her son Dibyasingha Deb's transportation for life in 1878, though the title of Rajas was used in some of the official letters and in some of the title of Maharajas, yet the general public were addressing the Rajas of her family as Maharajas and they were still addressing them as such. Again in the almanac of this country and also in the horoscope of the people the name of the Maharaja and his Anka are as a rule entered. Hence there is no doubt that the Rajas of her family were hereditarily called as Maharajas from time immemorial. Even under the British Govt. though they were addressed as Rajas in official papers, yet they were designated by the Public as Maharajas. The ancient Madala Panji, the almanac of the Country, the Histories of Orissa Sutton, Hunters, Pyarimohan Acharya and Shib Chandra Shome, the copy books of old documents in the Registration office, the documents filed herewith and the Settlement papers fully bear testimony to the foregoing fact i.e. the title of Rajas was hereditary in their family. Besides the statement which was prepared in your office

with reference to Govt. circular dated 20th June 59 containing the names of the titled chiefs of this district will show that the title of Raja was hereditary in her family.

2nd- The Parwana No. 577 found by the Collector of Pooree dated 16th July 77 shows that Govt. was pleased to grant her son Dibyasingha Deb a Sanad confirming his Maharaja title. That Sanad was however withheld for a short time only. You will see that they who hold the title of Rajas are invested by the Govt. with the title of Maharaja. There is no instance of titling one as Maharaja if he be not a Raja in the first instance. If Govt. had not accepted the hereditary title of Raja of her family then how could it grant the title of Maharaja to her son.

3rd – In the District of Pooree the Brahmins of 16 sasans and 32 parahs come to Pooree on Pousha and Gamha Purnima days to celebrate the ceremony of yearly coronation of the Maharajas of her family and present them with golden thread (Jagyoupabita, according to the dictates of the Shastras).

There has been a practice from time immemorial that in every fourth generation, the name of the Raja should recur. This will be borne out by the genealogy of her family, the old Madala Panji, the almanac of the country. Accordingly, her grandson being fourth in generation has assumed the name of Makund Deb.

According to the dictates of the Shastras, some of the nitis and sebas of Sri Jagannath Deb should be performed by the Raja himself or in his absence by his representative called Mudirath nominated by the Rajas. If the Gaddi be vacant, it will be difficult to appoint the next Mudirath. Consequently the religious usage of the nation will have to be interfered with. She was therefore compelled to raise her grandson to the Gaddi under the name and title of Raja Makund Deb according to the custom of her family. The Shastras, Narad's Pancharatna, Seeta Sanghita; Bamdeb Sanghita quoted in Niladri Mahoday are authorities on the subject. These facts may also be proved from the testimony of respectable Mohants, Sebaks and Rajas etc. That in raising her grandson to the Gaddi she has not disobeyed the orders of Government. This has been done simply to maintain her family usage to observe the dictates of Shastras. If the title be not granted she will unnecessarily be much disgraced in the eyes of the public.

In her second petition to the Collector of Puri dated 30 July, the Rani appended an extract from the *Madala Panji*, stating that in 1727 Raja Ramchandra Deb, because of his association with Muslims, was not allowed to perform the services of Jagannath or to enter the temple at Puri. He was replaced by his daughter's son who was installed as Raja during the lifetime of the former. Suryamani Patamahadei wrote:

> In continuation of my application in Uriya dated 12th July 1883, I most respectfully beg leave to state that should the convicted Rajah Dibyasingha Deb [be] released and allowed to return to his home, he would be, according to the custom of the country, disqualified to perform the ceremonies of Jaggernath for having associated with and taken the food cooked by "Mlechhas" i.e. persons other than Hindoos and it was on this and some other considerations already stated in my memorial to Government that I was compelled to install my minor grandson under the patronymical cognomen of "Rajah Makund Deb". I beg to enclose in original the opinion of the respectable Pundits and Mahants of the District declaring that the transported Rajah would be disqualified for the services (sebas of Jaggernath) in case he returns home.*

---

* This letter of Surymani Patamahadei can be found in Appendix 3 of this book. Along with this letter, there were two important attachments. The first one is an opinion of learned pandits and mahantas of monasteries opining about ineligibility of Raja Dibyasingha Deb to perform the service of Lord Jagannath in the event of his return being not consistent with the customs. The second one is an extract of opinion wherein the deported king having been associated with *mlechhas* has become disentitled to perform the services of the lord. Extracts from the *Madala Panji* can be found stating that in 1727 Raja Ramchandra Deb was not allowed to perform the services of Lord Jagannath because of his

As a precedent, I take liberty to bring to your notice that one of my ancestors named Rajah Ram Chandra Deb, who ascended the throne on 1649 Shakabda (AD 1727) having been compelled to associate with a daughter of the then Mahoamedan Nawab was not allowed to perform the services of Jaggernath or to enter the Temple. As he expressed his desire to worship the idol, the "Pattitapaban Deb" (a representative of Jaggernath) was set up at "Singhadwar" (Lions gate of the Temple) in order that he (the fallen Rajah) might be able to see and worship it from the outside. The Rajah having thus become disqualified to perform the religious and social ceremonies of the family, the officials of the palace brought down his daughter's son from Athagarh and installed him on the Gaddi as Rajah Bir Kishore Deb. The enclosed extracts from the old "Madla Panji" bear testimony on the subject.

In conclusion I beg to state that besides the documents I have already filed and the evidence already given a reference to the books specified in the accompanying memo would show that the title of Rajah is the hereditary title of family and I also presume the almanac of the country, histories of the Province and official correspondence would verify the above.

K.B. Gupta was the officiating Collector of Puri at this time. He gave a report to the Commissioner of Odisha on the petitions of Rani Suryamani Patamahadei, guardian of the minor.

I have the honour to acknowledge the receipt of your memo no. 939 dated 28th June last forwarding copy of the Govt. letter no. 417 P.D. dated 29th May regarding the assumption of the title of Rajah by the minor son of Raja Dibyasingha Deb.

2. The circumstances of which have given rise to the present question are set forth in your letter no.452 dated 4th April to the Govt. and I need not recapitulate the same here.

---

association with Muslims. These attachments, however, are not in proper condition to be reproduced. Source: Odisha State Archives.

3. The Govt., while refusing to allow the minor son assume without authority the title of Rajah during the lifetime of his father – the convict Rajah, have expressed their willingness to listen to any representations the family might make to have the title conferred on the minor.
4. Suryamani Patamaha Dei, mother of the banished Rajah and guardian of the minor son, was accordingly called upon to state her case in writing and adduce facts and considerations in support of it. This she has now done in two petitions dated 12th and 30th July respectively.
5. In the first place she claims that the title of Rajah is hereditary in the family; on this point, it may be said that the title, though not formally conferred by the Government, has been all along recognized in official usage. Ramchandra Deb, the first prince in the present family, reigned 29 years from AD 1578–1607 (*Hunters Orissa*, vol. II, Appendix VII, p. 190). He received the hereditary title of Maharajah from the Mugul Emperor (idem, p. 19) but this title has never been recognized by the British Government. The title of Rajah of Khordah is for the first time used in Sec 2 Regulation IV of 1809 by which the superintendency of Pooree temple was formally made over to the Khordah family, and the same style is used in Act V of 1840. In the list of the title holders called for by the Govt. of India in their circular dated 20th June 1859, the Rajah of Khordah was included as enjoying a hereditary title. A report to the same effect was submitted in this office No. 658 dated 4th October 1874 and the title has been in use in all official papers.
6. But the fact that the title of Rajah has in a manner been recognized by the Govt. as belonging to the family and could not justify the unauthorized assumption of that title by the minor son during the lifetime of his father, and the present difficulties are due to the hasty and ill-advised proceeding of the guardian in causing the investiture of the minor without reference to the Government. In the 3rd para of her memorial to the Government, the guardian gives her reason for the step

she took and in her petition to me she gives some further details, the purport of which is that as superintendent of the temple the Rajah to perform certain services to the idols but instead of doing them all by himself he is permitted by the shastras to appoint a substitute who goes by the name of Mudiratha and who must possess certain qualification and be formally installed by the Rajah himself. It will appear from the account given of the Mudiratha in the second memorial (dated 30 April 1883) that the office is liable to become vacant from time to time making fresh appointment to necessary. The guardian now urges that such a vacancy lately occurred but before the minor could make the necessary appointment it was indispensable that he himself should be formally installed Rajah – for none but the Rajah could appoint a Mudiratha. This contention is supported by extract (appendix to Memorial No.2) from a book called Niladri Mahoday which is an account of the shrine of Pooree and by the opinion in writing of some learned Pundits of the place (Exhibit C). The guardian and the Pundits go further for they hold that the convict Rajah has by his banishment, become permanently incapacitated from the service of Jagannath and should he ever be allowed to return to the country he would on no account be permitted to resume his duty in the temple. An extract has been given from the *Mandala Panji* or the historical record of the temple narrating the circumstances under which Maharaja Ramchandra Deb who had lost caste by his association with Musulmans was deprived of the service of the temple.

7. According to established usages and the sacred writings of the Hindoos it seems therefore necessary that there should be a duly installed Raja to carry on the services of the temple and appoint a Mudirath on a vacancy arising.

8. Under the circumstances, the recognition by the Govt. of the title and appellation of Raja Makund Deb assumed by the minor would be an act of grace which would not only be welcome to the family but be appreciated by the Hindoo

generally. The title may be conferred on him as a personal distinction to be enjoyed by him during the lifetime of his father at whose death he would inherit the family title.

9. As regards the petitions submitted by the guardian to His Honour the Lieutenant Governor, I do not think I need say much for, she has entirely misunderstood the attitude taken up by my predecessor Mr. Grant. While Rajah Dibyasingha Deb was still alive, the unauthorized assumption of the title of Rajah by his minor son could not be allowed and this was all he maintained. The point in question was not whether the title of Rajah was hereditary in the family but whether the minor could adopt it during the lifetime of his father. That the view taken by him was in the main the correct one has been amply proved and the guardian would have been well advised had she been more temperate and respectful in her language towards him.

Finally, the Lieutenant Governor gave his concurrence through his Secretary's dispatch dated 14 November 1883; therefore, the question of hereditary title was held in abeyance for the time being. The Lieutenant Governor recommended that the name and title of Raja Mukunda Deb be conferred as a personal distinction on the minor Raja. This would validate the action of minor's grandmother in installing him as the Raja and would enable the religious ceremonies of the temple to be properly carried on.[7]

In March 1884, Viceroy Lord Ripon conferred the title of 'Raja' as a personal distinction on Jagannath Jenamani. Rani Suryamani Patamahadei informed the Collector of Puri that she was willing to present *nuzur* of Rs 1,500 in gold *mohur*. Thus ended the dispute regarding the recognition of Jagannath Jenamani, the minor son of Dibyasingha Deb, as the Raja during the lifetime of his father.[*]

---

[*] The original letter in Odia dated 10 June 1884 and its English translation submitted to Collector, Puri, are attached as Appendices 4 & 5 to this chapter. Source: Odisha State Archives.

Metcalf's Mistake

The problems faced by the Rani did not end with the grant of title of 'Raja' to Mukunda Deb. In the meanwhile, the draft bill of 1881 for conducting the affairs of the Jagannath Temple was dropped, as the government did not want to introduce any legislation in connection with religious institutions in India. However, the issue of instituting a suit in the affairs of the Jagannath Temple in the court of the District Judge of Cuttack was not laid to rest. This issue came up on different occasions in the affairs of the government. The Government of India in a communication dated 5 May 1885 conveyed to the Government of Bengal that, 'The Governor General authorizes the institution of the proposed suit in connection with the proper superintendence and management of the Temple of Juggernath.'[8]

Pursuant to the above decision, Metcalfe, the Commissioner of Odisha, deputed Ram Prasad Singh, earlier *sheristadar* of his office, to enquire and report regarding the affairs of the Jagannath Temple. Ram Prasad Singh had earlier worked on deputation as the manager of the Jagannath Temple. He submitted his report stating that some of the ornaments, jewels and money received as *pindika* (presents by the pilgrims) are kept in the house of the Raja of Puri. The accounts of all the articles, ornaments, jewels, clothes, etc. and other valuables belonging to the temple in storerooms (new and old) and all its treasures including the *pindikas* are kept by the designated servants—the *Deula Karan*, the *Tarahu Karan* and the *Baithi Karan*. The temple officials along with the designated servants together received Rs 705 annually. These ill-paid servants should not have been entrusted with the accounts.

He mentioned that the keys of the storerooms should be kept by the Superintendent instead of minor temple officials, the Muduli and the Mekap. Ram Prasad Singh wrote: 'Rani never personally sees as to how and in what condition the valuable articles belonging to Juggernath are kept'. He complained that Dewan Ananda Mukherjee and the Deula Karan refused to show him the list of ornaments, jewels and other valuable articles. This refusal was 'under the strict order' from the Rani not to show any papers.

Ram Prasad Singh also threw light on the administration of the temple by the Dowager Rani. Because the Rani observed *pardah* (the practice among some Hindus and Muslims of secluding women from strangers), she was never directly in touch with the public and officials. Singh claimed that the proclaimed orders of the Rani could not be her real orders. He wrote that 'the ornaments of gold and silver, jewels and diamonds are in the hands of the low-paid servants of no moral training. It seems absolutely necessary that a fresh list should at once be prepared of these articles'.

He pointed out that the last list was prepared way back in 1819. 'Many ornaments have undoubtedly been made or received in the meantime. It seems to be the intention of Rani and her officials not to allow Government to know the exact value of the valuable property in the Temple'.[9]

After reading Ram Prasad Singh's detailed report, Commissioner C. Metcalfe decided to press for the appointment of a Receiver to take charge of the ornaments and valuable articles in the Jagannath Temple.

Suit No. 3 of 1886 was filed on 15 December 1886 in the court of J.B. Dragan, the District Judge of Cuttack. J.H. Savage, the officiating Collector of Puri, was the Plaintiff in the suit. Raja Dibyasingha Deb was the defendant. After his death, the defendants were Rani Suryamani Patamahadei, Rani Niladri Patamahadei (mother of Mukunda Deb), Ramachandra Santra (the Deul Karan), Yogi Mekup (the Bhandar Mekap), Gopinath Patnaik (the Deula Karan) and a few other persons. The following claim was made in the plaint.

Claim

That the valuables detailed in the plaint and such other articles of jewellery, gold and silver, belonging to the Temple which are not constantly in use in the services of the idols, might be deposited in the Court, or otherwise preserved and taken care of, and that, if necessary, a Receiver might be appointed for their preservation and custody; that the Defendants might be required to submit a full, true and particular account of all such articles of jewellery, gold and silver, as well as all money, coins and moveable property and accounts belonging to the endowments which were within their possession, custody and power; that the defendant Rani Suryamani might be required to submit a full, true and particular account of all estates which were in her possessions, appertaining to the said endowments; and that an account might be taken from her of all the revenues, profits and income and receipts whatever, whether received from the aforesaid estates and lands or from gifts and presents made to the idols – and all incomes and receipts whatsoever appertaining to the said trust received by her or for her use, from the time she took possession of the estates and took upon herself the charge of the said trust, and the said Rani might be required to account as how the money or things so received, have been applied or disbursed.

The Plaintiff moved to the Court asking defendant Suryamani Patamahadei to submit 'a list of all properties moveable and immoveable belonging to the Trust, and that all proper directions might be given and enquiries be made by the Court, and that the new Trustees might be appointed by the Court to exercise the same powers that were conferred on the Superintendent by Section 2 of Act X of 1840'.[10] The Court was requested to vest all properties of the Jagannath Temple, moveable and immoveable, in such trustees and to settle a proper scheme for the further management of the trust.

The Collector of Puri prayed for the appointment of a Receiver, Assistant Receiver and a Tahsildar to take charge of the temple property. The judge granted the prayer.

Raghunandan Ramanuja Das, the mahant of Emar Math, was appointed as honorary Receiver by the Civil Court on the recommendation of the officiating Collector J.H. Savage.* Nadia

---

* It is significant to mention here that the mahant of Emar Math had earlier led the protest on behalf of the other mahants by writing a

Chand Dutta, Sub-Deputy Collector, was appointed as Assistant Receiver and Ram Prasad Singh was named the Tahsildar.

The appointment of the Receiver was a blunder and was met with widespread protests. Metcalfe justified his action by stating that the object of the suit was to obtain through the Civil Court a scheme of temple management which could not be done through any other means. A Committee of management was to take the place of the Superintendent and till that Committee was formed, it was expedient to appoint a Receiver to take care of the endowments and properties of the temple to prevent their mismanagement. The editor of *Utkal Dipika* (18 December) commented that the Receiver was appointed under the apprehension that the Raja of Puri or his guardian would misappropriate the valuable articles of the temple. This apprehension was unbelievable. Meetings were organized against the removal of the Thakur Raja from the management of the temple by appointing a Receiver and trustees.

The Utkal Sabha* held a meeting in the second week of December 1886 at Cuttack. Baidyanath Pandit moved a resolution, seconded by Ram Shankar Ray,** that there was nothing wrong in the management of the Jagannath Temple to warrant interference by the government. The *Niladri Mahodaya* was quoted to highlight that without the Raja, worship could not be held in the temple and it would be rendered useless.[11] It was pointed out that the Raja of Puri had been an institution for centuries. The removal of the Thakur Raja would lower the dignity and status of the family, which would in turn wound the sentiments of Hindus. Copies

---

petition in 1882 protesting against the government move to appoint a committee of trustees to manage the affairs of the temple. The same person was now appointed as the Receiver.

*Utkal Sabha was an organization led by Odia luminaries to voice the aspirations of the native population and cause of Odisha.

**Ram Shankar Ray was the assistant editor of *Utkal Dipika* and he defended the Dowager Rani in the court of district judge along with Madhusudan Das.

of the resolution were sent to the Government of India and the Government of Bengal.

In this connection, a letter under an assumed name of *Golakhdanda* was published in *Utkal Dipika* on 18 December 1886. It is interesting that the letter was written in English and was published as such in the Odia paper. The identity of the writer is not known although the names of some important personalities associated with *Utkal Sabha* are speculated. The letter was meant to draw attention of the English to the sentiments and popular views on the issue. A copy of the letter is attached at the end of the book (Appendix 6).

A protest meeting was held in Gopalji Math at Cuttack, presided over by Jagneswar Chandra, the pleader. An estimated 5,000 people attended it. *Utkal Dipika* reported that such a large gathering was unprecedented. A resolution was passed saying the services of the temple could not be performed without the Raja. The speakers argued that there was no serious irregularity in temple administration to justify any interference by the government.

A large meeting was also held in Bada Akhada Matha in Puri in January 1887. That meeting too pointed out that the rituals of the temple could not be performed if the administration was taken away from the hands of the Raja as only he or his representative, i.e., the Mudiratha, was entitled to perform certain services for the Lord. Protest meetings also took place in interior villages. People participated in such meetings of their own volition and condemned the British Government over the administration of the Jagannath Temple.

Madhusudan Das, the Saviour

Rani Suryamani Patamahadei wasted no time in standing up to this challenge. She sought the help of eminent lawyer Madhusudan Das, who advised her to file a writ petition in the Calcutta High Court against the appointment of a Receiver. The petition prayed that the Government should be restrained from administering the temple till the disposal of the case in the court of the District Judge of Cuttack.

The High Court heard the case in the first week of March 1888. Barristers John Woodroffe, Evans and Sandell and lawyers Gurudash Banerjee, Amarnath Bose and Karunasindhu Mukherjee appeared for Suryamani Patamahadei. Advocate General Nanda Kishore Banerjee appeared for the Collector of Puri.

For Rani Suryamani Patamahadei, this was a case of immense significance. The prestige, honour and the future of the Gajapatis of Puri was at stake. It was also a difficult time for her financially as she did not have the economic means to fight the case. So dire was the situation that she had to borrow money to meet the daily *kotha bhog* expenses of the temple. Burdened by immense debt, the Rani's financial condition was dire. Madhusudan Das, who was helping her with the case, understood her predicament and empathized with her. It was not only the honour of the Gajapatis but the pride of Odisha that was at stake. So, Madhusudan Das stepped in to fight the case at his own expense.

Madhusudan Das faced resistance even from Woodroffe and Sandell, who represented the Rani, as they thought that the case had no merit. They did not have the slightest doubt that the government was on a very firm footing. Woodroffe was of the view that there was no impediment in the government taking over the administration of the temple and that there was no illegality involved in taking measures to streamline temple administration. Madhusudan Das's argument was that the action of the government was against the Governor General's assurance of non-interference in the temple affairs given at the time of the British occupation of Odisha. This did not convince Woodroffe, who raised a fundamental question—what was wrong in taking over the administration of the temple or in appointing a Receiver?

Madhusudan Das explained, based on previous discussions in the British Parliament, that an English Christian Government should not and need not keep any relationship with the Jagannath pagoda of Hindus. He made a counter argument to Woodroffe: 'Do you think that a Hindu priest will be appointed at the expense of a Christian Government?' Woodroffe retorted: 'You are a lunatic.' Both the English barristers emphatically told Madhusudan Das that he was fighting a 'lost cause'.

Madhusudan Das was not disheartened. He could understand that while the barristers viewed the matter from a narrow legal angle, the issue involved a wider canvas. He took up the case as a challenge and a personal mission. Nothing appealed to him more than lost causes.

For the budding young lawyer, a great deal was at stake. Although a Christian, he strongly felt that the pride and prestige of the Gajapati was paramount. The centuries-old right and privilege in the ritual tradition of the Jagannath Temple was involved. The crucial issue was non-interference by a Christian Government in the religious affairs of a revered Hindu temple. Another issue was his own standing and credibility in the eyes of the people of Odisha. He was the first graduate, the first post-graduate and the first lawyer from Odisha. So, for him, the case was a crucial testing ground.

Madhusudan Das wanted to create a bigger public impact. To influence public opinion in favour of the Rani's cause, he wrote two articles under the pseudonym of 'A Lunatic' in the Letters to the Editor's column of *Utkal Dipika*, the leading voice of 19th-century Odisha (the text of both these letters can be found in Appendices 7 and 8 to this book). Interestingly, although an Odia newspaper, these two letters were published in English.

The letters were composed in an allegorical style and employed dream motifs in order to not attract contempt of the court. The letters were noticed for their sharpness, biting irony and imaginative style. They betrayed his sharp mind and journalistic style. The letters denounced the British plot to divest the Puri Raja of his age-old honour. They had the desired effect as *Utkal Dipika* was widely read by people and government officials alike.

The Statesman on 15 March 1887 published a letter from a 'Wonderer' regarding the shrine of Jagannath. The writer referred to the declared policy of the government to sever all communication with the Jagannath Temple. 'How then can it be pretended in the face of this that the Government is interested in the Temple? Can there be appearance of connection?' This letter too was written by Madhusudan Das.

When the Calcutta High Court began hearing the writ petition by Rani Suryamani Patamahadei, Woodroffe argued that Section 539 of the Civil Code was not applicable to the Jagannath Temple. He extensively quoted records to prove that the Raja of Puri had proprietary rights in the worship of Jagannath. He refuted the allegation of misappropriation of valuable articles stating that the Commissioner had ordered the sealing of the storeroom of the temple a year earlier. This was done under the direction of Ram Prasad Singh. According to him, there was no need to appoint any Receiver and the Commissioner had no authority to do so.

Evans additionally stated that the Raja of Puri was made Superintendent of the temple first in 1809 and then in 1840. He argued that the British Government had already acknowledged the Rani as the legally competent custodian of the Jagannath Temple. Accordingly, there was no justification in seeking any further interference of the court.

The Advocate General countered that the custodian misused the property, necessitating the need for a Receiver. He argued that the government had no interest in the case and that the suit had been instituted on behalf of the public to protect the temple property from misappropriation and for proper management of temple services.

The Court gave its judgment in the end of March 1887, which *Utkal Dipika* reported on 2 April. The order of appointment of the Receiver was set aside by the Court. The Court ruled:

> We think that the order appointing the Receiver in this case must be set aside for the reason that in our opinion no necessity has been shown for the appointment. The suit is a suit which is brought by the Collector representing the public for the purpose of having a scheme fixed for the management of certain religious

endowment of a very extensive character on the ground that it is being mismanaged by the persons who are managing it. Now as to whether that suit can be maintained, or as to what the rights of the parties in this suit may be, we have no knowledge and no means of forming or expressing any opinion whatever, but this we do say that upon the affidavits before us.

With regard to the charge of mismanagement, the court held as follows:

It does not appear that there is any reason for supposing that the property of this endowment is being made away with or wasted in any way. What does appear is that there is a suspicion that there might be better management and it is charged that the managers of this endowment are mismanaging it. But no trace whatever is there of any specific charge of dishonesty or misconduct against them in the sense of dishonesty. Under these circumstances and having regard to the fact that the case of both sides is that the object of this endowment is to provide for a particular form of religious worship, and that it is not denied that this form of worship is carried out.

With regard to the appointment of Receiver, the Court further held:

We think that this matter of the Receiver ought to stand over until the decision of the suit when the rights of the parties will be finally decided and when it will be seen what is the proper scheme under which the endowment ought to be carried out; and therefore without expressing the slightest opinion to the merits of the case as to whether a *prima facie* case has been made out by the plaintiff or on the other hand a *bonafide* defence has been set up. On the part of the present Manager, we say that in our opinion there is no ground for the order appointing the Receiver in this case; and therefore we decree the appeal against that order and direct that that order will be set aside. The result will be that the rule and other proceedings will fall through because in as much as the order appointing a Receiver is gone. The action of the Receiver will also be gone and therefore it is unnecessary for us to say anything with reference to the rule except that the rule will drop; and especially we say that because we do not think it necessary to say anything about the costs in this case. If we deal with the costs we should have to assess them and at sum which will be very inadequate we think in the interests of justice. We should best not say anything about the cost.

The judgment was a historic one. It was a vindication of the stand which Rani Suryamani Patamahadei had so seriously been insisting upon. Madhusudan Das, the young lawyer, became an overnight hero among the people of Odisha. Barrister Woodroffe eloquently praised Das and publicly acknowledged the assistance he received from him to support and strengthen the case. There was celebration in Odisha and particularly in Puri over the judgment. *The Statesman* in an editorial of 5 April 1887 made a scathing criticism of the Lieutenant Governor while praising the High Court. The editor reported the outcome of the court proceedings and made a sharp attack on the issue of appointing a Receiver:

> The extent to which Sir Rivers Thompson was in the hands of his subordinates receives a very strong illustration from the permission presumably he must have given to the distant officers at Cuttack to take summary possession of the entire property and the whole administration of the great shrine of Juggernath.
>
> There can be no reasonable doubt that the administration of the Temple and the charge of its property have from time immemorial been vested in the Rajah of Khurda who is supposed for certain ceremonial purposes connected with the daily worship of the great shrine, to be the incarnation of the great MAHADEV JUGGERNATH himself.
>
> Without enquiry of any kind and in direct contravention of the whole tenor and spirit of our connection with the Temples of the country, the Collector and the Judge of Cuttack, by a

manifest understanding between them, summarily ousted the Maharanee of Khurda from the charge of the shrine and the custody of all the property connected with the Temple.

The record of this proceedings is before us and remembering that State interference of any kind with the affairs of the Temple is in direct teeth of the course which the Government has followed for the last thirty years under the order of Parliament.

We say advisedly that the proceedings are incredible. There is the strongest reason to believe that the Maharanee of Khurda—who is the guardian of the minor prince—is not open to any blame for her management of the shrine, her administration has been marked throughout by great unselfishness, self-sacrifice and devotion.

That the Collector can legally initiate proceedings of this kind is open to gravest question, while with such fervor did the Judge second him that it is positively entered in the record that the Judge directed his Sheristadar to lend the Collector's Vakeel the stamp fees required for the proceeding which the Vakeel had not (been) forthcoming.

The whole case seems to have arisen from the District authorities constituting the champion of Roghund Romaney Das and of a man named Ram Prasad Singh. Listening to the representation of these men, the Collector, summarily and in the most tyrannical manner, outsed (*sic*) the Maharanee, custodian of the Temple, from its charge, and made it over to these two men, who, so far as can be seen at present, have no right to the custody of the shrine, than the Collector or Judge who have acted in this extraordinary way. The slightest enquiry by Sir Rivers Thompson would have prevented the scandal.

The editor concluded that Her Majesty's judges very properly had set aside the orders of the district judge, but the outrage was an illustration of what officials would venture upon under a weak ruler such as Sir Rivers Thompson (the Lieutenant Governor then).

After Sir Rivers Thompson, Sir Stewart Bayley became the Lieutenant Governor in 1887. He was dismayed over the court's verdict and wanted a compromise in the case. He called for Madhusudan Das, the representative of the Dowager Rani, and Metcalfe, the Commissioner of Odisha. The Secretary of Bengal, Nolan, held discussions with Das and Metcalfe regarding the settlement of the temple suit. Madhusudan Das wrote in *The Statesman* on 20 April 1887:

> The public are anxious that our Lieutenant Governor should himself look into the suit regarding the Poore Temple, and I am glad to tell you that His Honor has already taken up the matter. On Saturday last Mr. Nolan, the Secretary, who has the management of the case, Mr. Metcalfe, the Commissioner of Orissa, and I talked over the matter, and it was decided that the case should be amicably settled.

Madhusudan Das thought it appropriate to bring his discussions with authorities to public notice. Therefore, he sent these letters to various newspapers. After consulting Rani Suryamani Patamahadei, he wrote to the Commissioner: 'The Rani wishes to have loan of the services of a Government officer to manage the affairs of the Temple till the Raja is of age. You are aware of the difficulty in getting an efficient Manager in a peculiarly constituted institution like the Temple of Jagannath.' He further mentioned that the manager should be a native of Odisha and believer of the orthodox Hindu faith. He conveyed the Rani's intention to have Babu Harekrushna Das as Manager.

Regarding the control and supervision of the priests, Madhusudan Das said the Rani with the new manager would be able to act in conformity with his authority. He made it clear that the proposed scheme would not extend beyond Raja Mukunda Deb's minority. A new scheme of management was to be embodied in the decree duly approved by Rani Suryamani Patamahadei. Metcalfe agreed with the draft and the Collector Puri moved a compromise petition on 3 October 1888.

The decree was passed on 15th December 1888. The suit was decreed on the terms mentioned in the compromise petition. The court verdict in the subsequent compromise petition showed the government and Rani Suryamani Patamahadei in different perspectives. It referred to the ill-advised step on the part of the government to appoint a Receiver, which triggered the writ petition. Rani Suryamani Patamahadei handled the case brilliantly by whipping up public sentiments and raising the cry of 'religion in danger'. She fomented public sentiment by raising the issue in the vernacular press. Madhusudan Das articulated and calibrated the case brilliantly. A large-scale propaganda machinery was put to use to convey that the Thakur Raja of Puri had an inalienable right in the Jagannath Temple. The government deliberately wanted to reduce the prestige and power of the Raja by taking away the administration of the temple from his hands. The compromise was seen as a victory of the Dowager Rani. It was agreed that a manager of her choice would be appointed and he would be dismissed if he went against her wishes.

Rani Suryamani Patamahadei turned out to be a great fighter and a person of tremendous intelligence and vision. As she was widowed at an early age, she might have ended up spending her life as a recluse. Instead, she became the custodian of the Jagannath Temple and of the Puri Raja's estates for a long period—from 1860 to 1897 (except in AD 1875–1878 when Dibyasingha Deb was in charge). She holds a unique place in the history of the Gajapati tradition by becoming the de facto superintendent and custodian of the Jagannath Temple during the minority of her adopted son from 1860 to 1874.

After the conviction of her adopted son in 1878, she again fought and became the custodian and the de facto superintendent of the temple for her grandson. She was a traditional woman who followed the *purdah* and was not exposed to the outside world. Therefore, during the minority of her adopted son, the initial years were difficult for her. But she learnt from experience and that improved the temple administration. Later, she was able to successfully improve relations with the temple *sebaks* that had worsened during Dibyasingha Deb's short reign. To retain and restore the prestige of the Gajapati family, she was able to mobilize public opinion in her favour and channelized her ideas through Madhusudan Das to take on the mighty British.

When the British Government was trying to assert its authority and supremacy by creating hurdles and finally threatening to take over the superintendence of the Jagannath Temple, Rani Suryamani Patamahadei followed a multipronged approach to resist the move. She made out a case of privilege of exclusivity and hereditary entitlement for the Puri Raja which was under challenge from the British Government. She generated effective, intelligent and widespread public opinion against the move. The writers, the media, the pundits, the mahants, the *sebaks*, the servitors and the people united with her in raising their voices against any interference in the traditional role and status of the Raja of Puri.

The ritual tradition, popular sanction and widespread support took the case of the Rani to a greater height of legitimacy. Scriptural sanction and authority of traditional texts such as the *Skanda Purana* and *Niladri Mahodaya* were quoted and relied upon, which provided authoritative credence to the cause the Rani was fighting for. She could gather the support of Madhusudan Das, which was invaluable to fight the historic case. That the Hindu religion was in danger from British interference and intrusion provided a rallying point of nationalist sentiments in Odisha. Rani Suryamani Patamahadei proved to be a master strategist and visionary fighter in restoring the pride and glory of the institution of Gajapati in Odisha.

Only when her grandson Mukunda Deb came of age in 1897 did she relegate herself to the background, gradually fading away and finally being lost in obscurity. She, however, left her indelible marks in the annals of the Gajapati history. However, fate had cruel designs for this strong-willed lady. Her twilight years were very painful as she lived a life of neglect and received only indifference from her grandson Raja Mukunda Deb. An incredible lady who fought for the restoration of the dignity of the Gajapati, she had to live a life of solitary confinement and neglect in her own palace, begging for a pension.

During the long years of Mukunda Deb's minority, Rani Suryamani Patamahadei carried out the administration of the Jagannath Temple well without much complaint. The temple administration was ably handled by the temple manager appointed by the Dowager Rani.*

Madhusudan Das, Baidyanath Pandit and Biharilal Pandit were given a General Power of Attorney on behalf of the Raja of Puri to supervise temple administration and the affairs of the Raja's estate in March 1891. Gokulananda Choudhury substituted Madhusudan Das in 1897, and the committee continued to function until Mukunda Deb attained maturity. Mukunda Deb was weak-minded and inefficient; he did not take any interest in the temple administration. In 1901, there was a major accident in the temple in which two persons died and five were seriously injured on the Mahastami day. The Magistrate of Puri blamed the Raja's mismanagement for the accident. K.G. Gupta, the Commissioner, wrote to the Chief Secretary, Government of Bengal, highlighting the need to appoint additional trustees for the management of the temple as suggested earlier. He also mentioned that the present arrangement and scheme would terminate with Mukunda Deb's death and his heir would have no legal status in connection with the temple.

Mukunda Deb died in 1926 and his adopted son took over the administration of the temple.

The decision of the court while restoring the dignity of Rani Suryamani Patamahadei enhanced the standing and stature of Madhusudan Das, who is popularly known as Madhu Babu

---

* Harekrushna Das, who joined as temple manager in October 1889, died after six months. Krushna Chandra Mohanty became the manager for three years. Gajendra Das Choudhury was appointed as manager in February 1894, and Nityananda Das succeeded him in 1895.

in Odisha. He was considered the saviour of the institution of Gajapati and protector of the pride of the Odia people. Although he was a devout Christian, he expressed that he was converted not to 'Churchianity' but to 'Christianity'.

He was moved by the dying words of Jesus on the cross: 'Father, forgive them. They know not what they are doing.' He was a great nationalist and the tallest leader of the state who fought for just causes irrespective of any religion. He was acutely conscious of the fact that Lord Jagannath and the Puri Temple occupied a pivotal place in the life of people of Odisha and any interference and intrusion in their religious affairs would amount to an insult to its people and institution. Madhusudan Das raised the fight to a higher level of Odia nationalism and pride. He made the Jagannath Temple a successful laboratory of living experiment in Odia nationalism, projecting Lord Jagannath as the heart, soul and symbol of every Odia transcending the barriers of caste, religion and other narrow identities.

After his success, whenever there was a major dispute, people thought of Madhusudan Das. There are innumerable instances when he played a key role in steering and handling a crisis and resolving it. He was, therefore, remembered as *Bipate Madhusudan*, meaning when there was a danger, distress or crisis, it was Madhusudan Das alone who was capable of saving the situation. There is no other example of a devout Christian fighting passionately for the protection of a tradition revolving around Lord Jagannath, the soul and identity of Odisha. He was fondly called 'Utkala Gouraba'—the Pride of the Utkal.

This is no occasion to write a commentary on this great leader and nation-maker. He became a legend in Odisha. Whenever a rustic Odia from a distant village returned home after a rare visit to Cuttack, the major metropolis of Odisha, one of the queries from his curious village friends would surely be: 'Did you see Madhu Babu at Cuttack?' And children in the villages all over Odisha used to sing the following modern folk song reflecting a dream:

Patha Padhibi, Okila Hebi,
Kalia Ghoda Re Chadhibi
Madhu Babu Sange Ladhibi

Study I must, a lawyer I must be
Will ride a black stallion
And fight against Madhu Babu!

This popular folk song was imprinted in children's mind over generations. In childhood Madhu Babu was the ideal and idol as well as the hallmark of reference for every child. It conveys Madhu Babu's astute acumen and deep intellect of a great lawyer. The aim of every child was to reach his stature so that they too could ride the black stallion/horse, a status symbol of achievement and pride.

Suryamani Patamahadei was an exceptional woman in the Gajapati history. Here, some aspects need reiteration and recapitulation. Firstly, she was the only woman who was the de facto ruler and the superintendent of temple for a long period of nearly 34 years. As an exception to the rule of primogeniture, she became the guardian of infant Raja and thus became the de facto superintendent of the Jagannath Temple. She became the only woman to enjoy this privilege, which by tradition was a forbidden space for a woman.

Secondly, she is the only person who witnessed five successive Gajapatis in her lifetime. Upon being married, she became the daughter-in-law of the then ruling Gajapati, Ramachandra Deb III (AD 1817–1855). She became Suryamani Patamahadei as the wife of Gajapati Birakeshari Deb II (AD 1855–1859). She was the guardian of her infant adopted son Dibyasingha Deb until he attained majority. On the deportation of Dibyasingha Deb, she became the guardian of her grandson Mukunda Deb III until he came of age. After the death of Mukunda Deb III in 1926, Ramchandra Deb IV acceded to the throne. Suryamani Patamahadei witnessed his accession but died thereafter on 24 November 1926 at the age of 108.[12] She witnessed a complete regnal block of four Gajapatis and the beginning of the next regnal block in 1926. From Ramachandra Deb III to Ramachandra Deb IV, a complete cycle took place in her lifetime, a rare phenomenon in the Gajapati history!

Thirdly, she will be remembered forever as an exceptional fighter for restoring the dignity and pride of the institution of Gajapati and the age-old ritual association of the Gajapati with the Jagannath Temple. At a critical juncture, when the tradition was challenged, she with the help of Madhusudan Das fought with exceptional fortitude and brilliance. She galvanized the society and secured their support.

Finally, she was always behind purdah. She was *asuryampasya* in true sense. It means a married lady who has not seen sunlight (that means who is confined to her home). She never met any male member outside the family besides her close blood relations. She always used to communicate her decisions through a female mediator with the outside world. When Madhusudan Das used to come to the Palace for consultation on several matters, she never came face to face with him. She used to stand behind a curtain and talk to him without seeing his face. It is a rare case that in 34 years of her rule, she was visible to very few. She stood out in her unique way despite such self-imposed handicap. These are some of the perspectives which endowed Suryamani Patamahedei a pride of place in the Odisha history.

14

PLIGHT OF PATTARANIS
The Sordid Story of Pension

Mukunda Deb turned out to be a weak man and an ineffective Gajapati. He didn't have much formal education and could only sign in Odia. He used to sign as 'Sri Raja Makund Deb' and not 'Raja Mukunda Deb', the acquired regnal name. He behaved shabbily with his wife Rani Padmavati Patamahadei and grandmother Rani Suryamani Patamahadei. The Gajapati was childless.

Mukunda Deb was fond of animals and birds. He reared many pigs, cows, buffaloes, goats, horses, elephants, deer and cats. He kept many birds like parrots, mynas and pigeons. Of all, he was particularly passionate about pigs and had a pigsty separately within the palace premises. Apart from indulging in this passion, he paid little attention to other matters and did not take much interest in temple administration, which as the custodian of the Jagannath Temple he was bound to do. He depended on his favourites to take care of his responsibilities but these people exploited and misguided him.

Mukunda Deb viewed both the Ranis with distrust and suspicion. After he came of age and took over the temple administration from Rani Suryamani Patamahadei, he started misbehaving with the Ranis, their servants and anyone close to them. He kept his wife and grandmother confined in the palace and their movements were restricted. This amounted to house arrest for them. The grandmother, Rani Suryamani Patamahadei, who had caringly and lovingly brought up Mukunda Deb, was abandoned and treated with malice and indifference by the Gajapati; even his wife was not spared.

This abominable behaviour on the part of Mukunda Deb was very intriguing. For the Ranis, the mistreatment made their lives unbearable. Articles of daily necessity were not provided to them and servants were not allowed to look after them. They were denied basic facilities such as getting their clothes washed regularly. For their food they were dependent on *Mahaprasad* from the temple.

The Raja received a monthly pension of Rs 2,133 meant for the upkeep of him and the two Ranis. But the Raja stopped giving a portion of the pension to the Ranis; only occasionally did he give them meagre amounts. Even the living quarters of the Ranis in the palace became uninhabitable. Their rooms used to leak profusely in the rainy season. For want of money, no repair work could be undertaken, forcing the Ranis to live in deplorable conditions. The Raja did not share a room with the Thakur Rani and lived in a separate quarter. The Ranis lived in abject deprivation, neglect and without liberty.

When the torture of Mukunda Deb became unbearable, the old Rani Suryamani Patamahadei, finding no other way, secretly sent a letter to Madhusudan Das in Cuttack through a maidservant, Lakshmipriya. Thakurani Rani, the wife of Mukunda Deb, had brought Lakshmipriya along with her from her paternal home when she got married. Lakshmipriya remained with her and served her since the day of marriage, faithfully and loyally. However, she was kept under close watch by Mukunda Deb as she was close to his wife. One day Lakshmipriya was fortunately able to slip out of the palace with Rani Suryamani Patamahadei's letter.

The translated version of the letter, which depicts the Rani's suffering and cry for help, reads as under:

My sufferings are great. If I have to suffer so much even when you are living whom else shall I look to for redress. Immediately on receipt of this letter, please come, bring the Collector and settle everything for me once for all. I should like to live under the same arrangements as before. I can't manage to live under the protection of the Raja. He will never listen to remonstrations, such has been the case on many occasions. I adopted you as my godson and you will kindly relieve me from my miseries in this fourth stage of my life. I entrust everything to your care.

Sd/Suryamani Patamahadei

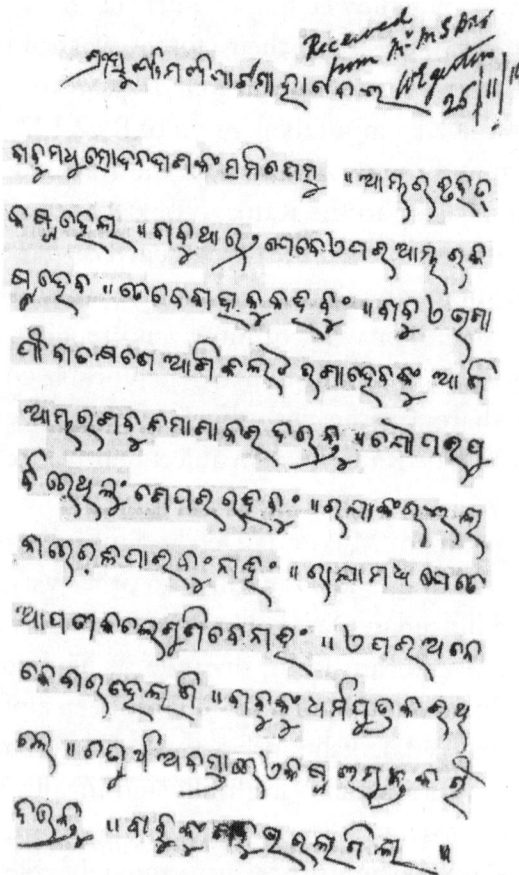

A copy of the original letter in Odia written by
Suryamani Patamahadei to Madhusudan Das

Madhusudan Das was seriously concerned after receiving the letter. He met W. Egerton, the Commissioner of Odisha Division, and handed over the letter to him. The right top corner of the letter shows that the letter was received and initialled by Egerton, on 25 November 1912. Egerton asked the District Magistrate of Puri to send a report after making necessary inquries.

Pundit Ramaballabh Misra, the District Magistrate of Puri, carried out an enquiry. He enquired about the condition of the Ranis from various people, matha mahants, the temple Manager and Lakshmipriya and elicited their views on how to address the situation.

Misra, in his report to the Commissioner on 15 December 1912, recorded the following deposition of Lakshmipriya:[1]

> The old Rani and the Thakurani Rani have asked me to tell you that they are drowned in a sea of troubles and unless you help them, they will be ruined. They are kept under lock and key and nobody is allowed to approach them. They find it difficult to procure for themselves the necessaries (*sic*) of life. All the money is going to Khandi and her relatives. They want that they should be separated from the Raja and that a boy should be adopted. They are not allowed to keep a maid-servant of their own with a view to forcing them to do their own menial work themselves. The Raja gives them nominally Rs. 200/- a month but on some pretext or other takes back most part of the money. They say that even prisoners are treated better in Jail by Government whereas they are kept confined and deprived even of the ordinary conveniences of life. I took a letter from the old Rani to Mr. Das. That day some sheds in the backyard were being repaired and the back door was open to allow the workmen in. So I managed to slip out with that letter. From that day I have not been able to go back inside the palace. I have been in the service of the Ranis since my childhood. I came to the palace at Puri with the Thakurani Rani from her father's house at the time of her marriage. The two Ranis live only on Mahaparasad. They are in great want. They have not enough

to live upon. All their rooms are leaking. During rains they find it difficult to live in them. They have not got money for repairs. The Raja uses very harsh and abusive words to both the Ranis. He does not sleep inside where the Ranis live.

The District Magistrate mentions that the maidservant saw him again on 21 December 1912. He reported:[2]

The maid-servant Lakshmi Priya saw me again this evening. She has not been able to return to the palace yet but her granddaughter is working inside. Through a hole in the wall she has had oral communications with the Ranis. She says they are waiting for relief by the Magistrate and Government and can't bear any longer. One fact the maid-servant specially emphasized. The Ranis are not allowed the services of Dhobi and Mehtar for months together. After 3 or 4 months, the Raja permits their clothes to be washed. The sweeper's entrance to the privies is kept under lock and key and opened with Raja's permission after very long intervals.

The Shankaracharya of Gobardhan Math, mahants of Emar Math, Dhakinaparswar Math, Uriya Math, Raghav Das Math and Radhakanta Math sent a joint petition to the District Magistrate on 20 December 1912. They mentioned that the Raja was under the evil influence of a low woman named Khandi and her son Madan Chhotra (more on them in the last section of the chapter). They reiterated that the Raja did not have good relations with his wife and grandmother. His pension was drawn by Madan Chhotra, who controlled the expenditure of the entire amount. A few rupees were doled out to the Ranis for their maintenance but the Raja took back most part of it under one pretext or other, which made it difficult for the Ranis to procure even the bare necessities of life.

They also mentioned that their condition was so intolerable that at times the Rani wanted to leave; but she was persuaded to abstain from taking such drastic steps for fear of giving rise to scandals. The petitioners proposed that a portion of the Raja's pension be paid directly to the Ranis and the Raja be ordered to live at Cuttack or elsewhere, so as to be out of the influence of Khandi and her people.[3]

After conducting the enquiries, the District Magistrate, as advised by Commissioner Egerton, submitted a detailed report recommending stoppage of pension to the Raja and suggesting that necessary provision be made for the Ranis out of the Raja's pension. Madhusudan Das also proposed to the Chief Secretary of Bengal requesting him to stop the pension of the Raja for some time. This letter of Madhusudan Das dated 14 October 1911 is reproduced below:[4]

> Pardon me for reminding you about the Puri Temple and the necessity of stopping for some time the payment of his pension to the Raja. I understand both Mr. Clark and Mr. Levinge are now in Darjeeling.
>
> For the safety of the numerous pilgrims who visit that temple and on other public grounds, the Bengal Government in the exercise of their executive powers compelled the Raja to delegate his powers of management to a Manager to be approved by Government. I was present when the matter was discussed by Sir John Woodburn at Cuttack. The Raja in the present suit wants by a side to invalidate his obligations to Govt.
>
> As for the power of Government to withhold the payment of pension till such time as the payee does not carry out any just order of the authorities, I beg to mention that this was frequently done during the minority of the present pensioner and also in his father's time. If necessary I shall give reference to records in the Government Offices.
>
> Act 23 of 1871 bars any civil suit for pension. This shows the executive armed with large powers in this matter.
>
> On political grounds it is not desirable that the management should pass into Bengalee hands. Not that I care to reserve the manager's post for an Oriya. That is not much. The Raja and

the priests have immense influence over the mass of the Hindu population of India. Both are stupid, ignorant and excitable and apt to be easily led astray by designing men. Here is the most suitable soil for the anarchist to sow his pernicious seed. The organization and the rites will safely hide the anarchist as the dark niches in the temple screen the owl.

I know more about this temple and its past history than people who think they know much. I was the pleader for defence in the memorable civil suit instituted by Government, which was watched by the whole Hindu population of India. The way in which the public appreciated my professional conduct and the compliment from the Chief Justice makes that brief specially valuable to me. I had in that case made a thorough study of the organization of the priesthood and of the history of the temple.

The detailed report of District Magistrate Pundit Ramaballabh Misra to the Commissioner of Odisha Division dated 22 December 1912 is significant:[5]

1. I have the honour to refer to your memo no. 125 dated the 5th November 1912, enclosing Government order no.3205 dated the 26th October 1912, on the subject of the suggested suspension of the political pension drawn by the Raja of Puri. Government desire that an attempt should be made to verify, by private enquiries, the rumours regarding the ill-treatment of the Ranis and that, as an alternative to the stoppage of pension, a special set of rules might be framed under Section 14(1) of the Act XXIII of 1871, whereby the woman Khandi and her son, who are now practically controlling the whole amount, might be kept out of it and a certain portion of it might be paid to the two ladies.

2. Owing to certain matters of a pressing character I had to keep out of headquarters a good deal since the receipt of these orders and have therefore been unable to take up this delicate enquiry as early as I wished.

3. I have since found out and examined the maid-servant who took to Mr. M. S. Das, C.I.E., the letter from the Raja's grand-mother, enclosed in original with your no.175 Con. dated the 25th November 1912 which I herewith return. It will be seen from the copy of her statement appended hereto that she was one of those who accompanied the Thakurani Rani (the wife of the Raja) from her father's house to Puri just after her marriage and has ever since been in her service. She fully corroborates the helpless condition of the two ladies. They nominally get Rs 200/- a month from the Raja who, on some pretext or other, takes back the major portion of the amount. They have to do their own menial service and have to go for months even without the services of a washer man and a sweeper. According to her version, they are in a worse plight than an ordinary prisoner in His Majesty's jail. Her escape from the vigilance over the palace on her perilous errand has the touch of a romance about it and she has not been able yet to re-enter the doors barred against her. After I examined her, I learnt that her absence attracted attention and that somehow or other it had reached the Raja's ears that she had gone on a mission to "Madhu Babu" in Cuttack. The Ranis naturally anticipated worst consequences and have therefore given it out as a ruse that they have made a complaint to Mr. Das against the impertinent behavior of a personal servant of the Raja who is on inimical terms with the Khandi and her party!!

4. Ras Behari Patnaik, Treasurer in the Manager's office, has stated to me that on 21st October last, Rs 1,500/- was advanced to the Ranis from the Temple funds on the security of the personal ornaments of the Thakurani Rani. I have verified the relevant entry in the account book and also inspected the ornaments in question. The Treasurer explained that the Ranis had contracted some debts at heavy interest which they wanted to pay off. They sent the ornaments to the Manager for pawning them and obtaining money at easy rates. The latter however decided to keep the ornaments,

advance the money from the Temple Treasury and charge no interest. Babu Raj Kishore Das fully corroborates this transaction. Indian ladies part with their ornaments only when all other resources fail.

5. Babu Jagabandhu Sinha, pleader and president of the Uriya Union Committee, came to see me the other day in connection with certain matters relating to the Puri Zilla school and casually I made enquires about the Ranis. He at once said that he heard it from trustworthy source that they were in great trouble and that Khandi and her son were reigning supreme in the palace to the great disgust of the local public. Another gentleman, Chowdhuri Kulamani Das of Bhingarpur, who is on the Durbar list of the District, went so far as to advise me that nothing short of deporting Khandi and her son from Puri would improve matters. According to him, the Ranis were in sad plight and the Raja entirely in the clutches of the old hag. This gentleman came only to pay me a complimentary visit and I took the opportunity of sounding him in the matter.

6. Babu Surendra Nath Mittra and Babu Harendra Kumar Chatterji, both Bengali pleaders, interviewed me this morning about a private affair of theirs and in the course of conversation I made a casual reference to the Raja and his affairs. They at once volunteered that matters have come to a sorry pass. The former said that the Ranis were in a pitiable position and so far as he knew were practically confined in the palace. Madan has got so much out of control that he is abusing respectable people right and left and that he (Surendra Babu) himself once avoided passing by his door while he was standing there simply for fear of being insulted. The other gentleman was the Raja's pleader in the Account suit but retired with Dhanapati Babu from it under circumstances already known to you. He related to me, from his own personal experience that Raja is so much under the thumb of Madan that nobody can approach the Raja against Madan's wish even if the Raja be anxious to see him.

7. The Deputy Superintendent of Police Babu Harekrishna Das and his senior Deputy Collector Babu Gopal Ballav Das—both Uriya gentlemen—have brought it to my notice from time to time that the Raja, though not an idiot in conversation, is for some reason or other quite helpless in the hands of the Khandi. I have seen the Raja twice and what they say confirms my own observations.

8. I have taken special care to acquaint myself with the views and sentiments of the local orthodox Hindus on the subject and among others have consulted the Mahants noted in the margin. With one voice they condemn the baneful influence of the Khandi and her son over the Raja and testify to the consequent deplorable conditions of the two Ranis. The Mahant of Emar Math has been approached more than once for loans by the elder Rani and has at time helped her with supplies. It is noteworthy that these gentlemen also lay stress on the fact that the Ranis have to do their own menial work and that on occasions they are denied the services of even Dhobi and Mehtar. All the Mahants are in great alarm as to the future of the Temple and the Raj family owing to the extraordinary control the Khandi and her son exercise over the Raja and are most anxious that the Raja should be removed from Puri for a time in order to be beyond their influence, that a boy should be adopted to perpetuate the family and that special provision be made for the two Ranis who are in so much distress. In order that their views may be placed before Government, they have given me a joint-statement in writing which has also been endorsed by the Mahant of Sankaracharya Gobardhan Math. I need not add that the last named Mahant is held in greatest possible esteem all over Hindu India, had the privilege of presiding over the deliberations of Bharat Dharma Mahamandal, in its inaugural session and is very well known to the Maharaja of Dharbhanga. His Holiness attended His Majesty's Durbar at Delhi and was among those who were there to convey to the

Throne the congratulations and the blessings of the Hindu orthodox.

...

11. The demoralization is complete; not only the Ranis but even the Raja himself is at the absolute mercy of Madan and Khandi who have full control of his purse. I have reasons to believe that at times the Raja wakes up to the realities of his situation but he is too weak and too much under the overpowering influence of the old woman to throw off the shackles and to play the man. Immediate removal from the present environments is likely to bring about a great and rapid improvement all round. But the obvious question to answer is how to achieve it and what is the remedy.

12. I would first advert to the alternative suggestion of regulating the payment of the pension under Section 14(1) of the Pensions Act. It is only with regard to the place and the time at which and the person to whom any pension shall be paid that any rule can be framed under this section and in the present case thereafter all that we can prescribe is that the pension due to Raja should be paid either to the Collector or the Temple Manager. Any other rule directing the manner in which this money should be disbursed would clearly be ultra vires. Even if it be prescribed that a certain portion of the pension should be paid to the Collector or the Temple Manager for payment to the Ranis there can be no guarantee that the money would actually reach the Ladies or remain with them. Under their present conditions they stand in such mortal terror of the Raja that it will be quite easy for the latter to extort a receipt from them without payment or the money itself from their custody. As to Khandi and Madan being kept out of it, it would be easy enough to frame a rule but it will always remain a dead letter because whatever money may be paid to the Raja for his household or pocket expenses would directly pass into their hands. The only procedure that may prove effective is to authorize the Temple

Manager to draw the whole of the pension and direct him to supply all necessaries both to the Raja and to the Ranis in kind. A draft of rules elastic enough to admit of this or any suitable procedure is enclosed herewith for consideration but I am afraid they go beyond the limits imposed by the law on which they are based.

13. The fact is notorious that the political pension which was granted to the Raja for the maintenance of himself and family in a suitable style is being drawn by his low favourites and flagrantly wasted. The meshes that the latter have woven round him have become so complete and strong that he himself is unable now to extricate himself from them and the poor Ranis find themselves in a hopeless corner. Half measures will serve only to render the confusion worst confounded.

14. In these circumstances, I venture most respectfully to reiterate my submission that nothing short of suspension of pension will have any appreciable effect on this unfortunate situation. Public opinion in Orissa will entirely endorse Government action in the matter and the Puri public will hail it with delight as an effective checkmate to the much-hated Khandi. Of course, a few Bengali pleaders who are egging on the Khandi and making a roaring trade will try to make a noise but it will be drowned in the chorus of grateful approval from the Uriyas themselves.

15. I would most strongly deprecate deferring any action until the disposal or the Account suit in the High Court. It may take months, if not years, and in the meantime the term of the present Manager will have expired. Several candidates are in the field and all are trying to secure Raja's nomination through Khandi. I have already reported to you that even Babu Gour Shyam Mohanty, whom the Raja had nominated in one of his letters to Government, has approached him through Khandi. In fact, in the present circumstances, the Raja is powerless to exercise his independent judgement and

we shall be confronted with a difficult position in May when the choice open to us will be either to accept the Khandi's nominee as Manager and perpetuate her boundless influence over the Raja or to resort to extreme measures.

16. In my humble judgment therefore, this is just the time for effective action and I venture to recommend that immediate orders may issue stopping the pension until such time as the Raja makes his submission, discards the Khandi, removes to Cuttack temporarily, allows effective provision being made for the Ranis from out of his pension and accepts the terms of Government as to the future management of the Temple.

W. Egerton, Commissioner of Odisha, wrote a confidential letter on 6th January 1913 to the Chief Secretary of the Government of Bihar and Odisha and gave his views on the District Collector's report. Egerton reported that the Raja of Puri had withdrawn the power of attorney given to the manager for dealing with his private income and instead executed a power of attorney dated 11th August 1911 in favour of Madan Chhotra, the son of Khandi. Accordingly, his pension of Rs 2,133 a month has since that date been drawn from the treasury by Madan Chhotra. While the pension was being drawn by the manager, he used to pay from it Rs 200 to the Raja's wife and in addition paid the household expenses and wages of the domestic servants. The power of attorney was changed because of some quarrel which arose between the Raja and the manager. Because of this change, it was the Ranis who suffered. The Raja's pension was granted for his own maintenance as well as his family's and not for the Raja alone. This was clearly understood and had been acted upon by manager Babu Raj Kishore Das until the dispute arose, and the Raja, no doubt acting on the advice of his pleaders, gave a power of attorney to Madan Chhotra.

With regard to stoppage of pension, which required a special set of rules under Section 14(1) of Act XXIII of 1871, the Commissioner observed:

There are obvious objections to stopping pension at the present moment, and it might not be expedient to take this drastic course. A reversion to the practice which obtained prior to August 1911, whereby a certain portion of the pension was disbursed by the Temple Manager to the Raja's wife and for the payment of household servants and for certain supplies seems desirable. I annex a copy of the statement prepared by Mr Clark, Collector of Puri, showing the particulars of disbursement of the Raja of Puri's pension, prior to the dispute.

Pursuant to this, the Board of Revenue issued a notification dated 9 September 1913 with the following rules:[6]

Rule I – The Political pension of Rs. 2,133-5-4* per mensem,** payable to Raja Makund Deb of Puri as the lineal descendant of the ancient Hindu Kings of Orissa for the maintenance of himself and his family shall, until further orders, be drawn and disbursed by the Collector of Puri.

Rule II – In disbursing the said pension a sufficient amount to be determined by the Collector of Puri, with the approval of the Commissioner of Orissa, shall be paid to the Raja's wife and grandmother for their proper maintenance.

Subsequently the local government approved the issue of the rule under which the Collector was required to pay Rs 500 to the two Ranis and Rs 1,000 to Raja Mukunda Deb; the balance was to be kept in reserve as a building fund, which was to be utilized for repairing the dilapidated palace.

Raja Mukunda Deb sent a memorial dated 16 October 1913 protesting against the drawing and disbursement of pension by the Collector. This was rejected. Mukunda Deb protested a second time

---

* This is how it used to be mentioned and recorded then. It is less than Rs 2134/-.

** Per mensem means every month or by the month

through a petition on 6 December 1913, which was also rejected by the Board of Revenue.[7]

In the meanwhile, the Collector started drawing and disbursing the pension to the Raja, which annoyed the latter. The Raja refused to provide a pension payment order to the Collector. A duplicate pension payment order was issued to the Collector and the original order was annulled. Another development took place in which the British government invited Raja Mukunda Deb to get the registration of the deed executed by him in appointing Gourashyam Mohanty as the manager of the temple. Disbursement of pension was made conditional upon his executing the deed appointing Mohanty as the manager. Mukunda Deb took this as an insult and he thought it was more honorable to live on loans than on such pension. He did not execute the deed and so did not get his pension.

A very strange situation arose as a result. Since the Raja did not get his portion of the pension, both the Ranis refused to receive their part of the pension. Both Ranis had a change of heart and thought it imprudent to receive their portion in spite of their pitiable condition for various reasons. Firstly, because of their sympathy for the Raja in spite of his adversarial behaviour towards them; secondly, due to the fear of retaliation from the Raja and his favourites; thirdly, the fear of the prospect of an unintended slander which could spread a rumour of separation of the Rani from Raja; and finally, because after the death of both the Ranis the pension amount may be curtailed depriving the future Ranis of their share. Two years passed in the meantime. The financial condition of both the Ranis as well as Raja Mukunda Deb went from bad to worse.

Raja Mukunda Deb sent a memorial dated 21 December 1914 addressed to the Viceroy praying for the cancellation of the rules issued by the Board of Revenue under Act XXIII of 1871 to regulate the disbursement of his political pension.[8] He raised the following important issues: (a) The Board of Revenue was not competent to issue the notification dated 9 September 1913 prescribing portion of the pension to be paid to the wife and grandmother of the

Raja. (b) According to the petition, it was beyond the provision of Clause 1 of Section 14 of Act XXIII. The Raja also challenged the issue of apportioning the pension between him and the Ranis and contended that the right to receive respective pensions of the wife and grandmother would be extinguished with their death. Section 14 of the Act did not contemplate appointment of a guardian of the memorialist and his family.

On this important issue, the government took the legal opinion of the Advocate General of Bengal, G.H.B. Kenrick, who said:

> I am of opinion that rules which (inter alia) prescribe that a portion of pension shall be paid to the wife and grandmother of Raja Mukunda Deb of Puri can legally be made under section 14(1) of the Pensions Act XXIII of 1871.
>
> That sub-section empowers the Board of Revenue with the consent of the Local Government from time to time to make rules consistent with the Act respecting the place and times at which and the person to whom any pension shall be paid.
>
> Under this power, a rule has been made giving a pension to the Raja for maintenance of himself and his family until further orders, and a second rule that 'in disbursing the said pension, a sufficient amount to be determined by the Collector of Puri with the approval of the Commissioner of Orissa shall be paid to the Raja's wife and grandmother for their proper maintenance'.
>
> The Raja contends in clause 27 of his Memorial that section 14(1) of the Act does not justify such a rule. I am unable to agree with this contention.
>
> There is the power to make rules as to the persons to whom any pension shall be paid. It would have been legally competent to grant pensions of specific amounts to the wife and grandmother of the Raja and to have granted a pension to the Raja less than the one actually granted by the sum of those amounts.
>
> In my opinion it is equally legal under section 14(1) to grant a pension to the Raja subject to the payment of certain portions to the wife and grandmother respectively.

In clause 29 of the Memorial, the Raja contends that if granted the right to the respective pensions of the wife and grandmother will be extinguished on their death. Whether it is so or whether the rule contemplates the continuance of full amount to the Raja without deduction after their death, is under section 14 which has the power to make new rules as to the pension from time to time.

Based on such opinion, the government decided to inform Raja Mukunda Deb that it did not see any reason to interfere on his behalf. The government, therefore, rejected the memorial of Raja Mukunda Deb.[9]

His extreme miserable condition finally forced Raja Mukunda Deb to write to the Collector on 6 December 1915 requesting him to pay the arrears of pension dues through the authorized Manager, Gourashyam Mohanty. The letter was written out of desperation and dire need. The Raja had not received any pension since September 1913. By the end of 1915, the arrears were to the extent of Rs 27,000. The Collector was sympathetic to the Raja's request. He told the Commissioner that the Raja was living in huge debts and badly needed money.

Madhusudan Das was always very sympathetic to the cause of the Ranis and was concerned about their plight. He lent money to the Ranis. He wrote a couple of letters to the Chief Secretary about the pension. The Chief Secretary replied to Das on 13 February 1916 that orders had been sent to the Commissioner regarding the payment of the Ranis' share of pension through him (Das) as he held a power of attorney. The same consideration would be applied for the share of pension payable to the Raja. The government could not refuse to pay anyone duly empowered by the Raja to take payment. If he had given a power of attorney to Khandi or her son Madan Chhotra, the authority would make over the money to him or her. They could not insist that the power must be given to a person approved by the Commissioner.[10]

Collector's Dilemma

An interesting development took place over the Raja's application for pension arrears. He was found to have executed another power of attorney in favour of Damodar Samartha, son-in-law of Khandi, and written to the Collector asking him to pay his pension to him. The translation of the power of attorney executed by the Raja dated 22 February 1916 is as below:[11]

> From the year 1913 up to this day I have not received the amount of pension due to me from Government. Now I want to take this amount as well as the amount in deposit with the Manager on account of my dues from the Temple. I hereby appoint Damodar Samartha as my authorized agent to receive payment of the above sums. The said agent will receive the amount of my pension from the Collector and give receipts thereof in his own handwriting. This will be taken as my own doing. He will also receive money from the Manager on account of my perquisites and give receipt in his own handwriting. This will also be regarded as my own doing and will be binding on me. If the Manager makes any objection with regard to my dues from the Temple, the agent is hereby empowered to take necessary steps for the realization of the same either by making an application to Government or by the help of the Civil Court and to engage Pleader on my behalf for the same. All these will be regarded as my own doing. Out of the amount of my pension the said agent will repay what is due to Mr Madhusudan Das on account of what he has personally paid to me and what he has spent on my suit and what I have borrowed on hand-note through his agency and will return the balance to me. The issue of personal orders and the tying of Sari (a ceremony performed to recognize the succession of a sebak) will be invalid if done without the knowledge of Damodar Samartha.

The Collector faced a dilemma as there were two powers of attorney: one in favour of the manager and another in favour of

Khandi's son-in-law. There were also two letters: In the first the Raja had asked the Collector to give his pension to the manager and in the second to Khandi's son-in-law. The Raja did not say anything in the second letter as to why he executed this power of attorney nor did he cancel the first letter. In the meanwhile, the Ranis' share had been paid to Madhusudan Das.

When the Raja's share was going to be paid to the manager, the son-in-law of Khandi came with the new power of attorney. The Collector observed that the Chief Secretary had ordered to pay the money to anyone holding a power of attorney. But a new situation had arisen where two persons had two powers of attorney with two covering letters addressed to the Collector, asking him to pay to two different persons. Under these circumstances, the Collector and the Commissioner wrote to H. McPherson, Chief Secretary, Government of Bihar and Odisha, suggesting that the Raja should personally come to take his money. 'I suspect that if the Raja is told to come personally, he will probably cancel the second power of attorney and ask that his portion of the pension should be paid through the Manager.' Cuttack Commissioner J.F. Gruning sought orders on this suggestion conveyed in his confidential letter dated 1 March 1916 addressed to H. McPherson.[12]

This anomalous matter was decided by McPherson in a letter dated 13 March 1916 to Gruning. He conveyed that:

> There is apparently nothing to prevent the Collector of Puri from paying Raja's pension to the Manager as he holds a Power of Attorney which has not been revoked, and ignoring the later power given to Damodar Samartha, which neither revokes the former nor gives exclusive powers to the holder. Should there be any further unforeseen complication about the two powers, the course suggested by you of insisting on the Raja's personal attendance may be followed.[13]

It may be relevant to mention here some details about the political pension which the Puri Raja was getting from the government. Gajapati Mukunda Deb II (1798–1817), the ancestor of the present Raja Mukunda Deb, was released by the British government from Midnapore jail and was shifted to Puri (see Chapter 10 for details). He lost all his estates of Khurda, which were taken over by the government. Therefore, by an order by George Dowdeswell, Secretary to the government, dated 5 March 1807, while releasing Raja Mukunda Deb II from confinement, he was granted an allowance equivalent to *malikana* or one-tenth of revenue of his estate.[14]

The allowance was fixed in 1807 at sicca Rs 1,200 a year and it was raised in 1819 to sicca Rs 24,000 or the Company's Rs 25,600 a year. This worked out to a monthly pension of around Rs 2,133, granted to the Raja of Khurda (subsequently known as Raja of Puri) for his maintenance in lieu of the estate which he lost. In 1873, the government of Bengal declared this allowance to be a political pension and not *malikana* on the grounds that the estate of Khurda had been confiscated absolutely. On 8 October 1873, the then Raja Dibyasingha Deb submitted a memorial against this order but the same was not accepted and the earlier decision was affirmed in a resolution released on 9 October 1876. Raja Dibyasingha Deb was sentenced to transportation for life for murder in 1878. His mother Rani Suryamani Patamahadei was permitted by the Government of Bengal, by an order dated 20 August 1878, to draw the political pension on behalf of his minor son. This political pension has remained unchanged since 1819 till today.

In 1958, Birakishore Deb (1956–1970) sent a memorial to the President of independent India requesting the revision of this pension.[15] He wrote:

> That the malikana was arbitrarily converted into political pension without taking into considerations the revenue of the territory of Raja of Puri and other natural considerations.
>
> That the meagre allowance of Rs. 2133-5-4 per mensem is also subject to income tax and other taxes. The sum fixed in

1873 has remained static, notwithstanding the abnormal rise of price level and other material considerations.

Your humble memorialist respectfully submits ... Govt. should forthwith convert retrospectively the political pension and malikana grant and to increase the same in proportion to revenue derived by the Government in the lost territory of the Puri Raj.

The Government of India did not consider this request. Even the present Gajapati, Dibyasingha Deb, had made a similar appeal to the government, which was not favourably considered.

Who Was Khandi?

We have come across references to Khandi and Madan Chhotra in this chapter, who had a decisive influence on Mukunda Deb. Khandi has been the villain who influenced Raja Mukunda Deb and fomented troubles between him and his family. Khandi's real name was Sadhavi and she was from a village named Suanla. Since she had a broken finger (a deformity) in her left hand, she was called Khandi in her village. She belonged to the Chasa caste, a farming community. She was married to Kapila Jena of Mirzapur village when she was a child. After his death, she married one Jagu Baral of Dasipada village, with whom she had one son, Madan, and two daughters, Pata and Rupei. After Jagu Baral passed away, she shifted to Gopalpur village near Puri along with her children.

Madan started to work as a servant at someone's place. Khandi used to come to Puri to sell cakes made out of cow dung. Later she resorted to begging in Puri to earn her livelihood. One day while Raja Mukunda Deb was distributing alms to poor, he happened to come across Khandi and heard her life story. He developed sympathy for Khandi and offered her and her daughters shelter in a hut near the pigsty in the palace.

Gradually Khandi took advantage of the situation and occupied an influential position. One day when Mukunda Deb was about to start his meal, Khandi came running and shouted, 'Don't touch that food; it is poisoned.' Mukunda Deb got up and threw the food into the courtyard. A crow was found lying dead there next day. The Raja became sure that people in the palace were conspiring to kill him. The incident instilled immense trust on Khandi and he started believing her blindly. He found her the only trustworthy person in the palace.[16]

Gradually, Mukunda Deb got more and more drawn to her and was dragged into the family affairs of Khandi. She exploited the situation fully and tactfully. Khandi married for the third time one Dasarathi Jena, a palace servant, at the instance of Raja Mukunda Deb. He was much younger than Khandi and the marriage was celebrated with pomp in the palace premises. On the request of Khandi, Dasarathi was appointed a police constable by the Raja. Dasarathi hardly did his duties and used to spend the whole day in the palace. For gross irregularity in service and in anticipation of dismissal, Dasarathi resigned from service in 1897.

The Raja in consideration of his weakness towards Khandi asked him to supervise the construction work in the premises of the Jagannath Temple. His surname was changed from Jena to Chhotra to enable this. The priests of the temple vehemently objected Dasarathi's entry into temple and his appointment. A police case was registered anticipating trouble. The police inspector of Puri filed a report before the Magistrate on 31 May 1901.

> I beg most respectfully to state that one Dasarathi Chotra, the husband of Khandi, the pet woman of the Raja, had this year been appointed the Head Engineer over all the building works of the temple of Jagannath. This woman Khandi having once been a beggar of the street has lost, according to the rules of Hindu religion, not only her caste but is not allowed to enter into the temple of any God of Hindu religion... This Dasarathi Chotra being the husband of the woman also met with the same fate. ... Just now one Damodar Pratihari, a Panda of the temple, lodged information to the effect that, with the favour of the Raja, this

Dasarathi will forcibly enter the temple. The Pandas, I am told, will resist him from doing so, even at the cost of their blood.

Khandi became more powerful. She started cornering the temple funds. The Raja was entitled to a share of whatever offerings were made in the form of money/gold. The Raja was also receiving directly gifts in the form of gold. Khandi started acquiring all these.

The growing influence of Khandi made everyone except Raja uncomfortable. Suryamani Patamadei and others sought the intervention of Madhusudan Das to arrest the situation. Das convened a meeting of Utkal Sabha to discuss the affairs of the temple. The *Utkal Dipika* carried a notice issued on 30 April 1898. Madhusudan Das told the meeting about the squandering away of temple property by Mukunda Deb. It was decided that a plan would be worked out after enquiring into the temple affairs. A committee was set up for this purpose.

After few days, a parallel meeting was called by the Raja of Puri to address the issue of mismanagement of temple affairs. A committee was also set up for this purpose. A peculiar situation arose where there were two committees for the same purpose and the purpose itself was defeated as the two committees achieved nothing.

Khandi being a beggar in the street had lost her caste and religion, according to the rules of the Hindu religion. Mukunda Deb made all attempts to bring her back to the fold of her original caste. The Chasa community of the villages of Kapileswarpur, Samagar and Batagaon agreed at the instance of the Raja to take her back as one of them. However, the same community from other villages opposed this. The community from other villages disowned and excommunicated their fellow caste members from Kapileswarpur, Samagar and Batagaon who accepted Khandi back in their fold.

One Kalu Samartha belonged to a caste called Malli. His son got married to the eldest daughter of Khandi. This enraged the Mallis, who disowned him from the community. Mukunda Deb, under the influence of Khandi, opposed the Mallis and started oppressing them.

The son of one Jogi Rout married the second daughter of Khandi. Being pleased with Jogi, the Raja appointed him as the tahsildar of Delanga and renamed him as Jogendra Chandra Routray. Khandi's son Madan's name was changed and the Raja named him Madan Mohan Chhotray Singh, in short known as Madan Chhotra. The Raja granted a lease of 75 acres of land to Madan and appealed to the state government to accord sanction for the lease. The Commissioner of Odisha Division rejected the Raja's request and did not recognize the lease in question, holding that the subject land was attached to the temple.

At the instance of Madhusudan Das, an Englishman J.C. Price was appointed the manager of the Raja in late November 1900 and took charge of Raja's private property as well as the property of temple. The Raja kept three villages under his own management—Kudiari, Kusumati and Chanaghara, belonging to the temple.

Mukunda Deb handed over these villages to Khandi who started collecting land revenue and rice from the villagers.[17] The largesse to Khandi and her family members continued. A large orchard was given to Khandi's son Madan in Kundheibenta Sahi for Rs 990. Khandi was also given a large homestead land in Dolamandap Sahi for Rs 1,500. Her son Madan was given the right to collect revenue from Batagaon mouza for 10 years.

Khandi and her son Madan were convicted in a case u/s 325 of IPC. They preferred an appeal in the higher court and were acquitted. This emboldened the mother and son while the acquittal came as a painful surprise to the public of Puri. Madan Chhotra started considering himself as above the law. He asserted himself by issuing a notice saying no one could enter the palace of the Raja without his permission. He put up a notice at the main entrance of the palace with the following message:[18] 'Madan Chhotra of Dolomandap Sahi, Puri authorized agent of Shri Raja Makund Deb, Superintendent, Puri (Temple) hereby informs the general public that admission of any outsiders into the Raja's palace is forbidden from this day. Any one doing so in unauthorized manner will be liable for punishment according to law.'

There are many more instances showing Raja under the control and influence of Khandi and Madan Chhotra. In a report of the Collector and District Magistrate of Puri, Pundit Ramaballabh Misra, dated 26 May 1913, there is a reference where Khandi got one Babu Ramchandra Chand appointed as *Dewan* to look after the Raja's personal affairs and also to work as a sort of personal secretary to him. However, at the request of Babu Raj Kishore Das, the then Commissioner of Odisha Division succeeded in making the Raja to agree to cancel the appointment forthwith.

There are many other such stories showing the influence Khandi and her son exerted over Mukunda Deb. It is very shocking and surprising that people like Khandi and her son could have such an impact and influence over the Gajapati. In fact, the downfall of Raja Mukunda Deb and the ignominy which he earned was greatly due to Khandi and her accomplices.

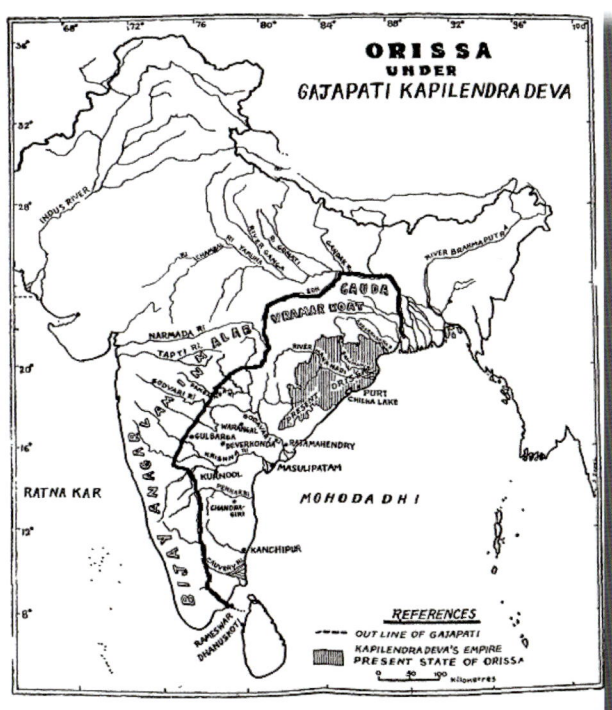

Odisha Empire of Gajapati Kapilendra Deb (AD 1435–1467)

Source: Wikipedia

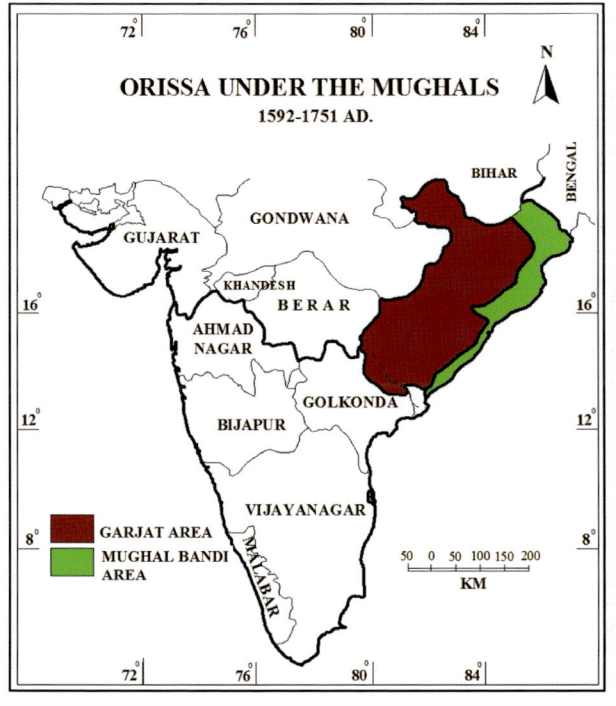

Source: S. K. Sheik Abdul Gaffar Ali, 'Aspects of Socio-cultural Life in Orissa under the Mughals (AD 1592-1751)'. Phd Thesis, 2015

The ancient Jagannath Temple—the abode of the Supreme Sovereign

Gajapati Ramachandra Deb IV

Gajapati Birakishore Deb III and Suryamani Patamahadei

ଗଜପତି ମହାରାଜା ଦିବ୍ୟସିଂହ ଦେବଙ୍କ ରାଜାଭିଷେକ ଓ ପ୍ରଥମ ଅଙ୍କ ପ୍ରଚଳନ ।

The coronation of the present Gajapati, Dibyasingha Deb IV, and introduction of first regnal year, on 8th July 1970

The royal insignia

A view of the palace courtyard with the traditional palanquin (Tamjhan) in which the Gajapati goes to perform the chherapanhara ritual

Nepal's last King and Queen Gyanendra Shah and Komal Shah along with Gajapati Dibyasingha Deb coming out of the southern gate of the temple after darshan. Nepal royalty enjoys special privilege at the Jagannath Temple

Gajapati Dibyasingha Deb at Snanabedi, where the deities are brought from the Ratna Singhasana

The three chariots—(from R-L) Taladhwaja, Devadalana and Nandighosha for Balabhadra, Subhadra and Jagannath respectively—getting ready to begin the annual Rath Yatra

The scene of Pahandi Bije — Lord Jagannath being taken in a ceremonial procession to the chariot Nandighosha for the annual Gundicha Yatra

Gajapati Dibyasingha Deb performing the chherapanhara (ceremonial sweeping of the chariot with a golden handle broom) at the annual Rath Yatra

The Gua Teka Niti ceremony in which Gajapati Dibyasingha Deb initiates the process of Nabakalebara—handing over a silver plate with a piece of gold, a coconut, some grains of rice, sacred thread and areca nut—to the Rajguru (royal priest)

Gajapati Dibyasingha Deb in royal attire, flanked by mahantas of different maths, during the ceremonial Sunia function

The Gajapati with some servitors in their traditional headgear at the commencement of the Nabakalebara event

The Gajapati coming out of the Singha Dwara (Lion's Gate) of the Jagannath Temple. The idol of Patitapabana can be seen on the right side just behind the entrance of the Lion's Gate

Lord Jagannath, the Supreme Sovereign, in His royal attire (Suna besa or Raja besa)

Solicitor General Tushar Mehta (centre) and the Supreme Court-appointed amicus curiae Ranjit Kumar (third from right) meet Gajapati Dibyasingha Deb to discuss reforms in temple rituals

Elephant Gangaram leading the procession of the Gajapati for the chherapanhara ritual

UK's Prince Charles being garlanded by elephant Laxmi at Pipli en route from Puri to Konark Temple

15

MUKUNDA DEB III
A Confirmed Oddity

In a judgment delivered about 100 years back in March 1921, T.D. Mukherjee, Additional Subordinate Judge, Cuttack, described Mukunda Deb as 'a man of weak character and a confirmed oddity'. Strong words indeed! Why did he say so? It involves a fascinating legal battle, the lower court deciding on facts and the higher court delving into intricate issues of law.

The story is about the adoption of a boy by Gajapati Mukunda Deb III. The tale is not just that of betrayal, greed and ego but also of an outstanding legal battle. The chapter unfurls with a brief background of the events as it happened surrounding the adoption of the third son of the then Bamra Raja. The case involves a detailed investigation of the adoption. The chapter ends with a second court case arising out of the appeal against the first. Both cases present outstanding expositions of great judicial minds and calibre.

In 1905, Puri Raja Gajapati Mukunda Deb evinced interest in adopting Lal Mohini Mohan Deb, the third son of Bamra King Raja Satchidananda Tribhuban Deb. Accordingly, he sent a proposal to Raja Satchidananda. However, the proposal did not fructify and was dropped in 1914.

After four years, the Gajapati revived his wish and sent his representative Dhanapati Banerjee to the Bamra Raja to plead on his behalf. Dhanapati negotiated the adoption matter with Bamra Raja Divya Sankar Sudhal Dev, who had acceded to the throne on the demise of his father Raja Satchidananda, and his private secretary Jogesh Chandra. Preliminary enquiries were made and the terms of adoption like the boy's age, absence of *Upanayana* (thread ceremony), providing separate quarters, his education and the government's sanction for adoption and amount to be paid to the adoptive father were discussed and settled by Dhanapati in August 1918.

During the discussion of these terms, Mukunda Deb's favourite Madan Chhotra (see Chapter 14 for details) was present at the Bamra palace along with others. After the final settlement, Madan Chhotra was sent to Bamra along with the Raja's priest for the *Barana* ceremony (formal acceptance of the proposal by conducting a *puja*) of the boy in September 1918. The Puri Raja executed a stamped agreement of adoption on 23 September 1918, which was accepted by the Bamra Raja after certain alterations.

Finally, the adoption ceremony was performed on 2 October 1918 at the Puri Raja's palace. Thereafter, Lal Mohini Mohan Deb was rechristened as Jagannath Jenamani, the title that is bestowed on the eldest son of a Gajapati which he retains till he acquires the regnal name on succeeding to the throne. Jenamani was accepted and treated as his own son by the Puri Raja.

Jenamani used to spend his days at the Raja's house from morning till evening. Rajamata, his mother, came to stay with him in a separate house in Puri. He used to be with her after his palace hours. The Puri Raja and his family started liking him and took good care of him. During the initial months, the health of Jenamani started deteriorating and he suffered a severe attack of pneumonia in January 1919. After this, he was confined to the seaside residence for treatment.

In late 1918 to early 1919, some nefarious steps were taken by some evil-minded conniving people within the Raja's inner circle that led to a souring of the relationship between the adopted son and the adoptive father. Rumours were spread which vitiated the Raja's mind. One rumour had it that Raja Mukunda Deb received a huge sum of Rs 80,000 from the Bamra King which he distributed among his favourites. A printed leaflet was circulated in Puri on 18 October 1918 in the name of Jenamani. It portrayed Jenamani as protesting against the Raja's conduct and threatening criminal prosecution against those who got the money. Jogesh Chandra, the private secretary of Raja Divya Sankar Sudhal Dev, sent a threatening letter on 21 October 1918 to Puri Raja about the wasted money, which greatly infuriated the latter.

An unusual incident took place on 3 February 1919. A number of articles supplied to Jagannath Jenamani and kept in his room at the Raja's palace were found scattered on a public road. Police took charge of these articles as unclaimed goods. The temple manager, who was informed, sent a note to the District Collector stating that the goods belonged to Jenamani. The articles were handed over to the temple *nazir* on behalf of Jenamani. This was witnessed by some mahants who requested the Raja to restore Jenamani to his former position as his successor and end the scandal. The Gajapati stunned everyone by denying that he ever adopted the boy. An insulted Jenamani did not return to his adoptive father's house and instead went back to Bamra.

A parallel case of adoption was put into motion. On 29 October 1918, court stamps were purchased by the Raja for an adoption deed. It was presented for registration by the Puri Raja in person at the Puri sub-registrar's office on 3 February 1919, on which day it was registered with the recital of the details of an adoption on a still earlier date, 2 March 1916. Through this deed, the Puri Raja claimed that Jagadananda Deb, the third son of Sri Krupamaya Deb, the Raja of Badakhemidi, was his actual adopted son whom he claimed to have adopted in March 1916.

In retaliation, Jenamani filed a criminal case against the Puri Raja before the court of Additional Sub-Judge of Cuttack.[1]

Jenamani became the plaintiff or the complainant and Raja Mukunda Deb and Jagadananda Deb, the newly claimed adopted son of the Puri Raja, the defendants.

Jenamani made the following prayers to the court:

1. He be declared the lawfully adopted son of Raja Mukunda Deb and as such entitled to all the privileges of an adopted son.
2. The alleged adopted son be declared fraudulent.
3. It be declared that the Puri Raja, Mukunda Deb, was a mere trustee for and on behalf of the plaintiff regarding the money paid at the time of adoption and was not entitled to deal with it in violation of the trust.

Both the Puri Raja and Jagadananda Deb denied every allegation. Mukunda Deb averred that on the date of alleged adoption of Jenamani (2 October 1918), he instituted a *Graha Shanti Homa* to propitiate the evil stars for his own health. He denied that he was connected with Jenamani's adoption. He repudiated the authority of Dhanapati Banerjee and Madan Chhotra to act on his behalf. Amid allegations and counter-allegations, the Judge framed the following issues:

1. Whether Raja Mukunda Deb executed the agreement of 23 September 1918 and whether it was valid and binding?
2. Whether Jenamani was adopted by Raja Mukunda Deb on 2 October 1918 and whether the adoption was valid and legal?
3. Whether Jagadananda Deb was adopted on 2 March 1916 and if so whether the adoption was valid?
4. Whether Raja Mukunda Deb was paid Rs 1 lakh as alleged by Jenamani? Was the Raja a trustee on behalf of Jenamani?

Before the case came up for trial, Jagadananda Deb died on 23 July 1920. Accordingly, he ceased to be entitled as the adopted son of Mukunda Deb. Therefore, on 24 July 1920, the Judge asked whether the Raja was stopped from questioning the validity of Jenamani's adoption now that Jagadananda Deb had died. The Judge held that the burden lay on the Jenamani to prove his own adoption. 'If he succeeds in establishing his adoption, it will be open to him to challenge and criticize the evidence regarding the alleged previous adoption of the deceased defendant and to invoke the legal aid of estoppel: otherwise the plaintiff will be entirely out of the court.'

The judge analysed and evaluated a vast amount of evidences, recorded statements of several witnesses, relied upon events, circumstances, testimonials and arguments of both the parties and delivered his ruling on 2 March 1921.

Negotiation

One of the key events that formed the protasis of this entire play was the negotiation that happened between the Puri Raja and Bamra Raja. In June 1918, Dhanapati Banerjee was asked by the Puri Raja to go to Bamra to negotiate with the Bamra Raja. His instructions were to see that the boy was fairly grown up and promisingly capable of looking after his affairs. The boy needed to be initiated into the sacred thread.

With this instruction, Dhanapati went to Calcutta and broached the subject with Jogesh Chandra, the private secretary of Bamra Raja. Dhanapati and Jogesh Chandra along with another pundit, Guru Charan Tarkadarsan, left for Bamra. There, Dhanapati interviewed the Raja and also the boy, whom he considered suitable.

The Bamra Raja approved the proposal and promised to pay Rs 1 lakh with certain conditions which required the assent and compliance of the Puri Raja on certain matters regarding the boy's education and a separate mess and quarters for him. The Puri Raja was to obtain the government sanction for the adoption, without which the Bamra Raja would not proceed. The Bamra

Raja authorized Dhanapati to negotiate with the Puri Raja on his behalf. Dhanapati was assured remuneration.

However, during trial, the Puri Raja denied Dhanapati's authority to negotiate on his behalf. The Judge wanted to know whether, under the cloak of being an agent of the Puri Raja, Dhanapati was playing the game of Bamra. Dhanapati deposed that he proceeded on his mission based on a written letter from the Puri Raja addressed to the Bamra Raja.

The interview was followed by a chain of events, correspondence and transactions. One such letter was affirmed by both Dhanapati as well as an officer of the Bamra Raja. Dhanapati met Raja Mukunda Deb several times and placed the counter-proposals offered by the Bamra Raja. Mukunda Deb did not agree immediately. He consulted the Ranis and then finalized the terms which were communicated to the Bamara King through Dhanapati.

Dhanapati wrote to the temple manager for moving the government for the required sanction for adoption on 8 July 1918. This was obtained on 16 July. The same day, the Divisional Commissioner of Odisha wrote to the Bamra chief stating that although the government could not influence or even advise the Puri Raja as to his choice, they would not raise any objection if the Puri Raja chose to select the third brother of Bamra Raja Divya Sankar Sudhal Dev.

Raja Mukunda Deb criticized the communication proceedings from the government and alleged that permissions were granted without proper care and inquiry, and provided a handle to a lot of unscrupulous elements 'to foist an adoption on the imbecile king by means of paper evidence which did not represent actual facts'. The Puri Raja alleged that the temple manager, Dhanapati, Madan Chhotra and all principal witnesses examined on Jenamani's side were influenced by Bamra money to create evidence in favour of Bamra.

The Judge delved deeper into the matter. He found that after getting the government's permission, the Puri Raja had sent Madan

Chhotra to Bamra with a letter dated 2 August 1918. This letter apparently requested the Bamra Raja to visit Puri with his mother and brother and bring with him the promised Rs 1 lakh. Dhanapati and the temple manager swore that Madan Chhotra went to Bamra on business. This was supported by the evidence of Madan Chhotra producing bills for travelling expenses for reimbursement.

According to the Judge, the circumstances connected with Madan Chhotra's mission and the part played by him in the affairs sufficiently indicated that he did not identify himself with Bamra's interest.

Preparation

The next evidentiary aspect was the deputation of a party to Bamra for the performance of the *Barana* ceremony of Jenamani. The group consisted of the Puri Raja's head priest Rajguru Raghunath Brahma, Madan Chhotra and others. Their tour was sanctioned by the Puri Raja in writing. The witnesses testified to the facts and circumstances connected with the visit to Bamra, the *Barana* ceremony and related events. It became clear that the Raja was fully aware of the negotiation and all aspects connected to it. The negotiation led to the execution of a stamped agreement by the Puri Raja on 23 September.

Another key event was the preparation for the *datta homo* ceremony. *Datta homo* is performed in Hindu adoptions. To complete the adoption, it is considered necessary. In the case of the twice-born classes no such ceremony is needed if the adopted boy belongs to the same *gotra* as the adoptive father. When the *gotra* of the adopted son is different from that of the adoptive father, *datta homo* is performed for a valid adoption.

The temple manager was sent for by the Raja and old Rani Suryamani Patamahadei to make arrangements for the ceremony. The manager wanted money as he could not get an advance from the temple fund. It was decided that money would have to be raised as a loan through Dhanapati's agency. The Raja raised a loan of

Rs 6,000 from Lokenath under a hand note dated 27 September. A *bedi* (mandap or raised platform) was constructed.

The Raja sent written instruction to the manager on 25 September to receive the Bamra family at the Puri railway station. Five days later, the old Rani sent written instruction regarding the special treatment to be accorded to Jenamani on the occasion of the ceremony. Her handwriting was proved by the manager.

The peculiarities related to the role of Jenamani were known to none else but the old Rani. All this showed the unmistakable fact that the adoption was a result of a mature deliberation not only on the part of the Raja but also the Ranis. The same day, a budget was prepared regarding the expenditure of adoption signed by the Raja. Dhanapati had also obtained a procession license on behalf of the Bamra Raja for 2 October 1918.

Agreement

The agreement was executed on 23 September 1918. Dhanapati was present on behalf of Bamra Raja on this occasion. He prepared the draft himself and explained it to the Raja who signed on every page. It was attested by Madan Patnaik, Madan Chhotra and Rajguru Raghunath Brahma. The Judge noted, 'There is no reason to entertain the suspicion in this case for the simple reason that the document was carefully signed by the Raja and witnessed by two of his faithful servants besides favourite Madan Chhotra.'

Adoption Ceremony

There was overwhelming evidence to prove that the Bamra family arrived at the Puri station on 1 October and was received by the temple manager, staff and Dhanapati. They went in a procession from the railway station to the seaside lodging. The boy was taken past the temple Lion Gate under the direction of the Puri Raja so as to enable himself and the Ranis to view him. On the day of adoption, there was a procession with music. Special constables were deputed to keep peace at the house of the Puri Raja. The Inspector of Police watched the procession himself.

The document of payment receipt was signed by the Raja in the presence of a number of persons, including Rebati Mohan, Registrar, Bengal Secretariat; Khitish Chandra Niogi, *Vakil* of the High Court of Calcutta; and Surendranath Chakravarti, Headmaster of Survey School.

There were discrepancies about the time of payment. The Judge did not attach much weight to this aspect. All doubts on this point were liquidated when the Raja of Puri admitted to the retired Collector, Manmohan Ray, that he had got Rs 1 lakh as a 'token of his dignity'.

The Raja of Puri stated that he held a ceremony of *Grahashanti Homo* at his house on a raised platform. Jenamani's contention was that a *Datta Homo* ceremony was performed on the same day on the same platform at the same place. So, was it *Grahashanti Homo* or *Datta Homo*? There were striking differences between the two. A *Datta Homo* is consummated by a formal ceremony of a vow on the part of the adopter before the sacred fire. In this case, that was done by the Puri Raja while doing *Purnahuti* with the boy by his side. No such thing was required to be done in a *Grahashanti Homo*, which was individual and bereft of any mutuality. The fact that *Datta Homo* was performed was proved by conduct, corroboration and other primary and secondary circumstances. Besides Jenamani, his second brother, his mother, Banerjee and Calcutta witnesses and many respectable men of Puri attended and testified to the performance of adoption ceremony. Premier mahants of Puri such as mahant Emar Math, Dakhinparso Math, Gopal Tirtha Math, Radhashyam Math, etc. also testified having attended the adoption ceremony.

Datta Homo was performed by Brahmins on the *bedi* inside the palace where the guests were seated. But *Adan Pradan* (exchange) and *Sankalp* (vow) took place behind the purdah. The Puri Raja came out of the purdah clasping Jenamani's hands in his own. Both walked to the *bedi*, mounted it and there the Puri Raja consummated the *Homo* which had commenced several hours earlier by offering *Purnahuti*. Both the Raja and the adopted son offered *puspanjali*.

The fact is that the Raja declared the holding of *datta homo* in the presence of the guests and recorded it on paper. It was also witnessed by the guests. It was argued that the recording of *Adan Pradan* was an unusual procedure and should be fully discredited as a matter of deception. This argument was rejected.

Adan Pradan was the most essential ceremony but it had to be done behind the purdah as the giver was the *Rajmata* of Bamra. This was testified to by the *Rajmata*, the adopted son and the Rajguru. This ceremony, though not required to be very ritualistic, juristically amounted to a corporeal transfer of the adoptee from the giver to the taker accompanied with words and actions. The adopted son and the Rajguru deposed to the physical delivery of the boy and the Raja's reply to the *Rajmata*'s offer.

Temple Visit and the Circumambulation

After the ceremony, the Puri Raja and Jenamani went to the Jagannath Temple in their palanquins. Jenamani's one was newly prepared. In the presence of the Lord, Jenamani was treated with special honours, which were only next in importance to those accorded to the Puri Raja. These facts were corroborated by the Puja Panda of Lord Jagannath. The Raja and Jenamani circumambulated the temple.

Invitation and Feasts

After the temple visit, verbal invitations were sent by the temple manager for a feast. Brahmins were fed at Bainkuth (inside the temple premises) on the day of adoption. Mahants were treated to *Mahaprasad* the next day at the Puri Raja's palace. Jenamani acted as the host. This was corroborated by the mahants. The sebaks were treated to a feast on the third day and others on the fourth day.

Other Supporting Evidence

There were other evidences to establish that adoption did take place. The Collector's letter to the temple manager enquiring about the ceremony on the very day of adoption was significant.

After the ceremony, Jenamani was treated with affection by the family. He confirmed that he received affectionate treatment from the Puri Raja and Rani during the first three months. His birthday ceremony, *Swanakhyatra*, was performed at the Puri Raja's house on 30 October 1918. Jenamani suffered a severe attack of pneumonia in January 1919 and was confined to the seaside lodge for treatment. He was not aware of any untoward action on part of the Raja until his belongings were thrown out on 3 February 1919.

The Alternate Adoption

The adoption of Jagadananda Deb by Mukunda Deb was alleged to have taken place on 2 March 1916 pursuant to an unstamped agreement executed on the previous day. A deed evidencing the adoption was engrossed on a stamp paper purchased on 29 October 1918 but registered on 3 March 1919. The claim of adoption was structured and found to be controverted by facts appearing from the papers of the Badakhimidi zamindar (Krupamaya Gajapati) who was siding with Mukunda Deb. One Durga Madhav brought a civil suit in the Behrampur Court in April 1916 for enhancement of maintenance against Krupamaya and his three minor sons. In the suit, the first son, Jubaraj, was shown as Defendant No. 2, Jagannath (second son) as Defendant No. 3 and Satyanarayan alias Jagadananda (third son) as Defendant No. 4. This Jagadananda was the boy who was alleged to have been adopted by the Puri Raja.

Krupamaya averred that his second son had been given in adoption to Sankhimidi and had said nothing about his third son

Jagadananda's adoption. The omission could be calculated as a damaging circumstance against the Badakhimidi adoption.

Krupamaya further claimed that after the adoption of his second son, he performed a ceremony to celebrate the Raj investiture regarding this third boy in 1917. This title 'Raja' belonged to the second son. But as he was given away in adoption to a different family, it was conferred on the third son. This contradicted his own claim. The title would never have been transferred to the third boy if he too had been given in adoption to another family.

Krupamaya belonged to a different *gotra* from that of the Puri family. Yet he gave the boy in adoption to the Puri Raja without the *datta homo* ceremony. To address this anomaly, Krupamaya devised a convoluted story. The Puri family, which belonged to Nagas *gotra*, adopted the Atriya *gotra* of Badakhimidi when Dibyasingha Deb (son of Khimidi Raja) was adopted by Birakeshari Deb. Krupamaya argued that the adopted son Dibyasingha Deb was his brother. Thus he was drafted to the Puri family by a special process of grafting not amounting to usual adoption. This was found to be specious and absurd.

Krupamaya also claimed that he refused to give his first son in adoption to the Puri Raja but later agreed to give away his third son. This contention too fell flat. In 1914 he had gone to Puri with the object of giving his first boy in adoption to Raja Mukunda Deb, but this was not accepted by Puri Raja family. He returned in anger and installed the same boy as 'Jubaraj' and shortly afterwards he gave away his second son in adoption to Sanakhimidi in November 1915. He had to admit these facts. These self-serving submissions turned out to be self-defeating for Krupamaya.

There were other evidences to contradict the claim of Jagadananda's adoption. Krupamaya had said that he left Digpudi on 28 February by a motor car for Berhampur with his three children and nurses besides a large number of servants. He reached Puri on 29 February. It was, however, proved from records that Krupamaya could not have left Digpudi on that date as the person said to have accompanied him to Puri in 1916 was sent to Sonepur.

It was contended that the agreement was executed in the presence of *sadhus*, mahants, *bhadralokas* (gentlemen) and so on. Not a single independent witness could be brought to the box. The statements of witnesses were found contradictory, inconsistent and untrue. On examination and cross-examination of witnesses, Krupamaya's deposition was found 'unreliable and scheming'.

Other Adoption Proposals: Government's Attitude

The Puri Raja was particularly coveted among the local royalty not so much for his wealth and emoluments (which were not considerable) but for the honour attached to his position from a religious and social point of view. There were many proposals for adoption from various principalities and kings such as Mayurbhanj, Salur, Surangi, Sonepur, Dharakot and Dhenkanal, besides Bamra and Badakhimidi. Proposals from Salur and Badakhimidi were discussed during the tenure of Raja Mukunda Deb from 23 February 1913 to 12 October 1916. Both fell through.

Dixon was the Collector of Puri for about one year till the middle of October 1917. There was a proposal of adoption from Surangi during his tenure but it failed. The Raja did not tell Dixon that he had already adopted a boy.

Manmohan Ray succeeded Dixon till a part of November 1919. He had knowledge of the Bamra adoption. He had heard about the proposal 3 to 4 months before it took place. But he had no information about the alleged Badakhimidi adoption. None of the district officers too knew anything about that adoption. No communication passed between the government and either the Puri Raja or Badakhimidi zamindar regarding the adoption. It was strange that the Puri Raja argued that there were some papers in possession of the government which, if produced, would show that they were aware of the Badakhimidi adoption.

The attitude of the government with respect to the Puri adoption was explained by the Divisional Commissioner and Ray, Collector of Puri. The government was interested on the issue of adoption because the then Puri Raja was in poor health and if he was to die without making any adoption, the affairs of the temple were likely to fall into confusion. The government had nothing to do with the secular and domestic affairs of the Raja; they could not advise about or interfere with any adoption by the Puri Raja nor could they influence such an adoption.

Nature of Payment

Having established that money was given in the adoption of Jenamani, it remained to be seen under what condition it was paid. Besides, Rs 20,000 paid in war bonds in the name of Jenamani, Rs 80,000 was paid in currency notes. It was paid to the Puri Raja for the adopted son; therefore, the Raja had no right to it except as the trustee on behalf of the adopted son. On this issue there was only an oral testimony of Dhanpati and there was nothing in writing to prove the condition. The Judge concluded that the money was paid as a consideration for adoption without any condition being attached.

After exhaustively dealing with all evidences, witnesses, material facts and circumstances, the Additional Subordinate Judge declared that 'Jagannath Jenamani, and not Jagadananda Deb of Badakhimidi, was duly adopted by Mukunda Deb and consequently the legally adopted boy was entitled to all the rights and privileges of an adopted son'.

Aftermath of Death and Decision

The matter did not rest with this judgment. The Raja filed an appeal in the Patna High Court.[2] His counsel did not question the findings of the Additional Subordinate Judge. But the Raja questioned the validity of adoption on legal grounds.

He contended that the age of the Jenamani, 18 years at the date of adoption, rendered the ceremony invalid according to Hindu Law amongst families of the twice-born classes.

Secondly, certain ceremonies essential to the validity of adoption under the *dattaka* form were not complied with.

Thirdly, the respondent's mother had no authority from her deceased husband to give her son in adoption.

Finally, the passing of money as a consideration for adoption is forbidden by Hindu Law and was contrary to public policy. This rendered the transaction void.

Chief Justice Dawson Miller, along with Justice H.F.E.B Foster, heard the appeal.

In support of the first point, reliance was placed upon a passage in the *Kalika Purana* quoted with approval by the author of the *Dattaka Mimansa*. The authority of *Kalika Purana* is unquestionable, and the treatise known as the *Dattaka Mimansa of Nanda Pandit* is regarded both in Bengal and amongst the followers of the Benares School of Hindu Law as a great authority.

Age, a Bar to Adoption or the First Issue

The meaning of the passage as explained by the author of the *Dattaka Mimansa* is: A son whose tonsure ceremony has been performed in the family of his natural father cannot validly be adopted as a son given, and; as this ceremony ought to be performed not later than the fifth year, no boy above that age is capable of being so adopted. This was the fundamental and strongest ground of challenge of the Raja of Puri for declaring the adoption as invalid.

Much controversy raged around this passage and much ingenuity was expended in explaining this rule which appeared to be at variance with actual practice. The Court dealt with this issue in detail and laid down the law by referring to diverse sources of Hindu law, judicial precedents and rigorous interpretation of texts and law.

a) The judges held that in the earliest *Smritis* there was no such prohibition. The only restriction imposed by Manu was that the adopted son should belong to the same class or caste as his adoptive father. According to them, the restrictions on age and marriage were unquestionably innovations of a later age.

b) Apart from the passage quoted from the *Kalika Purana* and adopted by *Dattaka Mimansa* and a few other treaties, there is no ancient authority for the preposition that a child over five years of age cannot be validly adopted in the *Dattaka* form. The authenticity of the passage was in question even before the date of the *Dattaka Mimansa* itself. *Dattaka Chandrika*, a work of equal authority, is of earlier date and prescribed no such restriction.

c) The reference to the fifth year is said to apply only to Brahmins seeking the fruit of holiness resulting from a study of the Vedas. Relying on Setlur's Complete Collection of Hindu Law Books on Inheritance, the court viewed that *Kalika Purana* on which the limitation as to age of the adopted son was based had been held to be spurious by the author of the *Dattaka Chandrika*. All the High Courts and many of the modern text writers were in agreement that the Hindu Law imposed no restrictions as to age and, whatever the age of the adopted son, it was now settled that his adoption was valid if made before *upanayana*, if he belonged to any of the regenerate classes, and before marriage if he belonged to the Sudra caste.

d) The judges even opined that the performance of the *upanayana* ceremony in the family of natural father was no bar to a subsequent adoption.

e) In 1887, Justice Mahmood of the Allahabad High Court concluded that the disputed passage in the *Kalika Purana* could not be relied upon as authentic and that the *upanayana* ceremony, which, in the case of Kshatriya, may be performed as late as the 22nd year, was the limit of age for a valid adoption.

f) The question over the *upanayana* ceremony of a Kshatriya did not arise as it was admitted that the respondent's *upanayana* had not been performed at the time of his adoption.

g) The court therefore held that the adoption of the respondent was not invalidated by reason of his age.

The Second Issue

The second point raised was whether the adoption ceremony was done according to the correct ritual. The omission urged were (1) that the Rajmata did not sit upon the *bedi* at the time when the *Datta Homo* was performed, (2) that the *Charu Homo* did not take place (3) that the *Sankalpa* was not done, and (4) that the *Putreshti Jag* ceremony was not performed. This was essential as the respondent's tonsure ceremony had taken place in the family of his natural parents. With regard to each of these points, the court viewed that except the last, there was no difficulty as there was evidence on record from which a decision could be arrived.

Regarding *Putreshti Jag* ceremony, there was no direct evidence from which it could be said whether it was performed or not. Although the court considered not allowing this question to be argued before them, the judges were cautious. The court put to itself for its opinion on the assumption that this ceremony was not done. The court rendered its views as under:

a) The foundation upon which its performance is claimed as a necessary adjunct to a valid adoption is based on explanation of a passage of the *Dattaka Mimansa*, which has been interpreted by some as meaning that adoption even after tonsure may be validated by the performance of the *Putreshti Jag*, or sacrifice for male issue, but not otherwise.

b) The only case in support of the appellant's contention was a ruling that *Putreshti Jag* was essential to the validity of an adoption in the Dattaka form amongst the three superior classes.

c) In a later case, the Calcutta High Court expressed the view that the words *Putreshti Jag* in a former judgement were inadvertently used for *Datta Homa* and on this assumption refused to follow it in the case of adoption of a son belonging to the same gotra as his adopted father.

d) The Calcutta High Court also held that the *putreshti jag* was not an essential element in the ceremony of adoption. But this was so for Sudras.

e) Apart from the dictum which had been characterized as a *lapsus lingua* in the same High Court, there was no direct authority in the appellant's favour on this point.

f) The judges finally held an adoption was valid provided the *upanayana* ceremony, the culminating point of the second birth, had not been performed although the other initiatory rites, including tonsure, had taken place in the natural family of the adopted son.

The Third Issue

The third point was the capacity of a widow to give her son in adoption. It was submitted that a widow could do so if her husband while alive had consented. It was argued that no such consent was there and hence the adoption was invalid. The court observed:

a) It was well settled that a mother could give her son in adoption even without her husband's express consent in cases where such consent could not be obtained.

b) In the text of Manu, the words 'with her husband's assent' do not appear. According to the court, he who is given by his mother with her husband's consent while her husband is absent or incapable though present, or without his assent after her husband's decease, or who is given by his father, or by both, being of the same class with the person to whom he is given becomes his given son.

c) The *Dattaka Mimansa* and the *Dattaka Chandrika* both recognize the right of a widow to give her son in adoption on account of the impossibility of obtaining her husband's consent.

d) The case-law is all to the same effect and no authority has been quoted in support of the contrary view.

The Fourth Issue

The last point was that the adoption was induced by a bribe. But the mere fact that the appellant had mixed motives for the adoption would not be sufficient in law to render it invalid.

Additional Issues

The counsel of Mukunda Deb contended that the appellant was mentally incapable of understanding the effect of his actions and so the adoption was invalid. This was a last ditch effort. The Chief Justice observed that this was not raised in the issues and the evidence did not support the contention. He refused to permit the question to be raised.

The counsel of the Puri Raja did not give up. He argued that there was no evidence that the *upanayana* ceremony had been performed as a part of adoption and this was in itself sufficient to invalidate the adoption. The Chief Justice refused to entertain this new plea.

Conclusion

This is a unique case of adoption battle anywhere and particularly in Gajapati history. It is really strange that a Gajapati of Puri for the first time having legally adopted a son disowned him. A childless Gajapati is required to adopt a son to succeed him without any discontinuity. On top of it, the Gajapati adopted another son or claimed to have done so. This resulted in a prolonged legal battle.

Before the case could come up for trial, the other adopted son expired. But it did not *ipso facto* recognize the claim of the first adopted son. The strangeness of the case is that the Raja of Puri made strong arguments against his legally adopted son. After losing the case in the trial court, the Raja moved the High Court against the validity of the adoption itself only to prove himself as a 'volatile person and confirmed oddity'.

The protracted litigation ended with the Patna High Court's decision on 17 February 1923 in favour of Jenamani. Gajapati Mukunda Deb died of smallpox on 14 February 1926.[3] Jenamani assumed the regnal name of Ramachandra Deb and was crowned the Raja of Puri. However, the government did not accord its approval to appoint him as the superintendent of the temple and did not confer on him the title 'Raja'. Finally, the government wrote to the Commissioner of Odisha Division, Cuttack, on 14 May 1926, 'The Governor in Council has now decided to transfer the management of the temple to Ramachandra Deb, adopted son of the late Raja Mukunda Deb of Puri, with the stipulation that he should submit to Government the name of any Manager whom he may propose to appoint.'

16

RAMACHANDRA DEB IV
Tryst with Gurudev, Fight with Priests

Raja Mukunda Deb died of smallpox on 14 February 1926. His adopted son Jagannath Jenamani, later known as Ramachandra Deb and was the son of Bamara King Satchidananda, succeeded to the throne. His appointment as the superintendent of temple was delayed because of the delay in the government order pursuant to the Patna High Court order resolving the dispute over adoption (see Chapter 15 for details). Finally, the government, on 14 May 1926, issued the order to the Commissioner, Cuttack Division, appointing Ramachandra Deb as superintendent of the Puri Temple.

Ramachandra Deb became the Gajapati at a crucial time. He was the last Raja during the British rule and the first after the country got independence. The management of the Jagannath Temple was stressed. He did his best in the given circumstances. Two instances show Ramachandra Deb in true perspective.

Honouring Gurudev

Gurudev Rabindranath Tagore had a century-long family connection with Odisha. Referring to it, the poet said, 'I belong also to Orissa. I entertain goodwill, love and affection for the people of Orissa. So I am closely watching the political developments in Orissa.' These were his words narrated by Biswanath Das, the then Prime Minister of Odisha (later designated as Chief Minister) when he met the poet to pay his respects in Calcutta. He invited Gurudev to Odisha.

After returning to Odisha, Biswanath Das urged the poet to visit the state as an honoured guest. The then Governor, Sir John Hubback, however, did not like the idea of treating a non-official person as a state guest. Biswanath Das disagreed and sanctioned necessary approval exercising his discretion to invite Gurudev as a state guest. Tagore did visit Odisha. Dr Harekrushna Mahtab, a former Chief Minister and a historian, wrote that Odisha was the first state in India to welcome Tagore as a state guest.[1] Tagore reached Puri on 19 April 1939 and was warmly received by the entire cabinet and government officials. He stayed at the Circuit House. This was Tagore's last visit to Odisha but he had made several trips earlier.

The Tagore family had a long association with Odisha. Rabindranath's ancestor Nilamani Tagore came to Cuttack as the first *sheristadar* of the British government. Nilamoni's grandson, the grandfather of Rabindranath, Dwarikanath Tagore, purchased the zamindari of Pandua near Jagatsinghpur in 1840. Debendranath Tagore, father of Rabindranath, came to Pandua to supervise his zamindari in 1851. Forty years later in 1891 Rabindranath made it to Odisha for the first time to oversee the Pandua zamindari. It was a memorable visit. He wrote *Chitrangada* then.

His next visit was in 1893 when he stayed in Cuttack and travelled to Puri in a palanquin. In Pandua, he wrote the poems *Anadruta, Nadipathe* and *Deul*. He came again to inspect the estate in the middle of 1896. Tagore's estate was divided by Debendranath when the sons of Gunendranath—Abanindranath, Gaganendranath and Samarendranath—attained majority. The Pandua estate fell to the share of the sons of Gunendranath. Consequently,

Rabindranath no longer supervised the affairs of the Pandua estate and his connection with Pandua came to an end.

He next came to Cuttack in 1931. On 9 May, a meeting was held in Cuttack to celebrate Tagore *jayanti*. Utkal Gaurab Madhusudan Das presided over the function. His next and last visit was in 1939. Each visit was interesting and historic, and Tagore wrote about the visits.

The poet's Puri visit was most memorable. On 8 May he was given an address on behalf of the women of Odisha. Tagore's birthday was celebrated on 9 May with great enthusiasm at a public function. After the inaugural song, the poet was welcomed with the chanting of Vedic hymns by the pundits of Sanskrit College. Oblations of flowers, sandal paste, vermillion and coconuts were offered. After the welcome address, Gopal Chandra Praharaj, Chairman of the Puri Municipality, presented a filigree casket on behalf of various cultural organizations.* Pandit Raghunath Misra welcomed him in Sanskrit and Sarala Devi in Odia.

The poet was very pleased with the reception. He expressed his satisfaction and gratitude. In his speech, he said that he had been warmly received in many places but the reception given that day by the people of Odisha had touched his heart as it was according to the traditional Hindu style. He would always cherish, he said, the memory of that welcome.

During his stay in Puri, another significant event was Gajapati Ramachandra Deb's gesture of honour for Gurudev. The Gajapati

---

* Gopal Chandra Praharaj mentions that when Rabindranath Tagore was presented with the title of 'Kabi Samrat' by the Andhra Research University, Vizianagaram, he himself as a fellow of the university presented a set of the work to the poet. The poet writes an appreciation on 20 July 1938 stating, 'The *Purnachandra Odia Bhashakosha* is an encyclopaedic dictionary which has been found extremely useful for the work of our Research Department in the Viswabharati. The compiler, G.C. Praharaj, and his collaborators deserve our sincere thanks for the excellent work done' (Gopal Chandra Praharaj, *Purnachandra Odia Bhashakosha* [Cuttack: Utkal Sahitya Press, 1940]).

wanted to hold a grand public function to honour Tagore. Since Tagore fell ill, it could not be organized. He sent his Dewan, Rajguru and the head priest of the temple in a procession to the Circuit House. After the recitation of a Sanskrit panegyric, a camphor garland, a headdress and a pair of silk clothes were offered on behalf of the Gajapati to Tagore. The Raja bestowed upon Tagore the title 'Param Guru' (Teacher of Teachers or Ultimate Teacher). A *manapatra* (scroll of honour) was also presented to Tagore. The scroll, in Odia, is preserved in the archives at Shantiniketan. Tagore was extremely pleased with the honour. The text of the scroll reads as under:

"ବୀର ଶ୍ରୀ ଗଜପତି ଗୌଡେଶ୍ୱର ନବକୋଟି କର୍ଣ୍ଣାଟୋତ୍କଳ ବୀରାଧୂବୀରବର ବର୍ଗେଶ୍ୱରାଧୁରାୟ ଭୂତଭୈରବ ସାଧୁ ଶାସନୋକ୍ଷୁର୍ଷ ରାଉତରାଜ ଅତୁଳ ବଳ ପରାକ୍ରମ ସଂଗ୍ରାମ ସହସ୍ରବାହୁ କ୍ଷତ୍ରୀୟ କୁଳ ଧୂମକେତୁ ମହାରାଜାଧିରାଜ ଶ୍ରୀ ଶ୍ରୀ ଶ୍ରୀ ରାଜା ରାମଚନ୍ଦ୍ର ଦେବଙ୍କର ଶ୍ରୀ ପୁରୁଷୋତ୍ତମ ବଡ଼ ଦେଉଳ ପରୀକ୍ଷାକୁ ସମସ୍ତ କାର୍ଯ୍ୟ ମାନଙ୍କୁ ସାମନ୍ତ ସତ୍ୟ ମହନ୍ତଙ୍କୁ ଚଉତରା ତହସିଲଦାରଙ୍କୁ ସୀତା କରଣଙ୍କୁ ସହର ସର୍ଦ୍ଦାର ନଗରନାୟକଙ୍କୁ ଚାରିବାଟ କରଣଙ୍କୁ ମାଝି ମିରିଧା ଗ୍ରାମ ପେଶ ଘାଟ ବିଶୋଇଙ୍କୁ ମଧ୍ୟ ଚିଟାଉ... ଭାରତ କବିକୁଳ ତିଳକ ବିଶ୍ୱବରେଣ୍ୟ ସୁଧୀପ୍ରବର ବିଶ୍ୱକବି ରବୀନ୍ଦ୍ରନାଥ ଠାକୁରଙ୍କର ଅସାଧାରଣ କବି ପ୍ରତିଭା ସସାଗରା ପ୍ରାଚ୍ୟ-ପାଶ୍ଚାତ୍ୟ ଧରା ପୃଷ୍ଠରେ ପ୍ରାଚୀନ ଆର୍ଷ ବିଭବ ମଣ୍ଡିତ ଭାରତବର୍ଷଙ୍କ ଦେଶୀୟ ସାହିତ୍ୟ କଳା, ଉତ୍କର୍ଷ ସାଧନ ଦ୍ୱାରା ଗୌରବାନ୍ୱିତ କରିଥିବୁ ବିଶ୍ୱକବିଙ୍କୁ ଆଗେ ଆନନ୍ଦିତ ହୋଇ ଆଜି ଏହି ସର୍ବଧର୍ମ ସମନ୍ୱିତ ନୀଳାଚଳ ଧାମରେ ପରମଗୁରୁ ଉପାଧିରେ ଭୂଷିତ କରି ଶାଢ଼ୀ ଶିରୋପା ଆଜ୍ଞା ଦେଲୁଁ ଏ, ପଦ ଅମଳ କରିବେ କେହି ଅଟକ ନ କରିବ ନ କରିବେ ଇତି ପଂଦର ବୈଶାଖ ଫଂଦର ଦିନ ନବମୀ ଶୁକ୍ରବାର ସ୍ୱ ୧୩୨୪"

ସାଲ ୧୧ ଙ୍କ ତା ୨୮ ୧୪ ୧୯୯୩୯ ୧୧୧

The English translation of the citation reads as below:

The Illustrious valiant and ever victor Hero, the Lord of Elephants, Hero of the Heroes, Sovereign of Bengal, Supreme Monarch over the rulers of tribes of Utkala, Kernata, and the nine forts, Absolute owner of Bargeswar, Originator and emanator of blood-curdling horror and terror, saintliest, highest spokesman of administrative acumen, lord of a thousand arms in the field of battle by his peerless and unequalled might, comet of the war adept Kshytriyas (martial race), King of kings Sri Sri Sri Ramachandra Deb's humble invitations to temple parichhas, priests, feudal lords, Mahants, representatives of landed gentry class, urban chieftains, all and sundry high class elites, Tahasildar and officials and all village heads, an open letter to you all... paragon of poets in India, world renowned, great intellectual, world-poet Rabindranath Tagore who ushered in modernist sensibility in the realm of world literature has inspired a whole generation of poets of Orient and Occident which is unprecedented in the annals of world literary history. He has resuscitated the ancient Indian tradition and heritage in its pristine purity and sanctity. The indigenous literature and art of India underwent metamorphosis having been magnified and glorified thousand fold by Tagore's unfathomable literary grandeur and splendor.

Hence we have been pleased to bestow the title of Parama Guru, preceptor of preceptors upon him by tying the Sadhi Siropa in this holy land of Lord Jagannath (Nilachala Dham) which is a confluence of myriad religious cults and syncretic spiritual undercurrents for his extraordinary literary talent. We specifically order that nobody will obstruct this endowment upon this Paragon of poets of the world.

Pronounced in this open ambience this fifteenth day of the month of Vaisakha, Navami, Friday, 1346 year.

Dated 28.4.1939

Overwhelmed by the hospitality in Puri, Tagore wrote:

Let me now tell you about myself. I have no work here nor am I of any use to anybody. Those who are taking care of me here expect no material advice from me. That salutary and refreshing effect with which sea breeze is touching my body and mind is the very symbol of the hospitality of the newly responsible Orissa Government. Administrative procedure has created no obstacle to it, nor has it been affected by the budgetary economy. Sitting on the first floor of the Circuit House, I have unhesitatingly given myself to pure idleness. The ministers here, having noticed the tired condition of my health, come every day to encourage me to spend my days without any purpose. The mentality of admitting human relationships even in the midst of pressure of work is still inherent in our country: and this has been felt by me specially after I have come over here.[2]

Tagore left Odisha in the second week of May 1939. While in Puri, he composed three poems entitled 'Pravasi' (The Outsider), 'Janmadin' (Birthday) and 'Epare Opare' (This Side and That Side).

Temple Administration

While Ramachandra Deb felt gratified by honouring Gurudev, he faced numerous challenges in the temple administration. He faced hostile sebaks who were averse to reform. One such instance is an unusual criminal case filed by the *puja pandas* (priests) which he handled.

On 21 March 1954, when the morning *dhupa* and *bhog* were offered to the Lord, some vessels containing the *bhog* were kept outside the inner sanctum (*Muruj*). According to the religious tenets and usages, such *bhog* is unfit to be offered to the Lord. *Puja pandas* who noticed the *bhog* kept outside directed their removal by the Brahmin sebaks known as *swars* (cooks) attached to the temple.

In the temple of Lord Jagannath, the *puja pandas* form a class of sebaks who alone, according to the customary religious practice, have the right to offer *bhog or neivedya* to the Lord. No other sebak, even if a Brahmin, was entitled to perform this function. But that day, in spite of their directions, the *swars* had the unfit *bhog* removed by *Sudra Bhojyas* instead of doing it themselves. The *pandas* objected to this and declared that this had polluted the whole temple, requiring a *Mahasnan* (sacred bath) to be performed by way of a purificatory ceremony. Until such *Mahasnan* was performed, the other daily *nitis* (rituals) offered to the Lord were held up.

When this was brought to the notice of Shri Jagat Ballav Das, dewan of the temple, he directed the performance of the necessary *nitis* without performing the *Mahasnan*. The temple commander, Shri Jagadeb Ray, supported the dewan and abused the *pandas* because they held up the *nitis*. The matter was brought before Gajapati Ramachandra Deb, the superintendent of temple. He supported the dewan and the commander of the temple. He felt that a *Mahasnan* would be expensive and that the other *nitis* might be performed by merely sprinkling sacred water around the temple premises.

The *pandas* as a group protested and refused to obey the Raja, saying it was against religious tenets. This led to an unusual situation. The Raja of Puri, thereafter, directed some of the *Pushapalak* sebaks to perform the remaining *nitis*. These sebaks initially protested but ultimately thought it was wise to obey the Raja. They did the daily *nitis*, including the offering of *bhog* to the Lord at the *Bhoga Mandap*. This *bhog* was subsequently sold to the public as *Mahaprasad*.

The *pandas* alleged that (a) the pollution of the temple had not been removed by proper purificatory rites, and (b) the *bhog* was not offered to the Lord with proper *mantras* by the *pandas* who had the exclusive right to offer such *bhog*. They alleged that other sebaks, namely *swars* and *Pushapalaks*, were aware of the religious practices and rituals and thus the *bhogas* offered at *Bhoga Mandap* would not be *Mahaprasad*. The *pandas* filed a criminal case against the Raja of Puri and the sebaks.

They alleged offences under Section 295, 295A and 420 of the Indian Penal Code (IPC) against the Raja and others (during the trial Section 295A was dropped). The main 'offence' was under Section 295, which says that a person will be guilty if he defiles any object held sacred by any class of persons with the intention of insulting the religion. The *pandas*' argument was that the object held sacred by all Hindus is the sacred food of Lord Jagannath, known as *Mahaprasad*.

A criminal case was linked with issues that were civil in nature. The religious practices, rituals, the role performed by sebaks as per the Record of Rights of the Temple and scriptural instructions relied upon for guidance were referred to for deciding the issue at stake. A case of cheating under Section 420 was also made out by the *pandas* in as much as they said the public was deceived into thinking that the *bhog* was *Mahaprasad*.

The main issue was to ascertain under what circumstances the need for a *Mahasnan* would arise. According to temple regulations, the temple would be considered seriously polluted if a pilgrim touches the holy image or if someone spits within the temple or if one passes stool or urine or vomits. *Mahasnan* then takes place and penalty is imposed on the culprit if he is traced. *Mahasnan* would also be ordered if accidentally a dog enters the temple, or a corpse or bone is found inside the sacred precincts. It was nowhere stated that for every act of pollution, even a minor one, *Mahasnan* should be performed.

The *pandas* relied on a passage from the *Niladri Mahodaya* which states: 'The *Archaka* shall thereafter worship the Lord according to the rites. He must place the articles that are to be offered as *Bhog* inside the *Mandala*. He shall not place them outside the *Mandala*. If by chance the articles for offering are placed outside the *Mandala*, they must be thrown out, otherwise they become the food of the *Rakshasas*.'

The court observed that the above passage in the *Niladri Mahodaya* only supported the view that the *bhog* kept outside the inner sanctum (*Muruj*) on the morning of the day of occurrence became unfit to be offered to the Lord and should be thrown out. It did not show that the mere removal of such *bhog* by Sudras would pollute the temple to such a degree as to require the performance of *Mahasnan* as a condition precedent to the performance of all other *nitis* inside the temple. It, however, was correct that the pollution would require some sort of purificatory ceremony. But the ceremony would depend on the nature of the pollution.

The *pandas*, according to the court, held an extreme view that *Mahasnan* should be performed for every act of pollution, irrespective of its nature. But the superintendent of the temple and other sebaks may hold the view that for minor acts of pollution—like in the present case—a mere sprinkling of sacred water would suffice.

The *pandas* relied on another passage from the *Niladri Mahodaya*, 'Oh, King, in the absence of the Acharya no other person shall perform the Puja karmas of Paramatma Vishnu. As in the absence of everybody, the Acharya can perform all the 'karmas': who can, Oh, King, performs His 'karmas' in his absence?'

This was pointed out by the *pandas* to highlight that none else other than them would offer the *bhog* and that *seba* by *Pushapalaks*, as directed by the Raja of Puri, was against religious practice.

Religious rules were quoted to counter the extreme position held by the *pandas*. It was emphasized earlier that the *bhog* can be offered only by the *pandas* and by no other class of Brahmins sebaks under any circumstances. But it was shown that though ordinarily *puja pandas* alone were entitled to offer *bhog* at *Bhoga Mandap*, during their absence, or on their default, Brahmins of other *gotras* could offer *bhog*. On one previous occasion, *Pushapalaks* were allowed to perform the *seba puja*.

A reference was made to an almost identical scenario decided by the Madras High Court. In that case, a goldsmith performed the *abhishekam* of a *Shiv Linga* by pouring coconut water over it. It was strongly objected to on the ground that only Brahmins were entitled to perform the *abhishekam*. The goldsmith was, however, acquitted by the lower court on the ground that he did what was considered to be a bona fide act of worship.

The guilty knowledge required for Section 295 could not be attributable to either of the parties in the case of the Jagannath

Temple. The Raja of Puri and the *pandas* in good faith held two different views regarding (a) the circumstances under which the purificatory ceremony known as *Mahasnan* would be performed, and (b) the circumstances under which the Brahmin sebaks known as *Pushpalaks* can offer *bhog* to the deity. Members of Mukti Mandap were consulted on this subject, who supported the Raja in directing the *Pushapalaks* to offer the *bhog* when the *pandas* refused to do so. As a result of the row, the ceremonies inside the temple were held up for several hours.

The court rejected the criminal appeal of Gopinath Puja Panda Samanta (on behalf of the *pandas*) and upheld the action of Raja Ramachandra Deb. The revision petition was dismissed.[3]

After this, Ramachandra Deb took several measures in bringing discipline among the sebaks for conducting various rituals in the temple. This led to a confrontation between the all-powerful *pandas* and the Raja. The *pandas*, though they had lost in the trial court, moved the High Court to insist that their refusal to obey the Raja's direction was correct. The Raja wanted to convey a message that an extreme position was unreasonable and untenable. He felt a need to bring in reformative orientation in various *sebas*. After a bitterly fought and protracted battle, Gajapati Ramachandra Deb was able to uphold his point of view.

17

GAJAPATI *VERSUS* GAJAPATI
Beginning and End of Hostility

The history of Odisha witnessed an interesting but lesser known story of hostility between two kingdoms, Khurda and Khimundi (Parlakhemundi)*. The cause of dispute was a common claim by their rulers—both assumed the title of Gajapati and this became a bone of contention and clash of ego. While the kings of Odisha—subsequently known as the Raja of Khurda and the Raja of Puri as their dominion diminished—have been using the title of Gajapati since the days of Suryavanshi kings with Kapilendra Deb being the founder of this dynasty, the Rajas of Parlakhemundi have claimed to be the true inheritors of the title. The kings of Khimundi have traditionally used the Gajapati both as a surname and a title. The rivalry between the two Gajapatis is rooted in history.

---

* Khemundi, Khemidi, Khimidi and Khemindi have been interchangeably used by different authors. They mean the same place. Similarly, Parlakhemundi, Parlakhemidi and Parlakhimindi have also been used interchangeably.

The Gangas came from the south of India and their original capital was Kalinganagar, located in Srikakulam in the present-day Andhra Pradesh. Chodagangadeva conquered Kalinga, Utkala and Kausal, becoming the *trikalingadhipati,* and established a massive empire. The Gangas constructed the Jagannath Temple, the magnificent Konark and the Lingaraj Temples and made significant contributions to the wealth, prosperity and welfare of the state. The Ganga period is known as the golden period in the history of Odisha.

The Gangas had five different branches ruling over various small states as independent kingdoms. The kings of Khimundi owe their origin to one of the branches and hence claim to be descendants of the Gangas—as inheritors and lineal descendants of the glorious founding Ganga kings, the rulers of Khimundi have been claiming to be the true Gajapatis. This conflict has expressed itself from time to time in various forms.

Confusion

The confusion was compounded after the death of Kapilendra Deb in AD 1464. Purushottama Deb, who succeeded him, was not the rightful claimant to the throne. Hamvira, the eldest son of Kapilendra Deb and a great warrior, was the natural choice. As a General in Kapilendra Deb's army, he had established his credential as a great warrior and conqueror in the south. To overcome the anomaly of Purushottama Deb ascending to the throne instead of Hamvira, the doctrine of divine elect was used: it was claimed that Purushottama Deb was the choice of Lord Jagannath, which was conveyed to his father Kapilendra Deb by the deity through a dream. This was used to select Purushottama Deb ignoring the rightful claimant.[1] This created a conflict between the two brothers and each tried to stake his claim over the Odishan kingdom. According to one tradition, 'Kala Hammira alias Narasimhadeva was eldest of Kapilendra's eighteen legitimate sons. When Purursottama became the king of Odisha after Kapilendra and ruled from his capital Cuttack, Kala Hammira established himself at a place called Gudari in modern Koraput district and laid the foundation of Khimundi kingdoms.'[2] There is a view that after the defeat of Hamvira, a compromise was reached under which Purushottama Deb allowed Hamvira to rule over Khimundi as his vassal.[3] This led to the notion that Hamvira and his successors formed a line of subordinate rulers under the Gajapati of Odisha.

Origin of the Khimundi King

This confusion needs to be addressed. It is, therefore, useful to understand the nature of the Khimundi kingdom and the genealogical character of the Khimundi kings. The kingdom existed independently from at least the 10th century AD. It is mentioned in the Dirghasi inscription of the time of Rajarajadeva, father of Chodagangadeva. In the inscription there is a mention of one Vanapati, Commander of the King of Kalinga, who captured areas like Kimidi, Gidrisingi, Kosala and Utkala. It is, therefore, clear that Khimundi was a separate region not under kings of Kalinga.[4]

When Narasimhadeva or Kala Hammira (Hamvira) began to rule Khimundi from Gudari Kataka, the kingdom consisted of the present taluks of Badakhimundi, Sanakhimundi, Parlakhemundi, Bastar and a portion of Koraput district. Kala Hammira's rule began in *Saka* 1167 (AD 1245) and continued up to *Saka* 1187 (AD 1265).[5]

Three researchers have prepared the genealogical tree of the Khimundi line: R. Sewell (*Archaeological Survey of Southern India*, vol. II, pp. 185–86ff.), B. Seshagiri Rao (*J.A.H.R.S.*, vol II, pp. 257–58ff.) and S. Paricha (*The Kalinga Sancika*, Telugu Edition, p. 416ff.).

The Khimundi rulers are shown below.[6]

A COMPARATIVE STATEMENT REGARDING THE PEDIGREE OF KHIMUNDI LINE

	Name of Kings	Sewell[1] (I) AD	Seshagiri Rao[2] (II) AD	Paricha[3] (III) AD
1	Narasimhadeva (Kala Hammira)	1245-1265	1245-1285	1245-1261
2	Madanadeva	1265-1290	1285-1320	1261-1281
3	Narayanadeva	1290-1309	1320-1355	1281-1296
4	Anandadeva	1309-1317		1296-1297
5	Ananta Rudradeva	1317-1325	1355-1386	1297-1311
6	Jaya Rudradeva[4]	1325-1367	1386-1431	1311-1344
7	Laksmi Narasimha Bhanudeva	1367-1392	1431-1456	1344-1364
8	Madhukarnadeva	1392-1432	1456-1488	1364-1388
9	Mrtyunjaya Bhanudeva	1432-1457	1488-1522	1388-1415
10	Madhava Madanasundara Bhanudeva	1457-1494	1522-1599	1415-1444
11	Candra Betala Bhanudeva	1494-1527	1599-1603	1444-1470
12	Suvarna Linga Bhanudeva	1527-1566	1603-1642	1470-1501
13	Sivalinga Narayanadeva	1566-1590	1642-1670	1501-1520

	Name of Kings	Sewell[1] (I) AD	Seshagiri Rao[2] (II) AD	Paricha[3] (III) AD
14	Suvana Kesari Narayanadeva	1590-1630	1670-1710	1520-1522
15	Makunda Rudra Narayanadeva	1630-1656	1710-1736	1522-1573
16	Mukundadeva	1656-1674	1736-1754	1573-1591
17	Ananta Padmanabha Narayanadeva	1674-1686	1754-1767	1591-1603
18	Sarvajna Jagannatha Narayanadeva	1686-1702	1767-1784	1603-1619
19	Narasimhadeva	1702-1729	1784-1811	1619-1646
20	Vira Padmanabha Narayanadeva	1729-1748	1811-1824	1646-1662
21	Vira Pratap Rudra Narayanadeva	1748-1766	1824-1842	1662-1693
		-13 ――― 1753 A.D.*	-89 ――― 1753 A.D.*	+60 ――― 1753 A.D.*

1. R. Sewell's *Archaeological Survey of Southern India*, vol. II, pp. 185–86ff.
2. *J.A.H.R.S.*, vol. II, pp. 257–58ff.
3. *The Kalinga Sancika* (Telugu Edition) p. 416ff.
4. Before Jayarudra, Nrsimharudra ruled for 30.5 years as per list II.

N.B.: It has been proved from other sources that the 21st king (Vira Pratap Rudra Narayanadeva) ended his rule in AD 1753. While comparing the three genealogies, it is seen that Sewell's list is more correct. The difference of 13 years in Sewell's list, from the total number of years, may be ignored in the face of the length of family line.

Source: Extracted from Dr S.N. Rajguru, *History of the Gangas*, Part II, pp. 80-81.

Five collateral branches of the Gangas began to establish their own kingdoms in Kalinga in five different provinces. This is supported by epigraphical evidence. Some copper plate inscriptions found near Gunpur, belonging to the time of Danarnava, and another found from Bagusala near Uppalada in Parlakhemundi taluk throw light on the existence of a separate kingdom of the Gangas.

This portion of the country, comprising Gunpur, Parlakhemundi and Tekkali, was separated from Kalinga-Dandapata in the regime of the imperial Gangas and the Gajapatis of Odisha. It is also found from the Parlakhemundi Vamsavali that a Ganga king, Subhalingabhanu or Sivalingabhanu, was the founder of Parlakhemundi line. From a Sanskrit work known as *Abda-duta*, composed by Krishna Shrichandan, one gets a short genealogical account of Ganga kings. The author was son of one Narayana Mangaraja and grandson of Ramachandra Mangaraja who acted as ministers of Khimundi. A commentary on this *kavya* was written by the king of Kimidi himself. According to this book, Badakhimundi and Sanakhimundi also belong to the same line of Subhalingabhanu.

Subhalingabhanu, who was a great warrior and a good scholar, had a brother, Ramachandra Anangabhima Keshari. Both brothers planned to conquer Odisha, since anarchy prevailed there after the death of Prataprudra Gajapati. They brought into their possession a large portion of Odisha towards the north of Khimundi and established their presence in Khurda Rathipur. The dominion lasted for a few years. The brothers divided the kingdom of their forefathers into two halves. Subhalingabhanu continued to rule from Nagarikataka while Ramachandra Anangabhima Keshari ruled in the tracts of Badakhimundi and Sanakhimundi.

Subhalingabhanu enjoyed the portion of Parlakhemundi, including Nagarikataka, Srikakulam and the present taluk of Gunpur.

Against this background, it is important to have clarity about Hammira or Hamvira. Hamvira, the rival brother of Purushottama Deb, appeared in the scene after the death of Kapilendra Deb in AD 1464. Narsimhadev or Kala Hammira, in different findings of genealogical research of the Khimundi line, reigned from AD 1245. When Hamvira was defeated and was reported to have had established Khimundi, research shows that Madhava Madanasundara Bhanudeva of the Ganga dynasty ruled Khimundi. Therefore, Hamvira of Suryavansa seems to be totally different from the Khimundi ruler of the relevant period. Therefore, 'The view that Hamvira and his successors formed a line of subordinate rulers under the Gajapatis of Orissa is not an established fact.'[7]

The Parlakhemundi Rajas had always claimed their descent from the Gangas and had never accepted the authority of the Bhoi Rajas. They always claimed the title of Gajapati as their hereditary right and disregarded the Khurda Rajas as inheritors of the title.[8] Some scholars feel that since the Khimundi kings belong to the Ganga dynasty and *Atreya gotra*, their family connection with the Suryavansi king Kapileswar Gajapati is only a myth.[9]

Conflicts Between Two Gajapatis

Conflicts took place between the two Gajapatis from time to time. For sake of convenience, the issue is analysed beginning with the British conquest of Odisha. The British occupation introduced a new equation in the relationship between the colonial regime and the Jagannath Temple. This impacted and influenced the role of the Raja of Puri and his relation with other kings, including the Gajapati of Parlakhemundi.

The East India Company occupied Puri with the assurance that they would not interfere in the administration, rituals and traditions of the Jagannath Temple. It procured the support of priests and pundits by assuring them that they need not entertain any fear over matters of the temple or religious sentiments. After Odisha came into British possession in 1803, the administration of Temple affairs was entrusted to the *Purchas*.

The East India Company, however, started facing difficulties in the administration of the temple. A debate began in October 1806 over finding a 'more satisfactory individual' in whom the 'control of Jagannath Temple consistent with the usages of the Temple can be properly vested'.[10] After deliberations and discussions, the Secretary of the Revenue Department in Calcutta informed the Board of Revenue in Cuttack in 1807 that the Governor General had decided to release the Khurda Raja from confinement and to reinvest in him the control of the temple. By a regulation IV of 1809, the Khurda Raja was appointed the superintendent of the temple and given control over the priests, internal economy and management.[11]

The re-establishment of the Khurda Raja in charge of temple administration brought a huge contextual change. The Raja was shifted and relocated to Puri and the Gajapati became the 'Raja of Puri'. As in the changed context the Gajapati became a king without any kingdom, he felt insulted and humiliated by the British for they went back on their promise of returning the four parganas (see Chapter 10 for details). The return of these promised parganas dispossessed during the Marathas would have restored some territorial legitimacy to the Raja of Puri but the British betrayed the Raja.

So a situation was created where the fallen king was trying to retrieve his lost dignity and pride and reposition himself by making an authoritative space for himself. The only leverage the Raja had in this context was his association and linkage with the Jagannath Temple. This leverage had to be calibrated by the Raja to create a niche for himself. The Raja had a dual identity and role—he was the Gajapati as well as the *Adyasebak* of Lord Jagannath. This dual identity had over time undergone a change in which the role of the Gajapati was subsumed in the new role of superintendent of the temple, while the traditional role of *Adyasebak* was retained.

This change in the Raja's dual role provided strength as well as challenges and was a difficult situation to navigate.

Against this background, a few instances are interesting.

In 1810, Raja Padmanabha Narayana Deo of Khimundi came to Puri with his three wives and mother to visit the Jagannath Temple. He was accompanied by a large troupe with all royal paraphernalia. He was in royal attire and led a procession accompanied by trumpets and other ceremonial musical instruments and *chattar* (umbrella). The Khurda Raja denied him entrance for *darshan* for three days.

The Khimundi Raja complained to the Settlement Commissioner, Charles Buller, against the Khurda Raja citing the humiliation suffered at his hands. On his complaint, the Collector of pilgrim tax, Samuel Busby, sent a report to Robert Mitford, Collector of Cuttack, indicted Raja for his 'atrocious behaviour'. Khurda Raja's attempt to justify his behaviour by making reference to *Madala Panji* was negated by Busby who reported:

> *Madlah Panjee* has no connection whatever with pilgrims coming to make *darshan* and that they should be entirely under the management of the Collector of tax and not for the Superintendent of the temple to interfere, but be limited solely to see that the *Bhoges* are properly supplied every day and at the different festivals, and he should always attend and see the nitty *sewas* or ceremonies of the temple are done agreeable to the recorded rules and institution of the temple.

Busby suggested that free liberty should be granted to everyone to come with their respective honour and perform religious ceremonies as they thought proper.[12]

The Khurda Raja responded to Busby's report and stated that the visiting chief had not applied for permission to enter the Temple as a customary courtesy. The *deula pariccha* (temple administrators appointed since the time of the Marathas) and priests supported the Raja's stand. Busby did not agree and asserted that since the region was under the control of the British government, the Khurda Raja had no right to issue 'original passes' on his own authority. The visiting Raja suffered further humiliation when the Khurda Raja prevented him from procuring *Mahaprasad*. The Khurda Raja persuaded the *swars* (temple cooks) not to cook *Mahaprasad*. Busby told the Collector, 'Upwards of four to five thousand of souls are now starving for want of necessary *Mahaprasad* including Rajah Padlabh Deo and his followers as it is not proper nor conformable with their religion to cook victuals at Pooree when they come on pilgrimage but only to live on *Mahaprasad*.'[13]

The Raja of Puri held a unique position of eminence among the kings of Odisha. Gadajat kings and other independent Hindu kings showed their loyalty and respect to the Khurda Raja because of the latter's access, engagement and linkage with the Jagannath Temple. Whenever visiting Rajas came for pilgrimage to the Jagannath Temple, they used to inform the Khurda Raja in advance as per established custom. Then the Raja used to arrange for the provision of various privileges in keeping with their status. The institution of the Raja and formal permission from him acted as a formal conduit for *darshan* of the lord. The Raja of Khimundi breached this protocol and broke the tradition and customary practice, which the Raja of Puri felt was an act of impropriety and discourtesy. By denying *darshan* and *Mahaprasad*, he asserted his customary privilege.

The Khimundi Raja also carried his royal insignia into the temple precincts without informing the Gajapati, thereby flouting his authority in his own territory. The Khurda Raja was exercising his authority as 'Protector of the divine order of the temple, which had been transgressed by the visiting chief'.[14]

The Gajapati had great command over the network of sebaks and service providers of the temple. Therefore, the priests and *deula pariccha* supported him. The *swars* too came to his help and did not cook the *Mahaprasad*. This deprived more than four thousand to five thousand pilgrims of food. The complex network associated with temple was a great asset, which the Raja of Khurda relied upon in asserting his traditional authority, which not only humiliated the Raja of Khimundi but also made the government come out in support of the latter. The Khurda Raja was reminded that the whole of Odisha including the temple was under the disposition of the British government.

The traditional personal enmity between the Gajapati of Puri and the Gajapati of Parlakhemundi was a living reality. The assertion of traditional authority by the Gajapati of Puri demonstrates a serious attempt to revive and restore his legacy in a changed context. Despite the loss of his kingdom, the loss of past glory and successive occupations by the Mughals, Afghans, Marathas and British, the Gajapati tried hard to retain his ideological authority. The Jagannath Temple, its rituals, traditions, network of support and patronage to the temple through various connections provided a solid ground; as the principal servitor of Lord Jagannath, the Raja of Khurda earned his respect, credibility and dignity.

While the government viewed the Raja's action from a legal administrative prism, the Raja created a broader framework for himself through which the people viewed him with respect and reverence. Collector Busby's view that the Raja of Parlakhemundi had paid pilgrim tax and he had every right to visit the temple was logically and legally correct; however, the Gajapati viewed it as an insult to his position, which he projected through his broader framework earning instant support. Compliance with the terms of the new regime violated the norms of tradition and practice giving rise to irreconcilable conflict and contradiction.

Moving to an earlier time, Jagannath Narayan Deb succeeded to the throne of Parlakhemundi in AD 1751. He lived and ruled at a critical period when there was a keen contest for power among the Marathas, French and English in that part of the country which the British won. Jagannath Narayan Deb tried to regain the past glory of Gajapati kings of his family who had once enjoyed suzerainty over the whole of Kalinga, including Utkala. He found that Birakeshari Deb of Khurda, who belonged to the Bhoi dynasty, was only a puppet king in the hands of the greedy Marathas and decided to attack the Khurda ruler.

From reliable palm leaf manuscripts,[15] a true picture of Jagannath Narayan Deb's invasion of Khurda has emerged. It is said that Jagannath Narayan Deb attacked the fort of Banapur, wherefrom he sent a messenger to Birakeshari Deb requesting him to join hands with him to crush the Marathas and the advancing European powers in Odisha. Birakeshari Deb refused to join him. So, Jagannath Narayan Deb marched his army against Birakeshari Deb towards Khurda and easily took possession of that fort. After this, Birakeshari Deb took shelter in Cuttack under the protection of the Marathas, whose soldiers were deployed against Jagannath Narayan Deb. A battle was fought near the fort of Chhatragada in modern Puri district, in which Jagannath Narayan Deb was defeated and retreated.

This story has another version. Seo Bhatt Sathe was the Subedar of Odisha during 1759–1764. During his rule, Gajapati Jagannath Narayan Deb, the Raja of Parlakhemundi, was very powerful. He used the title of Gajapati, claiming it belonged to him as a matter of right and hereditary privilege. He did not recognize the Raja of Khurda as the Gajapati. He staked claim on the throne of Khurda and invaded it. Gajapati Birakeshari Deb, the Raja of Khurda at that time, was defeated.

In distress, he sought the help of Seo Bhatt Sathe, the Maratha subedar. The subedar came to his rescue on the condition of payment of Rs 1 lakh to which Birakeshari Deb agreed. The Raja of Parlakhemundi was driven out of Khurda by the Marathas.

Birakeshari Deb, however, was unable to pay the promised money and so was forced to surrender to the Marathas the fertile parganas of Lembai and Rahanga, Purushottam Chattar and the 14 Gadajat areas. As a result, the Gajapati lost control over the Jagannath Temple of Puri too. The management of the temple of Jagannath, a privilege which was so long enjoyed by the Khurda Raja from ancient time, was placed under the Maratha government. Birakeshari Deb could not recover the lost territories or Puri, the 'Purushottam Chattar'. Despite several attempts, he could not retrieve the parganas either. He lived a life of distress and depression, finally going mad and killing his four sons. The historicity of these facts was a constant reminder of hatred and animosity between the Gajapati of Puri and the Raja of Parlakhemundi, who claimed to be the real Gajapati.

Prior to the fight with Khurda, in 1757, Raja Jagannath Narayan Deb of Parlakhemundi made an attempt to wrest the title of Gajapati from Raja Birakeshari Deb at the Rath Yatra held that year. Raja Jagannath Narayan Deb entered Puri with 2,000 people with all the insignia of royalty in clear defiance of the authority of the Puri Raja. The Parlakhemundi Raja arrived on an elephant to the beating of drums, a flagstaff and royal seat, and offered his gifts and prayers directly to priests. He even climbed the *rath* of the Lord for *darshan* which was the exclusive privilege of the Gajapati.

He demanded the holy garland offered to the deity, when it was by right the Gajapati's privilege to receive. The priests secretly sent the garland to their Gajapati, Birakeshari Deb, and gave tulsi and prasad to the Parlakhemundi Raja. The Parlakhemundi chief and his brother sat in the rath the whole day and stated their wish to enter the Jagannath Temple with their royal insignia and offer prayers, which was again the Gajapati's privilege. The priests were in utter distress and delayed all ceremonies, performing only the essential rituals. Finally, the Parlakhemundi Raja was allowed to enter the temple wearing royal costumes but could not perform various Gajapati *sebas*.

The uncomfortable relationship had another dimension. Birakeshari Deb died in 1859. Before his death, he adopted the infant son of Khimundi (Parlakhemundi) Raja as his successor. The adopted son was later known as Dibyasingha Deb. Dibyasingha Deb was convicted in a murder case and was given sentence of transportation (see Chapter 12). This was a black spot in the history of the Gajapatis. There came into being a psychological aversion towards any future relationship with the Parlakhemundi family.

Later, there was a proposal in 1914 that the childless Gajapati Mukunda Deb IV adopt the son of the Badakhemindi family. This was turned down by the Puri Raja. The Ranis, particularly the old Rani Suryamani Patamahadei, considered the proposal from Badakhemindi family to be inauspicious. Dibyasingha Deb's conviction was the biggest mental barrier to accept another child from the same family. History proved to be the most difficult hindrance.

Other Instances

It may be useful to know that such rivalry demonstrated by the Khurda Raja was not limited to the Gajapati of Parlakhemindi alone. The Raja of Khandapara, a tributary state, visited Puri with his family in 1814 to have *darshan* of Lord Jagannath. He entered the town with the insignia of kingship and demanded *Poorashood* for his family, a privilege where the visiting king and his family could have exclusive *darshan* of Lord Jagannath with the temple premises vacated by other pilgrims.

The Khurda Raja considered this demand to be a breach of protocol and an affront to his authority. He did not allow the Raja of Khandapara to enter the temple. The Raja complained to the British Collector 'that Rajah Mackoondeo prevented him from making *darshan* with his family in the mode he has been accustomed and that he is agreeable to the customs and rules of the Temple'.[16]

Collector William Trower issued orders to the Raja of Khurda and the *parichhas* not to object the Raja of Khandapara in performing his religious ceremonies in the usual mode. The Raja of Khurda was adamant and sent a letter to the Collector through Samuel Busby explaining the reasons for his objections to the admission of the Raja of Khandapara into the temple. Trower was furious and issued a *purwanah* to the Khurda Raja saying that in case he continued with his objection to the admission of the Khandapara Raja, he would take it upon himself to suspend him from the position as superintendent of the temple. Busby was also requested by Trower to ensure that the Khandapara Raja and his family did not meet any insult from the followers of the Raja of Khurda.[17]

Mukunda Deb, the Khurda Raja, gave in to the Collector's demands but did not keep quiet about the British way of handling the situation. He made a representation to the Board of Revenue against the conduct of the Collector of Cuttack. John Richardson was requested to investigate the matter. Richardson admitted that Trower, the Collector, had exceeded the limits of his authority by threatening suspension while admitting that the conduct of the Raja had been objectionable. Richardson, however, concluded that there could be no objection on the grounds of religion in denying the Khandapara Raja entry into the temple with insignia of kingship. He held that the resistance by the Raja of Khurda was based on personal enmity or other equally untenable grounds.

The Khurda Raja's opposition to the Khandapara Raja had a historical basis. During the reign of Gajapati Birakeshari Deb, the Khandapara Raja had visited Puri on pilgrimage in 1772. A *Chamu chitau* (royal order) was issued by the Khurda Raja announcing his visit to Puri and ordering that the visiting Raja be allowed an exclusive *darshan*. The family of the Khandapara Raja entered the temple accompanied by the Buxi of Khurda and the head of *Chatisanijoga* and performed rituals of *darshan* in their presence. The royal guests were offered a variety of sacred clothes, including a piece of the temple flag. In 1772, the tradition of protocol was followed by the Khandapara Raja to whom Gajapati Birakeshari Deb had extended all courtesy and reciprocal honours. In 1814, however, the Raja of Khandapara forgot the traditional convention.

Richardson, however, discussed at length the Khurda Raja's conduct. He was of the opinion that the misconduct and behaviour of the Raja of Puri was based on a belief that 'he will one day through the power and influence of Juggernath be restored to the supreme command and authority of the province of Cuttack, which tradition and family (oral or written) history state to have been invested in his ancestors'. He further wrote, 'These hopes, however chimerical, delusive and obtrusively viewed apparently innocent, have not only present ill effects, but they might possibly in the course of events at some critical juncture have further bad significances.'[18]

Richardson also opined that the Puri Raja had treated 'all the native hindu princes, Rajahs and Chiefs or men of rank with disrespect and contempt; which treatment, I am adequately informed, is one great excuse of the smallness of the number of pilgrims of First class which have resorted to this far famed Temple of Hindu worship since the Rajah's investiture in the superintendence of the Temple'.

Although Collector Trower was admonished by the Governor General for his interference in the affairs of temple, he made his remarks against the conduct of the Raja very clear in his report to Richardson. Trower very categorically mentioned that as long as the Raja retained any power in the temple, he would continue to 'prevent their visit and also those of many other persons'.

He also mentioned that the Raja of Khurda conveniently and cleverly quoted *Madala Panji* whenever he wanted to give trouble to others, but when it concerned his own interest he deliberately forgot the reference. Trower also said that the *Madala Panji* contained rules for the duties to be performed by sebaks and priests and had nothing to do with visits of pilgrims. He highlighted the 'extortion of Raja Mukunda Deb and [the] impertinence of his underlings'. Trower made out a case for which Richardson recommended to his Lordship in Council 'salutary restriction on the authority of Superintendent of Temple'.[19]

Let's take another example. Rani Muktadevi of Sambalpur lost control over her territory in 1805. She was granted the pragana of Panchagarh in the Khurda estate for her maintenance. When she visited the Jagannath Temple, the Raja denied her entry. This was because this area was lost by him to the Marathas and not returned by the British, wounding his feelings. The Khurda Raja could not reconcile to the situation.

End of Hostility

Odisha was separated from Bihar and declared an independent state on 1st April 1936. Until the constitution of a Representative House and a responsible Council of Ministers, Odisha was under the direct control of the Governor. Governor Sir John A. Hubback was appointed to look after the transition and interim arrangement from 1 April 1936 till 31 March 1937. A committee was set up to aid and advise the Governor. Maharaja Krushna Chandra Gajapati (also known as Maharaja Sir Krushna Chandra Gajapati Narayan Deb, KCIE), the king of Parlakhemundi and a member of the Madras Assembly, was appointed the advisor to the Governor.

The first meeting of the advisory committee was held on 8 May 1936 at the Raj Bhavan in Puri. Maharaja Krushna Chandra Gajapati reached Delanga, a taluk near Puri, on 7 May to participate in the meeting the next day. Parlakhemundi had a historical connection with Delanga. Maharaja Krushna Chandra Gajapati's father Gajapati Gourachandra Deb had purchased the zamindari of Delanga in 1885. The zamindari was looked after by Dewan Lakshmi Narayan Patnaik, the father of the late Biju Patnaik, the erstwhile Chief Minister of Odisha.

The purchase of the Delanga zamindari by the Parlakhemundi Raja was a source of bitterness for the Gajapati of Puri. In 1760 when the Marathas were ruling, the then king of Parlakhemundi, Jagannath Narayan Deb attacked Khurda. Gajapati Birakeshari Deb, with the help of the Marathas, drove away Jagannath Narayan Deb. Thereafter, the four parganas were lost to Birakeshari Deb for his inability to meet the Marathas' demand. His successors could not retrieve them. Under these circumstances, Parlakhemundi king Gajapati Gaurachandra Deb's purchase of the zamindari of Delanga, a part of dispossessed area of Raja of Khurda, re-opened the historical wounds and revived the old enmity.

This purchase caused friction between Parlakhemundi and Puri. Considering the sensitivity of the matter, no king of Parlakhemundi had ever visited Delanga. For the first time, to attend the meeting of the advisory committee at Puri, Maharaja Krushna Chandra Gajapati decided to spend the night at Delanga and left for Puri on the morning of 8 May. He went straight to the Raj Bhavan. After the meeting, he returned to Parlakhemundi.

He did not visit the Jagannath Temple as the wounded feeling of the past haunted Maharaja Krushna Chandra Gajapati. It was extremely unusual, quite unprecedented and exceptional for a Hindu dignitary or a king to visit Puri and not visit the temple. This happened 176 years after the erstwhile Parlakhemundi Raja, Jagannath Narayan Deb, his ancestor, had attacked Khurda in 1760.[20]

Governor Hubback invited Maharaja Krushna Chandra Gajapati to assume the office of the first Prime Minister of Odisha (later this post became Chief Minister) on 1 April 1937. He formed the first council of ministers with two ministerial colleagues—Gaurachandra Patnaik, the leading lawyer of Behrampur and Latifir Rehman, a lawyer from Puri.

After the swearing-in ceremony, Maharaja Krushna Chandra Gajapati sent a message to Gajapati Ramachandra Deb, the Maharaja of Puri, expressing his desire to visit the Jagannath Temple to have the Lord's blessings before plunging into official work. It became a tradition for the heads of state of Odisha, to visit Lord Jagannath, the supreme deity of the state, after assuming office.

Gajapati Ramachandra Deb accepted his request and expressed his pleasure in receiving him. Gajapati Ramachandra Deb led a massive procession, and with all royal paraphernalia and honour received Maharaja Krushna Chandra Gajapati at Atharanala on the outskirts of Puri. He gave a ceremonial welcome to the Maharaja with royal honour and courtesy and accompanied him to Shri Mandir.

A *Mahasud* was done at Shri Mandir and the entire temple was vacated of all visitors, a rare honour given to any visiting dignitary. The *sebaks*, the priests and the local people of Puri assembled in large numbers to witness and welcome the rare ceremonial procession where both the Gajapatis were seated together. The temple priests gave a fitting reception to Maharaja Krushna Chandra Gajapati after they had *darshan* of Lord Jagannath. As per the convention of the Gangas, Maharaja Krushna Chandra Gajapati threw gold *mohurs* at the *Ratna Singhasana*. This historic occasion marked the end of hostility between the two royalties.[21]

18

DIBYASINGHA DEB IV
The Golden Jubilee King

Gajapati Dibyasingha Deb IV, the present Gajapati, completed 50 years of his tenure on 8 July 2020. Such a long tenure is rare in the annals of Gajapati history. Birakeshari Deb is officially known to have had the longest tenure of 57 years from AD 1736 to 1793. However, his tenure was actually up to AD 1781 when he was imprisoned for killing his sons. His grandson Dibyasingha Deb II (AD 1793–1798) succeeded to the throne in AD 1781. However, the *anka* (regnal year) period of Birakeshari Deb was shown to have continued till his death. No Gajapati has completed such a long tenure so far. The only exception was during the pre-Gajapati Ganga era when Chodagangadeva (AD 1078–1150) had the longest glorious reign of 72 years. People feel joyous that their revered Gajapati, the jewel among the kings, has completed a splendid half a century.

When the Rath Yatra celebration was going on and the chariots were at the Gundicha Temple, Dibyasingha Deb's father Birakishore Deb breathed his last on 8 July 1970. As per the tradition, Badajenamani, the eldest son of the departed Gajapati, was crowned the next Gajapati. The seat of the Gajapati is perennially continuous and it can never remain vacant. The rule of primogeniture operates, by virtue of which the eldest son succeeds to the throne. No female member of the royal family can succeed to the throne.[1]

Badajenamani, whose recorded name was Kamarnava Deb, assumed the title and name of Gajapati Dibyasingha Deb IV at the age of 17. As per tradition, nominated Brahmins called *puabrahmana* carry out the funeral rites. This is a very peculiar tradition. A Gajapati appears to be an exception to the conventional Hindu law where the eldest son performs and observes the funeral rites and rituals of his departed father. This practice is not followed by the succeeding Gajapati. He does not perform or participate in the *Antyesti kriya*. A nominated Brahmin performs the rituals. He observes the rituals for 13 days, tonsures his head and even does the *pindadaan*.

When a Gajapati dies, immediately the successor ascends to the throne. The successor is informed, 'A guest had come and has departed (*Jane atithi asithile, chaligale*)'. The newly crowned Gajapati replies, 'Please take him outside through the backyard door (*Tanku badiduar dei baharaku nei jao)*.'[2] After this, the *karanas* carry the body of the Gajapati for the funeral. They observe all the funeral rituals. This tradition is followed to ensure that the seat of the Gajapati does not remain vacant even for a day. The uninterrupted and unbroken presence of the Gajapati is something which the tradition guarantees. It has been honoured since ages.

Although the Gajapati ascended the throne on 8 July 1970, he did not acquire the full right of being the *Adyasebak*. He had not had his *bratopanayana* (thread ceremony). In its absence, the ritual of *sadhibandha* (tying of saree or headdress) could not be performed. *Sadhibandha* is an important ritual which confers the Gajapati the honour and right to perform *seba* as the *Adyasebak* of deities. As per tradition and the Record of Rights, when a Gajapati cannot perform a *seba*, the same can be done by his representative called *Mudiratha* on his behalf.

A *Mudiratha* or *Mudrahasta* is a special *sebak* mentioned in the Record of Rights, prior to which the temple rituals were recorded in the *karmangi*. As per the *karmangi*, a *Mudiratha* can serve up to the age of 16 years. However, according to *Niladri Mahodaya* and *Bamadev Samhita*, a *Mudiratha* can perform *seba* from the age of 7 to 12. Whenever the Gajapati cannot perform a seba, the *mudiratha* can perform it in his absence but he cannot exercise any right independently. In the *Niladri Mahodaya* and *Bamadev Samhita*, he is referred to as *Agnisharma*.

The Gajapati's *bratopanayan* was performed on 29 November 1970. The chief priest of the temple then performed *sadhibandha* ritual. With these two functions, he acquired the status of a full performing *Adyasebak*.

Mystically Mysterious

The year 1972 was a memorable one. The Car Festival of that year is remembered for its mystery and relief. The real story has been described by Bihari Lal Patnaik, who was the Additional District Magistrate and in charge of temple administration. Patnaik had joined five months before the Car Festival. It was his first Car Festival. Sarangadhar Hota was the District Collector then.

As per the distribution of work, Patnaik was in charge of all the rituals inside the temple premises. The Collector was in charge of all functions and activities outside the temple. Once *pahandi bije* was completed and the deities were taken outside the temple, the responsibility shifted to the Collector.

The *pahandi bije* procession of the deities is very important. The deities are taken in a procession one by one to their respective chariots from the temple. The procession is accompanied by drums, trumpets, cymbals, chanting of *slokas*, brass bells and dances. It starts with the *bije kahali* or blowing of the royal trumpet. The deities, after elaborate rituals, are taken out in a rhythmic swing in a grand manner. Once the deities reach the base of the chariots, they are carried through the *charmala* (makeshift inclined ramp made of palm logs) to the pedestal of the chariots.

The timely performance of *pahandi bije* has always been of utmost concern and priority for the temple administration and *sebaks*. The district administration in collaboration with the temple officials and *sebaks* always strive to start it on time and avoid any indiscipline and irregularity. That year, Patnaik made all preparations ahead of time. Everything was ready and in order. At 8 a.m., the *bije kahali* (trumpet) of *pahandi bije* was sounded, signalling the start of the *pahandi* rituals.

On learning of this early start, Collector Hota got worried. The arrangements outside the temple were not ready by then. The chariots had not been cordoned off by police to prevent people from coming too near. Though the Collector was annoyed, he was helpless because the *pahandi bije* rituals had already started and could not be stopped. A minor altercation took place between Hota and Patnaik. Patnaik told the Collector, 'I was not told what arrangements have been done outside the Temple. Now that the *pahandi bije kahali* has been blown, the Lord will move.' The daitapati* in charge informed him that they had to start *pahandi*. Since the *pahandi* rituals had been initiated, all the three deities had started moving towards the chariots.

Lord Balabhadra, Lordess Subhadra and Lord Sudarshan climbed on the *charmala* to be seated on their pedestals in their respective chariots. Their *pahandi* was smooth and incident free. But Lord Jagannath was stuck on the *charmala*. Despite all efforts, Lord Jagannath did not move. Some daitapatis tried to pull the idol of Lord Jagannath but did not succeed. They suffered fractures in their leg. Patnaik was present at this time. He and the Collector got worried.

---

*Daitapatis are non-Brahmin *sebaks* who owe their origin to a Savara (an ancient tribe) chief called Viswabasu. The daitapatis play the most important part in Car Festival rituals right from the start of the festival till the deities return to the temple.

Though *pahandi bije* had started on time, the rituals on the chariot were getting delayed. Nandini Satpathy, the Chief Minister of Odisha who was present, inquired the reasons for the delay. Patnaik replied, 'Only the Lord knows. You can ask the Collector.'

The Chief Minister understood his helplessness and anxiety. She asked, 'Should I ask police personnel to help?' Patnaik replied, 'Daitapatis can lift the Lord and take Him to the chariot. It is not the job of policemen.' She spoke to the daitapatis, who tried to lift the idol but failed. The Chief Minister offered *Chadeinada tada*[*] to the Lord praying for Him to move.[3] But the Lord would not heed her prayer; He did not move an inch.

Deep worry engulfed the temple administration, the Chief Minister, *sebayats* (servitors) and millions of anxious devotees. The Chief Minister got anxious. The first female Chief Minister of the state had assumed office barely a month before the Car Festival. It was a big event for her. In such a tense moment, Patnaik started crying.

He heard someone asking him, 'Did you feel a sense of pride having performed *pahandi bije* so early?' These words struck him like lightning. He realised the truth, recollected that he did not care about anyone while performing the *pahandi bije* rituals; he did not even care about the Collector, his superior. He had felt very high and mighty having performed the ritual single-handedly and so early. He had considered the smooth and early start of *pahandi bije* as a feather in his cap and his ego had swelled for having achieving the rare feat.

He soon realised his guilt. Immediately, with folded hands, he sought pardon from the Lord over his inflated ego. In the meantime, the Lord continued to be on the inclined ramp without any movement. An idea flashed in Patnaik's mind. He requested a *daitapati*, Jaga Garabadu, who was standing nearby, to come along with him. When he was going down the ramp, a worried Chief

---

[*] This is a favourite sweet of Lord Jagannath.

Minister asked, 'Where are you going?' Patnaik replied, 'Madam, I will come back in no time.'

He and Jaga Garabadu reached the Gajapati's palace. Patnaik had remembered the legend that when wooden logs (*daru*) came floating, King Indrayumna had engaged servants to lift these logs. At that time, the Lord had said, 'I have come on your request and prayer. Why have you engaged servants?' Patnaik realised that now the Gajapati was the only hope. The Gajapati was getting ready for the *chherapanhara* ritual. Patnaik met and told him, 'Your honour, you have to come to the chariot. The Lord is not climbing the *charmala* and not moving to His pedestal in the chariot.'

The young Gajapati did not know what to do. He was advised by some people not to go. Some advisors told him that the Gajapati goes only once for *chherapanhara* and he could not go to the chariots before that ritual. One Sitaram Pandey told him, 'The Raja is the first *sebak* of the Lord. He cannot go on the request of the administration to work for the Lord.' At this point of time, *Rajmata*, the mother of the Gajapati, intervened and her advice came as a great relief. She advised the Gajapati to 'wear the golden necklace and go barefooted to Lord Jagannath'.

Gajapati Dibyasingha Deb went barefooted without any ceremonial rituals. When he reached the site, he first paid his obeisance to Lord Balabhadra, Lordess Subhadra and Lord Sudarsan standing on the ground without climbing the chariots. After that, he asked Patnaik, 'What should I do now?' Patnaik requested him: 'Your Honour! Please proceed as *Mahaprabhu* is on *charmala*, halfway.'

The young Gajapati climbed the *charmala*, reached *Mahaprabhu* and earnestly prayed to Him with folded hands, took his hand around the Lord's back and stood before the Lord praying, '*Mahaprabhu*, please move now. How much more we will be troubled?' These were the prayers of the first servitor. It was as if the Lord was waiting for this moment to put an end to the anxiety of his millions of devotees. The Lord was also waiting to convey a message of eternal truth: '*Gali mu sahai garba na sahai*' (I can tolerate your abuse [*gali*] but not your pride [*garba*]).'

After this, as soon as the daitapatis touched *Mahaprabhu*, He moved effortlessly to the chariot and was soon seated on the pedestal. The whole atmosphere was filled with resounding chants of 'Jai Jagannath' and the blowing of conch, cymbals, bells and drums. The atmosphere was electrifying. Devotees went mad with joy. The widespread relief lifted the spirits of devotees.

Patnaik accompanied the Gajapati back to the palace and thanked him profusely for saving the situation. He described this unforgettable incident as a miracle. Later during the day, the journalists surrounded him and flooded him with questions. He answered: 'Whatever you saw, I also saw that only.' This did not satisfy them. He then told the media that he would answer their questions with only two words and they should not ask any more question. He described the incident as 'Mystically Mysterious'.

The unique incident was a miracle witnessed by him and all others in the 1972 Car Festival. This was also the first time the new Gajapati experienced the miracle. This was the first time in the history of the Gajapati tradition and Car Festival when the Gajapati came twice to the chariot on the day of the Car Festival.[4]

Memory of a Lifetime

Gajapati Maharaja Dibyasingha Deb, before his coronation, was known as Kamarnava Deb. He was born on 6 February 1953. Dr Bina Dei, a famous surgeon of Odisha, writes about the birth of Kamarnava Deb in her autobiography *Akinchanara Jibana Smruti* (2001).

Bina Dei was born in 1904. On her day of birth, her father received the news that he had passed the medical degree examination. Bina Dei and her sister Jyostna Dei studied medicine at Lady Hardinge Medical College, Delhi, and Medical College, Lahore under Punjab University. Both passed the medical examination in 1933. She started her service in Raj Dufferin

Hospital in Champaran district in Bihar as there was no post of lady Assistant Surgeon then in the whole of Odisha. She was later posted in Odisha and joined Puri Hospital, then known as Puri Pilgrim Hospital. As lady Assistant Surgeon, she was very popular and famous in Puri. She became a household name in Puri town and adjoining areas for her commitment and dedicated service.

In her autobiography, she writes that one day she got a call from the palace, requesting her to medically check the young queen. 'I checked her and informed that the queen was expecting. This news brought waves of rejoice in the entire palace. The young queen took me to her bedroom and treated me with a liberal dose of various sweets. The young queen had a smiling face, was very charming and beautiful.' She told her to come to the palace from time to time and check her regularly. Since this was her first pregnancy, she was anxious and bit nervous. I told her, 'I will certainly come and it is my duty to do so.' She assured the queen that there was no reason to fear.

The young queen was the daughter of the brother of Basanta Manjari Devi, who was then the Health Minister. Dr Bina Dei writes that she developed intimate connection with the Puri Raja's family and both the young queen and her mother-in-law became very fond of her. The young queen had two large pet dogs. She was very fond of them. The two pets used to sleep on the queen's bed. Raja Gajapati Birakishore Deb was a jovial man and he used to interact with everyone very freely.

The day the queen developed labour pain, Dr Bina Dei was beside her at the palace. A nurse had accompanied her. 'In my hands she gave birth to her first son. His birth was welcomed with the blowing of conch shells. The whole palace came alive with joy and happiness.'[5] Bina Dei writes, 'As per traditional practice, the midwife or *dhai* of the palace was to cut the umbilical cord of the newborn. A gold coin was put beneath the chord as a support base. This gold coin is given as a gift to the *dhai*.'

Bina Dei says the *dhai* was wearing lots of gold bangles and had two or three rings on her fingers. Her nails were unusually long, untidy and dirty. For reasons of hygiene, she did not allow the midwife to cut the umbilical cord. The Rajmata (the King's mother) got worried as she was very particular about the tradition. Bina Dei suggested to the Rajmata that she would have the gold coin touch the navel of the new born and then hand it over to *dhai*. That would serve the purpose of following the tradition and she would cut the umbilical cord. The Rajmata concurred.

Bina Dei cut the umbilical cord of the newborn Jenamani. She would go every day to the palace to bathe the newborn and look after the mother. The nurse went thrice a day for dressing. 'Since that day, I have become a regular invitee to the palace in every occasion.' She writes, 'The toddler of that day is now the glorious Thakur Raja or the divine sovereign Shri Dibyasingha Deb. It is my great fortune that I am living for the last 93 years hearing the glory of the Thakur Raja. Admiration of Raja Saheb makes me proud as he was born in my hands. The Raja Saheb saw the first ray of light because of me and I was fortunate that he sat on my lap for the first time.'[6]

The baby grew up to be crowned as Gajapati Dibyasingha Deb on 8 July 1970. During the ceremony, he sat beside Senapathy Gadarodanga Bakshi as per tradition. His younger brother Sana Jenamani Ranarnaba Deb and Anangabhaskar Deb, son of his paternal uncle Thataraja Rajajaraja Deb, were also present on the occasion.

At the time of his coronation, he was studying at St Stephens College, Delhi. He started his education in Convent School of Puri (1957 to 1959). He then went to Rajkumar College, Raipur, and studied from 1959 to 1968. After graduation, he studied law in the Faculty of Law, Delhi University (1972–1975). After graduating from there, he joined the School of Law in North Western University, Chicago, and obtained a Master's in 1976. During this time, he used to visit Puri to perform his ritualistic service to Lord Jagannath for two important ceremonies: Ratha Yatra and Bahuda Yatra. He was unable to participate in the regular meeting of Shree Jagannatha Temple Managing Committee, of which he was the

Chairman. While abroad, he was not able to perform his service to Lord Jagannath. This was done in his absence by the *Mudiratha* as per tradition.

His father Gajapati Birakishore Deb III studied at Rajkumar College in Raipur and was its all-round athletic champion in 1945–1946. An avid football player, he represented Odisha in the Santosh Trophy championship in 1947–1948. He played for the Mohammedan Sporting Club of Kolkata. He was fond of horse riding and used to take part in equestrian events at the Kolkata Turf Club. He was also a tennis player, a painter and a lover of music.

Gajapati Birakishore Deb is the only Gajapati of Puri who fought the Assembly elections from Khurda in 1967 on a Jana Congress ticket and was elected an MLA defeating his powerful opponent.[7]

Except this solitary instance, the Gajapatis have assiduously tried to keep away from electoral politics and confined themselves to the service of Lord Jagannath. It is a conscious decision of the Gajapati not to dilute the traditional role for which he is revered and respected by the public. The present Gajapati, Dibyasingha Deb, has consistently maintained a stand that there should not be any unwarranted interference with time-honoured religious and traditional rituals and practices of the temple. He is, however, known for his progressive outlook in introducing reforms in the temple administration and improving services for devotees by bringing various measures, including discipline among *sebaks*.

Dilemma in Life

Once, Gajapati Dibyasingha Deb faced a dilemma—whether to adopt a spiritual mode in life by serving Lord Jagannath as His first servitor or pursue a career in law. The problem lay in taking up a compromised position of pursuing both. This was a tough call for the Gajapati when he was at a promising stage of his career. An interaction with Barrister Gobinda Das, the Advocate General at that time, changed his destiny.[8]

Dibyasingha Deb, who started his career as a junior lawyer to prominent senior advocates such as Ashok Sen, A.K. Ganguly and B.N. Kripal in the Supreme Court and Delhi High Court, started getting deep into the profession. One day, he received a message that Barrister Gobinda Das wanted to meet him. The young lawyer was very excited about the meeting as he hoped that it would open up new avenues in the legal profession. Das, however, had a different reason for seeking the meeting.

The awaited meeting took place. Das made the Gajapati comfortable with casual conversation and refreshments. At an opportune moment, Das drew his attention with a serious note. 'You are Gajapati Maharaja of Puri, the foremost servitor of Shri Jagannath. For this, you are revered by all Odias and devotees of Shri Jagannath. But while in court, as a lawyer you have to bow down before the judge and address "My Lord" or "Your Honour". As an Odia I find it very uncomfortable seeing you bowing before anyone except the Almighty Lord.'

The meeting with Das had an electrifying impact and was a defining moment for Dibyasingha Deb. The Gajapati is the Thakur Raja and he is loved and respected by people as the *Chalanti Vishnu*; he is the *Adyasebak* of Shri Jagannath. He can bow before his Lord, the one and only Lord Shri Jagannath. How can he bow before another artificial lord? Can there be a lord superior to Lord Jagannath? These questions churned in his mind.

The meeting with Das seemed like a message for him from the Lord. The divine message directed him to choose the right path. Dibyasingha Deb's ambition to pursue his cherished profession had to take a back seat as he realised the adage, 'Man proposes God disposes'. That meeting became the turning point in his life. He decided to willingly submit to the wish of *Mahaprabhu* Jagannath and spend more time in His service. The dilemma was resolved.

The Gajapati spent most of the time from 1980 to 1993 in Dehradun. He says, 'These 14 years (1980–1993) were almost *vanabasa* for me.' Yet, he adds, 'This period of mental twilight evolved me. It occurred due to the grace of Almighty. I decoded—now, service of the Lord is primary, all other things are immaterial.'[9]

He underwent a transformation. According to him, three catalysts contributed to this—*Sadgrantha*, *Sadguru* and *Satsang*. These aspects were essential elements in forming one's thought, action and knowledge. He evolved by imbibing knowledge from the *Dharmasastras* in which the spiritual teachers played an important role by imparting knowledge and explaining the texts. The company of learned men contributed to the deliberations, discussions and deductions, which brought clarity on many aspects of religious and spiritual matters. The service of the Lord is a difficult yet privileged honour of dedication.

Though he grew up in a spiritual environment during early childhood, the spiritual mindset remained dormant and was overshadowed by his education in school and subsequently at Rajkumar College, St Stephens College and North Western University. His secular education did not deter his spiritual leanings. He only required a spark to give vent to his dormant spiritual subconscious to enable the seed of divinity to bloom. He began to read the *Bhagavad Gita* and other spiritual texts.

He came across two great gurus. One was Swami Chidananda Saraswati, the main disciple of Swami Sivananda Saraswatiji Maharaj, the founder of International Divine Life Society of Rishikesh. The other was the revered Swami Chinmayananda Saraswati, the founder of the International Chinmay Mission of Mumbai. The Gajapati along with Maharani Lilabati Patamahadei took *diksha* from Swami Chidananda Saraswati in 1989. His association and involvement in these centres of learning had a transformative impact on him.

Sadgrantha, *Sadguru* and *Satsang* started to disperse all doubts from the Gajapati's mind. The dormant subconscious became active consciousness. He dedicated himself totally to the service of *Mahaprabhu* Jagannath as his foremost servitor.

Gajapati Maharaja Seva

As per the Record of Rights of the Jagannath Temple, the Gajapati Maharaja is the principal and foremost servitor of Lord Jagannath and this is the hereditary service of the royal dynasty. The most prominent service is called *Chherapanhara*, which the Gajapati performs by sweeping the chariots with a golden broom. On this occasion, the Gajapati offers worship inside *Raja Nahar* (his palace) to the family *istadevi* Kanak Durga, and puts on the sacred thread. Clad in white tunic, turban, and *kaustuva* necklace, accompanied by temple commanders and security employees, and holding the royal sword, the Gajapati comes out of the palace. He is carried in a palanquin named *Mahena* or *Tamjhan* to the chariot.

This royal procession is led by Behera Khuntia *sebaks* and accompanied by trumpets and drums. When the Gajapati is taken to the chariot through the crowd, there are chants of *Hari Bol* and traditional ululation. He is revered with utmost devotion by crowds who throng to have a glimpse of him. The Gajapati offers *aarti* before the Lord on a golden plate, then sweeps the platform of the chariot with a broom and consecrates the chariot by sprinkling sandalwood water. After he finishes the *Chherapanhara* ritual in all three chariots, he returns to the palace.

Besides the Car Festival and the Return Car Festival (Bahuda Yatra), the Gajapati may perform *Chherapanhara* on the festive days of Dola Purnima, Chandan Yatra and Devasnana Purnima.

The Gajapati has the privilege of performing service during several *besa*, i.e. decoration of the Lord. During such occasions, the Gajapati moves in the *Tamjhan,* which is kept at the Lion's Gate, and servitors like *karana, paricha* and others accompany him.

There is a special occasion when the Rani visits the temple. Her palanquin enters the inner sanctum (*bedhah*) of the temple and is parked near the banyan tree. The entire temple premises are evacuated of all other visitors. The *Mudiratha sebak* escorts the Queen and the King, and family members of the Gajapati accompany the Queen. This is known as *Gahana Bije*. This was solemnised on 8 April 2007 after a long gap of nearly 40 years when Gajapati Dibyasingha Deb and Rani Leelabati Patamahadei visited the temple along with other members of the royal family and offered prayers.

This *seba* is a privilege available to the Gajapati which has been continuing since long and retained even after Independence and enactment of the Shri Jagannath Temple (Administration) Act. While the Rani can visit the temple anytime, the *seba* of *Gahana Bije* is performed rarely and known to have been performed once in a lifetime. The Rani along with the Gajapati and other family members and invitees can perform the *seba*. The last *Gahana Bije* was performed in 1966 by the mother of the present Gajapati Dibyasingha Deb. Prior to that, the *Gahana Bije* was performed in 1933.[10]

The Gajapati can visit the Jagannath Temple anytime he wants. However, when he goes to the temple to perform a *seba*, he enters through the eastern gate. In normal times, he can enter through the southern gate.

The Gajapati's family enjoys certain privileges. On the birthdays of the children of the Gajapati, a special puja called *Swanakhyatra* is performed in the temple. On every *Ekadashi*, *Mahadeepa alati* (the great lamp offerings) is performed. After the evening *dhupa*, the puja *pandas* first perform *mahadeepa alati* near the *Ratna Singhasana*, go around it, pass through the Jaya Bijaya door and then go to the Bimala Temple with the lamp inside an earthen pot (*kalasa*). The puja *pandas* then give three *kalasas* and some tulsi (basil leaves) to Chunara *sebaks*. The Ghantua gives 12 *Chandraudiyas*.*

The *sebaks* climb up to the top of the temple with the *Mahadeepa* and the *Chandraudiyas*. Reaching the top and standing below the 'Dhandinauti', they offer tulsi and sandal paste to Neelachakra (blue wheel); then they go around it thrice and light

---

* Ghantuas are a type of *sebak* who prepare *chandraudiyas*, which are a special type of candle that sparkle and are lit on all four directions on the top of temple on every *Ekadashi* days.

three *Chandraudiyas* in each of the four directions. While moving round, they pray aloud, 'May the Lord save the King of Puri (the name of the ruling King is taken) sheltering him inside the conch shell, shielding him with the disc.'

There are other ritualistic connections of the Gajapati Maharaja in various festivals of the temple, namely Saradiya Durga puja, Vanajaga, Laxmi Narayan Veta (Bahuda Yatra), Champak dwadasi and Pausa Purnima.[11]

As per the traditional royal almanac, the time period of the Gajapati's ascension to the throne is calculated from *Shukla Dwadasi* of Bhadrab month, also known as *Sunia*, symbolising the beginning of the New Year as per Odia tradition. According to the tradition, since this is the birthday of King Indrayumna, all kings celebrate this day as New Year's Day. All the almanacs published from Odisha and palm-leaf horoscopes of newborns carry the name and reigning year (*anka*) of the Gajapati Maharaja.

Gajapati Dibyasingha Deb is a great patron and promoter of the Jagannath culture and tradition. According to him, the land of Odisha is blessed to have been the abode of Lord Jagannath, who is the Purushottama. 'There is a need to spread the Jagannath culture and I take it as my foremost responsibility since there is a huge spiritual vacuum.'[12] He is the Chairman of the Shree Jagannatha Temple Managing Committee for the administration of the shrine and promotion of Jagannath culture. Presently, he heads a team of scholars under the aegis of the temple administration with the title 'Shri Jagannath Tatwa, Gabeshana O Prasar Upasamithi' for spreading Shri Jagannath consciousness. He visits various places and groups and gives lectures on the greatness of the Jagannath culture, thereby creating better awareness about the temple.

Spiritual learning

The Gajapati emphasizes the importance of spiritualism in today's world. He is concerned that our country, the mother of spiritualism, is neglecting it. He feels that spiritualism is essential for building good human beings and hence for building a good society. He articulated his thoughts in a recent global virtual conference organized by the Odisha Society of Americas (OSA) in June 2021 on 'Spirituality in Our Lives'. Gajapati Maharaja Dibyasingha Deb spoke on spiritual learning in educational institutions.

He mentioned three factors that influence and shape the personality of a child or person. These are one's home and immediate surrounding like parents, grandparents, siblings or family. The second is educational institutions where one spends a crucial time of one's life. What they study, what their teachers teach and interactions with others influence a person's mind, shape his/her thoughts and frame the personality. Finally, the society at large—their place of work, cultural milieu and environment, living and experience is the biggest influence. In this context, he emphasized the need to address the all-important issue of spiritual education among children in school.

According to him, the Macaulay report of 1835 laid the foundation of education policy of the country. The aim of education, according to Macaulay, was 'to form a class who may be interpreters between us and the millions whom we govern; a class of persons Indian in blood and colour, but English in taste, in opinion, in morals and in intellect.' The policy emanated from an imperial mindset and colonial necessity.

Macaulay's approach introduced an education system to serve the English with a curriculum that covered a spectrum of subjects like history, geography and science. The system continued even after Independence. Cosmetic changes have not made any substantive dent on the character, content and context of the education policy. We are faced with a rote learning system that is purely examination-oriented to achieve a job or a career. The object of education today has given rise to learning through a prescribed matrix promoting secular, material education.

The question arises does it encourage inculcation of right values and right learning. The Gajapati says the education we learn is called *apaaravidya* that is modern science or study that addresses at the intellect level of a person. This may be important but not sufficient for preparing good human beings. Citing Vivekananda, he said the object of education should be to develop inner personality, building character and developing good humans. Einstein emphasized that the aim of education should be to improve people by making better human beings out of them.

The Gajapati highlights the need for and significance of spiritual education for building a good society. It is important that our education and learning ensures producing good people. While our present secular, material education addresses the outer aspects of our personality (*bahyakaran suddhi*) and emphasizes on *apaaravidya*, spiritual education is a deeply introverted process which promotes *paaravidya* based on internal process or *antakaran suddhi*. These two aspects are two sides of a coin. The problem with learning today is it is one-sided with neglect of the latter essential aspect.

Spiritual education is India's ancient ethos which was imparted through the *gurukul* system. It was aimed at unfolding and growth of inner personality. The need of spiritual education is more relevant today than ever before. The Gajapati says that it is important to impart spiritual education during the formative years of a child. Although it is time neutral, grown-ups also need to unwind to learn.

The Gajapati highlights challenges in imparting spiritual education in school in India. The first issue in such teaching appears to be extraneous to the curriculum. Therefore, spiritual education insofar as they don't form a part of a prescribed pattern be it CBSE or ICSE or any state board is difficult to impart in school. The second aspect is the character of such teaching or learning. If it is viewed as inconsistent with the secular concept of our curriculum, its acceptability is challenging. In view of such challenges, the Gajapati is of the view that there is a need to engage with other religious and reform groups and agree with a common denominator. He is optimistic. Spirituality is common to all religions. While different religions may view things differently, all of them lead to the same destination through different paths.

He says the solution lies with self. Each one of us lives in an individual world. If I change, my world will change for the better. According to him, we can blame the system, blame the society, blame the parents but a child is never to blame. He will learn by example, by experiencing. It is for us and the system to enable him to learn. Therefore, spiritualism has to be a passionate article of faith for all of us. We stop blaming others when we realize that buck stops with us.

Spiritualism lives in every one of us. It is in our conscious or subconscious mind lying silent, suppressed or dormant. It needs a spark. We need to change and orient ourselves. A baby step has to be put forward. Every great thing starts from a small step. It requires a conscious effort from each one of us to appreciate our profound scriptures, books, legends, folktales, religious discourses, *satsangha, satguru, satgrantha*, devotional literature, songs and *bhajans*. Our treasure is unlimited. They will arouse and awaken our mind to a spiritual direction, a direction towards *antakaran suddhi* (the purification of mind). They will guide and propel us to look inward for self-improvement. That should be our beginning to begin with.

19

AND IT NEVER ENDS...

History or literature does not have any last chapter as there cannot be any finality to it. A book, however, may end with a concluding chapter though it may not be the end of the story.

The Gajapati history in Odisha has followed a unique and unusual path. Throughout the book I have tried to explore and present various stories and facts through the prism of history. It is important, even at the cost of repetition, to have a bird's eye view of this trajectory.

The Beginning

Our story starts in the Ganga period when Chodagangadeva established the strong foundation of a Hindu empire in Odisha. His 72 years of reign, a truly remarkable feat, witnessed the building of a strong empire by conquest, consolidation and benevolent rule. A total of 188 inscriptions found at various places reveal the nature of the stupendous work, admirable administration and splendid contributions by this emperor. He started rebuilding the famous Jagannath Temple. It was completed by his successor Anangabhimadeva III.

For four centuries, subsequent Ganga kings strengthened and sustained the large empire which Chodagangadeva had founded. Under them, the vast Kalinga Empire stretched from the Ganges in the north to the Godavari in the south. The Ganga rulers not only consolidated the empire by subduing the feudatory rulers, annexing territories and creating military strongholds to check the inroads of the invaders, but they also established a sound administrative system. They brought economic prosperity to the region through inland and maritime trade and patronized art, architecture, learning, literature and religion. The Ganga period, therefore, has been epitomized as the golden age in the history of Kalinga.

Initially, the Gangas were Saivites who gradually converted to Vaishnavism in conformity with the predominant faith in Odisha then. It was also a necessity considering the centrality of the Jagannath Temple and Lord Jagannath, considered a representation of Vishnu, in the life of the Odiya people. The Gangas, particularly Anangabhimadeva III and his successors, held Jagannath as the supreme sovereign or ruler of the kingdom. The earthly king was designated as His *rauta* (deputy).

Ananagabhimadeva and his successors abdicated the throne, recognizing Lord Jagannath as their Supreme Sovereign, and did not have formal coronation ceremonies. This doctrine helped the Gangas secure legitimacy in the eyes of their subjects and helped them garner popular acceptance, which went a long way in contributing towards their empire-building exercise. As deputies, the Ganga kings followed a policy of attributing everything to the ultimate throne, which was adorned by Lord Jagannath and belonged to Him. They were acting as mere vassals or agents of the Lord. This ideology of subservience was the prime mover behind their great success.

Kapilendra Deb, the founder of the Suryavanshi dynasty, inherited a great empire from the Gangas. He, considered a usurper to the throne, faced insurmountable challenges. He was not a lineal descendent of his predecessor, the last Ganga King Bhanudeva IV. He was the first Gajapati in a conventional sense, although the term with its variations had been used by some Ganga rulers earlier. 'Gajapati' as a title and honour was adopted formally by Kapilendra Deb. This tradition is being followed by his successors till date.

Kapilendra Deb followed a multidimensional policy to take the empire to greater heights. He followed a humbler approach of positioning himself as a *sebak* of Lord Jagannath. He demonstrated that his empire and wealth belonged to the deity and the king was merely His servant; to legitimize his occupation of the throne after the last Ganga king, he popularized the theory that a new servant of the Lord, i.e., Kapilendra Deb, had merely replaced the previous servant, i.e., Bhanudeva IV.

By following this doctrine, Kapilendra Deb placed himself at the centre of the network of services and servants of the temple. This placed him in a role that was formalized and recognized by not only the entire network of servants but also the people at large. The outward manifestation of the Gajapati being the foremost servitor of the Lord is seen in the *chherapanhara* ritual, one of the most important services performed by the king for the Lord; it was glorified and glamourized during the reign of Purushottama Deb and that continues till date.

The doctrine of subordination and surrender also provided a great tool to the Suryavanshi kings to expand and consolidate their empire. Under Gajapati Kapilendra Deb, the Odishan Empire, which extended from the river Ganga to the river Cauvery, had reached its pinnacle. His successors Purushottama Deb and Prataprudra Deb somehow managed to hold on to this empire.

It is significant that while the Mughal invasion and expansion in the north as well in the south continued with various Hindu empires losing their independence, Odisha was an exception and retained its independent status for a comparatively longer period. This was primarily because of the strong foundation the Ganga rulers had laid; the Gajapatis of the subsequent Suryavanshi dynasty capably strengthened that inheritance.

The Turning Point

The year 1568 witnessed a turning point in Odisha's history as the region lost its independence to the Afghans. Mukunda Deb, the last independent Gajapati of Odisha, was defeated. This was immediately followed by the barbaric attack of the Afghan General Kalapahad on the Puri Jagannath Temple. After Mukunda Deb lost, due to internal rivalry and conspiracy, the history of Odisha took a different turn. Kataka (Cuttack), the traditional capital of the Gangas and the Suryavanshi Gajapatis, was occupied by the Afghans.

Ramachandra Deb, the first Gajapati under Afghan occupation, shifted his capital to Jagannatha Kataka near Khurda and he was re-christened as the Raja of Khurda. He had a semi-autonomous status with a much-reduced territorial domain—it extended from the Mahanadi River to the borders of Ganjam, comprising 129 killas apart from those situated in his own zamindari of Khurda. Ramachandra Deb restored and reinstalled the idols of the deities in Jagannath Temple, which had been desecrated by Kalapahad, and resumed the rituals that had been suspended for some years. For these acts, he was called 'Dwitiya Indradyumna'. Ramachandra Deb retained his legitimacy by demonstrating his devotion and servitude towards the temple and Lord Jagannath. In 1590, Mansingh, at the instruction of Mughal Emperor Akbar, recognized Ramachandra Deb as the Gajapati.

A new context was introduced after the death of Akbar by his successors Jahangir and Aurangzeb. In 1607, Odisha became a separate *subba* with Cuttack at its capital. Emperor Jahangir's ambition of expanding beyond Khurda and of annexing the southern kingdom Rajahmundry, which was under the control of Golconda, added another dimension to Odisha's history. The Khurda Raja and the Puri Temple became subjects of frequent attacks for plunder by the Mughal subedars stationed at Cuttack, with the objective of pleasing their master, the Mughal emperor in Delhi. Jahangir's ambition contributed to the loss of status for

Khurda as an autonomous state as a buffer between the Mughal Empire and the Golconda Sultanate.[1]

Foreign rule of 200 years—first by the Afghans and then by the Mughals—resulted in frequent attacks on the seat of power at Khurda and the Puri Temple. A detailed history of these attacks is outside the scope of this book. However, these attacks caused frequent shifting of deities to southern hilly regions, the islands in Chilka Lake, to deep jungles and other such places. The deities had great emotional and religious significance for the people, the priests, the *sebaks* and the Gajapatis. For them, they were not mere idols. They were living Gods for they contained the sacred and secret *brahma* inside them, which were changed at the time of Nabakalebara*. This period witnessed the priests secretly moving the idols to different locations to save them from the glare of invaders.

Also during this time, the Gajapatis moved away from their capital to hide in unknown places—not as cowards but to save their country and their deities and to divert attention of the invaders from the Puri Temple. Both the lord of the elephant (Gajapati) and lord of the universe (Jagannath) were on the run, exhibiting a sense of helplessness and desperation for survival.

The arrival of the Marathas in 1751 introduced another important phase in the history of the Gajapatis. For the Marathas,

---

*Nabakalebara means 'new body or new image', signifying the installation of the new bodies of four images, namely Balabhadra, Subhadra, Jagannath and Sudarshan, on the *Ratna Singhasana* of Shri Mandir. Many people entertain the wrong idea that this ceremony takes place once in 12 years. Nabakalebara took place in 1912, 1931, 1950, 1969, 1977 and 1996 in the last century. The first Nabakalebara in the current century took place in 2015. The year in which there are two *Asadhas* (intercalary month) witnesses the Nabakalebara ceremony. The Record of Rights of Shri Mandir mentions that Nabakalebara of the deities takes place in the year in which there are double *Asadhas* (one *Asadha* out of them is 'mala' and the *anasara* period continues for one month and a half, which is called *maha anasara*).

the Jagannath Temple was the centre of attention and attraction both from the point of view of religion and revenue. The temple generated huge amounts of pilgrim tax. The attack by Jagannath Narayan Deb of Parlakhemundi on Gajapati Birakeshari Deb in 1760 provided a golden opportunity to the Marathas to extend their control in the region. The Maratha help to Birakeshari Deb came with a price which the Gajapati could not pay, leading to the dismemberment of Khurda territory with important loss of the prized possession of Puri.

The Gajapati kingdom of Khurda survived a tumultuous Muslim rule of nearly 200 years. But during the Maratha rule, the Raja of Khurda was reduced to the status of an 'insignificant local zamindar'.[2] The Khurda Rajas continued to retain the nominal position as Gajapatis. At this time, the traditional role of Gajapati in the temple affairs received a jolt and the age-old traditional association between the Gajapati and the shrine was snapped. The management of the temple was assigned to three parichas Morar Pandit, Chief Paricha; Jagannath Rajguru, second Paricha; and Shewaji Ungits, third Paricha. Two of these parichas Marathas and one was from Odisha. Thus, the Gajapati was divested of his territory and deprived of his traditional role.

The Gajapati's link with the Puri Temple accorded him a special status among all feudatory kings in Odisha. They viewed him with honour and reverence. This position of the Gajapatis got substantially diluted with Maratha occupation when the temple management was taken over by the Marathas. This dilution was, however, addressed by the Raja of Khurda in a different manner; he followed a policy of outreach.

The Raja of Khurda obtained the support of the feudatory Rajas (*samant Rajas*) by involving them in various *sebas* and rituals of the temple. This was done by issuing *sanads/chhamu chitaus* to them, wherein not only new titles were conferred upon them but they were also given certain special rights. A Telugu text, 'Jagannath Sthala Varttanam', which mentions these *sanads* and was compiled for Colonel Mackenzie, is in a Madras archive.

Researcher S.N. Rajguru has done extensive work on the *sanads/chitaus*. Special rights are of various types, starting from the provision of land called *amruta manohi*, special manner of *darshan*, *sebas* and privileges of being accompanied with royal insignia, drums and other accompaniments. In this way, the Khurda Rajas were able to secure and sustain the involvement and participation of a large number of feudatory kings in the maintenance of the temple and its ritual framework. It also allowed the Khurda Rajas to retain their position of eminence to a considerable extent among the other feudatory kings.

British Era

The British conquest of Odisha in 1803 introduced a new era of uncertainty and volatility in the role of the Gajapati, who from then came to be known as the Raja of Puri. The possession of Puri, the temple as well as management of temple was taken over by the British. On conquering Odisha, the British directly managed the temple for the first few years. Mukunda Deb, the then Raja of Khurda, was deprived of the age-old ritual connection with the temple. This resulted in two-fold suffering of the Gajapati.

First, he continued to be deprived of the territorial domain over the precious four parganas lost to the Marathas during the reign of Gajapati Birakeshari Deb. The king was reduced to a mere status where he did not have any territorial domain. When all hope was lost that the precious parganas would be returned by Colonel Harcourt, Jayee Rajguru led a revolt against the British. Khurda was declared a *mugalbandi* area and was directly brought under the control of the British.

This situation led the British to arrest the young Gajapati Mukunda Deb along with his advisor Jayee Rajguru in 1805. Second, was the loss of the time-honoured privilege in relation to the Jagannath Temple over which the Gajapati had a ritualistic right, being the *Adyasebak*. The temple was managed initially by one paricha and later by a committee of three parichas by virtue of Regulation IV of 1806.

The British found it difficult to continue the temple management. It was inconceivable that a Christian government would be able to properly handle and administer a highly ritual-oriented Hindu temple. In fact, it was against the assurance not to intervene in religious matters made at the time of takeover of the province. Jayee Rajguru was hanged and Mukunda Deb was released from confinement in 1807.

The Khurda Raja was ordered to be stationed at Puri and was invested with the management of the temple. He was granted a *mallikana* of Rs 2,333 per month for the loss of his territory. The Raja (and his successors) was to hold the charge vested in him so long as he continued to conduct himself with integrity, diligence and propriety. The Governor General in Council had the power to remove the Raja or any of his successors from the superintendence of the temple on proof of misconduct.

The loss of power and province by the Gajapatis was compensated for by an apparent vesting of the management of internal affairs of the Puri Temple in his capacity as the Raja. However, the truth was that although the Gajapati was designated the superintendent of the temple, the ultimate power rested with the British government; particularly the functionaries at local level who held a view that the entire province including the temple was under the dominion of the British.

This gave rise to conflicting situations with frequent differences and disputes between the Raja of Puri and the local authorities of the British government, namely the Collector and the Commissioner, each trying to reiterate and reinforce their respective domains. The distrust and distance between the British and the Raja was palpable. Mukunda Deb was again arrested by the British government in 1817 to isolate him from the emerging Paik rebellion led by Baxi Jagabandhu. The foreigners feared that the Raja's support to and involvement in the rebellion would secure broad-based support, making it a bigger popular movement that would pose a huge threat to the British.

Mukunda Deb died in prison in November 1817. His son Ramachandra Deb became the superintendent and was in charge of the affairs of the temple. In the meanwhile, Christian missionaries started their proselytizing activities in India and the British association with the Jagannath Temple was criticized on the ground that it was akin to 'state sanction of idolatry'. Puri was held as a temple of superstition and source of propagating idolatry, 'the stronghold fountain head of [Hindu] idolatry'.[2] The missionaries held the view that 'a blow at the Idolatry here will prove to be a blow at the root'.

The pilgrim tax was the greatest cause of concern for the missionaries and a cause of worry for the administration. The proceeds of pilgrim tax being used for temple affairs were abhorred by the Christian missionaries and their supporters. This was viewed as a case of the Christian government sanctioning idolatry and that it went against Christian religious principles.

After persistent advocacy, the East India Company abolished the pilgrim tax by passing Act X of 1840. Although this Act abolished the pilgrim tax, it proclaimed that 'the superintendence of the Temple of Juggernaut and its interior economy, the conduct and management of its affairs, and the control over the Priests, officers, and servants attached to the Temple, shall continue to be vested in the Rajah of Khoordah for the time being'. The Raja of Puri was given full authority vis-a-vis the management of the temple and its property. The government declined to interfere with ancient grants and continued to make an annual payment to meet the expenses of the temple, which was hitherto being met using the proceeds from the pilgrim tax.

The government continued to pay a fixed subsidy of Rs 56,342 for the temple maintenance. The missionaries and the evangelical supporters both in Britain and India again raised the issue of 'connection and sanction' of idolatry. This forced the government to transfer the estate of the Satais Hazari Mahal to the temple in 1843 and also other estates in lieu of the annual payments.

In 1858 and 1863, Ekharjat Mahal* was transferred to the temple to defray the expenses of police establishments that provided security for the temple. The Raja of Puri as the superintendent of the temple was to possess these properties as *marfatdar*. This process reflected an apparent disconnection and dissociation of the British government from the temple affairs and the Puri Raja was given a little more independence and authority.

Apparent independence, however, came with insidious interference and control by the local government, discussed in the preceding chapters. The Raja of Puri was not the owner of these land parcels that were given to him for temple upkeep. He was merely a custodian or *marfatdar* and the revenue from these areas was meant to be utilized towards meeting expenses of the temple. The Puri Raja's long-cherished dream of repossessing his lost territories remained a dream.

The great famine of 1866 (known as *N'anka durbhikhya*) and the Famine Report in 1867 exposed the indifference, apathy and serious weakness of the British government in matters of administering the regions under its rule. The death of one third of the population was a telling commentary on the inability and inefficiency of the British administration. It was a turning point and a watershed moment in Odisha's history that rekindled the dormant collective consciousness. The birth of the Cuttack Printing Press in 1864 and the founding of the *Utkal Dipika* in 1866 provided the much needed channel to express public feelings and expose misgovernance. These contributed significantly to the birth of Odia nationalism.

The period witnessed two issues of seminal importance. The first was the proposal of the British government to remove the Raja and put in his place a committee of trustees in the wake of deportation of Dibyasingha Deb due to his conviction in the

---

* The word 'Ekharjat' is an Arabic word meaning 'expenses'. Ekharjat Mahal literally means land assigned for expenses. It comprises the whole of *zilla* Tapang and 34 villages of Rameshwar with a total *sadar jamma* of Rs 23,715-3-8 pies.

Siba Das murder case. The second, referred to as 'Metcalf's blunder' in an earlier chapter, took shape immediately after the first issue was resolved. This was the British proposal to appoint a Receiver in place of the Raja of Puri for the management of the temple. Both these issues were sensitive and significant and attempted to weaken the traditional linkage between the Gajapati family and the Puri Temple.

On both occasions, lawyer Madhusudan Das was engaged by Rani Suryamani Patamahadei as her saviour and spokesman. He viewed the proposal to remove the Gajapati as a ploy to deny and deprive the infant Mukunda Deb from his rightful claim to succeed as Raja. Das could read the ulterior motive of the British. He was convinced that the Rani's claim was justified and had the sanction of the text and support of the tradition.

Even in the case of the appointment of the Receiver, there was widespread resentment as people felt that the Raja was being deprived of his legitimate right; to prevent this, the bogie of Hindu religion being in danger was also raised, which garnered great public support. Madhusudan Das, however, pushed the matter to a different level. He recollected that such actions or proposals were contrary to 'anxious solitude and desire of the government' of no interference or intervention at the pagoda of Jagannath Temple by any act of British authority. He held that the former ceremonies and customs of the temple should be permitted and supported on every occasion as it affected the peace and happiness of a vast proportion of the inhabitants of the British dominion in India.[3]

Das viewed the proposed action of depriving the Puri Raja of his age-old ritual association with the temple as an act of interference in the religious affairs. He did not treat the issue merely as a religious affair. For him, Lord Jagannath was not merely a Hindu god. Jagannath was the heart, soul and symbol of Odias and He represented the pride and dignity of Odisha.

As an Odia himself, Das rose above his narrow identity of being a Christian. He viewed the Puri Temple not merely as a place of worship but as a laboratory of continuous experiment in Odia nationalism, an incubator of the nationalistic surge of Odias. Thus, on both the matters and particularly in the second issue, which is popularly referred to as the Jagannath Temple case, Das made a huge impact by articulating and securing the support of all sections of society by portraying them as a wider cause of nationalism against the British attempt to deprive the Puri Raja. The court case was made a touchtone of popular demand, a legal matter becoming a people's case at large.

The judgment that ultimately went in favour of the Puri Raja was a victory for Suryamani Patamahadei and was welcomed by one and all. It rekindled the pride and dignity of the Gajapati, who has been held in great reverence and veneration since time immemorial. The ruling was a validation and endorsement of the faith of the people and the restoration of the time-honored role of the Gajapati. It is a unique case where pressure by the missionaries and evangelists on the British government proved counterproductive. The root of Hindu faith, the Jagannath Temple, remained at its place and the ritual association with the temple made the Raja of Puri larger in image and stature.

The excessive obsession of a Christian government with a shrine of idolatry came under severe criticism from missionaries who began a powerful campaign against the administration. James Pegg wrote:

> How dishonourable to imperial Britain in the nineteenth century thus to degrade her sons by connection with shrines of gods of wood and stone! Where is the Alexander of the East who will have the wisdom and courage to draw his sword and cut in a minute the Gordian knot that binds Britain (*sic*) to be dragged after Juggernauth's car? Oh my country and my talented countrymen in India, my spirit feels indignant that you should affront high Heaven!

Colonial debates around the temple achieved political importance. In the *History of the Baptist Mission in Odisha*, Pegg wrote, 'On the contrary our struggle against Juggernaut led to the further importance of the cult.'[4] With intense political interaction and attention through history, Jagannath became a potent mobilizing factor for the people of Odisha. While the temple received political patronage primarily for economic purposes, Jagannath became a symbol for the nationalists. With increasing importance of the Jagannath consciousness, the institution of the Gajapati got a corresponding visible significance.

The importance of Jagannath as a cultural symbol overrides its religious significance. Taylor says, 'Politics tends out of necessity to find bases in society and proceeds through taking into aspects which are culturally specific.'[5] This connotes a broader, inclusive and secular view of Lord Jagannath, which is a unique feature where every section of the society has a relational attachment with the deity.

This aspect contributed to the greater association of people with the lord when their favoured ruler or associated institutions were under attack, be it from Mughals, Marathas or English. The greater the attack, the bigger was the cohesion and higher was the concern for their lord. This led to the enhancement of the image of Gajapati.

A very important and subtle aspect has been highlighted by writer Surendra Mohanty in his monumental work *Nilasaila*. He writes that in Jagannath consciousness *bhakti* (devotion) is insignificant compared to *sraddha* (affection). Every Odia has a personal relationship with Jagannath and has a right to call the lord their own. While he elaborated this aspect in the context of Gajapati Ramachandra Deb, who changed his religion and became Hafiz Kadir Beg, Mohanty's view has a significant appeal in Odia society.

The coexistence of both *bhakti* and *sraddha* is a pre-dominant feature in Odisha society. This is the reason why Jagannath has been a great source of inspiration to Odia nationalism. Therefore, when the ritual association of the Gajapatis with Lord Jagannath came under attack due to certain British initiatives, it was viewed as an attack and affront to the deity, thus invoking the larger cause of Odia pride and dignity which rose above narrow religious considerations. The actions of the Gajapati to take on the challenges thrown up by the British government not only brought wider support, publicity and acclamation but enhanced the image and perception of the Gajapati in people's mind. It is significant to mention that the misdeeds of Gajapatis were ignored by people for they viewed Gajapati from the perspective of his association with Lord Jagannath.

After Independence

Once India became independent in 1947, there was a necessity of bringing the temple, its rituals, administration and finances under statutory enactments. By then the temple administration was in a mess. The indiscipline in administration and poor financial condition were the main issues that needed to be addressed. The temple of Lord Jagannath at Puri is an institution of national importance.

The state government, after observing the continuous lawlessness and indiscipline in the management of the Shri Mandir, irregularities in the conduct of daily rituals and festivals and unusual delay in their execution, passed the Puri Shri Jagannath Temple (Administration) Act 1952 as a preliminary step to deal with the issues. A Bill was introduced in 1954 in the Assembly with a statement of objects and reasons as under.[6]

> The Puri Temple of Lord Jagannath which occupies an unique position not only in the state of Orissa but also in relation to the whole of the Union is in a sad plight.
>
> Abject mismanagement, a standing disgrace to the citizens and their administration, prevails in spite of all efforts to remedy it. There is no escape but that in the interest of the public, State Government must step in and take effective measures in order to save it from ruination.
>
> In the absence of any guidance from the Raja and sufficient contribution from him for the regular expenses of the Temple, the scheduled and disciplined performance of the *Nitis* has suffered beyond imagination and the Raja has practically lost all control over the different *sebaks* and other temple servants.

Economic rivalry and moral degeneration of the servants and *sebaks* has divested them of all sense of duty and co-operation. Specific endowments are regularly misapplied and misappropriated. Strikes amongst various classes are common occurrence. The non-availability at the appointed hours of the *Mahaprasad* coveted and adored by millions of pilgrims is always there these days. The lapses into unorthodoxy has resulted in extremely unhygienic conditions inside the Temple and commission of the heinous crimes even within the Temple precincts is not rare. Even the image of the deity has been at times defiled and its precious jewellery removed. Peace and solemnity inside the Temple has given way to sheer *goondaism* and it is mainly the servants of the Temple that make up the unruly elements responsible for such lawless state of affairs.

For the purpose of exercising effective supervision over the administration of the Temple and its endowments, a Bill was prepared and introduced in the State Legislature in June 1948. Provisions for constitution of a Committee with the Raja of Puri as Chairman, ex officio, was made for an effective administration of all the religious and specific endowments—jewels and the properties vested in the deity subject to the control of the State Government. Provisions for constitution of a Council of Religious Rituals was also made to settle disputes regarding rituals in the Temple. This Committee was required under the said Bill to report upon the disputes relating to the rights of *sebaks*, etc. and to control daily time-table relating to the performance of ceremonies in the Temple. This Bill was not, however, enacted and reasons are not known. The fact remains that the Bill fell through perhaps due to constitutional difficulties. All efforts from 1937 to 1948 to enact legislations have still failed due to initial difficulties as to the nature of rights and duties of the principal persons interested in the Seba-Puja of the deity and other idols....

According to the provisions of the Act, the government appointed a special officer who prepared the Record of Rights by making a study of the Shri Mandir, its services and puja rituals, donated property (endowment) and the rights and responsibilities of the *sebaks* and other personnel. He submitted his report to the government on 15 March 1954. Based on his recommendations and suggestions, the government passed the Shri Jagannath Temple Act, 1955 (Odisha Act No. 11 of 1955). All the earlier Acts, rules and regulations and prevailing system of management were declared invalid. Even though this Act was passed in 1955, it came into effect from 27 October 1960. The earlier Act of 1952 was integrated with it.[7]

Under the new Act, the management of Shri Mandir and all its moveable and immoveable property were entrusted to the Shree Jagannatha Temple Managing Committee constituted by the government. The Puri Raja became the hereditary chairman of the managing committee and the Puri Collector was made ex-officio vice-chairman. The committee was constituted with 12 members, including the chairman. It was stipulated that only Hindus could become committee members.

The Act was challenged by Gajapati Ramachandra Deb and subsequently his successor Gajapati Birakishore Deb in the High Court and the Supreme Court. They questioned the legal propriety and constitutionality of the Act. Puri Raja argued that the Jagannath Temple was his personal property. The government's action of withdrawing the Raja's right over his property without any compensation had resulted in the violation of Articles 19 and 31 of the Constitution. He also argued that this special Act was discriminatory as the common law of Odisha, Hindu Religious Endowment Act, 1952, was the law to govern the management of all Hindu temples and endowment properties, including the Jagannath Temple.

The High Court dismissed the contention. The court held that since the Raja happens to be the first and foremost *sebak* of the Lord, the aforesaid Act had not encroached upon his traditional service and rights due to him. Gajapati Birakishore Deb appealed against the High Court verdict.[8] The Supreme Court upheld the High Court ruling and dismissed the appeal of the Gajapati. In a historic judgment, a Division Bench headed by the Chief Justice of India along with two other judges held that the position of superintendent and *Adyasebak* were different. His position as superintendent had ceased to be and instead he has become chairman of the committee. The court held that his rights, privileges and perquisites as *Adyasebak* remained protected even if he ceases to be the chairman. His position as *Adyasebak* is safeguarded in the Act in as his much as rights and privileges in respect of *Gajapati Maharaja Seva* are protected.[9]

The Gajapati's claim that the Jagannath Temple was his personal property was surprising. The Gajapati probably realized the mistake and withdrew this claim. This was against the foundational philosophy of this great temple.

We are reminded of a legend from ancient times. Lord Brahma desired that King Indradyumna should ask for a boon after he consecrated the image of Lord Jagannath. He was pleased with the great efforts of Indradyumna in finding the sacred and secret image of Lord Jagannath. Indradyumna requested Brahma:

Tumbhe jebe bara deba maguchi muhin,
Mohara vanshare kehin na thibe gosain.[10]

As you desired to grant me a boon I asked for one:
let there be no descendant in my family/clan, in
other words, let there be an end to my clan.

It was very strange for a king to ask for such an unusual boon from the magnanimous Lord. He explained the reason why he made the request:

Putra nati bolibe je deula ambhara,
Ambhara bolante dharma jiba je mohara.[11]

My sons and grandsons will claim the temple to be ours, the moment they say 'ours' I will lose all my *dharma* or *punya*.

The king explained, 'My Lord, grant that my family might become extinct so as not to leave behind even one person to claim, in the distant future, that this temple was built by an ancestor of his!' He did not want that his son or grandson would claim this temple in future. Such a claim would take away the *dharma*. The king, whose long-cherished aim to discover and install the image of Lord Jagannath had been achieved, wanted the temple to belong to posterity. The magnanimous wish was granted.

This unique legend of Jagannath Temple has two great elements. One is the supreme sacrifice of King Indradyumna in asking for a boon to have no future progeny. Second, King Indradyumna wanted to profess and prove that this temple would not belong to any sect, individual, religion or king. By this act, he demonstrated that this shrine would be above any conflicting claims or narrow identities. Right at the beginning, he established that Lord Jagannath and the temple belonged to all and truly justified the deity's very name: 'Lord of Universe'.

This foundational philosophy was probably the realization and a reminder to Ramachandra Deb to drop the claim of ownership of the temple.

One of the reasons for the Odisha government's takeover was the abject mismanagement of the temple administration and indiscipline in performance of its rituals. The source of revenue of the temple after British dissociation became very limited. The transfer of Satais Hazari Mahal and Ekharjat Mahal provided some revenue for temple administration. However, over the years, with increasing expenses, the inelastic revenue sources resulted in growing deficit from year to year. The temple administration suffered.

It is important to note that the British dissociation under the pressure of Christian missionaries did not provide for meeting the increasing temple expense in future. This lack of foresight created problems later. This spilled over to indiscipline and disturbances in rituals and *nitis* of the temple. It is useful to refer to the Grome Report of 1805, which mentions about the strong temple administration when it was controlled by the Raja of Khurda during the pre-Maratha period. He writes, 'Even the slightest deviation from the prescribed duties was severely punished either by fine or corporal punishment.'[12]

The situation deteriorated after the Marathas took over and then during the subsequent British occupation. This pitiable situation was addressed after the Independence by the new Act during the time of Ramachandra Deb who was the last Gajapati under the British regime and the first Gajapati in post-Independence India. After his death in 1956, his son Birakishore Deb took over. The court cases were fought by these two Gajapatis.

With the new enactments and order of the Supreme Court, the role of the Gajapati changed—from being the erstwhile superintendent of temple he became the titular chairman of the multi-membered committee. His role as an independent authority ceased. The committee became the regulating, administrative and controlling authority.

However, the Gajapati's role in the domain of temple rituals remained intact. This role flowed from his privileged status as *Adyasebak*. In fact, his continued traditional role was codified in the Record of Rights prepared by the Special Officer appointed after the enactment of the Puri Shri Jagannath Temple (Administration) Act, 1952. The Record of Rights went a step further by a statutory incorporation of the Raja of Puri as *Chalanti Vishnu*. 'Raja of Puri is called *Chalanti Vishnu* because similar honour as to God Vishnu is shown to him when he enters the temple.'[13]

With the new Act in place, the 'Raja of Khurda' completely lost his relevance and the title ceased to exist. In its place, the Raja of Puri was statutorily recognized. The 'Raja of Puri means the person on whom rests for the time being the obligation of discharging duties of *sevak* in respect of Gajapati Maharaja Seva (service) as recorded in Record-of-Rights'.[14] The abolition of the title of 'Raja of Khurda' by the government of Odisha was probably the first such abolition even before the royal privileges and privy purses were stopped in India as a whole.

The Puri Raja is the first and foremost *sebak* of Shri Jagannath Temple and his service, *Gajapati Maharaja Seva,* is a hereditary function of the royal dynasty of Puri. His most important service is the *chherapanhara* in the three chariots on the days of Rath Yatra (Car Festival) and Bahuda Yatra (Return Car Festival). This refers to sweeping floors of the chariots with a broom having a golden handle. Besides, he performs the *chherapanhara* in the *snanabedi* (platform for bathing) and *dolabedi* (platform for swinging) during the Dola festival; he also does the same *chherapanhara* on the first and last days of the Chandan Yatra festival. In his absence, the *Mudrahasta* or *mudiratha sebak* can perform his services on his behalf.

The Raja can perform *Rajaniti* when he visits the temple on the occasion of Raja Besa (royal dressing). Gajapati Maharaja is regarded as *Chalanti Vishnu* (moving Vishnu). If the pilgrims have his *darshan* and present him a gift, it becomes his personal possession. Gajapati Maharaja can go to Shri Mandir in his palanquin accompanied by various musical instruments. When he goes to the temple, his palanquin is kept at the Lion Gate. *Sebaks* like *karana, parichha* and other servitors lead him to the temple in a grand procession accompanied by musical instruments.

If the Queen accompanies him, her palanquin goes straight to the banyan tree inside the compound. The people in the inner compound and outer compound are made to vacate the place before her visit. Only some specified servitors are allowed to stay. Only the *mudiratha* accompanies her and makes arrangement for the *darshan.* The Queen's *darshan* is called *Gahana bije.* The female attendants of the Queen can stay with her.

It is only when the King invokes the Lord with betel nuts and coconuts that the Brahmin priests initiate the *puja* in the temple of Maa Vimala and other goddesses in the month of Aswin (September–October). At the time of Nabakalebara, the Rajaguru gives the *daitas* areca nuts sanctified by the holy touch of the King (*Gua Teka Niti*) and thereafter the journey for the search of the *daaru* (sacred wood) for Nabakalebara ceremony begins. The King performs the ritual of *bandapana* at the palace gate on the occasion of *Lakshmi Narayana bheta* (meeting of Lakshmi and Jagannath) during the Bahuda festival. On the day after the *Rukmini Vibah* (marriage of Rukmini), i.e., on 'Champaka Dwadashi', the King takes both the bride and bridegroom inside from the palace gate. There the King performs a ritual called *Rajaniti*.[15]

The disengagement of the Gajapati with the management of the temple contributed to his enhanced role in the ritual and religious domain. He became free of possible blame and blemish of administrative ills of governance of the temple. He is completely insulated from the ills of bad administration and non-governance and their consequences.

The Story of two Elephants

The word Gajapati is derived from the word 'Gaja', meaning elephant. A book on the Gajapatis of Odisha may not be complete without recounting about the last two elephants belonging to the Gajapati and the Temple. One story is related to the death of Gangaram, or the *Pata Hati* (elephant of the palace), and the other is about Laxmi, the last elephant of the Temple.

Gangaram Dies

Gangaram and Moti (male and female) were brought by the Puri Raja as gifts from the Kalahandi royal family when they were five to six months old. They were cared for and loved in the palace. As Gangaram grew up, he was engaged in royal and ritual services. During Chandanyatra festival, a decorated Ganagaram used to be the torchbearer leading the procession. At the time of the Car Festival, Gangaram used to stand behind the chariots and gently use his weight to push the chariots to roll. When King used to proceed for *chherapanhara* in his ceremonial palanquin named

Tamjhan, Gangaram used to lead with his mighty gait in the front. At other times, the mahout would take Gangaram near the Lion Gate of the temple and let him rest there.

Visitors used to watch the decorated and gorgeous elephant before entering the temple. Many would offer bananas and coconuts. Coins and money would be accepted with his long trunk and passed on to the mahout. Gangaram was a popular and favourite sight at the temple. Whenever he went to any locality or *sahi*, people would come out of their houses and offer fruits, coconuts and vegetables to him. Children would fondly touch, caress and feed him. He was the darling of everyone. He was given special treatment and affection because he was the king's elephant.

It all changed for Gangaram one day. Moti, his companion, had died some time back. The lone Gangaram was declared mad one day. Word spread like wildfire in Puri town. Once loved and admired, Gangaram was now despised and rejected. People's love turned into hatred and anger. He became an object of attack and assault. No one received him or welcomed him the way they used to do earlier. People hurled stones at him, also attacking him with sharp objects. He was blinded in one eye with a sharp metal object thrown at him.

Crowds attacked him whenever the animal was spotted. He would run blind and hit people and houses which would invite fierce reactions. The animal's life became miserable. The municipality administration one day used fireballs and crackers and drove him away from the town towards Malatipatapur. The chase was the most pathetic and miserable plight for him. He reached Kanchinala, an offshoot of Bharagavi River. He probably found the place to be calm and far from the madding crowd. It was like lull before the storm.

That was when several shots were fired at him by the specially assigned snipers engaged by district officials. Gangaram fell silent. He struggled and gasped for life; but breathed his last in a few minutes. He was buried by the district administration soon thereafter at that place.[16]

Why did he go mad? Was he really mad? Or madness was a fiction? Many natives of Puri recall Gangaram's story. An eyewitness's description is as follows: One morning, when Gangaram was receiving visitors at the Lion Gate with the mahout astride on his back, a fisherwoman came close. She offered some coins to the animal. Gangaram extended his trunk toward the hand of the woman but as soon as it reached near her hand, he pulled his trunk back and did not accept the coins. It was apparently because the elephant did not like the pungent smell of fish.

The mahout did not care to go into the reason for his refusal. He got annoyed and coaxed Gangaram to accept the coins but he refused. This annoyed the mahout further, who did not take such disobedience well. With the *ankush* or elephant goad, a pointed object to train and guide elephants, the mahout hit near the right ear of the elephant and continued hitting repeatedly for his persistent refusal. In the meanwhile, the fisherwoman left without offering the coins, which infuriated the mahout more.

An angry Gangaram, annoyed and irritated with the continuous poking by the mahout, violently shook his body dislodging the mahout from his seat and dropping him down on the ground. The elephant roared and charged towards the mahout in fury. The man ran in fear. Gangaram pursued him. It seemed that Gangaram wanted to take revenge on his mahout. *Bada danda*, or the Grand Road of Puri, became a sight of horror. People ran helter-skelter and got hurt, shops got damaged. And, thus, rose the cry, Gangaram had gone mad.

This happened in 1971.

Laxmi Dies

Charles Grome's Report in 1805 is the first report on the Jagannath Temple after the British occupation of Odisha in 1803. The report contains details of the working of the temple, organization structure, details of *seba* and temple servants, *nitis* and category of pilgrims. List 13 describes the establishment of the temple and mentions various *sebas*. At serial no 209, there is a mention of Hauty Mahoot Sebuck or Elephant Mahout Servitor.

The report says the temple had six elephants to carry out various ceremonial rituals. These elephants were managed by mahouts who were considered as servitors of the Lord. Gromes's report talks of categories of service without describing the service. This category of servitor does not find any mention either in the Record of Rights that came after 1952 or in Karmangi, which was in force before the Record of Rights came into existence.

While all temple services can only be performed by Hindus, the role of mahouts of elephants are exclusively reserved for Muslims. Records say that Muslims were given priority to be engaged as mahouts. Only if a Muslim candidate was not available was a Hindu considered. Researcher Dr Mahesh Prasad Dash writes,

> The Temple of Jagannatha was a unique centre of cultural synthesis in this regard. It may be mentioned here that the mahunta seva of the temple was usually entrusted to a person belonging to Muslim Sect. Raja of Puri, who was the Superintendent of the Jagannatha Temple, once passed an order to appoint a Hindu in case a person from Muslim community was not available to perform the Mahunta Seva.[17]

This is an exceptional instance of engaging a non-Hindu in a Hindu temple to perform a particular service to the Lord. Mubarak Khan was the last mahout employed in the Jagannath Temple. He was appointed on 1 December 1972 and retired on 31 May 2003. There is no mahout now. The temple has no elephant. Mubarak was the mahout of Laxmi. Laxmi died on 31 July 1987 at age 72. She was the last elephant owned by the temple administration. After her death, Mubarak was engaged in other works by the temple administration.[18]

The death of the Gangaram in 1971 and Laxmi in 1987 brought an end to an important facet of a tradition. The Gajapati became dispossessed of his iconic association with Gaja, an inalienable part of his identity. The title Gajapati became a misnomer, a title only. Second, the visible sign of an elephant being a part of our ritualistic symbol in ceremonies of the temple stopped. For a few years, the temple administration tried to engage elephants borrowed from Nandankanan Zoological Park but it did not work out. Third, a great tradition of employing and engaging Muslims as a servitor of the Lord as mahout stopped.

Gajapati Lives in the Hearts of People

The Gajapati, the lord of elephants, does not own an elephant today; yet, he is called the Gajapati. He is a king without any kingdom; yet, he is called the Raja of Puri. He has no empire, no army, no power or status of yesterday; yet, he is addressed as *Shree Shree Shree Virashree Gajapati Gaudeswara Nabakoti Karnatotkala Kalabargeswar Viradhivirabara Bhuta Vhairaba Sadhu Sasanotirna Rautaraja Atula Bala Parakram Sahasra Bahu Kshetriyakula Dhumaketu Maharajaadhiraja*……

He is probably the only king in independent India who has some sort of statutory recognition as his service is recorded as *Gajapati Maharaja Seva* in the Record of Rights. He is a unique king, a Gajapati Maharaja whose elephant, power, riches and position is of no relevance to a common man. In peoples' perception he enjoys respect and recognition much above all these.

He has an identity, a stamp of devotional connect. He is the *Chalanti Vishnu*, an image that is very dear and close to peoples' heart. This image of him remains etched in the hearts and minds of the average man. People yearn to have his *darshan*. A glimpse of his person makes one feel humbled and people prostrate before him as they think that they are having the *darshan* of Vishnu. The depth of reverence and devotion commanded by the Gajapati is indescribable. And all these because he is the *Adyasebak* of Lord Jagannath. The inseparable link between Lord Jagannath and

Gajapati, between two lords, makes his position very unique and unparalleled.

The faith and reverence are so deep rooted that the temple almanac is prepared every year and runs from the *sunia* day that is the beginning of the New Year called *anka* of Gajapati. The horoscope of a child at the time of his birth used to be prepared on the palm leaf in the name of Gajapati. The practice is even prevalent today. Such connection, so deep and durable, is a part of tradition and life in Odisha.

Today, as part of the Jagannath tradition, people of Odisha relate to two icons or two images. One is of Lord Jagannath and the other of the Gajapati as *Chalanti Vishnu*. The veneration and reverence for the Gajapati is immense and emotive. The linkage between these two images in people's mind is associative as well as parallel. The associative linkage between these two identities, complementing each other has become stronger over the years. However, within the duality of the identities, the role of Gajapati has become secondary and less significant while magnifying his traditional role of *Adyasebak*.

The present disconnect between his historical administrative duties and servitor duties allows him to focus on spreading, propagating and disseminating Jagannath consciousness among people. The close involvement of the present Gajapati in spreading Jagannath consciousness across India and abroad has helped raise his stature. In people's esteem, the position of the Gajapati remains unchanged. This has helped the reverence for the Gajapati to go up in people's perception and esteem. Such a phenomenon does not find any parallel elsewhere.

APPENDICES

APPENDIX 1

Translated version of letter No. 345 from Puri priests to Lord Wellesley dated 24 July 1804

May the Illustrious LORD, the Sovereign of the Universe, be our refuge

May the sincerest felicitations of the entire population of this city of the Supreme one, wealthy, pious and noble, of the whole sect of the Vaishnavas, of countless Brahmanas headed by the Royal preceptor and lastly, of all the attendants of the Deity, like Krishna Chandra Mahapatra the Chief of the thirty-six holy offices, shed brilliant lustre on the exalted (personage) Governor-General, Marquess of Wellesley, known by the following titles, "one-with-everlasting-fame" (lit. may-his-glory-continue) "the ruler universally accepted," "chief among all nobles" and "wielding lofty titles"; who is devoted to (the task of) bearing the burden of the earth which testifies to the (unique) virtue of worshipping his illustrious patron deity; who is the repository of a host of virtues which are being sung by numerous women, who have been turned into his chattels, in consequence of his having extinguished the splendour of the orb that his enemies are, included in the globe of the earth, itself held in fee by the exhibition of his majesty derived from the prowess of his own arms; to whom the entire world is devoted on account of the repeated recounting of his noble fame; who is the unrivalled sun that has caused to bloom the lotus that the English race is ; and who has besides taken the vow of protecting the gods, the Brahmanas and the Vaishnavas.

Supported as we are by the solicitous attention of the English power, our predominance has been established in the holy temple of our Divine Master Jagannatha partly through the grace of the Supreme Lord, the illustrious Sovereign of the Universe and partly through the desire of the esteemed ruler. It is on this account that security and comfort have come to us according to our luck. Therefore, we, the people of the holy city are ever engaged in pronouncing our benediction and we wish to send our felicitations to your lordship. Further, we cherish but this desire that your authority over this holy city may continue in this way forever. Previously, while pondering on your Lordship's reputation, we became convinced of (the inevitability of) your control over the holy temple from reports, discussion, the sacred texts and the trends (of current events). We are now beholding with our own eyes exactly what we foresaw. In no instance did we witness nor shall we ever discern such prowess as we saw when your forces were preparing for war and again at the time of the defeat and the expulsion of the enemies. During this period the entire population was protected by you in such a manner that not a single soul suffered even the slightest loss, and we who were employed in attending on our Lord were not even aware that a war was raging in the land. While in the previous regime we had to meet with obstruction oven in the smallest matter, we enjoy happiness now in every respect under your government. Sincerely do we hope that your lordship will establish justice in the same way as it was done (of yore) by Brahma and other gods and that having heard of the security in which our lives and properties are, thanks to the care of the British authority, people from other places like Vrindavana, Varanasi, Ramanatha and Dvarika will all come to this city and having viewed the Deity will ascend to Vaikuntha. And we here are praying night and day to God that the supremacy of the English power may last forever, that the Lord by placing your lordship under his lasting protection may promote your steady advancement and that, we your well-wishers, being rid of all fear (worries) under your rule may ever remain engaged in the service of the Sovereign of the Universe:-

Verses

Such is the virtue of this city of the Supreme Being that here indulgence (of the senses) brings the same reward as asceticism, taking of meals in disregard of (caste) rules serve only to clean the stains of birth and the dust of a slave girl's feet is capable of purifying even the gods. (1)

The journey (of life) has been rendered difficult by the Vedas and the Dharma-Sāstras. In vain, oh wise men, have you pursued (your path), Of what use is this labour? On this sea-coast, beneath the banyan tree, is available the nectar of absolute truth for anyone to drink in with his eyes. (2)

(Here) The purifying food even if dropped from a dog's mouth should be eaten by Brahma and other gods if by luck they find it. (3)

The light which flashes like lightning in the firmament of the soul of the ascetic, shines on the Blue Rock in the form of wood. (4)

Glory to the Lord of the Universe, in partaking of the leavings of whose food the bars of proximity do not operate between the (various castes) beginning with the Brahmanas and ending with the dog-eaters. (5)

Where there is prosperity there is no learning; where both co-exist liberality is wanting ; If three of them happen to occur in one place in consequence of numerous meritorious deeds (done), courtesy does not manifest itself; and where the last-named is found piety is sure to be absent. But it is in you alone, that all these shine together through the grace of God. (6)

APPENDIX 2

Translated version of petition filed by Gajapati Mukund Deb II for release

That your petitioner, in conformity to the custom of his ancestors and to prove himself deserving of the favour of the Honourable Company, has been always on amicable terms with the Magistrate at Ganjam, and according to the dictates of friendship, your petitioner's Vakeel resided with the above gentleman and in return his, resided with your petitioner. When your petitioner's father died, your petitioner was very young, and on this account the Rajgooroo having been appointed Mookhtar for directing the affairs of the country, placed your petitioner on the Musnad. During the Mookhtarship of the Rajgooroo, your petitioner except the name, had not any of the power of Raja. At this time the English forces attacked the fort of Cuttack and Col Harcourt, W. John Melville and the Magistrate at Ganjam, having summoned your petitioner's Vakeel, acquainted him that they had intention of taking the city of Cuttack, and directed him to request his master to withdraw himself from the Marathas, and afford a clear passage to the English. The above Vakeel, in conformity to the orders of the above gentlemen, made known these circumstances to your petitioner. Immediately on hearing this your petitioner being greatly rejoiced, sent to the above Vakeel to represent, that the Marathas had by violence and force of arm wrested from your petitioner Sri Purusotum, and other places, altogether four Mahals; and that on this account, your petitioner being desirous of meeting with the favour of company, prayed night and day, that the country might fall under the dominion of the company, and that then your petitioner would have justice due to him. Agreeably to your petitioner's wishes, the Kanoongoh of the Company advanced. Your petitioner was in hopes that according to the hereditary custom, your petitioner would have the above Mahals granted to him. To the representations of the Vakeel, the above gentlemen observed with kindness that the four Mahals and a lakh of rupees in cash, should be given to your petitioner, provided that your petitioner should form no alliance with the Marathas. In consequence of hearing this, your petitioner afforded them a safe passage and Colonel Harcourt with a large army advanced and gained possession of the Fort of Cuttack. During these circumstances your petitioner Vakeel was with the above gentlemen - after this the Rajgooroo went to Cuttack, and having had an audience, laid a petition requesting, according to promise, the delivery of the Mahals. Colonel Harcourt in answer observed that not span of land should be given up and that from the lakh of rupees a part should be given then and the remainder at some future time. God knows how much money was given to the Rajgooroo, your petitioner knows not. That which he did receive he expended on the pay of the troops in his service. He then return from Cuttack and said to your petitioner "I at first warned you from forming an alliance with the commander of the Company's troops, and from affording him is safe passage. Now Colonel Harcourt has not given up the Mahals and has also intentions of taking from you what hereditary country remains in your possession." During this Colonel Harcourt sent the Kanoongoh, Suddar, Mahashai to draw up a quirarnama and agreeably to his wishes your petitioner signed the quirarnama with the knowledge of Rajgooroo and told the Rajgooroo to dismiss the troops in his service, for that your petitioner has determined to discharge the obligations of a well wisher, and subject to the Company and that by this means, your petitioner would become fortunate and prosperous. Having heard the substance of your petitioner's speech the Rajgooroo was displeased and told the troops to receive their pay from your petitioner. Accordingly they violently demanded their pay and deprived your petitioner of food and clothing for two or three days. Under these circumstances your petitioner told them that he had not retained them in his service, but that the Rajgooroo had, and desired them to demand their pay from him. The Rajgooroo was enraged at this and by way of procuring money for their pay, led the troops into those Mahauls which the Marathas had by force taken up possession of and attacked and plundered them. In these Mahauls, the troops of the Rajgooroo fought and skirmished with Company's force who were stationed there. Being informed of this Colonel Harcourt attacked the fort of Khoordha, on which account your petition determined to have a conference with him. Hearing this the Rajgooroo returned from the Mahauls and consulted to confine your petitioner in prison and fight the Company's army. Your petitioner, having been made acquainted with this, abandoned the fort and took the road into the jungles. At length the affairs of the unskillful and imprudent Rajgooroo were ruined and he was put to flight. Colonel Harcourt having taken the fort, plundered the whole of your petitioner's property and possessions. After this the Ryots of the Country, who had been much harassed by the tyranny of the Rajgooroo, seizing the opportunity caused him to be confined and sent to Colonel Harcourt.

Colonel Harcourt asked him whether he had caused these disturbances of his own accord or at the instigation of the Raja, your petitioner. He answered that the Raja was a child and that what had been done had been done by himself. After this your petitioner sent his Vakeel with intent to request an audience of Colonel Harcourt, who detained the Vakeel as prisoner. Your petitioner then sent his Dewan for the same purpose, who was also detained as prisoner. Having no remedy your petitioner sent Fateh Mohammud, a Jamadar, a servant of the Company and ambassador to Mr. Betun to procure an audience of Colonel Harcourt.

He, by the order of Colonel Harcourt, came himself to your petitioner and comforted and encouraged him. In spite of this, Colonel Harcourt, not deigning your petitioner an audience, imprisoned him in the fort of Cuttack. Now being a prisoner at Midnapore, your petitioner passes his time in great distress, and his family being also in confinement in the city of Cuttack are in great trouble. The men who had acted as Mookhatars, in not having attended to the orders of your humble petitioner, were deserving of punishment from the Company. They have met with the due punishment of their deeds. Your petitioner is innocent and with the name of Raja, had no power, no influence, in the direction of the country, although your petitioner attended the Commander of the Company's forces, he is confined, and suffers much distress. The whole age is acquainted with the justice of the Company and until now the British Government has never deprived a Zamindar of his Estate, without his being guilty of some offence. Your petitioner, therefore, praise that a copy of this petition may be laid before the Governor General, and that your petitioner being found deserving of compassion, may be freed from prison. May you order this and may the sun of your prosperity shine bright.

Appendix 3

Letter of Suryamani Patamahadei to Collector of Puri dated 30 July 1883 clarifying that the transported raja would make him disqualified to perform the services of the temple in case he ever returned

(Copy)

To

The Collector of Poore

Sir,

In continuation of my application in Ooriya dated 12th July 1883, I most respectfully beg leave to state that should the convicted Rajah Dibyo Singh Deb be released and allowed to return to his home, he would be, according to the custom of the country, disqualified to perform the ceremonies of Juggannath for having associated with and taken the food cooked by "Mleches" i.e. persons other than Hindoos, and it was on this and some other considerations already stated in my memorial to Govt. that I was compelled to install my minor grandson under the patronymical cognomen of "Rajah Mukund Deb". I beg to enclose in original the opinion of the respectable Pundits and Mahants of the District declaring that the transported Rajah would be disqualified for the services of the [temple] in case he returns home.

As a precedent, I take [liberty] to bring to your notice that one of my ancestors named Rajah Ramchandra Deb who ascended the throne in 1649 Sakabda (1727 A.D.) having been compelled to associate with a daughter of the then Mahomedan Nabab

Nabab, was not allowed to perform the services of Jagannath or to enter the Temple — and as he expressed his desire to worship the idol, the "Patitpaban Deb" (a representative of Jagannath) was set up at "Singhadwár" (Lion gate of the Temple) in order that he (the fallen Rájáh) might be able to see and worship it from the outside. The Rájáh having thus become disqualified to perform the religious and social ceremonies of the family, the officials of the palace brought down his daughter's son from Athgar and installed him on the Gáddi as Rájáh Bir Kishore Deb. The enclosed extracts from the old "Madla Lángi" bear testimony on the subject.

In conclusion I beg to state that besides the documents I have already filed and the evidence already given, a reference to the books specified in the accompanying memo would shew that the title of Rájáh is hereditary in the family and I also presume that the histories of the Province and official correspondence would verify the above.

I beg to remain
Sir
Your most obdt. servant

Coonee
Raghiri, the 30th July 1883.

Sdf. Sarjamoni Patmahadei
(True copy)
Her obedt.
Head clerk

Sdf. Ananda Chandra Gu Mhoy
Dewan & authorised
agent of Rani Surjyamoni
Patmahadei of Coonee

APPENDIX 4

Letter in Odia from Rani Suryamani Patamahadei to the collector of Puri dated 10 June 1884 agreeing to pay *nuzur* of 1,500 rupees in gold mohurs for confering the title of 'Raja' to her grandson Makunda Deb

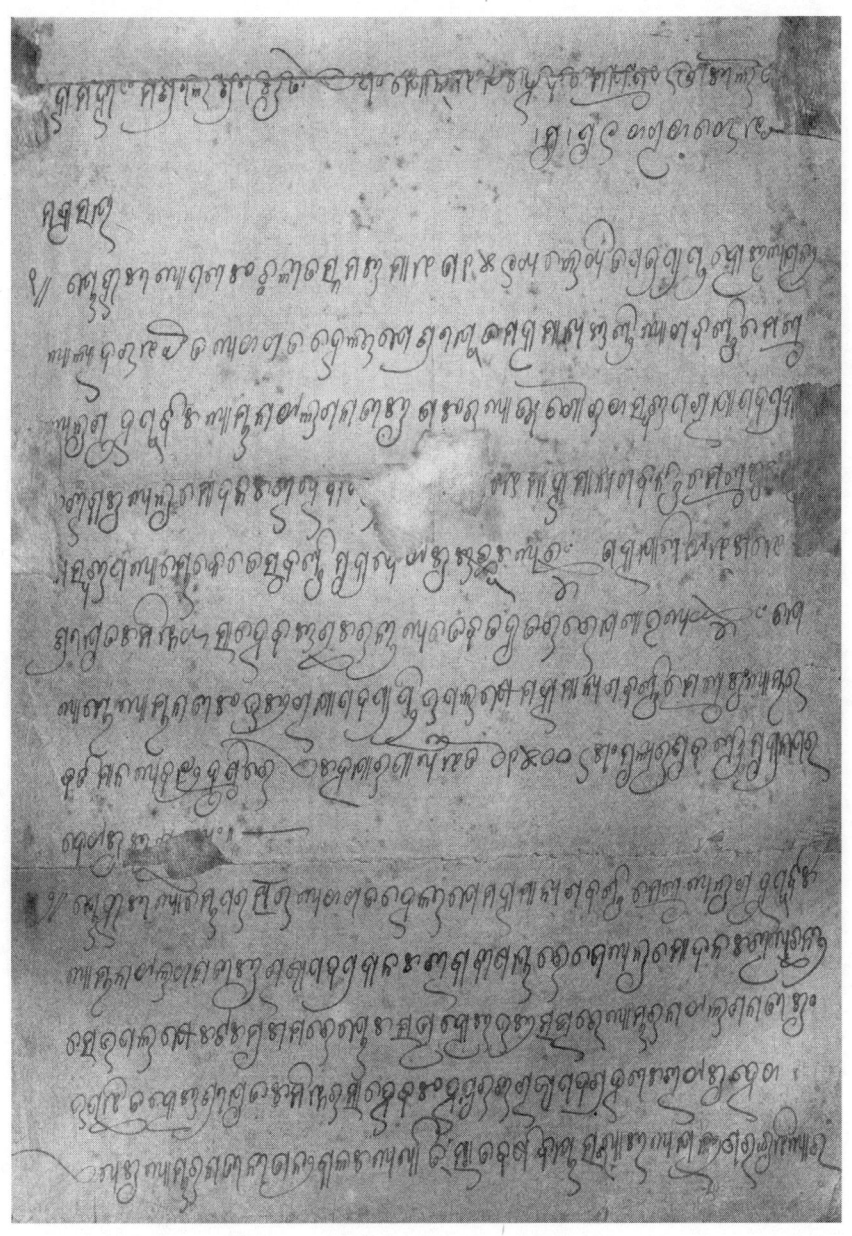

Appendix 5

Translated version of the letter of Rani Suryamani Patamahadei submitted to Collector, Puri

Translation of the letter from the Ranee to the Collector of Pooree

No. 478/2

From

Ranee Suryamani Patmahadei
Pooree

To

F. Jones Esquire
Collector Magistrate
Pooree

Pooree, dated 10th June 1884.

Sir,

In acknowledging receipt of your letter dated 15th May 84, I am very glad to learn that the Govt. of India has been pleased to confer on my grandson the title of Rajah, as a personal distinction. The Commissioner of Orissa Division desires to know what amount of Nuzzer in gold Mohurs I am willing to present to Government. In reply I have the honor to state that with a view to circumstances I am at present in, I am willing to present to Govt.

a Nuzzer of Rs. 1500/- in gold mohurs.

2d - I am told that a durbar will be held at Cuttack for the purpose and my grandson will have to attend it, to receive the said title from the Commissioner of Orissa. As he is a boy only 7 years old, and is very much attached to me and is not yet familiar with Hakims (Govt Officers) he is unable to attend the Durbar. I would therefore request the favour of your making proper arrangements to have the title conferred on him by the Commissioner or by yourself in your Bungalow.

Sd. Suryamani Patmahádei

True Translation

Bhagirathee Naik
Head Clerk.

APPENDIX 6

Letter of Golakhdanda to the Editor of *Utkal Dipika* published on 18 December 1888

Sir,

I shall be much obliged if you kindly make room in your journal for the following lines.

It is a matter of great regret that the Orissa Association has to protest against the intended policy of Govt. as regards the affairs of Jagannath Temple. No doubt can be entertained that its intention is good. It cannot be otherwise. To secure the greatest possible happiness to its people is the avowed object of ruling powers. It does not, however, necessarily follow that they are not likely to be misinformed and misled. Charity has not altogether banished fault finding spirits from the world. Rumour is a dame that always sees objects through a magnifying glass of great power. Hands are ever ready to distort everything that comes to them, either from their sinister motives or from their evil nature. What is to be most deplored is, not that the millennium is not come when angles only are to be met with everywhere, but that these evil genii should exercise so great an influence over British Government as to make it forget its own nature and principles. This is, however, no matter of wonder. Government consist of human beings and Satan was successful in his trick upon Adam and Eve.

This must not be taken to mean that there is all perfection in Puri Temple. It is under the management of a human being. Human nature is human nature everywhere. Had it been otherwise, it is well known that the throne would have been a bed of ease, there would have been no Legislature, no Police and no Court of Justice. Had it been perfect, there would have been no necessity for dissolving parliament, no necessity for amending laws, no provision that judges in England should continue during their good behaviour, no remark from it from R.W. Emerson that there is in Oxford "gross favouritism; many chairs and many fellowships are made beds of ease." It is from one to another human agency that Government is likely to transfer the management of temple affairs.

The fallibility of human nature for furnishes indeed no ground to let off delinquents with impunity. For the sake of public interest justice should be done to them. But this justice is prescribed by the British coronation oath to be tempered with mercy. Charity again comes in and puts forward her claims to make allowances for special circumstances. These noble principles are a sealed book to those who try to mislead our benign Government. Their jaundiced eye does not see that the management of the Temple affairs has been for years in the hands of a woman, who is not Mrs Bilasini Karformar, who has never seen male faces except those of her father, husband and son, who has never been beyond the four walls of the Zannana, who does not hold any university diploma and who is not versed in the science of Government. They forget that the temple is the large establishment with various ceremonies to be performed by numerous hands; that it is visited during the yatras by thousands and thousands who never dreamt of one another's face and who differ as much in habit, custom, manners, and temper as a Newzealander from a Laplander. The faults, if any, in the management are not such as to confer the intended remedy. In support of my this assertion I beg to refer to the resolutions passed in the recent meeting of Orissa Association where the flowers of Orissa met for the express purpose of discussing the question.

No one can deny that it will be gross injustice to apply no remedy to the defects, if there be any, in the management. It will, on the other hand, be equally so to deprive the Puri Raj family of a privilege which it has been enjoying long since and which was as sacred from the religious fury of the Mahomedans, who preached with the Koran in one hand and sword in the other, as from the fingers of the Marathas whose cupidity knew no bounds. No such passion can possibly be worked upon in British constitution. It's best part has consequently been appealed to, much against their own nature, by those of the neither religion from whose quadrimanus activity nothing is sacred. They have taken their stand upon mismanagement, forgetting that this is an evil to be met with wherever there is human agency. Hundreds and hundreds of human beings are, either crushed to dust by railway accidents, or unceremoniously buried in the depths of the sea. Such calamities are in most cases ascribed to the screw being somewhere loose. But in no case Governments are invoked to apply such remedy as in present instance; a railway is not transferred; a shipowner is not prohibited from plying his ships. For the sake of public interest laws are made, rules are laid down and proprieties are directed to take proper care and precaution. They have as much to deal with the public as the Puri Raja. No more legal right can be claimed in their favour than in that of latter. Legal rights is a creature of the sovereign will. It can as easily transfer the management of railways and steamers as that of the Puri Temple. There is an appeal, not to law, but to morality against the sovereign, who always tries to make his dictates as for as possible harmonious with those of morality. There seems to be as much moral right to appeal to morality on behalf of Puri Raja as that of any other body. While others are seen to be furnished with rules for guidance and to go off with punishments other than forfeiture of property, it appears to be cruel and morally unjust to deprive the Puri Raj family of a long enjoyed privileged on the ground of mismanagement if there be any, in the hands of an old Oriya Hindoo woman. Though this step has been advised by evil spirits, it is hoped that angels will come forward to lead in the path prescribed by morality.

There is no better way than to appeal to the noble feelings of the sovereign. But if it pleases our Government not to give up the intended course, we beg its permission to say that it cannot place the Temple affairs in the hands of angels; nor can it, as far as we see, secure the service of a Gladstone or Lord Ripon; the sovereign power is, however almighty. But it is as certain as the sun rises that Jagannath Himself cannot afford to pay for the service of such men. The greater probability is that incompetent hands of far inferior nature will be appointed to the trust. No one can assure that there will be no necessity for rules, inquiries, dismissals and punishments. The chances are that there will be no Darogahs, Inspectors and others with titles from the fairy land will sponge and batten upon Jagannath who will be inch by inch made to learn how to keep fasts.

It is imagined that the Temple affairs will be placed in the hands of a committee like that of Bhoobaneshwar Temple. I am not inclined to criticise the conduct of the existing one. I beg to appeal only to a principle of British Constitution, a principle which displaces the unquestionable wisdom and sagacity of the English nation. Stephen says in his commentaries on Blackstone that the Executive power in England has been "wisely placed in one hand for the sake of unanimity, strength and despatch." Although so high a character can by no means be claimed for the functions of Puri Raja, they are undoubtedly of an analogous nature. There is no doubt that he has not to make laws or manage a municipality. Had it been so, he could be properly replaced by a body of persons. On the contrary he has the charge of an establishment which is a mere household on a large scale, the duties being only to see that peace and order are preserved among the Temples servants and that *Nities* are regularly perform. There are great misgivings whether household business can be properly carried on by a number of persons working at a time. The English proverb says that too many cooks spoil the broth. The committee cannot but resign the whole trust one hand reserving to itself the superintendence only.

The same supervision can be well exercised by Government without recourse to the intended course. No one can question its this right of oversight. The sovereign, is vested with the guardianship over its subjects. Does not this relation exist between our Government and Puri Raja? Is he not a minor? Has he forfeited his claim to parental protection? Have counsels been thrown away upon him? It is becoming enough is it becoming a parent to go to court of justice in order to take away its own gift from its own child? It is merely to hold a candle to sun to speak of regal duties to British Government well known for its wisdom, virtue and tenderness of his subjects.

I may, however, be allowed to draw attention to the relation between Jagannath and Puri Raja. They are popularly believed by the Hindus to be inseparably connected. Let it be ascertained how far their separation will affect the worship of Jagannath. For this purpose let no page of shastras be left unturned and let no feelings be left unconsulted either in the court or in the cottage, in matters of religion of Maharaja of Cashmere being on the same footing with the meanest subject of Her Majesty. The proclamation of the Empress and the non-interfering policy of British Constitution in matter spiritual encourage the hope that our religious feelings will be tenderly attended to and that our external happiness in the world to come will not be sacrificed for mere temporary convenience in this world of misery and woe. We pray Jagannath to bless our Empress that Her Majesty gives us an opportunity to secure our bliss in His world of joy.

Cuttack

8-12-88

I beg to remain Sir
Yours faithfully
GOLAKHDANDA

APPENDIX 7

The first letter of the 'Lunatic' published in *Utkal Dipika* on 26 March 1887

Sir,

I have read a good deal about the Juggernath Temple case in the Vernacular and English papers of the several presidencies of India. I think a collection of these in the form of a pamphlet will be acceptable reading to the public. One evening I was just trying to guess the real object of Government in instituting this suit. I am neither a philosopher nor a lexicographer and I have never been able to grasp the distinction between motive and object, so pardon me, Mr. Editor, if I have wrongly used the word object. I tried to examine the several motives attributable to Government by the different classes of Indian population from the highest Government official to the poorest "Chasa", but none of these explanations seemed reasonable to me. Some people say the object of the suit is to improve the ceremonials; this I cannot believe, for it will be unworthy of Christian Government and opposed to the policy which Government has always pursued in regard to religious matter. I am sure we are not going to have Hindu chaplains in the Government of India's pay. Besides, the Government of India is bound by a most serious pledge to the Christian public both in England and in India not to revive its connection in any form with this temple. This pledge may be read in the minutes of the Governor General of the time, in the minutes by the Members of the Council, in the dispatches by the Court of Directors, in the letters to the representatives of the Christian assemblies in India, in the returns to House of Commons and in the speeches in the House by the Hon'ble Messrs Ingles and Kinard. I cannot believe that the object of the suit is to improve the management of the Temple. But there are many people who believe it and not only here, but even in England, some people believe this to be the object of the suit. I have heard that the matter has attracted the notice of the Christian people in England and they believe this to be the object of the suit.

Some people believe that the object of the suit is to prevent the spread of disease and consequent loss of life from the consumption of unwholesome food in the shape of stale Mahaprasad. I cannot believe this, for I cannot understand how this can be effected. The Hindus believe Mahaprasad to be the most sacred food, no part of it, ought to be thrown away. Pilgrims carry this sacred food thousand of miles to be given to relatives as a most acceptable present. By the time the food reaches its destination, it becomes unfit for human food. How can any system of management in the temple at Puri prevent the consumption of unwholesome food in the Punjab or in the Bombay Presidency.

The only effectual means to prevent this evil will be the addition of a section to the Penal Code making the consumption of this unwholesome food punishable. But will the Legislature have the courage the courage to do this?

While musing and amusing myself in this strain I fell asleep and saw a dream. I saw Sir George Campbell hold a serious conversation with a person whose official designation was the Settlement Officer of Khurda but whose name I could not learn. I heard the latter point out to Sir George the difficulty of increasing the revenue of Khordah by reason of a portion of that Estate having been made over unconditionally to the Temple. Sir George seemed anxious to raise the revenue by resettlement of the Estate. The Settlement Officer was willing to carry out Sir George's orders, but how could he enhance the rents of a portion of the estate, when the other portion which had been made over to the Rajah of Khordah was exempted from enhancement under the terms of the deeds of transfer. Sir George seemed to think that those deeds of transfer purported to be assignment of revenue and not of land, and this construction seemed to please the Settlement Officer. Just at this moment I was disturbed by it sound. I woke and both Sir George and the Settlement Officer vanished. I again fell asleep and strange to say the scene changed. Sir George appeared with another gentleman, who I learnt was the Secretary of State for India. This gentleman in a very serious tone disapproved of the forced construction put up by Sir George on the deeds of transfer and of the conduct of the Settlement Officer in treating the portion of Khordah covered by those deeds as much under Khas management as the rest of it. Here I was again disturbed by the sound which I discovered this time was caused by a big rat which had entered the drawers of a toilet table and was trying to get out.

A few minutes after I again fell asleep and I saw an altogether new scene. I saw a number of gentleman with Sir Ashley Eden at their head sitting in solemn and serious deliberation over this Khordah Settlement question. It will not interest you to know the opinions of the several gentlemen present at this meeting, and I am not sure whether I shall be able to reproduce a dream correctly but the resolution arrived at was that the recourse should be had to legislation for the purpose of removing the Rajah of Khordah, to whom a portion of this estate had been assigned over, from the management of the temple and thus get out of this difficulty in the settlement of Khordah. It was dawn, the cock crew, I woke up, to this world of state secrets never to be admitted again to the privilege of listening to the conversation of angels.

This dream puzzled me very much and I tried to ascertain if this dream had any reality. All that I could learn was that for some years subsequent to the transfer of a portion of Khordah to the Raja as Superintendent of the temple, Government undertook the management of this portion of the estate as well, realized arrears of rent by the certificate procedure, surveyed the lands, in short, treated the deeds of transfer as assignments of revenue and not conveyances of lands.

Mr. Editor, do you know anyone who could read this dream for me? Or do you know any Government official who could enlighten me as to whether this vision is a mere dream or has a corresponding reality on the red tape world.

Yours Sincerely
A lunatic

APPENDIX 8

The second letter of the 'Lunatic' published in *Utkal Dipika* on 9 April 1887

Sir,

Thanks for your publishing my last letter. It is no small encouragement to a lunatic to see that his wild thoughts are acceptable to the Editor of a newspaper. I don't believe I am a lunatic, but some people say I am one. I once had a discussion about the Juggernath Temple case with a European gentleman who is considered one of the cleverest man in India, he called me a lunatic. I challenged him to a discussion by correspondence and we had a long correspondence. At last this gentleman admitted I was right and remarked to a friend of mine that he thought I was an exceeding clever fellow. Thus I came to consider myself a lunatic.

I don't like anything second hand. A second handbook I don't care to read because it comes tainted in marginal pencil notes with the views and ideas of its first reader, just as a second hand wife imbibes the views of her first husband. For the same reason I don't believe in second-hand opinions and feelings general, popular or individual. By second-hand opinions, I mean the opinions and feelings of some men as reported by others. If you tell me that the present suit regarding the Temple of Juggernath is very popular with the Hindu community I won't believe your report; that would be against the rules of the asylum of which the lunatic is an inmate. I would go and mix freely with the people so as they may throw off all reserve and communicate to me their views and feelings in the matter. Owing to my dislike for everything second-hand I have got into the habit of picking up in my morning and evening walks little bits of torn paper that lie in the streets and about the houses of men. I always buy the contents of wastepaper baskets because these enable me to learn directly the views and feelings of authors of the torn manuscripts contained in the such baskets. I compare the views and opinions disclosed in the tattered contents of waste paper baskets and those expressed in the resolutions, letters and despatches written for the public or for the Government, and the result of such comparison is always grateful to me.

I put all the collections in the box which I have labelled as "Hodge-podge box". The collection consists of torn letters, stray leaves of book, portion of documents and all odds and ends of lazy and busy literature. It is no small task to make this odds and ends fit into one another; it resembles the task of adjusting the several parts of a geometrical figure in a Chinese puzzle. I give you Mr. Editor the contents of some of my valuable documents and leave it to you and to your readers to make these odds and ends fit into one another.

No. 1 is a portion of a printed leaf evidently from a book found in the grand trunk road to Khordah. It contains the following : "Policy indeed would suggest that the remembrance of the former rank and power of his family should, as much as possible, be obliterated from the minds of himself and all the natives of the districts; at least that no positive measures should be taken tending to keep alive the impression of his high rank and political consequences, and that it should be made an object to confine as far as practicable the veneration felt by natives towards the person of the descendent of their ancient sovereigns, to his office and situation as Superintendent of the peculiarly sacred and celebrated temple of Juggernath."

No. 2 is the manuscript found near the Lal Bagh gate. It runs thus: "As far as the question of strict right is concerned Government has determined that the Raja cannot claim under any regulation or order to engage on any more favorable terms than as a Zamindar at a fixed and comparatively easy Jumma, with reference to the ordinary principles of assessment. It may be added that the family, it is believed, have long ceased to expect that they will ever be readmitted to the possession of the estate on such highly favoured terms as alone would render it worth their having. The arrangement suggested for their support and maintenance in the letter regarding Lembai is sufficiently liberal and combined with pecuniary and other advantages resulting from the Superintendency of the temple must entirely preclude all just ground of complaint."

No. 3 is the cover to a bottle of whisky received from No. 5 Bankshall Street Calcutta. The contents are: "I am indeed to suggest that this object may be attained without putting the (original is torn here) in possession of Khordah, relinquishing to him Zemindar's allowance or Malikana of 35 per cent on the rental which under the orders of (the original torn) was found as the minimum rate for the Zemindars of these provinces and resuming per contra the personal allowances of (original torn) Rupees and the donation to the temple. The Raja, therefore, would not demur to an arrangement by which he would be a considerable gamer."

No. 4 is a manuscript. I don't remember where I picked it up. It runs this : "But it is to be borne in mind that he has been entirely uncontrolled and has been led to regard the temple as a sort of private property."

No. 5 came to me as cover to a pair of boots from Parliament Street London. It contains these words:"An act of legislation, the repeal of an act, cannot affect the rights and interests of the Raja to the management of the temple."

No. 6 is a page from manuscript copy of what seems to be a revised edition of the Holy Bible. This page is headed "hard swearing."

The contents of the first are as follows "I don't quote verbatim but give the purport in my words: "I swear that the Raja is a trespasser in the temple, he has no business to be there, that he is about to run away with bricks and mortar in the temple."

The contents of the second page are: "I swear that the God Juggernath invoked my aid to save him and his endowments from the act of misappropriation and sacrilege by the Rajah."

The content of the third page is a drawing. I am not an artist and cannot paint the picture but I shall describe it as well as a lunatic's pen can do the work of the artist's pencil. The Rajah is seated in the attitude of devotion before the idol Juggernath, a policeman seizing him by his left arm and a large crowd attacking the policeman, having evidently come to the rescue of Rajah.

Now Mr. Editor, I believe all the above including the picture are by the same person, may not be the same natural person, but at least they are by the same juristical person. If you ask me why I believe this I simply answer because I am "A lunatic".

NOTES

1. GAJAPATI

1. Andrew Sterling, *Orissa: Its Geography, Statistics, History, Religion and Antiquities* (Jagatsinghpur: Prafulla Pathagar Publications, 2004), p. 88.
2. Ibid., p. 89.
3. D.C. Sircar, *Indian Epigraphy* (Delhi: Motilal Banarsidass, 1965), pp. 338–339, quoted in Phillip B. Wagoner, *Tidings of the KING*, p. 178.
4. Sircar, *Indian Epigraphy*, quoted in Wagoner, *Tidings of the KING*.
5. L. Sprague de Camp, *An Elephant for Aristotle* (London: Dobson, 1966).
6. For details, see https://www.thehindu.com/children/Unforgettable-GIFT/article16388768.ece.
7. a) Moreshwar Ramchandra Kale, *Raghuvansam of Kalidas* (Mumbai: Gopal Naryan & Co., 1932); b) Haraprasad Das, *Odia Jatira Jibana Katha* (Bhubaneswar: Pashima Publications, 2011), pp. 248-49.
8. K.C. Panigrahi, *History of Orissa* (Cuttack: Kitab Mahal, 1986), p. 63.
9. Ibid., p. 92.

10. P. Sensharma, *Kurukshetra War: A Military Study* (Calcutta: Naya Prokash, 1975), p. 130.
11. H.C. Das, *Military History of Kalinga* (Calcutta: Punthi Pustak, 1986), p. 12.
12. Das, *Military History of Kalinga*, p. 12.
13. Panigrahi, *History of Orissa*, p. 179.
14. Ibid., p. 183.
15. Prabhat Mukherjee, *The History of the Gajapati Kings of Orissa and Their Successors* (Cuttack: Kitab Mahal, 1981), p. 2.
16. Dr S.N. Rajguru, *Odishara Sanskrutika Itihasa (1100–1568 AD)*, 4th Part (Bhubaneswar: Odisha Sahitya Akademi, 1986).
17. Raja GCH Jagadeb, *Utkal Empire Under Ganga Kings, A Book Dedicated to All Scholars and Students of History on the Occasion of the History Congress at Bhubaneswar*, 1977, p. 18.
18. Das, *Military History of Kalinga*, p. 288.
19. A.L. Basham, *The Wonder That Was India* (London: Sidgwick & Jackson, 1954), p. 130.
20. Sri Dhrubacharan Jaysingh Paikaray, *Bharatiya Swadhinata Sangramuka Khurdar Abadana* (Cuttack: Chitrotpala Publication, 2007), p. 256.
21. B.C. Ray, *Mogal Odisha Itihas O Sanskruti* (Cuttack: Vidyapuri, 2020), p. 23.
22. Chakradhar Mahapatra, *Utkala Itihasara Ek Ajnanta Adhyaya* (Cuttack: Friends Publishers, 1969), p. 126.
23. Das, *Military History of Kalinga*, pp. 298-99.
24. Debabrata Swain, 'Elephants in Art, Architecture and History of Orissa', *Orissa Review*, vol. LXIV, no. 11 (June 2008), pp. 36-49.
25. Mukherjee, *The History of the Gajapati Kings*, p. 3.
26. D.C. Sircar, 'Kapilas Inscriptions of Narasimhadeva', *Epigrahica India*, vol xxxiii (1959-1960), pp. 43–44.
27. R. Subrahmanyam, *The Suryavanshi Gajapatis of Odisha* (Waltair: Andhra University, 1957).
28. Mahimohan Tripathy, *Gajapati Maharaja Mananku Upadhi*, Shree Mandir, Kartik Edition, 2013, p. 22.
29. Mukherjee, *The History of the Gajapati Kings*, p. 14.
30. Rajguru, *Odishara Sanskrutika Itihasa*, p. 45.
31. Mukherjee, *The History of the Gajapati Kings*, p. 15.
32. Rajguru, *Odishara Sanskrutika Itihasa*.

33. Jagabandhu Singh, *Prachina Utkal* (First Part) (Bhubaneswar: Odisha Sahitya Akademi, 1982), p. 34.
34. Subrahmanyam, *The Suryavanshi Gajapatis of Odisha*.
35. Ibid., p. 174.
36. Tripathy, *Gajapati Maharaja Mananku Upadhi*, p. 23.
37. Sterling, *Orissa: Its Geography*, p. 103.

2. GAJAPATI KING: THE FOREMOST SERVITOR

1. Mahimohan Tripathy, 'Jagannath, State Deity of Odisha', in *Cultural Heritage of Odisha*, vol. xii, Shri Jagannath Special Volume (Bhubaneswar: Vyasakabi Fakir Mohan Smruti Sansada, 2010), p. 933.
2. N. Mukunda Rao, *Kalinga under the Eastern Gangas* (Delhi: B.R. Publishing Corporation, 1991).
3. D.C. Sircar, 'Nagari Plates of Anangabhima III; Saka 1151 and 1152', *Epigraphia Indica*, vol. xxviii, p. 243.
4. Artaballabha Mohanty, *Madala Panji*, second edition (Bhubaneswar: Utkal University, 1969), pp. 26–27.
5. D.C. Sircar, 'No. 5, Bhubaneswar Inscription of Anangabhima III; Anka year 34', *Epigraphia Indica*, vol. xxx (1953–54), pp. 17–23.
6. D.C. Sircar, 'No. 39, Bhubaneswar Inscriptions of Bhimadeva', *Epigraphia Indica*, vol. xxx, pp. 232–36.
7. D.C. Sircar, 'Puri Inscription of Anangabhima III, Saka 1147 and 1158', *Epigraphia Indica*, vol. xxx, p. 199.
8. Dr S.N. Rajguru, *Inscription of Odisha c. 1045–1190 AD*, vol. 3, Part 1 (Bhubaneswar: Odisha Sahitya Akademi, 1960).
9. Dr Harekrushna Mahtab, *The History of Odisha*, vol. II (Cuttack: Dr. Harekrushna Mahtab Foundation, 2000), p. 126.
10. R. Balakrishnan, 'Sri Jagannath: The Divine Face of Pluralism', *Odisha Review* (June–July 2018), p. 32.
11. Kailash Chandra Dash, *Kingship of Purushottama-Jagannatha in Odisha in Legend, History and Culture of India: : Based on Archaeology, Art, and Literature* (Calcutta: Punthi Pustak, 1997), pp. 219–37.
12. Sri Satchidananda Misra, 'Theocracy of Jagannath: A Study in the Retrospect', in *Cult and Culture of Lord Jagannatha* by D. Panda

and S.C. Panigrahi (Cuttack: Rastrabhasa Samanvaya Prakashan, 1984), p. 167.
13. Misra, 'Theocracy of Jagannath', p. 168.
14. G.N. Dash, 'The Evolution of the Priestly Power', in *The Cult of Jagannath and the Regional Tradition of Odisha*, ed. Anncharlott Eschmann, Hermann Kulke and Gaya Charan Tripathi (Delhi: Manohar, 2014), p. 286.
15. M.M. Chakravarty, *Journal of the Asiatic Society of Bengal*, vol. LXIV, 1901, p. 175.
16. Mahtab, *The History of Odisha*, vol. II, p. 132.
17. H. Kulke, 'Jagannatha as the State Deity under the Gajapatis of Orissa', in *The Cult of Jagannath*, ed. by Eschmann, Kulke and Tripathi, p. 277.
18. Misra, 'Theocracy of Jagannath', p. 177.
19. K.B. Tripathi, 'A Study of Early Oriya Inscriptions', PhD Thesis, School of Oriental and African Studies, University of London, 1952, p. 445.
20. Tripathi, 'A Study of Early Oriya Inscriptions', pp. 452–54.
21. Ibid., p. 450.
22. Kulke, 'Jagannatha as the State Deity', p. 280.
23. R. Subrahmanyam, *Inscriptions of Suryavanshi Gajapatis of Orissa* (Delhi: ICHR, 1986), p. 122.
24. Tripathi, 'A Study of Early Oriya Inscriptions', p 471.
25. Kulke, 'Jagannatha as the State Deity', p. 280.
26. Panigrahi, *History of Odisha*, p. 216.
27. Dash, 'The Evolution of the Priestly Power'.
28. Subrahmanyam, *Inscriptions of Suryavanshi Gajapatis*, pp. 159–60.

3. SURYAVANSHI GAJAPATIS: GRANDEUR AND GLORY

1. Subhramanyam, *The Suryavanshi Gajapatis*, pp. 31–32.
2. Panigrahi, *History of Odisha*, p. 194.
3. N.K. Sahu, 'The Imperial Ganga and the Gajapati Rule in Odisha', *OHRJ*, vol. III, no. 4, 1955, p. 173.
4. Subrahmanyam, *The Suryavanshi Gajapatis*, p. 59.
5. Sharmila Das, *The Cultural Contributions of the Gajapatis* (Delhi: New Age Publications, 2007), p. 77.

6. Mayadhar Mansinha, *The Saga of the Land of Jagannatha*, Fourth Edition (Cuttack: Mass Media (P) Ltd., 2020).
7. Das, *The Cultural Contributions of the Gajapatis*, p. 79.
8. Sarala Dasa, *Mahabharat, Santiparva* (Cuttack: Dharmagrantha Store, 1970), pp. 11–12.
9. R.D. Mukherjee, 'Purusottama Gajapati', *JBSR*, vol. 32.
10. Subrahmanyam, *The Suryavanshi Gajapatis*, p. 66.
11. Panigrahi, *History of Odisha*, p. 209.
12. Subrahmanyam, *The Suryavanshi Gajapatis*, p. 76.
13. Paes and Nuniz do not mention her name. She is called Tukka in the poem *Tukka Panchakam* and in the *Krishnaraya Vijayamu*, Jaganmohini in the *Rayavachakamu*, and Lakshmi in the *Kaifiyat of Kondavidu: A Forgotten Empire*, p. 247.
14. C. Mahapatra, *Utkala Itihasara*, p. 42.
15. Ibid., p. 44.
16. Phillip B. Wagoner, *Tidings of the KING: A Translation and Ethnohistorical Analysis of the Rayavacakam* (Honolulu: University of Hawaii, 1993), p. 155.
17. Ibid., p. 155.
18. Ibid., p. 156.
19. Das, *The Cultural Contributions of the Gajapatis*, p. 230.
20. K.K. Goswami, *Chaitnya Charitramrita* (Cuttack: Edward Press, 1910, p. 248.
21. (a) Das, *The Cultural Contributions of the Gajapatis*, p. 232; (b) Dr D.C. Sen, *Chaitanya and His Companions* (Calcutta: University of Calcutta, 1917), p. 12.
22. Sen, *Chaitanya and His Companions*, p.13.
23. R.D. Banerji, *History of Odisha: From the Earliest Times to the British Period*, vol. I (Calcutta: S.K. Das Prabasi Press, 1930), p. 332.
24. Mukherjee, *The History of the Gajapati Kings*, p. 103.
25. Dr Harekrushna Mahtab, *The History of Odisha*, vol. I (Cuttack: Dr Harekrushna Mahtab Foundation, 2000), p. 154.
26. Prabhat Mukherjee, *History of the Jagannath Temple in the 19th Century* (Calcutta: Firma KLM, 1977), p. 107.
27. Subrahmanyam, *The Suryavamsi Gajapatis*, p. 171.

4. MUKUNDA DEB: THE LAST INDEPENDENT HINDU KING

1. Panigrahi, *History of Orissa*, p. 240.
2. Mahtab, *The History of Orissa*, vol. II, p. 170.
3. Abu'l Fazl-i-Allami, *Ain-i-Akbari*, vol. II, trans. Col H.S. Jarrett (Calcutta: Asiatic Society of Bengal, 1891), p. 127.
4. Das, *Military History of Kalinga*, p. 312.
5. Abu'l Fazl-i-Allami, *Ain-i-Akbari*, vol. II, p. 128.
6. Al-Badaoni, *Muntakhab-ut-Tawarikh*, trans. by W.H. Lowe (Calcutta: Asiatic Society of Bengal, 1884), pp. 166-67.
7. Neamet Ullah, *History of the Afghans* (Persian), trans. by Bernhard Dorns (London: John Murray, 1829), p. 181.
8. K.N. Mahapatra, 'Gajapati Ramachandra Deva I', *Orissa Historical Research Journal*, vol. VI, no. 4 (Jan 1958), p. 236. A point to be noted here is that the description of the demolition of the Temple of Jagannath as recorded in some historical accounts is not correct because the temple is still standing in spite of several invasions. The fact of the attack on the temple and damage and desecration of the idols are, however, well supported by evidence.
9. http://magazines.odisha.gov.in/Orissareview/2011/july/engpdf/82-89.pdf.
10. Haraprasad Das, *Odia Jatira Jibana Katha* (Bhubaneswar: Pashima Publications, 2011), p. 218.
11. Krupasindhu Misra, *Fort of Barabati* [in Odia] (Cuttack Trading Company, 1955).

5. RAMACHANDRA DEB I: ABHINAVA INDRADYUMNA

1. K.N. Mahapatra, 'Gajapati Ramachandra Deva I', p. 233.
2. Artaballabha Mohanty, *Madala Panji*, fourth edition (Cuttack: Prachi Samiti Grantha I, 1940, 2017), p. 45.
3. Sterling, *Orissa, Its Geography*, p. 78.
4. Mohanty, *Madala Panji*, p. 46.
5. Kedarnath Mahapatra, *Khuruda Itihasa* (Cuttack: Grantha Mandir, 1999), p. 11.

6. S. Pattanaik (ed.), *Chakada and Chayani Chakada* [in Odia] (Cuttack: BinodBihari Publisher, 1959), pp. 101-102.
7. Records indicate that during his visit to Cuttack in 1510, Chaitanya had *darshan* of these idols.
8. Mahomed Kasim Ferishta, *History of the Rise of Mahomedan Power in India till the year AD 1612*, trans. John Briggs, vol. III (Calcutta: R. Cambray & Co. 1910), p. 466.
9. Abu'l Fazl, *Akbarnama*, vol. III, trans. by H. Beveridge (Calcutta: Asiatic Society of Bengal, 1907), pp. 967-68.
10. Kedarnath Mahapatra, 'Two Little Known Sanskrit Poets of Orissa', *Orissa Historical Research Journal*, vol. I, pp. 52–56.

6. PURUSHOTTAMA DEB: THE MOST ATTACKED KING

1. Mirza Nathan, *Baharistan-i-Ghaybi*, trans. Dr M.I. Borah (Guahati: Government of Assam, 1936), p. 36.
2. Ibid., p. 38.
3. Henry Beveridge (ed.), *Tuzuk-i-Jahangiri or Memoirs of Jahangir*, trans. Alexanders Rogers (London: Royal Asiatic Society, 1909–1914), p. 21. See also https://archive.org/stream/tuzukijahangirio00jahauoft/tuzukijahangirio00jahauoft_djvu.txt.
4. K. Mahapatra, *Khuruda Itihasa*, p. 48.
5. Beveridge (ed.), *Tuzuk-I-Jahangiri*, p. 433.

7. GAJAPATIS ON THE RUN: TURBULENT TIMES FOR BOTH THE LORDS

1. K. Mahapatra, *Khuruda Itihasa*, p. 61.
2. Jadunath Sarkar, *Studies in Mughal India* (Calcutta: M.C. Sarkar, 1919), p. 210.
3. Prasanna Kumar Swain, *Bhaktakabi Salabega* (Bhubaneswar: Odisha Sahitya Akademi, 2002), p. 62.
4. Sitakant Mahapatra (trans. & ed.), *The Alphabet of Birds: Hymns for the Lord of the Blue Mountain* (Delhi: National Book Trust, 2003), p. 83.
5. Sarkar, *Studies in Mughal India*, p. 208.
6. Ibid., p. 209.

7. Ibid., p. 210.
8. Ibid., p. 214.
9. Jadunath Sarkar, *History of Aurangzeb*, vol. III (Calcutta: M.C. Sarkar, 1912), p. 265.
10. Sarkar, *Studies in Mughal India*, p. 227.
11. K. Mahapatra, *Khurda Itihasa*, p. 106, quoting *Tabsirat-ul-Naizirin* in Rajendralal Mitra, *Antiquities of Orissa*, vol. II, p. 112.
12. K. Mahapatra, *Khurda Itihasa*, quoting *Tabsirat-ul-Naizirin* in Rajendralal Mitra, *Antiquities of Orissa*, vol. II, p. 111.

8. RAMACHANDRA DEB II: FALLEN KING, UNFAILING DEVOTION

1. K. Mahapatra, *Khuruda Itihasa*, p. 152.
2. Ibid., p. 153.
3. As by then Ramachandra Deb II had converted to Islam.
4. C. Mahapatra, *Utkala Itihasara*, pp. 207-08.
5. Ray, *Mugol Odisha Itihas*, p. 86.
6. Mahimohan Tripathy. 'Sri Mandir Sikharare Mahadeep and Mahadeep Boli' in *Pourush*, July 2016.
7. A note on a bilingual royal letter (*Chamu Citau*) issued by the Raja of Khurda granting special privileges to the King of Athagada, Ganjam, by Shishir Kumar Panda, *Proceedings of the Indian History Congress*, vol. 55 (1994), pp. 916-20.
8. Mahimohan Tripathy, *Shree Jagannath* (English) (Bhubaneswar: Ama Odisha, 2018), p. 279.
9. K. Mahapatra, *Khuruda Itihasa*.
10. C. Mahapatra, *Utkala Itihasara*, pp. 257-59.
11. Surendra Mohanty, *Satabdira Surya*, 3rd Edition, Cuttack: Lark Books, 1986), p. 252.

9. BIRAKESHARI DEB I: GAJAPATI GOES MAD

1. Ghulam Hussain Salim, *The Riyazu-s-Salatin (A History of Bengal)*, vol. I, trans. Maulavi Abdus Salam (Calcutta: The Asiatic Society, 1902), p. 331.
2. Ibid., p. 331.

3. B.C. Ray, *Orissa under the Marathas [1751-1803]* (Allahabad: Kitab Mahal Publishers, 1960).
4. T. Motte, 'A Narrative of a Journey to the Diamond Mines at Sumbhulpoor in the Province of Orissa', *OHRJ*, vol. 1, no. 3 (1953), p. 28.
5. Rajaram Pandit, who had by then become the Maratha Governor of Odisha, dissuaded the Ganjam chief Padmalakshmi Raju from coming to the aid of Birakeshari Deb.
6. Ray, *Orissa under the Marathas*, pp. 102-03.
7. Andrew Sterling, 'An Account Geographical, Statistical and Historical, of Orissa Proper, or Cuttack', *Asiatic Researches*, 1825, p. 93.
8. Mahapatra, *The Alphabet of Birds*, pp. 45–46.
9. Ibid., pp. 46–47.

10. MUKUNDA DEB II: THE FALL OF THE LAST PILLAR

1. Ray, *Orissa under the Marathas*, pp. 106-07.
2. Ibid., p. 107.
3. Major William Thorn, *Memoir of the War in India* (London: T. Egerton, Military Library, 1818), p. 253.
4. B.C. Ray, *The Foundations of British Orissa* (Cuttack, 1960), p. 21.
5. Fakir Harichandan, *Khordha Itihasara Antarale* (Cuttack: Bharat Bharati Publication, 1999), p. 41.
6. Bijay Chandra Rath, *Jayee Rajguru and Anti-colonial Resistance in Khurda* (Bhubaneswar: Sisukalam, 2017), p. 58.
7. Ray, *Orissa under the Marathas*, p. 67, in translation of Persian record no. 398, 6 September 1798.
8. Harekrushna Mahtab and Sushil Chandra De (eds.), *History of the Freedom Movement in Orissa*, vol. 1 (Odisha: State Committee for Compilation of History of the Freedom Movement, 1957), p. 73.
9. This refers to Ram Chandra Mahapatara, a famous priest of the Temple, who was head of Chhatis Niyoga and might have been dead since Jagannath Tarkapanchanan's last visit to Puri (Surendranath Sen and Umesha Mishra, *Sanskrit Documents* [Allahabad: Ganganatha Jha Research Institute, 1951], p. 12).
10. Jagannath Pattnaik, *Odisha Itihasara Ketoti Romanchakara Kahani* (Cuttack: Nalanda, 1999), p. 14.

11. Melville to Government, Bengal Secret and Political Consultations, 11 September 1803, No. 13 as given in Mukherjee, *History of the Jagannath Temple*, p. 34.
12. Mukherjee, *History of the Jagannath Temple*, p. 35.
13. This information can be found in the petition the Khurda Raja wrote to the British and the text of this petition can be found in Appendix 2—Turner to Government, 10 October 1806, Board's Collections, vol. 318, no. 7214, p. 4 quoted in Ray, *The Foundations of British Orissa*, p. 50.
14. G. Toynbee, *A Sketch of the History of Orissa from 1803 to 1828* (Calcutta: Bengal Secretariat Press, 1873), p. 7.
15. P.K. Pattanaik, *A Forgotten Chapter of Orissan History (with special reference to the Rajas of Khurda and Puri 1568–1828)* (Punthi Pustak, 1979), p. 127.
16. Ray, *The Foundations of British Orissa*, pp. 52-53.
17. Mukherjee, *History of the Jagannath Temple*, p. 44.
18. Yaaminey Mubayi, *Altar of Power: The Temple and the State in the Land of Jagannatha* (Delhi: Manohar, 2005), p. 161.
19. Harcourt to Shawe, 6 October 1804, Add.MSS.13610, p. 81.
20. Ray, *The Foundations of British Orissa*, pp. 57-58.
21. Rath, *Jayee Rajguru and Anti-colonial Resistance*, pp. 98-99.
22. Surendranath Sen and Umesha Mishra (eds), *Sanskrit Documents*, Allahabad, Ganganatha Jha Research Institute on behalf of National Archives of India, 1951, pp. 26–29 (Sanskrit text), pp. 90–92 (English translation).
23. Letter from Fortesque to Charles Grome, 7 December 1804, Odisha State Archives, Jagannath Temple Correspondence.
24. Letter from Fortesque to Charles Grome, dated 15th December 1804, Odisha State Archives, No. 3, Jagannath Temple Correspondence.
25. Mukherjee, *History of the Jagannath Temple*, p. 44.
26. Ray, *The Foundations of British Orissa*, p. 72.
27. Rath, *Jayee Rajguru and Anti-colonial Resistance*, p. 118.
28. Petition of the Raja of Khurda to the British government for mercy (translated from Odia), Odisha State Archives, Bhubaneswar.
29. Letter of George Dowdeswell to Magistrate of Midnapore, 5 March 1807, Odisha State Archives.
30. Pattanaik, *A Forgotten Chapter of Orissan History*, p. 162.

31. Pritish Acharya, 'Paika Revolt of Khurda, 1817', in *Paika Rebellion: Precursor to Freedom Struggle in India*, ed. B.K. Pradhan, Bhubaneswar: Uktal Vikas Parishad, 2017.
32. Mukherjee, *History of the Jagannath Temple*, pp. 120–121.
33. Sushil Chandra De, *Guide to Odishan Records*, vol. III (Odisha State Archives, 1962), pp. 82–83.
34. Son and successor of the imprisoned Mukunda Deb II.
35. Yaaminey Mubayi, 'The Paik Rebellion of 1817: Status and Conflict in Early Colonial Orissa', in *Paik Rebellion – A Documentary Study* (Odisha State Archives, 2017), p. 388.
36. Harichandan, *Khordha Itihasara Antarale*, p. 41.
37. G. Mastindell and W. Ewer to Government of Bengal, 8 December 1817, Board of Revenue Records.
38. 'Urzee of the Raja of Khoordah Ram Chandra Deo', (received) 20 January 1818, in Board of Revenue Records Judl-18 (January–April 1818).
39. Board of Revenue Records, Rev-17, W.Ewer to Government of Bengal, 18 May 1818.
40. S. Pati, 'Raja Rama Chandra Dev: A Victim of Khurda Rising of 1817', *OHRJ*, vol. XXVIII.

11. THE FORT OF BARABATI: THE PRIDE AND THE PRISON

1. S.N. Rajguru, 'The Age of Cuttack City', in *Cuttack: One Thousand Years*, vol. I, ed. Behera, Pattnaik and Das, pp. 198–205.
2. Sterling, *Orissa: Its Geography*, p. 98; Mohanty, *Madala Panji*.
3. Hafizullah Newalpuri, 'Cuttack as Known from Persian Sources', in *Cuttack: One Thousand Years*, vol. I, ed. Behera, Pattnaik and Das, p. 50.
4. M.N. Das, *Glimpses of Kalinga History* (Calcutta: Century Publishers, 1949), p. 163.
5. H.C. Das, 'Military Significance of Cuttack', in *Cuttack: One Thousand Years*, vol. I, ed. Behera, Pattnaik and Das, p. 89.
6. Ibid.
7. Das, *Military History of Kalinga* (Calcutta: Punthi Pustak, 1986), p. 28.

8. Das, 'Military Significance of Cuttack', p. 82.
9. Abu'l Fazl-i-Allami, *Ain-i-Akbari*, vol. II, p. 150.
10. Mohanty, *Madala Panji*.
11. Sterling, *Orissa: Its Geography*, p. 100.
12. Das, 'Military Significance of Cuttack'.
13. Al-Badaoni, *Muntakhab-T-Tawarikh*.
14. Abu'l Fazl, *Ain-i-Akbari*, p. 127.
15. Motte, 'A Narrative of a Journey to the Diamond Mines at Sumbhulpoor', p. 17.
16. Das, *Military History of Kalinga*.
17. Ibid.
18. K.C. Panigrahi, *Cuttack: The Historic Capital of Orissa*, in *Souvenir*, Cuttack Municipality, 1977, p. 16.
19. Misra, *Fort of Barabati*, pp. 59–60.
20. Mahtab, *The History of Orissa*, vol. II, pp. 177–78.

12. DIBYASINGHA DEB III: CROWN TO CONVICTION

1. Mukherjee, *History of the Jagannath Temple*, pp. 330-31.
2. Supriya Prasanta, 'Print Media in Colonial Odisha: A Brief Study', in www.academia.edu.
3. Pyarimohan Acharya, *Odishara Itihasa* (in Odia), New Edition (Cuttack: Orissa Book Store, 2012), p. 176; See also, 'Odisha Famine (Na'anka): A Documentation of Primary Sources' (Bhubaneswar: Odisha State Archives, 2016), p. xxiii.
4. 'Odisha Famine (Na'anka): A Documentation of Primary Sources', pp. 911–39.
5. Mukherjee, *History of the Jagannath Temple*, pp. 336-37.
6. Ibid., p. 336.
7. Ibid., pp. 338-40.
8. Ibid., p. 341.
9. Loke Nath Ghoshe, *The Modern History of the Indian Chiefs, Rajas, Zamindars, & C. Part II, The Native Aristocracy and Gentry* (Calcutta: J.N. Ghose, 1881), p. 452.
10. J.P. Das, *A Time Elsewhere* (Delhi: Penguin, 2009), p. 247.
11. District Magistrate Armstrong's Report to Commissioner on 6 March 1878 (Bhubaneswar: Odisha State Archives), p. 407.

12. District Magistrate Armstrong to Commissioner dated 9 March 1878 (Bhubaneswar: Odisha State Archives), p. 408.
13. John Beames, *Memoirs of a Bengal Civilian* (London: Chatto and Windus, 1961), p. 273. John Beames was the Magistrate and Collector of Cuttack for nearly nine years till 1878, when he was transferred to Chittagong. He wrote his memoir in 1896.
14. *Utkal Dipika*, 30 March 1878.
15. Jagannath Pattnaik, *Odisha Itihasare Ketoti Romanchakara Kahani* (Cuttack: Nalanda, 1999), p. 151 quoting *Utkal Dipika*.
16. *Utkal Dipika* dated 6 April 1878.
17. Ibid. dated 6 April 1878.
18. Ibid. dated 6 April 1878.
19. Das, *A Time Elsewhere*, pp. 257–58.
20. *Utkal Dipika* dated 13 April 1878.
21. This was another name for the Cellular Jail, a colonial prison in the Andaman and Nicobar Islands.
22. *Utkal Dipika* dated 13 July 1878.
23. Kunja Bihari Das, *Kunja Bihari Granthabali* (Cuttack: Odisha Book Store, 2008), pp. 636–37.
24. Das, *A Time Elsewhere*, p. 294.
25. Ibid., p. 335.
26. Mohanty, *Satabdira Surya*, p. 333; British library blog dated 4 June 2012, https://blogs.bl.uk/untoldlives/2012/06/prisoners-released-for-diamond-jubilee.html.

13. RANI SURYAMANI PATAMAHADEI: WOMAN EXTRAORDINAIRE

1. Armstrong to Commissioner, 1 June 1878, JTC Pt V, quoted in Mukherjee, *History of the Jagannath Temple*, p. 346.
2. Ibid., p. 347.
3. Secretary, Board of Revenue, to Secretary, Government of Bengal, Revenue Department, 29 August 1881, JTC Pt. V, quoted in Mukherjee, *History of the Jagannath Temple*, pp. 369–370.
4. Mukherjee, *History of the Jagannath Temple*, pp. 372–373.
5. Ibid., p. 373.
6. Odisha State Archives, No. 476.

7. J.B. Peacock to Secretary, Government of India, Foreign Department, 14 December 1883, No. 1467, JTC Pt. V, quoted in Mukherjee, *History of the Jagannath Temple*, p. 381.
8. F.S. Daukes to Secretary, Government of Bengal, Revenue Department, 5 May 1885, No. 694, JTC Pt. VII, quoted in Mukherjee, *History of the Jagannath Temple*, p. 388.
9. R.P. Singh to Commissioner, 27 October 1885, JTC Pt. VII.
10. Mukherjee, *History of the Jagannath Temple*, p. 392.
11. Mohanty, *Satabdira Surya*, p. 320.
12. Jagannath Mohanty, 'Rani Suryamanai Patamahadei—A Revolutionary Queen in Puri Gajapati Dynasty', *Odisha Review*, July 2008.

14. PLIGHT OF PATTARANIS: THE SORDID STORY OF PENSION

1. Manimohan Tripathy, *Shrimandira Itihasara Keteka Chhina Prustha* (Cuttack: Roopambica, 2007), p. 72.
2. Ibid., p. 73.
3. Letter of 20 December 1912 addressed to Pundit Ramaballabh Misra, District Officer, Odisha State Archives.
4. Odisha State Archives.
5. Odisha State Archives. See also Tripathy, *Srimandira Itihasara*, pp. 62–70.
6. J.A. Hubback, Secretary, Board of Revenue Bihar and Orissa, notifies on 9th September 1913 to Mr W. Maude, ICS, Member-in-charge, conveying consent of Lieutenant Governor in Council to publish the Rules in exercise of powers conferred by Section 14(1) of the Act XXIII of 1871, Odisha State Archives.
7. Odisha State Archives.
8. Memorial dated 21 December 1914 addressed to His Excellency the Viceroy praying for the cancellation of the Rules issued by Board of Revenue under Act XXIII of 1871 to regulate the disbursement of his political pension, Odisha State Archives, 553.
9. The letter from F. Noyce, Esq. ICS, Under Secretary to Government of India, to Chief Secretary to Government of Bihar and Orissa

dated 18th September 1915 enclosing the opinion of Advocate General of Bengal G.H.B. Kenrick dated 31 August 1915, obtained through Mr C.H. Kesteeven, Solicitor to Government of India, and conveying the decision of Government of India not to interfere in the matter, Odisha State Archives.

10. D.O. No. 481 P.T. from H. McPherson, Chief Secretary, to J.F Gruning, Commissioner of the Orissa Division, Cuttack, dated 13.02.1916, in File of Government of Bihar and Orissa, Political Branch, 1916, transferred as File No LXXIX-6/63, Board of Revenue, Orissa, Odisha State Archives.
11. Odisha State Archives.
12. D.O. No. 133, Con. from J.F. Gruning, Commissioner, to H. McPherson, Chief Secretary to Government of Bihar and Orissa, dated 1st March 1916, Odisha State Archives.
13. D.O. No. 909 P., from H. McPherson to J.F. Gruning dated 13th March 1916, Odisha State Archives.
14. Letter of George Dowdeswell, Secretary to government, addressed to the Magistrate of zillah of Midnapore, dated 5th March 1807, Odisha State Archives.
15. Tripathy, *Srimandira Itihasara*, p. 22.
16. J.P. Das, *A Time Elsewhere* (New Delhi: Penguin, 2009), p. 410.
17. Jagannath Prasad Das, *Desha Kala Patra* (Bhubaneswar: Prachi Prakashan, 2004), p. 477.
18. Tripathy, *Srimandira Itihasara*, p. 20.

15. MUKUNDA DEB III: A CONFIRMED ODDITY

1. Jagannath Jenamani v. Raja Makund Deb, Suit No. 538 of 1919, order passed by T.D. Mukherjee, Additional Subordinate Judge, Cuttack, dated 2.03.1921.
2. Raja Makunda Deb v. Sri Jagannath Jenamani, order passed by Patna High Court on 17 February 1923.
3. *Utkal Dipika*, 20 February 1926.

16. RAMACHANDRA DEB IV: TRYST WITH GURUDEV, FIGHT WITH PRIESTS

1. Dr Harekrushna Mahtab, *Sadhanar Pathe*, Part I (Cuttack: Dr Harekrushna Mahtab Foundation, 2016), pp. 191-92.
2. P. Mukherjee, *Tagore in Orissa* (Cuttack: Dr Harekrushna Mahtab Foundation, 1961), p. 19.
3. *Gopinath Puja Panda Samanta* v. *Ramchandra Deb and Ors*, AIR 1958 Ori 220.

17. GAJAPATI *VERSUS* GAJAPATI: BEGINNING AND END OF HOSTILITY

1. Subrahmanyam, *The Suryavanshi Gajapatis*, p. 69.
2. Eschmann, Kulke and Tripathi (eds.), *The Cult of Jagannath*, p. 291.
3. Subrahmanyam, *The Suryavanshi Gajapatis*, p. 76.
4. Dr S.N. Rajguru, *History of the Gangas*, Part II (Superintendent of Museum, Bhubaneswar, 1972), pp. 75–76.
5. Rajguru, *History of the Gangas*, Part II, pp. 76–78.
6. Ibid., Part II, pp. 80-81.
7. Panigrahi, *History of Odisha*, p. 220.
8. Mubayi, *Altar of Power*, p. 116.
9. Rajguru, *History of the Gangas*, Part II, p. 90.
10. Mubayi, *Altar of Power*, p. 171
11. Ibid., p. 172.
12. Busby, Collector of Tax, to Robert Mitford, Acting Collector Zilla, Cuttack, dated 15 May 1810, Odisha State Archives, Doc. No. 20.
13. Mukherjee, *History of the Jagannath Temple*, p. 97.
14. Mubayi, *Altar of Power*, p. 174.
15. For details, see Rajguru, *History of the Gangas*, Part II, p. 118.
16. Mukherjee, *History of the Jagannath Temple*, p. 103.
17. Ibid., p. 104.
18. Ibid., pp. 106-07.
19. Ibid., p. 111.
20. Satyanarayan Mohapatra, *Gajapati Krushna Chandra Deb* [in Odia] (Cuttack: Vidyapuri Publication, 2020), pp. 374–75.
21. Ibid., pp. 386–88.

18. DIBYASINGHA DEB IV: THE GOLDEN JUBILEE KING

1. Bhaskar Mishra, 'The Traditional Role of Gajapati Maharaja in Shri Jagannath Temple in Cultural heritage of Orissa,' *Shri Jagannath Special Volume*, vol. XII (Bhubaneswar: Vyasakabi Fakir Mohan Smruti Sansad, 2010), p. 803.
2. Dr Sidheswar Mohapatra, *Puriboli* (Bhubeneswar: Odisha Sahitya Akademi, 2019), p. 52
3. Sarat Ch. Mahapatra, 'Jagannath Temple after Independence', in Janaki Ballav Patnaik's *The March to a Modern Odisha*, ed. Soumya Ranjan Patnaik and Wasbur Hussain (Bhubaneswar: Ama Odisha, 2013), p. 23.
4. Bihari Lal Patnaik, 'Sri Jaganathankara Ananya Leela', in *Anathanatha Sri Jagannath*, ed. Pitabas Routray, 2014.
5. Dr Binapani Dei, *Akinchanara Jibanasmruti* (in Odia) (Cuttack: Kahani, 2001), p. 95.
6. Dei, *Akinchanara Jibanasmruti*, pp. 96-97.
7. https://sambadenglish.com/gajapati-maharaja-of-puri-in-khurda-electoral-battle.
8. *Lord Jagannath: Great Mystic of Mystics*, Advisor Chandrasekhar Pati, Compiler Ramesh C. Pradhan (Bhubaneswar: Sisukalam Publisher, 2019), p. 93.
9. Asit Mohanty, 'Sri Jagannath's Foremost Servitor', *Orissa Review*. July 2019, p. 73.
10. Tripathy, *Shree Jagannath* [English], p. 71.
11. Ibid.
12. Interview, *The Times of India*, 1 July 2011.

19. AND IT NEVER ENDS...

1. Eschmann, Kulke and Tripathi, *The Cult of Jagannath*, p. 417.
2. Mubayi, *Altar of Power*, p. 54.
3. Mohanty, *Satabdira Surya,* p. 248.
4. Kulke, 'Jagannath: The State Deity of Odisha', p. 25.
5. Charles Taylor, *Social Theory as Practice* (Delhi: OUP, 1983), p. 32.
6. Report of the Special Officer under the Puri Shri Jagannath Temple (Administration) Act, 1952 (Odisha Act XIV of 1952), GoO, Law Department, 1961, pp. 3, 4.

7. Tripathy, *Shree Jagannath* [English], p. 306.
8. *Ram Chandra Deb* v. *The State of Odisha*, AIR 1959 Ori 5.
9. *Raja Birakishore* v. the *State of Odisha*, 1964 AIR 1501.
10. Tripathy, *Shree Jagannath*, p. 325, quoting Deulatola of Shishukrushna Das.
11. Ibid.
12. K.S. Behera, M.P. Dash, H.S. Pattnaik and R.K. Mishra (eds.). 'Charles Grome's Report on the Temple of Jagannatha, 10 June 1805' (Bhubaneswar: Odisha State Archives, 2002).
13. Record of Rights III, Form D, Published in Odisha Gazette (Extraordinary), Cuttack, 14 October 1955, p. 12.
14. Section 4(1)(C) of Shri Jagannath Temple Act, 1955.
15. Tripathy, *Shree Jagannath*, pp. 70-71.
16. Debi Prasanna Nanda, 'Rajaghara Hati-Gangaram Hathi Prasanga', in *Ekabarnee*, 1971, pp. 96–99.
17. Dr Mahesh Prasad Dash, 'Temple of Jagannatha in the eyes of Maharaja Ranjit Singh of Punjab and Mahmud-Bin-Amir Walo of Balkhi' in *Studies in the Cult of Jagannath*, ed. K.C. Mishra (Bhubaneswar: Institute of Orissa Culture, 1991).
18. Mahimohan Tripathy, *Shri Jagannathanka Haathi*, Srimandir Kartik issue. 2016.

BIBLIOGRAPHY

'Cultural Heritage of Orissa', vol. XII. *Shri Jagannath Special Volume*. Bhubaneswar: Vyasakabi Fakir Mohan Smruti Sansad, 2010.

'History and the Present: Rethinking Society, State and Region in Odisha'. Odisha Panel, Proceedings of 74th session of Indian History Congress held at Cuttack from 28th to 30th Dec 2013 (4).

'Odisha Famine (Na'anka): A Documentation of Primary Sources'. Bhubaneswar: Odisha State Archives, 2016.

Acharya, Paramananda. *Studies in Orissan History, Archeology & Archives*. Cuttack, 1969.

Acharya, Pritish. *Odisha Etihash*. Bhubaneswar: Ama Odisha, 2018.

Aiyangar, S.K. *Sources of Vijayanagar History*. The University of Madras, 1919.

Al-Badaoni. *Muntakhab-ut-Tawarikh*. Translated by W.H. Lowe. Calcutta: Asiatic Society of Bengal, 1884.

Ali, Sk. Abdul Gaffar. 'Aspects of Socio Cultural life in Orissa under the Mughals (1592 to 1751 AD)'. PhD Thesis. Department of History, Aligarh Muslim University, 2015.

Aurobindo, Sri. *The Chariot of Jagannath*. https://www.aurobindo.ru/workings/sa/04/0020_e.htm

Balakrishnan, R. 'Sri Jagannath: The Divine Face of Pluralism', *Odisha Review* (June–July 2018).

Basham, A.L. *The Wonder That Was India*. London: Sidgwick & Jackson, 1954.

Beames, John. *Memoirs of a Bengal Civilian*. London: Chatto and Windus, 1961.

Behera, K.S., M.P. Dash, H.S. Pattnaik and R.K. Mishra, eds. 'Charles Grome's Report on the Temple of Jagannatha, 10 June 1805'. Bhubaneswar: Odisha State Archives, 2002.

Behera, K.S. and A.N. Parida. *Madalapanji: The Chronicle of Jagannath Temple (Rajabhoga Itihasa)*. Bhubaneswar: Amadeus Press, 2009.

Behera, K.S., Jagannath Pattnaik and H.C. Das, eds. *Cuttack, One Thousand Years*, vol 1. Cuttack: Cuttack City Millennium Celebration Committee, 1990.

Behera, Subhakanta. *Construction of an Identity Discourse: Oriya Literature & the Jagannath Cult (1866-1936)*. New Delhi: Munshiram Manohar Lal, 2003.

Behera, Subhakanta. 'Oriya Literature and the Jagannath Cult, 1866-1936: Quest for Identity'.PhD Thesis. Univerity of Oxford, 1999.

Beveridge, Henry, ed. *Tuzuk-i-Jahangiri or Memoirs of Jahangir*. Translated by Alexanders Rogers. London: Royal Asiatic Society, 1909–1914.

Das, H.C. *Military History of Kalinga*. Calcutta: Punthi Pustak, 1986, 2006.

Das, Haraprasad. *Odia Jatira Jibana Katha*. Bhubaneswar: Paschima Publications, 2011.

———. *Odia Jatira Jibana Chinta*. Bhubaneswar: Paschima Publications, 2020.

Das, J.P. *A Time Elsewhere*. Delhi: Penguin Books, 2009.

Das, Jagannath Prasad. *Desha Kala Patra*. Bhubaneswar: Prachi Prakashan, 2004.

Das, M.N. *Glimpses of Kalinga History*. Calcutta: Century Publishers, 1949.

Das, Madhusudan and Surendra Mohanty. *National Biography Series*. New Delhi: National Book Trust, 1972.

Das, Manoj. *My Little India*. New Delhi: National Book Trust, 2002.

———. *Myths, Legends, Concepts and Literary Antiquities of India*. New Delhi: Sahitya Akademi, 2009.

Das, Sharmila. *The Cultural Contributions of the Gajapatis*. Delhi: New Age Publications, 2007.

Dash, Gaganendra Nath and Ranjan Kumar Das. *Jagannatha and the Gajapati Kings of Orissa*. Delhi: Manohar, 2010.

Dash, Kailash Chandra. *Legend, History and Culture of India: Based on Archaeology, Art, and Literature*. Calcutta: Punthi Pustak, 1997.

De, Sushil Chandra. *Guide to Odishan Records,* vol. I & II. Odisha State Archives, 1961.

———. Guide to Odishan Records vol. III. Odisha State Archives, 1962.

———. Guide to Odishan Records vol. IV. Odisha State Archives, 1964.

———. Guide to Odishan Records vol. V, VI & VII. Odisha State Archives, 1965.

Deb, Gajapati Maharaja Sri Dibyasingha. 'The Tradition of Lord Jagannath'. Swami Sankarananda Memorial Lecture. Ramakrishna Mission Institute of Culture, Kolkata, 2004.

Dei, Dr Binapani. *Akinchanara Jibanasmruti* (In Odia). Cuttack: Kahani, 2001.

Eschmann, Anncharlott, Hermann Kulke and Gaya Charan Tripathi (eds.). *The Cult of Jagannath and the Regional Tradition of Orissa*. Delhi: Manohar, 2014.

Fazl-i-Allami, Abu'l. *Ain-i-Akbari*, vol. I. Translated by Blochmann H. from the original Persian. Calcutta: Asiatic Society of Bengal, 1927.

———, Abu'l. *Ain-i-Akbari*, vol. II. Translated by Colonel H.S. Jarrett. Calcutta: Asiatic Society of Bengal, 1891.

———, Abu'l. *Ain-i-Akbari*, vol. III. Translated by H. Beveridge. Calcutta: Asiatic Society of Bengal, 1907.

Ghose, Loke Nath. *The Modern History of the Indian Chiefs, Rajas, Zamindars & C. Part II The Native Aristocracy & Gentry*. Calcutta: J.N. Ghose, 1881.

Government of Odisha. 'Report of the Special Officer under the Puri Shri Jagannath Temple (Administration) Act 1952 (Orissa Act XIV of 1952)'. Law Department, 1961.

Harichandan, Fakir. *Khordha Itihasara Antarale*. Cuttack: Bharat Bharati Publication, 1999.

Hunter, W.W., Andrew Stirling, John Beames and N.K. Sahu. *A History of Orissa*. Bhubaneswar: A.K. Mishra Publication, 2005.

Jagadeb, Raja GCH. *Utkal Empire Under Ganga Kings*. Dedicated to All Scholars and Students of History on the Occasion of the History Congress at Bhubaneswar, 1977

Janana Chautisa, *Shri Jagannath Bhajan*. Bhubaneswar: Govt. of Odisha.

Juge Juge Rathayatra. Sri Jagannath Mandir Prasana, Puri, 2001.

Kale, Moreshwar Ramchandra. *Raghuvansam of Kalidas*. Bombay: Gopal Narayen & Co., 1932.

Kar, Rajat Kumar. *Janajibanare Jagannath*. Cuttack: Basanta Publications, 2006.

Mahapatra, Chakradhar. *Utkala Itihasara Ek Ajnanta Adhyaya*. Cuttack: Friends Publishers, 1969.

Mahapatra, Kedarnath. *A Descriptive Catalogue of Sanskrit Manuscripts of Orissa*. Bhubaneswar: Orissa Sahitya Akademi, 1960.

Mahapatra, Sitakant (trans. & ed.). *The Alphabet of Birds: Hymns for the Lord of the Blue Mountain*. New Delhi: National Book Trust, 2003.

Mahapatra, Kedarnath. *Khuruda Itihasa*. Cuttack: Grantha Mandir, 1999.

Mahtab, Dr Harekrushna. *Sadhanar Pathe*, Part I & II. Cuttack: Dr Harekrushna Mahtab Foundation.

———. *The History of Orissa*, vol. I & II. Cuttack: Dr Harekrushna Mahtab Foundation.

Malinar, Angelika, Johannes Beltz and Heiko Frese. *Text and Context in the History, Literature & Religion in Orissa*. Delhi: Manohar, 2004.

Mansinha, Mayadhar. *History of Odia Literature*. New Delhi: Sahitya Akademi, 1960.

———. *The Saga of the Land of Jagannatha*, Fouth Edition. Cuttack: Mass Media(P) Ltd., 2020.

Marglin, Frédérique Apffel. *Wives of The God-King: The Rituals of the Devadasis of Puri*. Delhi: OUP, 1985.

Meeshraw, Dr Amoolya Krushna. *Ahe Nila Saila O' Anyanya Bhajana*. Cuttack: SB Publication, 1997.

Mishra, Bhaskar. *Shree Jagannathanka Sanskrutika Itihasa*. Cuttack: SB Publications, 2006.

Mishra, Dr Prabodh Kumar. *Odia jatira itihas o sanskruti* (in Odia). Cuttack: Vidyapuri, 2008.

Mishra, Dr Surendra Kumar. *Shri Jagannath Eithiya Sataka*. Bhubeneswar: Odisha Sahitya Akademi, 2015.

Mishra, K.C., ed. *Studies in the Cult of Jagannath*. Bhubaneswar: Institute of Orissa Culture, 1991.

Mishra, Binayak. *Indian Culture and Cult of Jagannath*. Calcutta: Punthi Pustak, 1986.

Misra, Aswini Kumar. *Shree Jagannath*. Bhubaneswar: Odisha Sahitya Akademi, 1982.

Misra, Krupasindhu. *Fort of Barabati* (in Odia). Cuttack: Cuttack Trading Company, 1955.

Misra, Narayan. *Annals and Antiquities of the Temple of Jagannath*. New Delhi: Sarup & Sons, 2005.

Mohanty, Artaballabha: *Madala Panji*, second edition, Bhubaneswar: Utkal University, 1969.

——: *Madala Panji*, fourth edition. Cuttack: Prachi Samiti Grantha I, 1940, 2017.

Mohanty, Bishnu Charan. *Parala Pratibha*. Calcutta: Priyadarshi Prakasan, 1991.

Mohanty, Surendra. *Madhusudan Das*. New Delhi: National Book Trust, 1972.

——. *Satabdira Surya*, 3rd edition. Cuttack: Lark Books, 1986.

——. *Nilasaila*. Cuttack, 1996.

Mohapatra, Dr Sidheswar. *Puriboli*. Bhubeneswar: Odisha Sahitya Akademi, 1996.

Mohapatra, Satyanarayan. *Gajapati Krushna Chandra Deb* (in Odia). Cuttack: Vidyapuri Publication, 2020.

Mubayi, Yaaminey. *Altar of Power: The Temple and the State in the Land of Jagannatha*. Delhi: Manohar, 2005.

Mukherjee, P. *Tagore in Orissa*. Cuttack: Dr Harekrushna Mahtab Foundation, 1961.

Mukherjee, Prabhat. *History of the Jagannath Temple in the 19th Century*. Calcutta: Firma KLM, 1977.

———. *The History of the Gajapati Kings of Orissa and their Successors*. Cuttack: Kitab Mahal, 1981.

Narvane, V. S. *The Elephant and the Lotus: Essays in Philosophy and Culture*. London: Asia Publishing, 1965.

Nathan, Mirza. *Bahiristan-i-Ghaybi* (Persian). Translated by Dr M.I. Borah. Guahati: Government of Assam, 1936.

Odisha State Archives. *The Paika Rebellion: A Documentary Study*. 2017.

Padhi, Dr A., ed. *Nabakalebara: An Archival Document*. Bhubaneswar: Odisha State Archives, 2015.

Paikaray, Prof. Dhrubacharan Jaysingh and Prof. Prafulla Kumar Paikaray, *Bharatiya Swadhinata Sangramaku Khurdar Abadana*. Cuttack: Chitrotpala Publications, 2007.

Paikaray, Prof. Dhrubacharan Jaysingh. *Odishara Aitihya*, Bidya Prakashan, 2011.

Pal, Dr Bharati. *Inscriptions of Odisha*. Odisha State Museum, 2020.

Panda, D. and S.C. Panigrahi, eds. *Cult and Culture of Lord Jagannatha*. Cuttack: Rastrabhasa Samanvaya Prakashan, 1984.

Panda, Harihara. *Rajaghara Katha*. Bhubaneswar: Pen In Books, 2020.

Panigrahi, K.C. *History of Orissa*. Cuttack: Kitab Mahal, 1981, 1986.

Parija, Ganesh Prasad. *Juge Juge Jagannath*. Bhubaneswar: A.K. Mishra Publication, 2008.

Patnaik, Janaki Ballav. *The March to a Modern Odisha*, edited by Soumya Ranjan Patnaik and Wasbur Hussain. Bhubaneswar: Ama Odisha, 2013.

Patra, Kishori Mohan, Purna Chandra Das, Hemant Kumar Parija and Bandita Devi. *Glimpses of Odishan History & Cultural Heritage*. Cuttack: Kitab Mahal, 2019.

Pattanaik S. ed. *Chakada and Chayani Chakada* (in Odia). Cuttack: BinodBihari Publisher, 1969.

Pattanaik, P.K. *A Forgotten Chapter of Orissan History (with special reference to the Rajas of Khurda and Puri 1568-1828)*. Calcutta: Punthi Pustak, 1979.

Pattnaik, Jagannath. *Odisha Itihasara ketoti romanchakara kahani.* Cuttack: Nalanda, 1999.

Pegg, James. 'A History of the General Baptist Mission Established in the Province' in *Orissa, Its Geography, Statistics, History, Religion and Antiquities* by Andrew Sterling. London: John Snow, 35, Paternoster Row, 1846.

Pradhan, B.K., ed. *Paika Rebellion: Precursor to Freedom Struggle in India.* Bhubaneswar: Uktal Vikas Parishad, 2017.

Pyarimohan Acharya. *Odishara Itihasa* (in Odia). Cuttack: Orissa Book Store, 1925, 2012.

Rajguru, Dr S.N. *Odisha ra Itihasa* (in Odia). Cuttack: Grantha Mandir, 1985.

———. *History of the Gangas,* Part I & II. Superintendent, Orissa State Museum, 1968 & 1972.

———. *Inscriptions of the Temples of Puri and Origin of Sri Purusottama Jagannath* (In 2 Volumes). Puri: Sri Jagannath Sanskrit Viswavidyalaya.

———. *Odishara Sanskrutika Itihasa (1100-1568 AD),* 4th Part. Bhubaneswar: Odisha Sahitya Akademi, 1986.

Rao, Dr N. Mukunda. Simachalam Temple Inscription, 1986.

Rath, Bijay Chandra. *Jayee Rajguru and Anti-colonial Resistance in Khurda.* Bhubaneswar: Sisukalam, 2017.

Ratha, Tarinicharan. *Annapurna.* Berhampur: The Students Store, 1934.

Ray, B.C. *Mogal Odisha Itihas O Sanskruti.* Cuttack: Vidyapuri, 2020.

———. *Orissa under the Marathas (1751-1803).* Allahabad: Kitab Mahal Publishers 1960.

———. *The Foundations of British Orissa.* Cuttack, 1960.

Ray, Dr Dipti. *Prataparudradeva: The Last Great Suryavanshi Kings of Orissa (AD 1497- AD 1540).* New Delhi: Northern Book Store, 2007.

Roy, Kumkum and Naina Dayal, ed. *Questioning Paradigms, Constructing Histories: A Festschrift For Romila Thapar.* Delhi: Aleph, 2019.

Sahu, Bhairabi Prasad. *The Making of Regions in Indian History: Society, State and Identity in Premodern Odisha.* Delhi: Primus Books, 2020.

Sahu, N.K. 'The Imperial Ganga and the Gajapati rule in Orissa'. *OHRJ,* vol. III, no. 4, 1955.

Sarkar, Jadunath. *History of Aurangzeb*, vol. III. Calcutta: M.C. Sarkar, 1912.

———. *Studies in Mughal India*. Calcutta: M.C. Sarkar, 1919.

'Satabdira Nabakalebara (1912-2015)', Sri Jagannatha Chetana Gabesana Pratisthana Saradhabali, Puri, 2015.

Sen, Surendranath and Umesha Mishra, ed. *Sanskrit Documents*. Allahabad: Ganganatha Jha Research Institute, 1951.

Sewell, Robert. *A Forgotten Empire (Vijayanagar): A Contribution to the History of India*. London: Swan Sonnenschein & Co., Ltd., 1900, reprint: 2002.

Sewell, Robert. *Vijayanagar*, edited by Vasundhara Filliozat. New Delhi: National Book Trust, 1999.

Shrichandan, Dilip and Janmejaya Choudhury. *Srimandir O Sri Jagannath* (in Odia). Pakhi Ghara Prakashan, 2012.

Singh, Upinder. *Kings, Brahmanas and Temples in Orissa: An Epigraphic Study AD 300-1147*. New Delhi: Munshiram Manoharlal Publishers, 1994.

Sircar, D.C. *Indian Epigraphy*. Delhi: Motilal Banarsidass, 1965.

Somayaji, Vasudeva Ratha. *Gangavamsanu Charitam (Campu Kavyam)*. The Directorate of Tourism & Cultural Affairs, Odisha, 1979.

Sterling, Andrew. 'An Account Geographical, Statistical and Historical, of Orissa Proper, or Cuttack'. *Asiatic Researches*, 1825.

———. *Orissa, Its Geography, Statistics, History, Religion and Antiquities*. Jagatsinghpur: Prafulla Pathagar Publications, 2004.

Subrahmanyam, R. 'Inscriptions of Suryavanshi Gajapatis of Orissa'. ICHR, 1986.

———. *The Suryavanshi Gajapatis of Orissa*. Waltair: Andhra University, 1957.

Sutton, Amos. *Orissa and its Evangelisation: Interspersed with suggestions respecting the more efficient conducting of Indian missions*. Calcutta: Derby, Wilkins and Son, 1850.

Swain, Prasanna Kumar. *Bhaktakabi Salabega*. Bhubaneswar: Odisha Sahitya Akademi, 2002.

Swami, Bhakti Purusottama. *Sri Jagannath*. Mayapur: Bhaktivedanta Book Trust, 2006.

Taylor, Charles. *Social Theory As Practice*. Delhi: OUP, 1983.

Thorn, Major William. *Memoir of the War in India*. London: T. Egerton, Military Library, 1818.

Toynbee, G. *A Sketch of the History of Orissa from 1803 to 1828*. Calcutta: Bengal Secretariat Press, 1873.

Tripathi, K. B. 'A Study of Early Oriya Inscriptions', PhD Thesis. School of Oriental and African Studies, University of London, 1952.

Tripathy, Lopamudra. 'Literature and the Politics of Identity in Orissa 1920 -1960'. PhD Thesis. School of Oriental and African Studies, University of London, 2003.

Tripathy, Mahimohan. *Shree Jagannath* (English). Bhubaneswar: Ama Odisha, 2018.

———. *Shrimandira Itihasara Keteka Chhina Prustha* (in Odia). Cuttack: Roopambica, 2007.

Ullah, Neamet. *History of the Afghans* (Persian). Translated by Bernhard Dorns. London: John Murray, 1829.

Wagoner, Phillip B. *Tidings of the KING: A Translation and Ethnohistorical Analysis of the Rayavacakamu*. Honolulu: University of Hawaii Press, 1993

White Whispers: Selected Poems of Salabega in Odia. Translated by Niranjan Mohanty. New Delhi: Sahitya Akademi, 1998.

Yamin, Mohammed. *Impact of Islam on Orissian Culture*. New Delhi: Readworthy, 2009.

INDEX

Abhinava Yajatinagara 187
Abu'l Fazl 3, 83–84, 90, 100, 187, 190–91
Act 10 of 1840 205
Act 23 of 1871 265
Act of 1952 367
Act XI of 1858 200
Act XL of 1858 229
Act X of 1840 199, 219, 228–31, 244, 360
Act X of 1877 230
Act XXIII of 1871 266, 272, 274–75
Act XX of 1863 201
Adan Pradan 293–94
Adoption 285–305
    alternate 295
    Badakhimidi 296–97
    ceremony 286, 292–93, 301
    deed 287
    Jagadananda's 296
    proposal of 297
    proposals 297
Adyasebak 31, 37, 44, 215, 322, 335–36, 344, 358, 368, 370, 376–77
    role of 322, 377
Afghans 11, 43, 80–82, 85–87, 89–92, 97–98, 325, 355–56
    invaders 82

Ain-i-Akbari 3, 91, 97, 187
Akbar, Mughal King 3, 11, 80–81, 84, 91–93, 98–101, 104, 150, 187, 190, 355
    death of 101, 355
Akinchanara Jibana Smruti 340
Allahabad High Court 300
Amuktamalyada 63
Anagabhim Deo 188
Anangabhimadeva II 22
Ananga bhimadeva III 22
Anangabhimadeva III 22, 26–27, 42, 48, 187, 352–53
    consequences of ideology 27
Anangabhima III 22–24, 29
Andamans xxii, 137, 223, 225, 227, 229
Andhra Pradesh 13, 16, 24–25, 47, 50, 52, 61, 63, 70, 128, 153, 184, 316
Antagonism 60
Anti-British confederacy 147
Anti-colonialism 167
Art and architecture 12, 48, 83, 309, 353
Attacks and disturbances 11, 25, 29, 34, 43, 70, 81, 84, 86, 89–90, 95, 98–99, 101–05, 108–11, 113, 116–17, 119–22, 124, 126–29,

139, 141, 154, 158, 164, 168–70, 183, 185, 188, 190, 193, 251, 286, 295, 326, 355–57, 364, 369, 373, 384
Audaka 185

Aurangzeb, Mughal King 115, 117–20, 122, 355
Bahmani Empire 38, 59, 61
Bahmani kingdom 15, 41, 52
Bahuda Yatra 110, 342, 346, 348, 371
Balabhadra Deb 18, 114–15
Bamadev Samhita 336
Bamanda state 57
Bamra King 285, 287
Barabati Fort 83, 88, 126–27, 134–35, 142, 145, 150, 155, 161, 174, 185, 188–99
  demolition of 194
Barana ceremony 286, 291
Battle of Plassey 153
Baxi Jagabandhu Bidyadhar Mahapatra 173
  role of 177–78
Bengal 7, 9, 15, 17, 27–28, 50–52, 61–62, 75, 78, 80–81, 84, 86, 102–03, 107–09, 118, 124, 141–43, 147, 153–55, 159, 169–70, 179, 188–90, 193, 199, 206, 210, 228, 230–31, 242, 246, 253, 256, 265, 275, 279, 293, 299, 308
  political turmoil in 62
  politics of 80
  Sultanate 9
Bhagabata 149
Bhajans 109, 111, 351
Bhakti 71–75, 94, 109, 111, 149, 364
Bhakti cult 71, 73–74
Bhanudeva I 13
Bhanudeva III 9–10
Bhanudeva IV 9, 13, 32, 33, 49–50, 353–54
Bhanu II 23
Bhaskar Pandit 191
Bhauma-Kara period 7
Bhog 205, 247, 310–14
Bhoga Mandap 311, 313

Bhoi dynasty 75, 78, 80, 89, 92, 220, 235, 325
Bichitrabharat 149
Bidar 15, 52
Bihar 28, 109, 141–42, 153, 155, 199, 272, 278, 331, 341
Birakeshari Deb 18–19, 44, 131, 133, 141–52, 156–57, 196, 200, 226, 258, 296, 325–27, 329, 331, 334, 357–58
  death of 148
  descent into madness 145
  imprisonment of 148
  insanity of 146
  reign 149
Birakeshari Deb I 18, 44
Birakeshari Deb II 18, 200, 258
Birakeshari Deb III 18–19
Birakishore Deb 18–19, 279, 334, 341, 343, 367, 370
Birakishore Deb III 18–19, 343
Biswanath Das 306
Bratopanayan 336
British betrayal 161
British government 158–65, 168, 170–72, 175, 179–80, 200, 204–05, 208–10, 225, 227, 232, 234–35, 239, 246, 249, 255, 274, 279, 306, 324–25, 359, 361, 363–64, 384, 391, 394
  accession of the 235
Burhan-i-Ma'asir 10
Calcutta High Court 219, 221, 223, 246, 249, 302
Car Festival 31, 39–40, 96, 102, 121, 128, 131, 133, 167, 204, 224, 336–38, 340, 346, 371–72
Ceremonial procession 94, 333
Chaitanya Charitamrita 71, 72, 74
Chaitanya movement 74
Chalukya dynasty 77, 79, 115, 220
Chamu Citau 131–32
Chandan Yatra 93, 120, 346, 371
Charu homo 301
Chauhan, Prithviraj 28
Chedi dynasty 36, 53
Chhattisgarh 27

Chherapanhara xx, 31-32, 40, 45, 131, 339, 346, 354, 371-72
Chilika Lake 84, 98, 105, 112, 120, 127, 153
Chodaganga, Anantavarman 13, 22, 183–84
Chodagangadeva, Anantavarman 10, 13, 21–22, 24, 47–48, 183–84, 187, 316–17, 334, 352–53
  rule of 183
Christian government 172, 359–60, 363
Christian missionaries 360, 369
Civil Code 249
Collector's Dilemma 277
Conflicts 42, 52, 60, 77, 81–82, 92, 104, 143, 157, 164, 204, 316, 321, 325
Confusion 62, 114, 271, 298, 316–17
Conspiracy 44, 76–79, 107, 109, 125, 146–48, 219, 355
Council of Religious Rituals 366
Credibility 50, 80, 248, 325
Culture and custom xxi–ii, 3–4, 6, 20, 24, 40–42, 71, 109–11, 113–14, 180, 233–34, 236–37, 324, 348, 382, 392
  ancient 4, 180
  devotional 111
  diverse xxii
  inclusive 113
  Indian 3
  Jagannath xxi, 20, 41, 71, 348
  Vaishnava 111
Culture and tradition xix–xxii, 4, 14, 19–24, 26–27, 29–31, 37, 42–45, 48, 109–11, 113, 120, 137, 184, 196, 218, 225, 248, 254–55, 257–59, 309, 316, 324–25, 329–30, 332, 334–35, 340, 342–43, 348, 354, 362, 375–77
  cultural 20
  Indian 4, 309
  Jagannath 110, 377
  Odishan 110
  of kingship 29
  religious 20
  royal 4, 26, 30
  social 20
Cuttack
  accounts of 182
  occupation of 154, 161

Daitapatis 30, 337–38, 340
Dakhinparso Math 293
Dardhyata Bhakti Rasamrita 149
Das, Madhusudan 137–38, 245–49, 251, 253–57, 259, 261–63, 265, 276–78, 282–83, 307, 362
Dasarathi Chotra 281
Datta homo ceremony 291, 293–94, 296, 301–02
Dattaka Chandrika 300, 303
Dattaka Mimansa 299–301, 303
Debasnana 120
Deccan 2, 25, 29, 52, 61–62
Deception 294
Demoralization 270
Deva Raya II 50–52
Devasnana Purnima 346
Devotion 40, 43, 71, 73, 86, 109–11, 135, 252, 346, 355, 364, 376, 400
Dhakinaparswar Math 264
Dhanavana 185
Dhanvadurga 184
Dibyasingha Deb 18–19, 46, 118–20, 122–23, 137–38, 145, 148, 156–57, 200, 202, 204–05, 208, 210–13, 215–17, 223–25, 227–29, 234–38, 241, 243, 254–55, 258, 279–80, 296, 327–28, 334–35, 339–40, 342–44, 347–49, 361
  childhood of 202
  conviction of 210, 224, 228
  death of 156 – 57
  deportation of 227, 258, 361
  dilemma in life 343
  transportation for life 235
Dibyasingha Deb I 18, 118–20, 122
Dibyasingha Deb II 18, 334
Dibyasingha Deb III 18, 137
Dibyasingha Deb IV 18, 334–35
Differences and disputes 49, 86, 159, 293, 359, 366
Dignity 4, 41, 89, 184, 232, 245, 256, 259, 293, 322, 325, 362–64

Diksha 345
Diplomacy 154
Divya Sankar Sudhal Dev 286–87, 290
Dolabedi 371
Dola festival 371
Dola Purnima 205, 346
Dol Jattra 207
Dukha Nasana He 151
Dvadasi 30, 206
Dwitiya Indradyumna 95–96, 355
East India Company 11, 153, 155–58, 161, 164, 167, 178, 218, 321–22, 360
　administration 164
Ekadashi Tradition 45
Ekharjat Mahal 361, 369
Ekram Khan 118–20, 122
Elephants 3–14, 17, 56, 67–68, 83–85, 104, 113, 151, 186, 190, 260, 308, 327, 356, 372–76
　commodities of trade for Odisha 7
　corps 8, 11–12
　hunt 9
　importance of 9, 12
　in Indian culture 3
　in the history of Odisha 7
　Odishan 8–9
　role in warfare 10 –11
　significance of the use of 8
　war 5, 7, 11–12
　white 12
Emar Math 232, 244, 264, 269, 293
Expedition 9, 21, 35, 39–41, 52, 58, 85, 108–09, 160, 189

Faith xxiii, 20, 25, 40, 43, 80, 86–87, 113, 149, 177, 253, 314, 351, 353, 363, 377
　Hindu 253, 363
Famine of 1866 202, 361
Feudatory
　chiefs 51, 63, 160, 208
　kings 33–34, 36, 51, 148, 357–58
　Rajas 357
　rulers 81, 353
Folklores xxi, xxiii, 38, 55, 87

Fortification 185
Fort of Barabati 161, 185, 188–89, 191, 194, 198
Forts 8, 15–17, 39, 52, 60, 62–63, 67, 78, 82–83, 85, 88, 90–92, 98, 105, 115–16, 124–27, 131, 134–35, 142, 145, 150, 154–55, 161, 169–70, 174, 184–99, 308, 326, 382–84
　desert 185
　forest 185
　hill 185
　importance of 185
　types of 184
　water 185
Friendship 6, 81, 101, 382

Gahana Bije 346–347
Gajapati and Lord Jagannath 20, 44
Gajapati and the Puri Temple 357
Gajapati Maharaja xxii, 31–32, 210, 340, 344, 346, 348–49, 368, 370–71, 376
Gajapati Maharaja Seva 346, 368, 370–71, 376
Gajapatis
　childless 303, 328
　conflicts between 321
　dignity of 256, 363
　ineffective 260
　loss of power and province by 359
　manifestation of 354
　name of the xx
　of Odisha xix, xxiii, 2, 13, 18, 21, 134, 187, 320, 372
　personality of the xix
　pride and dignity of 248, 255, 363
　role of 173, 322, 358, 363, 370
　Suryavanshi 1, 47, 49, 355
　the protector of idols 127
　title of 1, 12–14, 16, 52, 60, 143, 315, 321, 326–27
　tradition xix, xxi, 109, 218, 254, 340
Gajapati versus Gajapati 315

INDEX 433

Ganga dynasty 3, 10, 13–14, 21, 24, 32–33, 47–48, 53, 188, 321
Ganga emperors 42
Ganga Empire 27
Ganga king 13, 24, 32, 36, 49–50, 320, 354
Ganga kingdom 9, 48
Ganga kings 13–14, 23–25, 30, 32, 37, 48–49, 60, 316, 320, 353
Gangaram 372–75
   death of 372, 375
Gangavansanucharitam 49
Gaurachandra Deb 331
General Power of Attorney 256
Giridurga 184–85
Gitagovinda 41, 42
Glimpses of Kalingan History 183
Glory xx, 39, 47, 66–67, 184, 198, 255, 325, 342, 379, 381
Gobardhan Math 264, 269
Golakhdanda 246, 391
   letter to the Editor of Utkal Dipika 391
Gopal Tirtha Math 293
Gopinath Deb 18, 123, 166
Gopinath Misra 233
Gopinath Puja Panda Samanta 314
Government of Bengal 179, 210, 228, 230–31, 242, 246, 256, 279
Government of India 210, 230, 242, 246, 280, 395
Government order no. 3205 266
Govinda Vidyadhara 75, 77–78, 90, 146
Govt. circular dated 20th June 59 236
Grandeur xx, 14, 47, 309
Grome's Report of 1805 369, 374
Gundicha Temple 31, 102, 334

Hafiz Kadir Beg 134, 364
Harekrushna Deb 18, 123
Harihara Chaturanga 12
Hindoos 159, 206, 233, 237, 240
Hindu Desa Katha Sangraha 16
Hindu kingdoms 1, 28–29, 36, 48, 81, 102
Hindu kings 2, 28, 44, 324

Hindu Religious Endowment Act, 1952 367
Hindus xxi–ii, 32, 80, 85, 87, 97, 104, 110, 118, 120, 122, 135, 190, 217, 232, 243, 245, 247, 269, 312, 367, 375, 394–95
History of Oriya Literature 55
History of The Afghans 85
History of the Baptist Mission in Odisha 363
Hostility 141, 143, 165, 167, 315, 331, 333
   end of 331, 333
Humiliation 69–70, 87, 103, 106, 135, 162, 218, 323–24

Identity 1, 14, 25, 42, 53, 113, 246, 257, 322, 362, 369, 376–77
   narrow 257, 369
   political 14
   social 14
   sovereign aspect of 25
Ideology 22, 24–25, 27–28, 32, 42, 353
   professed 27
Idolatry 360, 363
India
   colonial rule in xxii
   history of xxii, xxiii
Indian history xxii, xxiii
Indian Penal Code (IPC) 214, 219, 283, 311
Inscription from the Bhimeswar Temple in Draksharamam 79
Inscription II 23
Inscriptions
   Athagarh 92
   Bhimeswar Temple 80
   Bhubaneswar 23
   contemporary 62
   copper plate 320
   Dirghasi 317
   epigraphic 57
   Ganga kings 30
   Gopinathapura 34
   Gopinathapura Stone 33, 49
   Jagamohana 33
   Jagannath Temple 15, 51, 53, 59

Kalachuri kings 2
Kalahasti Temple 63
Kapilas 14
Kapilash Temple 13
Mangalagiri temple (Vijayawada) pillar 63
Persian 192
pillar 63
Puri 38, 42
rock 186
Ronanki stone 10
Simhachalam 13
Integrity 27, 28, 359
Islam xxi, 84, 103, 134–35, 137, 139, 190, 196

Jagadeva, King Jagannath Harichandan 129–33
Jagannath cult 42–43, 109
Jagannath Jenamani 197, 228–29, 233–34, 241, 286–87, 298, 305
Jagannath Narayan Deb 143–44, 325–27, 331–32, 357
Jagannath Tarka Panchanan 159
Jagannath Temple, Marada 129
Jagannath Temple of Puri
   administration of 227, 243, 246–47, 251, 254, 256, 260, 310, 322, 336–38, 343, 348, 365–66, 369, 375–76
   affairs of 1, 161, 199, 204–05, 227, 230–31, 247, 252–53, 282, 322, 357, 360–61, 391–93
   control over 326
   custodian of 99, 148, 167, 228, 249, 254, 260
   importance of 364
   management by committee of trustees 231
   management of 145, 171–72, 199, 205, 228–31, 242, 245, 256, 272, 304–05, 326, 357, 359–60, 362, 372, 392, 395, 397, 400
   order to demolition of the 118
   regulations 312
   rituals and traditions of the 321

Jahangir, Mughal Emperor 85, 101, 103–04, 107, 109, 355
Jaladurga 184
Jaunpur 9
Jayee Rajguru 156–58, 161, 163–64, 167, 179, 358–59
Jenamani, Jagannath 197, 228–29, 233–34, 241, 286–95, 298, 304–05, 342
Jharkhand 108
Juggernaut 360, 363

Kaala Pani Jail 221
Kaifiyat of Jagannatham 49
Kalachuri king 27
Kalapahad 81–82, 84–90, 94–95, 98, 189–90, 355
Kalinga Empire 183, 353
Kamarnava Deb 335, 340
Kanchi Abhijana xx, 38–40, 60
Kanchi-Kaveri expedition 41
Kapilendra Deb xix, 2, 10, 14–18, 33–39, 47, 49–58, 60–61, 315–17, 321, 353–54
   death of 38, 57, 316, 321
Karnata 2, 15–17, 52, 187
Katakaraja-vamsavali 49
Kautilya 7–8, 185, 186
   Arthashastra 7, 185
   classified forts 185
Keshari, Raja Nrupa 182–83
Khandapara Raja 328–29
Khandi 263–72, 276–78, 280–84
Khan-i-Dauran 108, 115–17
Khemidi kingdom 60
Khilaut-i-Maharajagie 180
Khiljis 29
Khimundi kingdom 317
Khimundi kings 317, 321
Khurda
   campaign against 107
   capture of 116
Killa Khurda 91
King and the deity 42
Kingdom of Orissa 34, 85
King Krishnadevaraya 16, 61–70, 73
King of Gauda 80
King of Khurda 1, 99

King of Parlakhemundi 331–32
King Raghuji Bhonsle 142
Kingship 4, 29, 42, 72, 89, 328–29
    survival of 42
Konark temple 48
Krupamaya 287, 295–97
Krupamaya Deb 287
Kshetra Mahatmyam 233

Lalbagh Palace, Cuttack 108
Lal Mohini Mohan Deb 285–86
Languages xxii, 6, 53–55, 150, 202, 241
    Devbhasa 53
    Lokbhasa 53
    Odia 53, 54
    Rastrabhasa 53
    Sanskrit 23, 30, 53–54, 65, 67, 70, 96, 98–99, 109, 126, 149, 159, 166, 307–08, 320
    vulgar 202
Laxmi, death of 374–75
Legends xxiii, 20, 55, 86, 351
Legitimacy 25, 34, 38, 49, 51, 58, 89, 94, 100, 174, 177, 185, 255, 322, 353, 355
Legitimization 51
Letter No. 345 379
Literature 2, 12, 43, 53–55, 68, 70–71, 75, 83, 99, 109–11, 149–50, 152, 309, 351–53, 399
    devotional 110–11, 351
    Odia 53–55, 71, 109, 149
Lord Balabhadra 39, 337, 339
Lord Shri Jagannath
    dedication of the throne to 28
    devotion to 40, 135
    festival of 30, 110
    overlordship of 32
    servant and representative of 36
    servitors of 29, 37, 45, 325, 346
    sovereign supremacy of 29, 31, 38
Lord Vishnu xxii, 95, 121
Lotus 4, 111, 113–14, 150–52, 166, 380
Loyalty 36, 43, 58, 92–93, 99, 102, 104, 126, 135, 177, 215, 324

Macaulay report of 1835 349
Madala Panji 21–23, 30, 33, 49, 57, 68, 75, 77, 84, 90–91, 93, 95–97, 105–06, 108, 114–15, 119, 121–25, 134, 141, 146, 182, 184, 188, 235–37, 323, 330
Madan Chhotra 264, 272, 276, 280, 283–84, 286, 288, 290–92
Madhura Nirudha Natakam 149
Madras Presidency 153
Mahabharata 54–56
Mahadeep alati 120
Mahaparasad seba 121
Mahaprasad 96, 261, 294, 311–12, 324, 366, 395
Maharaja Krushna Chandra Gajapati 331–33
Mahasnan 310–14
Mahidurga 184
Makunda Deb 18–19, 138, 234, 387
Makunda Deb III 18–19
Makund Deb 235–37, 240, 260, 273, 283
Mallikana 171, 359
Malwa 9, 50
Man Singh 11, 91–93, 97–101
Marada Temple 131
Marathas 2, 44, 98, 142–45, 147–48, 153–55, 157–58, 160–62, 189, 191–95, 218, 322–23, 325–26, 330–31, 356–58, 364, 370, 382–83, 392
    and Alivardi Khan 142
    arrival of 356
    in Odisha 142
Marriage 40, 43, 60, 64, 67–70, 103, 120, 134, 261, 263, 267, 281, 300, 372
    ceremonies 120
Memo no. 125 266
Metcalf's blunder 362
Metcalf's Mistake 242
Midnapore Fort 170
Militarism 53, 184
Military campaign 109, 115
Mir Habib and Birakeshari Deb 143
Monuments xxii, 124
Moti 372–73

Mughal-Maratha warfare 144
Mughals 43, 49, 80, 91–92, 102–04, 117, 120, 122, 124, 126–27, 139–43, 195, 325, 356, 364
  administration 101, 124
  court 80, 100
  emperor 11, 81, 92–93, 98, 100–105, 107, 118, 355
  empire 3, 356
  invasion and expansion 354
Muhammad Ghori 28
Mukti Mandap 94, 97–98, 130–31, 314
Mukunda Deb 18–19, 44, 76–83, 87–93, 96, 115–18, 131, 156–58, 161–64, 167–72, 174, 177–80, 189–90, 194, 196–97, 199, 227–28, 233–34, 241–43, 253, 255–56, 258, 260–61, 273–76, 279–90, 295–98, 303–05, 328–30, 355, 358–60, 362
  abominable behaviour of 261
  accession to the throne 77
  achievements 82
  death 87, 90, 256
  death of 83, 87, 90– 92, 190, 199, 258
  extortion of 330
  mistake of 79
  torture of 261
Mukunda Deb I 18–19, 114, 115
Mukunda Deb II 18, 44, 156–58, 161–64, 167–72, 174, 177–79, 196, 279, 382
  arrest of 174
  conduct of 178
  petition filed by 382
  petition for release 170
Mukunda Deb III 18–19, 199, 258, 285
Mukunda Deb IV 328
Muslim 7, 9–10, 21, 27–29, 60–61, 62, 74, 86–87, 89–90, 102, 110–12, 120, 129, 135–36, 139, 196, 220, 357, 375
  attacks 29
  invaders 28, 112, 220
  power 27, 61–62

Muslims 7, 9–10, 21, 27–29, 60–62, 74, 86–87, 89–90, 102, 110–12, 120, 129, 135–36, 139, 188–89, 196, 220, 237–38, 243, 357, 375–76
Mystery 70, 145, 152, 178, 336
Myths 20, 55

Nabakalebara 226, 356, 371-72
Nabakoti xix, 15–17, 46, 52, 187, 376
Narasa Nayaka 61-2
Narasimha Deb 13, 18, 76, 107–09, 114–15
  death of 108
  tenure of 109
Narasimhadeva I 13, 48
Narasimhadeva III 13
Narasimhadeva IV 13
Narasimha I 13
Narasimha IV 32
Narayan Deb 143–44, 325–27, 331–32, 357
Nationalism 257, 361–64
  Odia 257, 361–62, 364
Natural calamities 202
Nawab of Bengal 142–43
Negotiation 154, 158, 289, 291
Niladri Mahodaya 233, 245, 255, 312–13, 336
Nilasaila 364
Nine forts 15–17, 52, 308
Nizam of Hyderabad 153
Non-Hindus xxi, xxii, 32, 110
Northern Sarkars 153 –54
North India 29
Nrdurga 184
Nrusingha Purana 149

Odisha
  Afghan conquest of 1, 84
  British conquest of 1, 321, 358
  colonial administration in 202
  conquest of 1, 74, 84, 153, 321, 358
  Gajapati history in 49, 352
  Gajapati tradition of xix
  history and heritage 113

history of xxi, 13, 15, 30, 71, 100, 150, 182, 226, 315–16, 355
Maratha government in 193–94
Maratha occupation of 143
occupation of 143, 154, 247, 374
pride and dignity of 362
state deity of 22
takeover of 44
turning point in history 355
war against 62
Odisha Act No. 11 of 1955 367
Odishan Empire 32, 36, 39, 53, 70, 76, 182, 187, 189–90, 354
Odishan kingdom 48, 50, 62, 70, 73, 97, 316
Odisha Society of Americas (OSA) 349
Orissa: Its Geography, Statistics, History, Religion and Antiquities 17
Orissa's Cultural History 10

Padlabh Deo 324
Padmanabha Deb 140–41, 147
Padmanabha Narayana Deo 323
Pahandi bije procession 336
Paika Bidroha (Rebellion) 172–74, 178–97
Pandas 45, 110, 112, 310–14, 347
Parlakhemundi 51, 60, 315, 317, 320–21, 325–27, 331–32, 357
and Puri 332
Parvata 185
Parwana No. 577 236
Patajoshi Mahapatra 165
Patalesvara shrine 23
Patita Pabana Bana 150
Patna High Court 298, 304–05
Pension 145, 256, 261, 264–66, 270–80
drawing and disbursing the 273–74
suspension of 271
Pensions Act 270, 275
Perwana No. 329 235
Pilgrims 34, 121, 199, 204–08, 210, 242, 265, 323–24, 328, 330, 366, 371, 374

Political
exigency 64
pension 266, 271, 273–74, 278–80
Power of attorney 272, 276, 277, 278
Prataprudra Deb 12, 16, 18, 41, 42, 61–64, 68–79, 93, 97, 320, 354
Prema Tarangini 149
Pride xx, 53, 111, 141, 195, 197, 227, 247–48, 255, 257–59, 322, 338, 340, 362–64
Princely races 2
Princess 7, 40, 64–65, 69, 86, 134
Muslim 86
Odishan 69
Privy purses 370
Property 28, 34, 50, 200–201, 228–29, 243–44, 249–52, 282–83, 360, 367–68, 383, 393, 400
custody of 252
Devasva 28
landed 228
Punishment 163, 170, 218, 224, 229, 284, 370, 384
Puri, occupation of 144, 159
Purificatory ceremony 310, 313–14
Puri Raninkara Rodana 221
Puri Shri Jagannath Temple (Administration) Act, 1952 365, 370
Purushottama Deb xx, 18, 38–42, 56–61, 64, 97–98, 101–06, 189, 316–17, 321, 354
accession of 58
Kanchi expedition 40, 189
notable aspects of regime 60
personal humiliation 106
reign of 38, 354
Purushottama-Jagannatha 21–23
Purusottam Samrajya 23
Putreshti Jag 301–02
Putreshti Jag ceremony 301

Qadam-E-Rasool 124
Queen Victoria 209–10, 225
Quli Khan 109, 129, 141–43
defeat of 142
Quli Qutb Shah 70, 73

Qutb Shahi dynasty 70

Radhakanta Math 264
Radhashyam Math 293
Raghav Das Math 264
Raja Daityari Singh 226
Raja Ghanabhanja 140, 141
Rajah of Khoordah 179, 231, 360
Rajah of Khurda 251
Raja of Bamanda 225
Raja of Berar 154, 164
Raja of Gumusar 141
Raja of Khandapara 328–29
Raja of Khimundi 323–24
Raja of Khurda 1, 43–44, 91–93, 99, 101–03, 105, 114, 116, 123–26, 128, 131–32, 134, 136, 138, 140–45, 155–57, 161–65, 167–71, 173–74, 178, 194, 196–97, 208, 230, 279, 315, 322–26, 328–31, 355, 357–59, 370
Raja of Kimedy 200–202, 225
Raja of Kujang 194
Raja of Nagpur 147–48
Raja of Parlakhemundi 60, 143–44, 325–27
Raja of Puri 1, 44, 60, 171, 199–200, 204, 209, 215, 218–21, 227, 230–31, 233–34, 242, 245, 249, 254–56, 266, 272–73, 279, 282, 293, 299, 304, 311, 313–15, 321–22, 324, 329, 358–63, 366, 370, 375–76
   criminal case against the 287
   misconduct and behaviour of 329
Rajaraja III 22
Rajguru, Jayee 11, 31, 94, 97, 126–27, 130, 135, 149, 156–59, 161–68, 170–71, 178–79, 291–92, 294, 308, 357–59
   and Baxi 178–79
Ramachandra Deb I 18, 89–101
   accession of 91
   achievement of 94
   a pious ruler 93
   becoming the Gajapati 90
   conflict with Man Singh 98
   man of letters 99
   title of Abhinava Indradyumna 100
   title of the Raja of Khurda 92
Ramachandra Deb II 18, 124–31, 134–40, 147, 196
   accession 124
   converted to Islam 137, 196
   rises from the dead 136
Ramachandra Deb III 18, 197, 199–200, 226, 258–59
   death of 200
Ramachandra Deb IV 18, 259
Ramananda Raya 71–74
Ramchandra Deb IV 177, 258
Rani Leelabati Patamahadei 347
Rani Muktadevi 330
Rani Suryamani Patamahadei xxii, 19, 134–35, 137–38, 200, 202, 210, 226–29, 232–34, 237–39, 241, 243–44, 246–47, 249, 251, 253–56, 258–60, 261–62, 279, 282, 291, 328, 362–63, 385, 387, 389
   letter to Collector of Puri 385, 387, 389
Rath Yatra xx, 31, 45, 96, 110, 121–22, 224, 327, 334, 342, 371
Raya, Saluva Narasimha Deva 58
Rebellion 33, 78, 82, 90, 92, 107, 170–71, 173, 177, 359
Rebellious feudatories 34
Record of Rights 130, 312, 335–36, 346, 356, 366, 370, 375–76
Reddys 50–52
Regulation IV of 1806 359
Regulation IV of 1809 239, 322
Religion 3, 6, 8, 25, 28, 32, 74, 86, 136–37, 159, 232–33, 254–55, 257, 281–82, 311, 324, 329, 353, 357, 362, 364, 369, 392, 394
   Hindu 3, 232–33, 255, 281–82, 362
Religious
   affairs 44, 181, 248, 257, 362
   discourses 351
   mendicant 72, 164
   practices 311–12
   sentiments 231, 322

Return Car Festival 346, 371
Right and hereditary privilege 4, 24, 36, 43, 137, 140–41, 144, 151, 162–63, 172, 229, 248, 252, 254, 263, 268, 275–76, 283, 298, 303, 310–11, 321, 324–27, 335–37, 358, 362, 367, 374, 392–94, 398–99
Rites and rituals xx, xxii, 1, 4, 20, 22, 26–27, 30–32, 41–42, 44–46, 86, 94–95, 112, 120–22, 129–31, 134, 137, 200, 205, 233, 246, 248, 255, 259, 301, 311–12, 314, 321, 325, 327, 329, 335–39, 343, 346, 354–55, 357–59, 362–67, 369–70, 372, 375
    association xxii, 1, 259, 362–64
    chherapanhara xx, 131, 339, 354
    funeral 179, 335
    pahandi bije 337–38
Royal
    dynasty 346, 371
    officials 58, 172
    privileges 370
    procession 4, 121, 346
Royal Titles Act 1876 209
Royalty xxii, 2–4, 11, 19, 21, 215, 297, 327, 333
    trappings of xxii
Rukmani barana nitti 120

Sabdabrahmagita 149
Sacrilege of 84
Saivaism 24
Saivites 353
Salabega 109–14
    poems 111
Saluva Narasimha xx, 39, 41, 58–61, 64
Samartha, Damodar 277–78
Sanctity 44, 98, 309
Sankalpa 301
Sannad 208, 210
Sanskrit Bhatti-kavya 126
Santosh Trophy 343
Sarala Mahabharata 55
Satchidananda Tribhuban Deb 285, 305
Saviour 150, 246

Sculptural depictions 48
Sebaks 29, 32, 35–38, 41, 45, 51, 53, 56, 84, 93, 96, 106, 130, 137, 204–05, 231–32, 255, 277, 295, 310–14, 324, 330, 333, 336–37, 339, 343, 346–47, 354, 356, 365–67, 371
    Brahmin 310, 314, 337
    non-Brahmin 337
Secret Committee of the Court of Directors 154
Self-improvement 351
Self-respect 53, 113
Servitors 29–30, 37, 45, 93, 204, 255, 338, 346, 371, 375
Shah, Hushang 9
Shah III, Sultan Mohammad 38
Shah Jahan, Mughal emeror 11, 107–08
Shah, Shamsuddin Ilyas 9
Shah, Sultan Nasiruddin Mahmud 15
Shaista Khan 115, 117
Shankaracharya of Gobardhan Math 264
Shree Jagannatha Managing Committee 44
Shree Jagannatha Temple Managing Committee 342, 348, 367
Shri Gundicha Yatra 128
Shri Jagannath Temple Act, 1954 44
Shri Jagannath Temple Act, 1955 367
Shuja-ud-Din, Mughal emperor 124, 134, 141
Shyam Sundar Deb 157
Simhachalam Temple Inscription 13, 69
Sirat-i-Firuz Shahi 9, 10
Snanabedi 371
Solar dynasty 14
Solitary confinement 256
Somavamsi kings 53
Somavanshi kingdom 48
South India 18, 29
Sovereignty 2–3, 11, 15, 32, 95, 158, 162
Spiritual
    education 349–50
    learning 348–49
    values 75

Spiritualism 71, 348, 351
Spirituality 349–50
Sraddha 364
Sri Chaitanya Mahaprabhu 71–75, 94, 149
Srikrushnalilamruta 149
Stampede 205
Statecraft 28
Suit No. 3 of 1886 243
Sulamania Gurzani 189
Sun dynasty 33
Sun Temple at Konark 48, 108, 188
Supremacy 29, 31–32, 38, 54, 62, 101, 117, 147, 158, 167, 255, 380
Supreme Court of India 344, 367, 370
Suri Sarvasvam 100
Suryavanshi dynasty 33, 353–54
Suryavanshi Gajapatis 1, 47, 49, 355
Suryavanshi kings 24, 315, 354
Suzerainty 26, 93, 107, 143, 325
Swami Chidananda Saraswati 345
Swars 30, 310–11, 324

Tagore, Gurudev Rabindranath 305–10
   function to honour 308
   Tagore jayanti 307
Taqi Khan 98, 124–26, 128–29, 134, 140–41, 146–47, 191
   death of 141
   machinations of 124, 140
Tarikh-i-Jadid-i-Subah-Orissa 183
Tax 34, 59, 129, 141, 145, 160, 172–73, 279, 323, 325, 357, 360
   chaukidari 59
   income 279
   pilgrim 129, 141, 145, 172, 323, 325, 357, 360
Temples xxii, 28–29, 48, 67, 85–86, 88, 113, 117–18, 130, 138, 184, 367
   Hindu 117–18, 138, 367

Thakur Raja 45, 93, 96, 135–36, 196, 208, 219, 245, 254, 342, 344
Titles
   Aswapati 2
   Chhatrapati 2–3
   Gajapati 13
   Gaudeswar 15
   Kalabargeswar xix, 15–17, 52, 187, 376
   Nabakoti Karnata Kalabargeswar 15–16, 187
   Nabanabati Sahasra Gunjaradhisvara 10, 13
   Narapati 2, 3
   of Khetriyabara 141
   of Nabakoti Karnata 52
   royal 2
Tonsure ceremony 299, 301
Tughlaq dynasty 9
Tughlaq, Sultan Firoz Shah 9
Tughluqs 29
Tukka Panchakam 65

Udayagiri 39, 62, 69
   fall of 62
Uriya Math 264
Utkal Dipika 203, 215, 221, 224–46, 248–49, 282, 361, 391, 395, 398
Utkal Sabha 245–46, 282
Uttar Pradesh 9, 28

Vaishnavism 24, 71, 73–74, 94, 353
Vana Durga 185
Veligalani plates 16
Vijayanagar 3, 15–16, 22, 39, 50–52, 58–59, 61–62, 64, 68, 74
Vijayanagar emperor 50
Vivekananda 350
Vrksadurga 184

Zamindars 115–17, 148, 155, 160, 168, 173–74, 176, 208, 225, 295, 297, 331, 357, 384, 399

NOTES